Rob van Tulder

Skill Sheets

An Integrated Approach to Research,

Study and Management

Also published by Pearson Education

- Monique Dankers-van der Spek, *Study Path Development – Building Vocational Skills*, 978-90-430-1297-3 (English)

- Monique Dankers-van der Spek, *Studieloopbaanontwikkeling – Beroepsgeschikt*, 978-90-430-1157-0 (Dutch)

- Monique Dankers-van der Spek, *Studieloopbaanontwikkeling – Stagebekwaam*, 978-90-430-1158-7 (Dutch)

- Monique Dankers-van der Spek, *Studieloopbaanontwikkeling, van stage naar afstuderen*, 978-90-430-1548-6 (Dutch)

- Sheila Cameron, *The Business Student's Handbook – Learning Skills for Study and Employment*, third edition, 978-14-058-4719-3 (English)

- Sheila Cameron, *Vaardigheden voor studie en loopbaan*, derde editie, 978-90-430-1298-0 (Dutch)

- Liz Harris-Tuck, *Brand You*, fourth edition, 978-01-318-5700-1 (English)

- Liz Harris-Tuck, *Brand You*, 978-90-430-1395-6 (Dutch)

Rob van Tulder

Skill Sheets

An Integrated Approach to Research,

Study and Management

PEARSON
Education

ISBN: 978 90 430 1461 8
Uniform Dutch-Language Classification (NUR): 163
Key words: research skills, study skills, management skills

This is a publication by Pearson Education Benelux bv, Postbus 75598, 1070 AN Amsterdam
Website: www.pearsoneducation.nl – email: amsterdam@pearson.com

Interior: RAM Vormgeving, Asperen
Cover: RAM Vormgeving (Jan van Waarden), Asperen
Cartoons: Kafak

First print run: August 2007
Second print run: December 2007
Third print run: August 2008

This book is printed on non-chlorine bleached paper in a bid to reduce the impact of production on the environment.

Preface		VII
Skill Sheets: the website		X
The Challenges		1
The Format		11

Series A Research **25**

A1	Principles of Good Research	27
A2	Research Aims: Basic or Applied?	31
A3	Personal Research Aims/Ambitions	33
A4	Creativity in Research	35
A5	Steps in Research Projects	38
A6	Feasibility Study	41
A7	Research Strategies	45
A8	Choosing Appropriate Methods	50
A9	Choosing Appropriate Questions	53
A10	Formulating the Research Question	55
A11	Organising Files	58
A12	Barter in Research	60
A13	Online Databases	62
A14	Search Engines: Googling Around	65
A15	Internet or Internot?	67
A16	Validation and Verification as Barter	70

Series B Study and Self-Management **73**

B1	Principles of Virtuous/Lifelong Learning	75
B2	Self-diagnosis: Attitude	80
B3	What does the Teacher want?	84
B4	Learning Report and Contract	87
B5	Study Strategies and Learning Styles	89
B6	Memory and Mind Maps	92
B7	Concentration	96
B8	Good Time Management	99
B9	Procrastination	103
B10	Study Planning: Week	106
B11	Study Planning: Semester	109
B12	Health and Energy Balance	111
B13	Generating/Receiving Feedback	113
B14	Learning Contract II: Peer Feedback	115

Series C Reading **117**

C1	Principles of Active Reading	119
C2	Book Selection: Authors	121
C3	Book Selection: Contents	125
C4	Newspapers and Magazines	128
C5	Large Amounts of Material	131
C6	Identifying Argumentation	133
C7	Organisation of the Argument	136
C8	Fallacies in Argumentation	138
C9	Translation Programmes	140
C10	Active Note-making	142
C11	Speed Reading	145
C12	Evaluation: Correction Symbols	148

Series D Listening **151**

D1	Principles of Constructive Listening	153
D2	Preparing Interviews	156
D3	Managing Interviews	159
D4	Asking Questions	163
D5	Body Language	168
D6	Processing Interviews	171
D7	Attending Lectures	175
D8	Listening for Feedback	179

Series E Writing **181**

E1	Principles of Powerful Writing	183
E2	Plagiarism	187
E3	Reporting: Opening Parts	189
E4	Reporting: Main Body	193
E5	Reporting: Final Parts	195
E6	Argumentation	198
E7	Rewriting	201
E8	Style: Common Errors	203
E9	Style: Phrasing Problems	207
E10	Spelling: Common Errors	209
E11	Quotations and Paraphrasing	212
E12	References	216

E13	Abbreviations and Acronyms	219
E14	Tables, Figures and Boxes	223
E15	Bibliography	226
E16	Layout	231

Series F Presentation   **235**

F1	Principles of Effective Presentation	237
F2	Preparation	240
F3	Presentation Formats	246
F4	Presentation Design	253
F5	Design (PowerPoint) slides	256
F6	Last-minute Presentation Checklist	259
F7	Effective use of Practical Tools	262
F8	A Balanced Approach to Questioning	266
F9	Body Language	268
F10	Dealing with Disasters	273

Series G Team and Project Management   **277**

G1	Principles of Effective Team Management	279
G2	Forming: Members, Roles and Dependencies	283
G3	Brainstorming	288
G4	Norming: Tasks and Roles	291
G5	Decision-making	294
G6	Basics of Effective Negotiations	297
G7	Group Contract	301
G8	Effective Meetings	305
G9	Feedback and Coaching	311
G10	Unhealthy Group Dynamics	317
G11	Dealing with Conflicts	321
G12	The Final Stage: Tasks and Roles	324

Contributors	327
Bibliography	328
Index	333

At the beginning of the 1990s, I was challenged by my own students to further elaborate a set of 'Skill Sheets' that I had written for them (primarily because I did not want to explain how to write footnotes again!). The student syllabus became bigger, included more topics and was finally published as a big red binder. Since 1991, thousands of students at the Erasmus University Rotterdam and a number of other universities have been using consecutive versions of the Skill Sheets collection. The Skill Sheets functioned as a practical aid for individual students, but were used also by teachers as an easy way to specify the skill requirements linked to their courses.

These Skill Sheets are written by a research practitioner – an International Business professor to be precise. The 'rules', advice, challenges, tips and 'principles' which are delineated result from personal experience with teaching and collaborating with students from several universities around the world. They also build on twenty-five years of conducting and publishing own research, carried out for a considerable number of organisations in business, politics and civil society, in collaboration with a large number of scientists and covering an extensive range of large economic and political topics. On the basis of this experience, I have come to realise that skills are not a goal in themselves. Their value derives from their practical *use* when doing research, studying, preparing a presentation, managing a project, or advising policy makers. The proof of the pudding is in the eating.

The Skill Sheets in their present form are also the result of the collective experience of many fellow practitioners and students. I have made use of hundreds of 'hand-outs' written by colleagues, consulted hundreds of websites, and read hundreds of books and practical guides (of which only a fraction is included in the bibliography). In a separate annex I have listed the names of the colleagues whose brains I have gratefully 'picked' for the particular Skill Sheet. Often sources were brought to me by enthusiastic students who challenged me to add specific information to the original Skill Sheet collection. In the 2004-2007 period, a large number of students at my present department (department of Business-Society Management) were asked to write their own Skill Sheet on complementary topics. Some of their contributions have been included in this Skill Sheet collection – and acknowledged as such in the same annex. With every consecutive edition of the Skill Sheets, the formula matured more.

This fifth and completely revised version of the Skill Sheets contains a number of novelties. Firstly, the format is now solidly founded in the relevant literature. Two core techniques are consistently used throughout the book: the skill circle and the reflective cycle of research and learning. The second introductory chapter ('The Format') explains this formula in considerable detail. Secondly, the need for an integrative approach to skill development is more explicitly addressed and related to the modern dilemmas that universities and students face in the so-called 'bargaining society'. The first introductory chapter ('The Challenge') explains this background in more detail. Thirdly, the loose-leaf format has been abandoned. In the past ten years, the loose-leaf format became less and less satisfactory – including the big binder that did not fit into students' bags. The coming of age of Internet provided an alternative. With a basic book and an interactive website the present version of the Skill Sheets combines the soft flexibility of the web with the hard solidity of a more manageable book. Fourthly, this edition identifies the levels of skill proficiency you normally would have to obtain when going through the consecutive phases of your academic training. The Skill Sheets can be used throughout the university curriculum and beyond. The various levels of skill proficiency are specified in the introduction of each skill series. It should help you in identifying your present skill level. Fifthly, the present edition of the Skill Sheets remains part of an ongoing process of updating, experimentation and renewal. The interactive website (www.skillsheets.com) comprises additional skill sheets, gives exercises and many more web links. A new organisation called 'Skill Solutions' was founded to help create and sustain a more modern and interactive version of the Skill Sheets. Skill Solutions (www.skillsolutions.nl) is managed by Geert van Deth, Wouter Klinkhamer and Riena Buikema. Their efforts will hopefully carry the Skill torch further than I can individually. Finally, the Skill Sheets changed publishers. By moving to Pearson – the world's prime publishing house in educational books – the Skill Sheets finally have reached the appropriate platform. This move was made easy by the enthusiasm and patience of Cees Stoppelenburg, Annemarie Geerling and Wendelien Van Voorst van Beest.

The interdisciplinary nature of the Skill Sheets could not have been achieved without the help and inspiration of many colleagues: Gerd Junne, Winfried Ruigrok, Linda van Klink, Cynthia Piqué, Mariska Keus, Jeroen van Wijk, Ans Kolk, Arnoud Monster, Eric Waarts, Ad Breukel, Bettina Wittneben, Jordan Otten have contributed ideas for new Skill Sheets and have sometimes written parts of Skill Sheets themselves. The latter in particular applies to Simone Schenk, who has been particularly helpful in my thinking about study skills. Suzanne Bax gave considerable input for the management skills series. Vitas Kersbergen showed me the importance of giving 'creativity' a more prominent place in the Skill Sheets formula. Michel Lander and Stefan Leliveld inspired me to link Belbin's team roles with the research(er) roles and skill profiles, increasing the integrated nature of the Skill Sheets even further.

Over the years, a number of assistants have helped me to compile the sheets and upgrade them, in particular Bayard Hollingsworth, Claire Dumas, Patrick Hardy, Samantha Williams, Fabienne Fortanier, Michiel Hogerhuis, Geert van Deth, Eva Oskam, and Esther Kostwinder. Numerous student-users of the Skill Sheets and many peer-teachers and first year tutors who have participated in my teaching programmes, have provided me with valuable feedback from the user perspective. This has enabled me to improve the Skill Sheets and encouraged me to add many extra topics. The students in particular have motivated me to do much more than I had initially planned. As with other academics who have written *ad-hoc* hand-outs on skills to support teaching programmes and research projects, it was not my intention to write a whole collection of Sheets. The Skill Sheets have taken their present shape as a result of the enthusiasm *and* skills of my assistants, the continued complaints of the students, and thanks to the financial support of the Rotterdam School of Management. The illustrator (Kafak) also contributed to my motivation: with so many telling and excellent illustrations I had no alternative but to come up with supportive texts. Sometimes, even in scientific projects, it can be very useful to begin with the illustrations!

Rob van Tulder,
Amsterdam/Rotterdam, August 2007

The *Skill Sheets* book provides the core of an integrated approach to skills development. The book specifies minimum skill requirements, and explains how they can all be linked in virtuous learning and research cycles. Awareness and understanding, however, always need to be complemented with practice and further elaboration. The 'hard' and relatively inflexible book is therefore complemented by two 'soft', flexible and more interactive websites aimed at 'skill solutions' for practical and day-to-day use: (1) for students and (2) for teachers.

1 Students: www.skillsheets.com

The student website has an open format. It is primarily problem-oriented, and is aimed at assisting students in tackling the skill problems they encounter in their study activities (and helping tutors support them effectively). It contains web-based exercises – offering practical exercises online to help students assess and enhance their skill levels. The *Skill Sheets* website contains a large number of examples of Skill-related problems, questions and challenges that every student encounters from time to time, and provides guidance on how to deal with these challenges. The Table provides examples of how personal questions can be linked to relevant Skill Sheets. These questions can be updated regularly on the basis of what proves to be relevant for students around the world.

Examples of personal skill problems	Relevant Approach
'I have problems formulating a good research question'	Skill Sheet A9, A10
'How and when should I use theory?' 'When should I use statistics?'	Skill Sheet A7
'I do not know how to prepare for an exam'	Skill Sheet B3
'I face serious concentration problems"	Skill Sheet B7, B12
'I do not know where to start reading a study book'	Skill Sheet C5
'I do not know how to prepare for an interview'	Skill Sheet D2
'How to use references in texts'; or 'how should I refer to Internet?'	Skill Sheet E12
'I always write down my complete presentation'	Skill Sheet F2
'One of the team members is hardly doing anything for the assignment'	Skill Sheet G10

The website also offers you self-assessment exercises, checklists for practical purposes and lots of further reading suggestions and references. The website material is often based on more practical situations than the book can offer. The website also allows for extensive cross-referencing to other websites. Many of the Skill Sheets in the book specifically refer to the website for further guidance and personal checks [⊕➔www.skillsheets.com].

2 Teachers:www.skillsolutions.nl

The challenge for teachers, tutors, coaches and professors regarding skill development is often twofold: (1) how to specify minimum requirements for a course, a paper trajectory or a project, (2) how to stimulate students to acquire and develop new skills (maximum requirements). This challenge is particularly big in case the teacher is not a specialized skills teacher, and not specially dedicated to the training and acquisition of skills – this is what actually covers most of the curriculum at institutes of higher education. The website for teachers gives further guidance on how to use the Skill Sheets effectively, at what time in the curriculum, and for what type of courses. In particular the integrated approach to skills development will be further elaborated, and practical examples of how to train this with students in a research setting will be given. The checklists that are available to students will be complemented with a number of checklists especially dedicated to tutors.

The Challenges

Contents

1 The Need for Integrated Skill Development
2 Entering a Calculating Learning Environment
3 The University as a Positive Learning Environment

1 Introduction: The need for integrated Skill Development

These are challenging times. Globalisation – induced by technological change and political, cultural and economic integration – is bringing world communities together, but has also severely complicated their management. An 'international bargaining society' is materialising (cf. Van Tulder with Van der Zwart, 2006) – a society in which more and more assertive stakeholders are willing and capable of bargaining over the rules of the game and its outcome. Table 1 lists a number of related concepts that have been introduced to grasp the nature, dynamics and outcome of present-day societal change. As a short introduction of these concepts will illustrate, the present era presents opportunities, but also major threats and challenges. In any case, it necessitates a higher level of skills proficiency than ever before. Luckily this is obtainable for anybody willing to understand and invest in an integrated approach to skill development. This is the approach proposed by the Skill Sheets.

General characteristics

A networked knowledge society is rapidly coming of age (cf. Castells, 1996). Instead of hierarchies, relatively open communities increasingly interact with each other. The access to knowledge is increasing, partly due to the spread of internet, but also due to the breaking down of ideologies and other shared values. Communities of peers pragmatically get together to interactively produce joint knowledge. This trend is best exemplified by the Wiki-phenomenon in which an open community of often unregistered participants – aided by collaborative software and the internet – generate knowledge through quickly adding, removing and editing content. 'Wiki' in principle means 'able to be edited quickly'. In some instances, quick and open Wiki networks have already provided better and more accessible knowledge results than the slower networks of closed communities dominated for instance by scientific peers. The networking society has multiple centres of power and decision-making, which however also makes it more difficult to change its course once it takes the wrong route. The declining number of shared values can lead to the disintegration of societies that were build on these values, with nothing replacing them (cf. Etzioni, 1998). The power vacuum produces an institutional void, in which the lack of common rules and practices can also lead to chaos (cf. Van Tulder, with Van der Zwart, 2006).

Table 1 The Bargaining Society: Synonyms and Statements

☐ The Network society	You are who you know.
☐ The Knowledge economy	Access to knowledge is abundant and decisive for active participation.
☐ The Wiki Society	Quick and open is better than thorough and closed.
☐ The Open Society	Interrelated open networks create better results than closed, isolated, networks.
☐ A peer review society	Absolute quality does not exist, it is all in the eye of the beholder.
☐ The Benchmarking society	Doing it right is relative to the 'best-practices'.
☐ The numeracy society	What counts is what you can measure even the unmeasurable.
☐ The Deadline-society	It is only relevant if it can be achieved within the deadline.
☐ The Pseudo-intellectual society	It is not about being right but be proved right.
☐ The Knitting Society	It is more effective to network than to work.
☐ The Mediacracy	What/who you appear to be is more important than what/who you are.
☐ The calculating society	Getting it right is only right if it takes the least amount of effort.
☐ Multi-individualist society	Everybody opportunistically bargains with everybody else.
☐ The low-trust society	Low mutual trust in skills and integrity.
☐ A second opinion society	Two is more than one.
☐ The Debate society	You don't have to win a debate, but don't lose it in any case.
☐ A Protestocracy	If you do not protest, you will be ignored (and hit twice as hard).
☐ The Cynical society	Commenting is more important than commitment.
☐ The Risk Society	A society that is preoccupied with the future, 'manufactures' risk and distributes it unevenly.
☐ The hyperkinetic Society	Fast thinking is more important than deep thinking.

If quick and open becomes more pervasive, it could also jeopardize the creation of more thorough and deep knowledge, which sometimes requires rather closed networks of dedicated and committed peers that engage in dialogue to develop knowledge. Wikipedia as the most advanced global application of the Wiki-principle has been criticised for being susceptible to manipulation and electronic vandalism. So the first challenge of the bargaining society is to increase the reliability and relevance of open knowledge exchange, without losing its flexibility and low entry barriers. It requires high skill levels to use the abundance availability of knowledge, to access and produce *relevant* knowledge.

Principles

Networking changes the traditional selection criteria for identifying the quality and the relevance of knowledge. Absolute quality is becoming less relevant than relative quality, not in the least because there is no mutually accepted authority anymore that can define absolute quality standards. Increasingly benchmarking and rankings are used to distinguish 'best-practices' and help individual participants specify their own rules of engagement. But who is defining the 'best-practice' and who compiles the rankings? It has been shown that the more independent ranking agencies are, the more reliable knowledge they produce. However, in a bargaining society independence is a very relative concept. At the same time so-called 'peer reviews' act as an increasingly important mechanism through which information and influence is regulated. In media, accountancy, the medical and legal trades, science in general, even as regards whole countries, peer reviews are considered the only feasible way to come to judgements. But how independent are those peers and who defines who 'the peers' are? Networks of peers often constitute rather closed communities, which in turn limits the trend towards 'openness'. There is, finally, a constant quest for producing ratios, rankings, exact measures. What counts is what you can measure, and in the bargaining society that also applies to the unmeasurable. The resulting 'numeracy society' creates another (bargaining) problem – that of an increasing number of innumerate people. Innumeracy is the 'inability or unwillingness to understand basic mathematical ideas involving numbers of logic as they apply in everyday life' (Dewdney, 1993). It is the mathematical parallel or illiteracy. In bargaining processes actors (companies, governments, special-interest groups, the media) increasingly use mathematics – in numbers, surveys, percentages – to sell their ideas and products. But the use can easily turn out into abuse, as actors exploit innumeracy of their audience by twisting logic and distorting numbers (ibid: 2). The second challenge of the bargaining society, therefore, is to produce high quality and relevant knowledge on the basis of peer review and benchmarking. It requires high skill levels to identify, select and reproduce *reliable* knowledge.

Dynamics

The bargaining society can empower skilful participants. But as a societal model, it seems to come at a considerable price. Knowledge creation and diffusion is basically a slow process. In the bargaining society there seems to be less time available for slow progress. Under the constant pressure of media, customers, funding agencies, people are often stimulated to put more emphasis with timely than relevant information. The concept of a 'deadline society' is another expression of this phenomenon: relevant knowledge is only what can be produced within the deadline. In a deadline society, 'being right' is less important than to be proved right by your peers. This leaves tremendous room open for so called 'pseudo-intellectuals' and the rule of the 'mediacracy' – in which appearances are more important than the actual reality. The spread of pseudo-intellectualism is a sign of intellectual sloppiness that is feeding the bargaining society in a particular way. One of the mechanisms through which pseudo-intellectualism operates is through easy abstractions and superficial judgements (Barzun, 2002). 'Mediacracy' sounds remarkably the same as 'mediocracy' (or 'mediacrazy'). Instead of collaboration and dialogue, the bargaining society becomes governed by the principles of a 'debate society', in which sound bites and smart one-liners are more important than solid argumentation. At the same time this spurs a high degree of 'negativity', criticism and cynicism. This trend is based on a fundamental human trait, i.e. that people tend to remember four negative memories for every positive one (Roberts et al, 2005). This makes distant and negative commenting for instance easier than committed and positive feedback. The mediacracy gets further fed by these tendencies. Research comparing the contents of British media over time, found that the ratio of negative versus positive articles moved from 3:1 in 1974 to 18:1 in 2001 (Kamp, 2005). Based on these figures the present bargaining society can also be labelled as a 'cynical society'

Consequently, the level of opportunism in societal interactions increases. Enter the idea of a 'low trust' society (Troman, 2000). The intensification of mutual relationships in a bargaining society leads to calculating behaviour in which participants – in case they still want to get it right – want to do this with preferably the least amount of effort. Often, this is easier to obtain in a closely knit network of people, which further precipitates the concept of a 'knitting society' in which it proofs easier to 'network' than to 'work'. Sociologist Kees Schuyt refers to this phenomenon as the 'multi-individual society' in which everybody negotiates with everybody else, but on the basis of bleak convictions. Strategic behaviour – that can involve misrepresenting one's preferences in order to vote against the least preferred outcome – prevails. The flipside of the debate society is what sociologist Henk Becker has called the 'protestocracy'. Societal actors have to speak up in order to be heard, or to be allowed to participate on one of the (manifold) bargaining tables at which decisions are made. When faced with negative consequences of specific measures, you have to share the protests or risk to be hit twice as hard. It leads to interactions that are largely guided by tactical and short-term considerations.

The low trust society gives room to a 'second-opinion' society. Basically the search for second opinions highlights the growing assertiveness and research orientation of people that acknowledge that there can be more sides to an issue or a problem and that quality levels are not objectively established. Second opinions can lead to more informed choices. However, in practice the 'second opinion' society also leads people to search for a second opinion if they do not like the first opinion they get – whatever its quality is. The principle of *competitive bidding* increasingly applies to participants of the bargaining society even in the private realm of personal health (sometimes with devastating effects for the individual involved). As a consequence, quackery and charlatanism are on the rebound in many societies. The 'scientific method' (of proving what you claim to be true or relevant) gets under pressure.

So the third challenge of the bargaining society entails producing relevant and reliable (controllable) knowledge for specific audiences. It requires high skill levels to produce (often together with others) *timely* knowledge with sufficient independence.

Outcome

What is the outcome of all of the above parallel developments? Two final societal concepts are relevant in this respect: the risk society and the hyperkinetic society. The term 'risk society' was first coined by Ulrich Beck (1992). He focussed on competing scientific and political ways in the management of the increasing risks associated with modern society. Modern risks are 'manufactured' and much more the result of human activity than in the past. The operation of the risk society contains a boomerang effect, in that individuals will also increasingly be exposed to these risks. But the distribution of the causes and consequences of risk can be unequal. In the view of Beck, the unequal distribution of risk is fundamentally dependent on the knowledge and access to information of individuals. This brings us back to the above mentioned skill challenges. To what extent can individuals become aware of the threats and opportunities of the risk society? Here the challenge can become very personal.

The present risk society has also manufactured a 'hyperkinetic society' (cf. Hallowell, 2005) in which fast thinking is more important than deep thinking. The demands on time and attention of the human brains have exploded over the last two decades. Life has accelerated tremendously. According to Hallowell (2005) the human mind is filled with noise and the brain gradually loses its capacity to fully and thoroughly do anything. The human brain can be improved, but can also be destroyed due to societal stress. An increasing number of people complaints about loss of memory and concentration. According to neurologist Margriet Sitskoorn, these complains are caused by a mismatch between existing skills and the demands imposed upon us by the rapidly changing environment. The cognitive brain might perfectly understand the operation of the bargaining society, the emotional brains not (yet). As a result, even smart people tend to under-perform and suffer from serious attention deficits. Only under stress can they perform. Stress stimulates the production of adrenaline which resembles the chemicals used to treat Attention Distraction Disorder – a neurological disease. Firms, universities, society at large ask people 'to work on multiple overlapping projects and initiatives, resulting in second-rate thinking' (Hallowell, 2005). The hyperkinetic society tends to reward those that do much and punish those that try to focus.

As a consequence of the comming-of-age of the bargaining society in many countries, managers, students, teachers, researchers, administrators, parents, and politicians are increasingly operating in a continuous 'survival' mode. This affects the functioning of your brain, which in turn further precipitates calculating behaviour. In a bargaining society everyone has to become a calculating person to a certain extent. You can do that smartly or not. For instance engaging in many activities at the same time requires priority setting and management, which in turn requires smart calculating. Calculating is a fact of life in a multi-faceted, rapidly changing society. It is difficult to attach negative or positive connotations *per se* to calculating behaviour.

The fourth challenge presented by the bargaining society, therefore, entails the production of *shared knowledge* that takes into account the outcome of societal processes, and assesses their desirability in order to come up with effective solutions. In the words of Douglas Englebrecht, key contributor to the internet revolution: 'for coping with critical, global problems (...) a higher order of shared intelligence is essential' (quoted in Business Week, September 6, 2004). For an individual student this challenge implies that you are intimately aware of the positive as well as negative consequences of the hyperkinetic society for yourself and capable and willing to make effectively use of the knowledge developed by others and yourself. This requires an integrated approach to skills, for which this book is intended to give you sufficient support.

Four Skill Challenges

1 **Relevance**: Use the abundant availability of knowledge to access and produce relevant knowledge;
2 **Reliability**: identify, select and reproduce reliable knowledge;
3 **Timeliness**: produce together with others timely knowledge with sufficient independence;
4 **Sharing**: production of shared knowledge that takes the outcome of societal processes into account.

2 Entering a calculating learning environment

At the start of any type of advanced study after high school, you face the challenge of a significant change in attitude. The information load you are facing is often overwhelming; you are expected to study large amounts of material in a disciplined manner, gather information yourself, work together with other students that come from different places (and cultures sometimes) and create new information. With relatively little external control or incentives from the educational institution, the responsibility for personal development and academic achievement rests largely on the individual student. There are no laws forcing you to study and your parents are hardly able to check whether you are doing your 'homework'. Tutors can enthuse and encourage students to study, but in the end it all comes down to your own *intrinsic motivation* and your ability to adapt to this new style of learning. Moreover, academia is less and less a place where in splendid isolation from the outside world, scientists and students can pursue 'the truth' and accumulate knowledge and skills. Academia has also become part and parcel of the *international bargaining society*.

What are the implications of the bargaining society for the academic environment? Faculty staff members often find themselves caught up in a 'publish or perish' rat race and strugge with an increasing and diverse set of demands and activities. Students increasingly bargain over grades, the content and in particular the work load of courses - confronted as they are with an increasing and diverse set of demands and ambitions in a complex society with a wide range of options and possibilities. Higher education as public good is getting increasingly mixed up with a private mode of organising and financing. Higher education in many countries around the world is becoming a *hybrid* form in between public and private – with all its opportunities, but also with all its drawbacks. By blending into the international bargaining society, academia also becomes susceptible to one of its dominant mechanisms – participants engaging in calculating behaviour and seeking to maximise output through minimum effort. The wider academic community in principle consists of the following actors: students, staff (administrators, teachers, researchers) and financiers (governments, business, parents).

Table 2 The Academic Community as a Calculating Society

Calculating...	Characteristics	Possible consequences
Students	Only doing what is required; trying to make maximum use of any ambiguities in a programme; engaging in free-rider behaviour; CV-building (extra-curricular activities are more important than actual study to distinguish yourself in the job market).	Lengthy appeal procedures; lack of time for effective studying; constant demand for lower intensity of classes and less frequent exams; plagiarism; increasing number of pseudo-intellectuals; grade-inflation.
Administrators	Kissing up, kicking down; not laying down clear rules so as to manipulate them to own advantage; not engaging in evaluation exercises; networkers.	Lack of transparency; lengthy meetings; atmosphere of mistrust; lower productivity; increased overhead expenditures.
Scientists/teachers	Refraining from engaging in small group tutoring (too much work); preference for mass lectures (highest returns per contact hour) and strict grading systems; multiple-choice exams; limited availability; scientist as a bureaucrat.	Limited commitment to students; hierarchical; rule-oriented rather than content-oriented; stricter rules; lowered quality of exams; growing gap between teaching and research.
Scientists/ researchers	Choosing 'easy' topics that lead to easier publications or easier funding for consulting research; use of junior researchers; free-rider on the efforts of colleagues in their own institutions; networkers in the academic community and funding organisations.	Publishing as an act of extreme pleasing of referees (or 'prostitution'; cf. Frey, 2003); 'old boys' network in research funding; (top) scientists become administrators; gap between academics (know a lot about little) and intellectuals (know something about a lot) increases.
Governments	Budgetary problems in funding universities not in the least because more people study – and they study longer; trying to 'rationalise' education, cutting back on funding of scholarships and involving private parties in funding; stricter selection or admission criteria; privatisation of higher education.	Race between universities to attract additional funding; decline in cooperation in periods of rationalisation; lack of funding through scholarships force students to work, often with negative consequences for their studies.
Business	Due to decreased government funding, business gets more involved as sponsors (buildings, facilities), but also as customers for research. Scholarships of firms select the 'best' students. Choice of master's studies is strongly influenced by job opportunities. Thesis topics reflect business interests.	No fundamental but only applied research is done. Interests of business become the leading research questions. Scientist becomes 'guru'. 'Market conformity' of the university triggers more calculating behaviour. 'Best students' are defined from the perspective of future employers, not necessarily with reference to scientific requirements.

| Parents | Quid pro quo: support in financing higher education as retirement scheme and way to exert control over children. | Parental affection channelled through scholarships and dependency relations; only interested in the grades and consecutive career – not in the topic. |

Table 2 illustrates the various forms of calculating behaviour exhibited by these stakeholders and the possible sub-optimal consequences of this behaviour. See whether and to what extent this image corresponds to your academic environment. It will help you to determine the extent to which you should develop a strategy to escape the negative consequences of a calculating academic community.

This environment can have negative and positive consequences for students. An overly calculating environment implies high transaction costs and increases the propensity towards free-rider behaviour of all involved. The problem is that you only understand what you have missed out on during your studies long after graduation. Whilst the bargaining/knowledge society is also characterised by the continuous need for education and re-education, missed opportunities at university level do not easily get compensated in your post-graduate career. The choices made at university often have a lasting impact on an individual. The lasting impact does not apply to the academic discipline chosen – there is an abundance of examples of post-graduates who established a career in a completely different area to the one they were trained for. A more lasting impact exists in terms of the skills and attitude you have developed during these extremely important formation years – the years from approximately the age of 18 until the age of 25. Whatever attitude you develop in this period, including the social networks you become involved in, will shape your future in a more profound manner than the exact study you choose.

3 The University as a Positive Learning Environment

So far for the 'realistic' scenario. In particular a university environment should be able to make the best out of the bargaining society, provided you are able and willing to effectively apply the four Skill challenges presented in the first section of this chapter. The university can provide excellent preconditions for a continuous and virtuous learning process (➔B series). There are five dimensions to this issue: the staff; the library; the free haven function of the university; the peers, and the application of quality standards.

- **Outstanding and committed staff**: Universities make it their business to attract the best intellectual resources available. Even in remote areas around the world, academic staff is dedicated to the combination of research and teaching. Their commitment is not dependent upon their status and often not even upon the remuneration they receive. Calculating students who project their, somewhat distorted, expectations upon staff members tend to assume that the faculty is generally not very eager to invest much time in supporting students, certainly not in bachelor and undergraduate students. If you approach a 'teacher' to bargain about your grades in an ostensibly calculating manner – you received a 5.2

and start negotiating to be awarded a 5.5 [the minimum requirement to pass in most countries] - it should not come as a surprise that the teacher also behaves in a calculating manner. The teacher or faculty will be absent or will create other barriers to discourage students from claiming higher grades. It has been shown however, that faculty members at some of the top universities in the United States – including even a number of Nobel Laureates – proved to be very receptive to students' concerns, provided that these students entered their room with an informed question and/or showed that they had done their homework (having read some of the professor's academic writings). The inaccessible professor suddenly became very accessible.

Making use of the great potential of academic staff requires that (1) you are willing to listen to and learn from people who are more experienced or more intelligent than you; (2) you are prepared to invest time and energy to reap the rewards of interacting with existing staff and (3) you do not view staff as 'teachers' – as a burden you have to bear in order to get a sufficient grade – but as 'researchers', 'advisers', 'mentors', 'writers' – which is much closer to their identity and ambition...

- **Dedicated libraries and librarians**: Notwithstanding the financial limitations of your particular university, most of the time the university is the place where you will find the best equipped libraries and the best trained librarians *relative* to other nearby places. Why? Because universities make it their business to invest in 'knowledge', and academic staff deals with relatively well informed customers (you), which prompt them to continuously request good library facilities. Librarians are trained to be of assistance to you and their self-esteem is often dependent on the degree to which they are capable of assisting you in your research efforts. Librarians around the world also have a professional interest in finding things on the Internet; so their advice can be very useful before you start 'Googling around' to find information. Besides, large amounts of relevant information cannot be found through the Google search engine(s). Many students who did internships at international organisations, ministries, companies and the like found out that these organizations often have no access to very sophisticated databases and sources. They return to the university library to find the relevant information.

Making use of the often excellent university libraries and librarians requires that (1) you know where the library is; (2) you know your way around the library, i.e. you have spent some time in understanding the system and its manifold applications and (3) you understand why the librarians are there...

- **An intellectual free haven**: The university – no matter how it is structured – often provides an opportunity to develop your intellectual capacities, thus furnishing you with the competencies to belong to the 'thinking' segment of society. The societal elite of a country strongly corresponds with the intellectual elite of a country. This requires a relatively safe and secure environment to experiment and get feedback on complex issues that necessitate a large number of skills. When you go to university you extend your 'learning' period with the aim to reach higher competencies than you would normally attain; you must learn to walk before you can run.

An intellectual free haven is only relevant to you if you (1) are interested in independent thinking; (2) want to think in the first place and (3) are willing to learn and receive feedback...

- **Interesting peers**: A university is a meeting place of interesting peers; everybody comes to the university with specific ambitions and ideals; some might be more calculating, but in general no student has ever entered a university just for economic reasons – the alternative being to get a job and earn some 'real bucks' straight away. Moreover, your fellow students come from all over the country (or even the world) and have most probably already had some interesting life experiences. It is a matter of tapping into these 'stories' and experiences, and your university experience will become a 'micro cosmos' of what you will encounter the rest of your life – although right now in a somewhat more controlled environment. Didactical research has found that you often learn more from your fellow students than from lecturers. It might start with 'how to bake an egg' (if you have left the parental home for the first time), but can proceed into very rewarding exchanges of insights and experiences on 'how to analyse society' and 'how to come up with interesting solutions to real problems'.

Making use of interesting peers requires that (1) you understand the basics of 'peer teaching' and the way in which you can profit from an intelligent exchange with your peers and (2) are prepared to act as a peer to your fellow students as well...

- **Promoting high standards**: Universities are increasingly competing to establish and maintain high standards; in the bargaining society they are judged on the basis of peer reviews (visitation commissions) of their educational, research and administrative quality. Whether or not these systems are fair and effective is contingent upon a large number of variables. But it implies in any case that there is a strong sense for quality control at most universities around the world. As a student you can make use of this awareness by demanding the highest possible quality in teaching, examinations and related activities.

The commitment to high standards requires that you are interested in the quality (1) of life; (2) of your environment and (3) of the activities in which you participate...

Contents

1 The Skill Circle
2 The Skill Circle as an organic whole: creating linkages
3 Skill Development as managing circular cycles
4 Goals of the Skill Sheets collection

1 The Skill Circle

To survive in a bargaining society you have to be a smart negotiator capable of maximizing your short-term benefits (get good grades for your exams and assignments). But academia as a learning environment can be so much more. To move beyond a mere survival strategy you have to work on and master a set of basic skills at a sufficiently high level. These skills can be identified by a Skill Circle that can be depicted by two overlapping scales (Figure 1). First along a *social scale* skills can be positioned from purely individual to group skills. Secondly, skills have a *process scale* that runs from input oriented to output oriented skills. This basic distinction results in seven relevant basic skills: research skills, study and self-management skills, reading, listening, writing, presentation and team and project management skills.

Figure 1 The Skill Circle

At university you are often supposed and challenged to develop all these skills *simultaneously*. But the degree to which you develop and master these beyond the minimum (calculating) level largely depends on your own efforts. At most universities, for instance, presentation skills and project/team management skills are fostered much less than listening skills (in big classes) or reading skills (large amounts of literature for a written multiple-choice exam). Project management in teams – even at universities that have adopted small study groups – often comes down to a fixed division of labour between study friends who team up repeatedly. Experience shows that this type of division of labour is not conducive to individuals correcting the deficiencies in their Skill Circle. Many a student realizes only during the thesis-writing period – when you cannot fall back on a team – what kind of skills they never practised. This explains why a considerable number of students do not finish their studies despite only having their thesis left to write – in other words, with 95% of all course work already completed at a 'sufficient' level. It also explains why some tutors always complain that students are not 'ready' for their thesis.

The 'Skill Highway' constitutes the central vertical axis of the Skill Circle. It runs from study/self-management skills via research skills to team/project management skills. 'We can know others only by knowing ourselves, but we can know ourselves only by knowing others' (Whetten et al., 2000: 79). The challenge of mastering these skills is that they have a somewhat complicated process dimension – lying in between input and output. Research skills are the core competency of anybody following an academic training. These skills are the *prerequisite* necessary for giving reliable advice, but also constitute the basis for effective self-management and team-management. Mastering research skills has individual as well as social ingredients. It first implies that you are able to learn from your own experience. Any learning experience commences with *personal awareness* (self-management) and is followed by a number of learning phases: from relatively incompetent (but blessed in their ignorance of that incompetence) to often agonising periods of awareness of incompetence to a phase of awareness of competence (Figure 2).

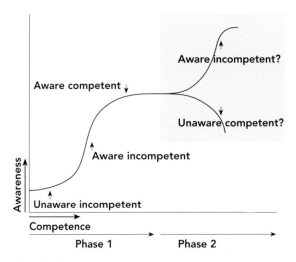

Figure 2 The Learning Cycle

Then you enter a new phase (2) and begin a new cycle of learning new competencies. In learning psychology it is considered that the ultimate stage of the learning cycle is when you reach the stage of being unaware of your competence. This is perhaps important in the event of having to perform complex physical tasks – for instance when driving a car – but is not very functional when you have to engage in the continuous learning process that most managerial and research tasks demand. So the challenge after you for instance have successfully finished a course is to understand that you might have received a sufficient grade, but that it does not mean that you have mastered everything. It is time to move into the so-called 'discomfort' zone again, certainly if you want to address a complex issue to which there is no simple answer. Going through the cycle time and again requires a solid research orientation, which will help you throughout the development of any other skill as well.

But research skills only acquire a meaningful and relevant content in a social setting. It is not sufficient for instance to study literature intelligently and contemplate solutions for problems. You should be capable of communicating what you have read and the ideas that you have formed in such a manner, that it has impact on the problem which you want to address. Moreover, the image of the solitary researcher writing analyses in an ivory tower, away from everyday problems, does not hold any longer in a bargaining society. Research itself is increasingly becoming a group process. Organisations demand that university alumni present facts that can be of practical relevance and are involved in the execution of ideas. Participatory experience in group processes can also give you valuable insight into the interaction of people and organisations. There is always value in participatory observations, as long as you are capable of *systematically* using these insights as *input* for further research.

Input oriented Skills are often the first skills that have to be acquired in academia. First, *reading skills* are the easiest skill to learn. Reading can be done almost everywhere on an individual basis. Reading presents the most effective way of acquiring knowledge accumulated by others, but is also a means of developing a personal approach. Reading represents the highest speed of processing information (much higher than listening for instance). By gaining insight into what others have found or thought, it becomes possible to figure out what you can (or should) add to that, and thus slowly start developing your own approach. Not all relevant information, however, is presented in written form, or the information on paper or on the website is biased. So the second input oriented skill is the ability to obtain information from presentations and by *listening* to others. Effective listening is a social activity that requires that you understand that what you hear is partly the result of your own constructive communication skills. Listening skills are interactive.

Output oriented Skills aim at communicating the results of your research and learning processes. The most effective way is in written form. Writing skills are not only important for the organisation or person that you do the research for, but also for yourself. The writing process itself gives you the most concrete feedback about your level of understanding of the topic at hand. Famous novelists like George Orwell or Stephen King are known for having stated, 'I write to find out what I think'. By writing in a scientific manner, your knowledge in any case becomes reproducible. Enabling reproduction is a basic characteristic of any science which strives for the accumulation of relevant knowledge. Committing your research results and ideas to paper creates the best preconditions for getting feedback from others.

The other method of communicating your research results is by oral *presentations*. Presentations are the least effective in making your knowledge reproducible. But it is often a better, and more direct, way of getting instant feedback from your audience. This applies in particular in case you are still in the middle of a learning cycle. In that case, the presentation can enable the formulation of further research questions. A presentation also provides you with information concerning your own understanding of the topic, particularly when your presentation leads to debate and an interaction of opinions. Good presentations are, therefore, always aimed at co-production together with the audience. A bad presentation, on the other hand, at best gives you feedback on your inability to present information, but most of the time does not lead to any meaningful feedback at all ('questions? no questions!').

2 The Skill Circle as an integrated whole: creating linkages

Output-oriented skills (writing and presentation) are a necessary precondition for becoming a skilled person. However, they are never sufficient preconditions. They should have meaningful contents, which is based on input oriented skills such as reading and listening. Dealing with skills effectively means *linking* the various parts of the Skill Circle. Skills can and have to be distinguished, but it is problematic – even foolish – to separate them. Specialised skills training programmes often lack effectiveness when they are devoid of content, good feedback and lack awareness of how they are linked to other skills. If you become aware of this mechanism, the Skill Circle becomes an organic whole and skill development a natural and daily phenomenon. Two types of linkages can thereby be distinguished: horizontal and vertical linkages.

Horizontal linkages. Reading and writing are linked through self-management skills. Listening and presentation are linked through team management skills. By reading intelligently one also accumulates knowledge on how to write. An effective reader, for instance, thinks about the composition of the text read, or considers whether a particular argument is more convincing than another. The next step then is to use this experience as *input* for improving the writing *output*. Good writing, therefore, implies the ability to re-read, (self) manage feedback and consequently re-write texts. Critical writing requires critical reading. A capable reader is often a better writer and, as a result, a better researcher. Writing and reading to a certain extent draw upon the same cognitive systems in the brain (Berninger et al.,

1994). There has to be a balance between the two activities. Too much reading without the other skill activities makes the mind lazy. In the words of Albert Einstein: 'reading after a certain age, diverts the mind too much from its creative pursuits. Any man who reads too much and uses his own brain too little, falls into lazy habits of thinking' (www.brainyquote.com/quotes/authors/a/albert_einstein.html, consulted 5 May 2007). Good readers and writers have comparable abilities in effectively organising their personal environment.

The same applies to listening and presentation. Good listening provides input for your own presentation skills. If you attend a lecture and can analyse during the lecture why you like it (for instance because of the structure of the argument or the supportive communication contained in the body language of the speaker) it provides you with input for your own presentation skills. In preparing your own presentation you draw on these other lectures. Skilful presenting, moreover, necessitates the ability to listen. Some managers think that they can learn by talking, but without using any of the other linkages (either reading or listening) this tends to become a rather small and isolated learning path. Some students think that they can learn by passively listening. There has to be a balance between talking/presenting and listening. In case students for instance talk through the presentation of a teacher (on another topic than is lectured about), this in turn discourages the teacher to commit him/herself to the class. By adopting a positive posture and actively intervening in the speech, listeners are able to influence the speaker positively and thus make it more worth their while. Effective presenters and listeners actively shape the social environment that they operated in. The best interpersonal relationships are based on so called 'congruence' between listening and speaking and between verbal and non-verbal communication (Whetten et al., 2000: 238).

Vertical linkages can be established if you are for instance aware that listening and reading have a lot in common in terms of concentration skills. Listening and reading are the skills that you have to master earliest in your studies. They will take up most of your time initially. When you want to know what you are good at, it is important to understand that most people have their strength either in reading or listening – rarely in both (Drucker, 2005). By establishing vertical linkages between the two a higher level of competence can be achieved. An interesting technique in this respect is by reading aloud the text one has written. If you feel uncomfortable with the way the text 'sounds', it is often an indication of a poorly formulated argument. If it sounds intelligible, you might have written something legible.

Table 3 Skill Linkages: Examples

HORIZONTAL	Reading and writing	• 'Easy reading is hard writing' (Ernest Hemingway) • 'Effective writing requires re-reading time and again' • 'Sorry for the long text, I didn't have time to re-read it and consequently shorten it'
	Listening and presentation	• 'One advantage of talking to yourself is that you know at least somebody's listening' (Franklin P. Jones) • 'Make sure you have finished speaking before your audience has finished listening' (Dorothy Sarnoff) • 'Courage is what it takes to stand up and speak; courage is also what it takes to sit down and listen' (Winston Churchill)
VERTICAL	Listening and reading	• 'I learned to write by listening to people talk' (Gayl Jones) • 'Effective PowerPoint presentations require a good balance between listening and reading what is projected' • 'The reading of all good books is like conversation with the finest men of past centuries' (Descartes)
	Presentation and writing	• 'Before one starts talking, others should be able to read off one's face what is going to be told to them' (Marcus Aurelius) • 'Bad presenters stick to their written text' • 'I present my writing to receive direct feedback from people that otherwise would not have taken the time to read the whole text' • 'Our thoughts are half-formed and unexamined when they're still inside our heads. Through talking about them, writing them down, debating them, teaching them (...) we work out our beliefs and ideas and make them better' (Ephilosopher.com, consulted 13/9/2005)

3 Skill Development as managing circular cycles

Research skills are the undisputed 'linking pin' of all other skills (Figure 1). The learning cycle of research can also be portrayed as a 'reflective' circle or cycle (Figure 3). Going through the cycle in the right order is vital to the learning process: from problem, via problem definition, diagnosis to the design of a possible solution. Only then you can implement solutions and evaluate them. This can be dubbed the 'virtuous circle' of research. In every research project – no matter how small it is – you go through the reflective cycle; sometimes more than once. The idea of the reflective cycle closely resembles the famous learning cycle of David Kolb (1976). Kolb developed his learning cycle as a sequence that moves from concrete experience, reflective observations, via abstract conceptualisations, towards active experimentation and testing. Whetten et al. (2000) further specified Kolb's learning styles into four basic questions that need to be asked in the right sequence and follow a comparable logic as the reflective cycle of research: (1) Why? (problem definition), (2) What? (diagnosis and design), (3) How? (implementation) and (4) If? (evaluation and next problem). Kolb comes to the conclusion that successful managers or administrators are not so much distinguished by any single set of knowledge or skills, but by the ability to 'adapt to and master the changing demands of his job and career – by his ability to learn' (Kolb, 1976:21). Linking Kolb's ideas to the reflective cycle of research specifies the skill highway: good research is a matter of adequate management and self-management skills.

People in the bargaining society, however, are strongly inclined to go through the reflective cycle in a different order. For instance, as a guru you are only interested in providing 'solutions' – catchy concepts, quick scans, simple methods – which do not always clearly relate to the problems at hand. You run the risk of the 'consultancy disease' which is also phrased as: if you have only a hammer at your disposal, you define every problem as a nail. A comparable problem appears in the so-called 'neurotic spiral' (cf. Fensterheim, Baer, 1975). People adopt self-doubts because they take inadequate action. If they only analyse this by benchmarking and evaluating against the action of others, the change is imminent that they develop seriously disturbed feelings, heighten their self-doubts and thus engage in

Virtuous Circles/Cycles

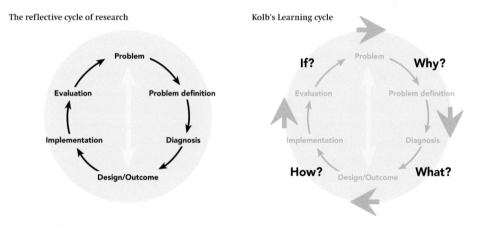

Vicious Circles/Cycles

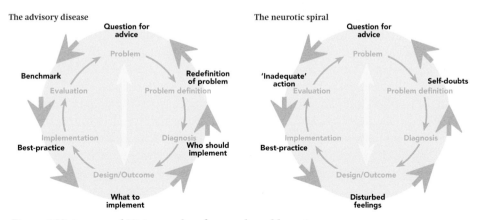

Figure 3 Virtuous and Vicious cycles of research and learning

further inadequate action. Going through the reflective cycle the wrong ('left') way can actually trap you in a 'vicious circle'. It contributes to many of the societal problems that have been analysed in *The Challenges*. 'The more tolerant people are of novelty, complexity and insolubility, the more likely they are to succeed as managers in information-rich, ambiguous environments' (Whetten et al., 2000: 71). Tolerance of novelty implies going through the reflective cycle the 'right' way.

Mastering all other skills progressively along the Skill Circle displays a comparable (reflective) sequence. Figure 4 shows the related circles for each of the six skills. The figure also shows the ambition level of the present approach for each Skill and the way to obtain this:

- **Lifelong learning** through effectively self-managing your own study and learning processes – the process through which you change yourself and your capabilities (Parker with Stone, 2003). This is also known as 'generative' or 'double loop' learning. Generative learners are concerned with learning how to learn. It requires the following sequence: (1) that you are always aware of your 'learning gaps' (the difference between where you are and where you want to be and the ability to question old models of learning), (2) make decisions on the basis of different perspectives, (3) translate that into action, and (4) organise solid feedback (either by yourself or through your peers) on a more or less continuous basis.
- **Effective team and project management** through (1) forming: the appropriate team, (2) storming: taking adequate time for brainstorming over possible dimensions (causes as well as consequences) of the project, (3) norming: deciding on the basis of more or less objective 'norms', (4) performing: implement it, after which (5) the team can be adjourned, provided they performed well.
- **Active reading** always (1) first requires the choice for the most appropriate source (no brainless reading of everything that is available) that can be linked to the issue at hand; (2) after which you come to a selection of what you want to know, which is aided by (3) your identification of structures and argumentation in the read material. Active reading is always accompanied by (4) writing at the same time, either as notes or directly as input for the paper you write (never read only to read), after which you (5) evaluate the usability of what you have read and come to the choice of further sources.
- **Constructive listening** is part of constructive communication techniques in general. It starts with (1) deciding whether a meeting is necessary (i.e. whether there are no other instruments that can be used to establish the communication), (2) good preparation of the content and (3) organisation of the meeting. The actual listening effort should be aimed at (4) co-production of what is communicated, otherwise the meeting will be much less effective. This requires for instance (5) so-called 'supportive listening', which shows that you are aware of the effect of your listening attitude on the person(s) you communicate with. After the actual meeting (6) digesting and evaluating the information in an effective and appropriate manner is as important as getting the actual information.
- **Writing with power** (Elbow, 1981) implies that your writings are aimed to have an effect on the reader. It requires a state of mind and the application of a num-

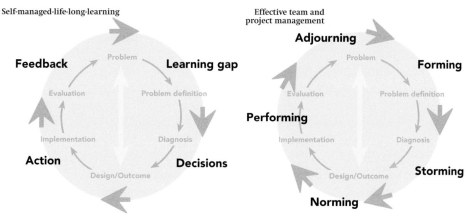

Self-managed-life-long-learning

Effective team and project management

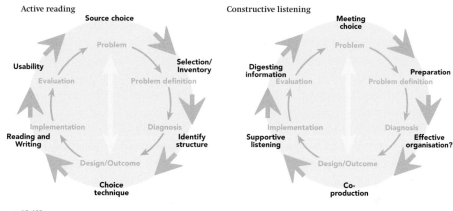

Active reading

Constructive listening

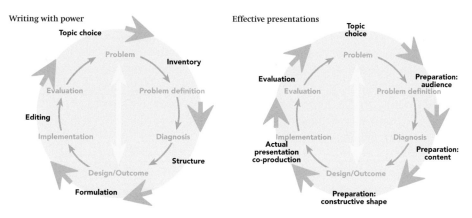

Writing with power

Effective presentations

Figure 4 Skills as Reflective Cycles

ber of organisational principles that also apply to effective project management: after your topic choice, first (1) come to an inventory of what you have prepared; start brainstorming over possible lines of argument; (2) then decide upon a clear structure (norming); (3) start formulating completely from scratch your arguments (performing); (4) after which you take sufficient time to edit the text written. Each of these phases takes approximately the same time. Only then can your writings become powerful – no matter how much or how little time you have available. The same rules apply for writing a joint paper. With group papers the danger of engaging in a vicious cycle looms much larger than with individual papers.

- **Effective presentations** also apply the rules of constructive communication. In this case, however, you are more responsible for creating the right preconditions for communication. It requires that you not only (1) choose a topic, but (2) try to figure out who your audience exactly is and what the circumstances are under which you make your presentation. This is vital (3) for the type of content you prepare and the (4) constructive shape (informal, graphical, formal, discussion) in which you design your presentation. The actual presentation (5) then can become an act of co-production, after which (6) you always organise solid feedback on the effectiveness of your presentation. Only then can you confidently move to the next presentation.

Weakest links. In the bargaining society, people not only tend to go through these reflective cycles the other way round, but they also tend to undervalue two stages in particular in the cycle: the problem definition and the evaluation stage. The problem definition or brainstorming stage, firstly, is one of the most underrated stages of activities. If not organised appropriately the remainder of the process lacks depth and creativity. Effective brainstorming is the basis for all creativity. Not brainstorming often implies that you do not even become aware of old habits, and start up a very handicapped learning loop.

Many projects, secondly, are not evaluated – or only marginally evaluated – for sometimes opportunistic and defensive reasons. Project organisers fear criticism, certainly when the evaluation triggers more critical negotiations over new projects. In case major projects do get evaluated, it is often already because of the perception of a problem. The formation of such evaluation commissions is always part of a complex bargaining process. The same sometimes applies to calculating teachers who do not engage themselves in evaluating their teaching out of fear for generating criticism. Not evaluating, however, increases the risk that you get stuck in old habits and unfinished learning loops.

4 Goals of the Skill Sheets collection

The Skill Sheets collection has been designed as a practical tool to help students work through the skill circle and linking the various skills at ever higher levels of mastery and sophistication. Once you have understood the basic logic of this approach, you will find it hard to stop learning! None of the skills is solely 'product' or 'process' oriented. Sometimes the skills are easy to develop and master, but more often they require intensive training over longer periods of time. They always have to be linked to real research and content, otherwise you will only learn a number of 'tricks' without substance. The Skill Sheets are designed to support tutors and students in this training process. It aims at five results.

1 **Quick reference guide**. Firstly, the Skill Sheets should be used whenever a question arises with regards to a particular skill. The research practitioner should be able to find reminders, pointers, tips and general criteria on these skills 'at a glance' and should not have to go through whole libraries of information. In less than five minutes every relevant question should be answered by the information in the Skill Sheets. For this reason a detailed index has been included. If you have more time available, a system of references in the text (indicated by an arrow and the number, for instance: ➲A6) points at other relevant Skill Sheets. If you have even more time available, or in case you need more detailed guidance, you can consult the website [⊕➲www.skillsheets.com] for many more references, exercises and related tools.

2 **Selective**. Secondly, the collection has selected those skills that are considered to be of prime importance for students and researchers. In this Skill Sheets collection, very basic instrumental skills such as data processing skills or detailed knowledge of statistical techniques have more or less been taken for granted. Specialized skills training often lack effectiveness when they are devoid of content, good feedback and lack awareness of how they are linked to other skills.

3 **Identification of Skill levels**. Thirdly, the collection presents various *levels* of Skill requirements throughout the studies. Everybody goes through the reflective cycles time and again, and hopefully at ever higher levels of sophistication. Table 4 portrays a number of generalisations on this path per separate skill. These characteristics account for the learning experience of the 'average' student.

Table 4 Learning Cycles in Skill Development

	From...	To...
A Research	The questions of others; own experience	Your own questions; other people's experience
B Study/self-management	Learning to digest knowledge; teacher/tutor-oriented; fragmented	Knowledge to generate further learning; assertive/self-oriented; integrated
C Reading	Reproducing; memorizing for exam	Gathering; input for research
D Listening	Passive; consumption; teacher-oriented	Active and interactive; co-production; research-oriented
E Writing	Simple; process-oriented	Advanced/sophisticated; content-oriented
F Presentation	Based on your own experience; aimed at knowledge transfer	Based on your research; co-producing knowledge
G Team/project management	Simple; directive; assignment and input-oriented	Sophisticated; reflective; project output-oriented

You all move from relatively simple, passive, and reproduction or consumption-oriented skills toward far more (inter)active, complex and production-oriented skills. These processes are intimately related to your research skills. Academic research skills for instance develop from addressing questions of others on the basis of your personal experience, to addressing your own questions on the basis of other people's experience; and from subjective towards objective or inter-subjective knowledge accumulation. Study skills develop from a fragmented and teacher-oriented digestion of pre-arranged knowledge towards a more assertive attitude that aims at life-long learning in the knowledge society.

In the introduction to every series of Skills four levels of skill proficiency will be specified:
- **Level 1**: Approximates the entry level of a Bachelor
- **Level 2**: Exit level Bachelors
- **Level 3**: Exit level Masters
- **Level 4**: Postgraduate level

These specifications will help you to identify where you are in your skill development trajectory. On the website (www.skillsheets.com) further checklists will be published with which you can assess your strengths and weaknesses on a much more detailed level. Secondly, some of these checklists have already been filled out by previous generations of students. The average patterns of their assessments per level will be revealed on the website. It provides an excellent benchmark for an individual assessment of the skills profile that you are likely to attain in the next phase of your studies. Even in your first year, you can start comparing yourself with your peers. This benchmark provides you a starting point for – call it – a 'bargaining session' with yourself over the kind of goals and priorities you should/could adopt per skill. It also enables you to ask for advice from your peers or staff members on whether your particular skills profile – for instance in case it really deviates from the average – should be cause for alarm or for comfort. Treat these 'bargaining benchmarks' as a guideline, a challenge or source of inspiration, never as an objective measure.

4 **Systematic and integrative**. Fourthly, this collection helps the student-user to work towards acquiring these skills *systematically*, during their time at university. Some of the skills referred to in this collection may already be included in the programmes offered by the university, others may not. The result of making most skill requirements *clear* is that students *themselves* will be able to systematically assess in which areas they need extra training or where they should organise feedback. In the series on self-management and study skills, some supporting sheets for this goal have been added. While some of the skills appear to be quite basic and self-evident in practice this rarely proves to be the case.

5 **Tutor orientation**. Lastly, the Skill Sheet series should enable *tutors* to refer to specific sheets when they make comments and suggestions. This is particularly useful with regard to the lack of time available for practice and sufficient feedback in individual research, speech and writing skills at many universities. Using the Skill Sheets as a basis of focused feedback should allow teachers to use

their time effectively, as they do not have to waste time by continually repeating the same information.

Skill Mottos

o   *Everyone can acquire a minimum mastery of all relevant Skills. It is a matter of attitude.*

o   *You are as strong as the weakest Skill in the Skill Circle and as the weakest link in the Reflective cycle.*

o   *'A person is not shaped by the skills (s)he has, but by the choices (s)he makes on the basis of these skills'*
    (cf. Boers, Lingsma, 2003).

o   *Skills can't be taught, but they can be learned.*

o   *Practice, practice, practice? No, the impact of quality always prevails over quantity.*

Series A Research

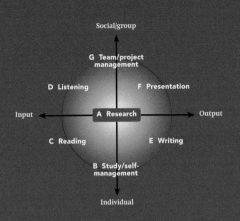

The Reflective Cycle of Research

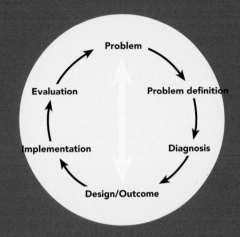

	Problem definition	Diagnosis	Design/ outcome	Implementation	Evaluation
A1 Principles of Good Research	■				
A2 Research Aims: Basic or Applied	■				
A3 Personal Research Aims/Ambitions	■				
A4 Creativity in Research	■				
A5 Steps in Research Projects	■	■			
A6 Feasibility Study	■				
A7 Research Strategies		■	■		
A8 Choosing Appropriate Methods		■	■		
A9 Choosing Appropriate Questions			■		
A10 Formulating the Research Question				■	
A11 Organising Files				■	
A12 Barter in Research				■	
A13 Online Databases				■	
A14 Search Engines: Googling Around				■	
A15 Internet or Internot?				■	
A16 Validation & Verification as Barter					■

Research Skill Levels

Level 1

- ○ Research on questions formulated by others/the teacher
- ○ Own experience forms the prime basis of research
- ○ Link general knowledge (secondary school) to prime object of research of the university
- ○ Understand the reflective cycle as concept
- ○ Can make distinction between 'good' and 'bad' research, and between 'science' and 'journalism'
- ○ First use of basic Internet search methods and (online) libraries
- ○ Understand and able to use the relationship between model and reality (inductive and deductive reasoning)

Level 2

- ○ Research on the basis of (simple) own questions
- ○ Experience of fellow students forms additional basis of and input for research
- ○ A broad spectrum of research methods is understood and applied; choice of the best method concerning the research topic
- ○ Accession requirements of Master are known
- ○ Mastering in particular the descriptive part of the reflective cycle
- ○ Use Internet and other search engines effectively in combination with a systematic use of (online) libraries

Level 3

- ○ Translation of other people's experience into own research questions
- ○ Commitment to a specific research master
- ○ Knowledge of master specific skills and research methods
- ○ The whole reflective cycle is mastered; understanding of the balance between description and prescription
- ○ Mastering advanced research methods on Internet and in libraries (in particular as regards finding relevant scientific articles)
- ○ Knowledge of important other sources of information

Level 4

- ○ The graduated Master remains research-oriented, invests in attitude and creates the right preconditions for good research
- ○ Applies the reflective circle with an emphasis for the prescriptive dimension (based on solid descriptive research)
- ○ Is part of a network of informants and is capable of intensifying and de-intensifying this network in order to access relevant information
- ○ Feedback on research by contractors

In principle, there is no wrong or right research. Likewise, there are no wrong or right theories, nor wrong or right methods. There is only good, mediocre or bad research. Good research selects the most appropriate theories and methods for the problem at hand. It links methods to theory and problem definition to problem. Bad research claims more than can be done on the basis of the used methods, or chooses overly quantitative methods for a primarily qualitative problem. *Always* take the following eight basic rules of good research into account.

1   Dare to build upon the research of others
2   Dare to make *motivated* choices
3   Always define the most important concepts
4   Explain flaws in the research yourself
5   Make a clear distinction between analytical and normative judgement
6   Strive for the highest possible integrity
7   Be critical
8   Good research is disciplined and realistic

1 Dare to build upon the research of others

Many research questions have been addressed before. And most social science problems are very complex. Each individual researcher is, in a way, an intellectual 'dwarf'. Be brave enough to admit this. You can stand on the shoulders of giant predecessors and in doing so, if you are also brave enough to take previous ideas into account, get a splendid view of the research problem at hand. Science is intended to be cumulative. In the early stages even of a small research project, get an overview of the most relevant approaches (➲A7). Very often there are good textbooks which can give you this overview in a few hours. If you are an inexperienced researcher, ask a supervisor, a tutor or even the librarian for clear guidance (➲B13)

2 Dare to make *motivated* choices

Research is a continuous choice process. For every problem there is an abundance of solutions, depending on the stakeholder, time and place (➲A6). Likewise a large number of equally valid approaches, methodologies and perspectives exist. You have to dare to make a choice, otherwise nothing will come out of your research. The worst thing you can do, besides not daring to make choices, is *not* specifying choices. Revealing *all* your choices is a minimum requirement for a good research project. It enables other researchers to repeat your research steps, and your research results are then as objective as possible. Basically this is what distinguishes the *scientific method* of research from other methods, for example those of journalists and often also of consultants (Emory, Cooper, 1991:15). Ideally *each one of these choices is explained in the introduction of the research report*. Table A.1 shows the basic choices that you need to make in any research project.

Table A.1 Research Choices

Topic	Choice and motivation
The problem	Choice of a problem definition: why have you defined the problem like this?
Research aim	☐ basic; ☐ applied; ☐ action-oriented; ☐ evaluation (➔A2, A3)
Level of analysis	☐ micro; ☐ meso; ☐ macro; ☐ meta; ☐ a particular combination
Theories	If available, make a choice from at least **three** related approaches
Methods	Specify your choice for one or a combination of methods e.g. by stating the strengths and weaknesses of each method
Stakeholder perspective	Whose perspective do you want to take into account in this research project? Make your choice of a particular actor (manager, trade union, government) clear. Be selective
Sources	What kind of sources did you search for in particular: ☐ primary, ☐ secondary, ☐ tertiary. What is the strength and the weakness of these sources? (➔A6, E1)
'Audience'	Who are you addressing with your research? Is your audience the same as your stakeholder? Or do you consider the research project valuable for others as well?

3 Always define the most important concepts

Social sciences focus very much on argumentation. Words and concepts which form these arguments can have many meanings. The dictionary definition of a concept is often inappropriate for research, because the dictionary is too general and frequently gives definitions based on circular reasoning. Use definitions from the relevant literature and explain your choice of a particular definition if more than one definition exists (which is often the case). Make the definition operational, i.e. understandable and open to testing. Remember: definitions do not usually develop in isolation. Always consider the context in which a definition is introduced.

4 Explain flaws in the research yourself

If you explain the choices that you have made, you should also make clear the flaws in the research design that you have chosen. You should include this information in your conclusion. Do not leave this for the reader to discover by themselves. If you do this it will not only lessen your credibility as a researcher, but also reduce the credibility of your research (see also point 6). If you come to the conclusion that you have chosen a methodology that is not appropriate – although often used in comparable research projects – you should not necessarily have to begin your research again. The fear of having to start again is a mistake that many students make and sometimes results in them failing to reveal the choices they have made. To conclude that a particular methodology is not particularly useful can also be an important result of your research effort. Your research aim has only changed to one of lesser advance (➔A3).

5 Make a clear distinction between analytical and normative judgement

Avoid the inclination of many researchers to come to prescription on the basis of weak or very limited description of empirical phenomena. Conclusions can *only* be based on the results of the research. A limited research project can only lead to limited conclusions. Always specify the conditions under which you think your research results hold true. Since you have stated this in the earlier parts of your research, your conclusion should be the logical end-result of your research. *Speculating* on the basis of your research results could be valuable and interesting, but can only be done after the conclusions, and should be explicitly stated as such.

6 Strive for the highest possible integrity

Every researcher should be aware of the ease with which data and figures can be manipulated (➔A7). You frequently make use of data collected by others for instance, often at high levels of aggregation. So you should adopt a high level of integrity when assembling qualitative and quantitative data. Likewise, always take into account the possibility that data and arguments are manipulated by others. The more the researcher uses the criteria for good research the higher the credibility of the research report. Integrity is valuable even for short research essays. Work on your reputation as a reliable researcher. You should demonstrate your experience of doing research in the research project at hand. If you are inexperienced, at least state your personal motivation for doing this research in the preface of the report (➔E3).

7 Be critical and creative

Good research is critical research. A good researcher is not afraid to ask tough questions. Never stop asking the 'why' question: why is this problem a problem? Why should I choose this particular approach for tackling this problem? Why do I see what I see? As children ceaselessly ask their parents the 'why' question, researchers should be capable of doing the same with the (societal) problems that they want to address. A skilled researcher should be capable of expressing doubt and asking 'why' questions without annoying the recipient of the research question (as is so often the case with parents and children!). As René Descartes already stated in the early 17th century, 'doubt is the basis of wisdom'. Research refers to the effective management of doubt. Apply the basic rules of critical thinking (box next page). Critical research sometimes necessitates developing creative research approaches, but only when the traditional methods do not hold (➔A4).

Ten Principles of Critical Research

1 Continuously ask the 'why' question (at least three times in building up an argument)
2 Be sceptical of the reliability of sources
3 Always know the background (either editorial, personal or otherwise) of your sources.
4 Think! Evade obvious questions
5 Prepare!
6 Always question arguments
7 Always check the appropriateness of quantitative data
8 Be realistic about what you can achieve as an individual researcher
9 Make sure that your research can be replicated and your hypotheses refuted (falsified)
10 Be modest regarding what you can know as a subjective human being

8 Good research is disciplined and realistic

Managing doubt is not easy. You may hope to be inspired by the aims you set for yourself (➲A3). But always keep in mind one final 'rule of thumb', which is applicable to most research projects even if you realise that this rule suggests an exactitude that is difficult to obtain in most real-life research projects:

Good research is the result of 80% perspiration and 20% inspiration.

The type of research project you want to undertake depends as much on the problem you address, as on the type of researcher you want to be/become. What are your aims in a research project? This is *always the first question* that you should ask yourself when beginning a research project. Two general research aims can be distinguished: basic and applied research. A basic research project is aimed primarily at understanding the problem at hand. An applied research project focuses more on the outcome of the problem, and the design of possible solutions.

Aims of basic research

- **Aim 1: Problem definition** This type of research deals with semantics and philosophy. You ask questions like: 'What is the *nature of the problem* I would like to address?' 'Which areas of research are involved?' 'Which *key words* and *concepts* should be considered?' You often need to go beyond the problem experienced by the people who are directly involved, and find out the context of their problem in order to formulate the appropriate problem definition.
- **Aim 2: Diagnosis** This type of research aims at analysing all the ins and outs of a particular problem. You ask questions like: 'What *causes* the problem to appear?' 'Why is there a discrepancy between the actual, and the desired situation of the actors involved?' 'What level(s) of analysis should be considered, in order to find the cause of the problem?' 'Which theoretical approaches (lines of argument) and methodologies are available to analyse this kind of problem?' You can also ask for the *consequences* when the problem persists.

Aims of (more) applied research

- **Aim 3: Design** This type of research aims at giving advice, but from a distance. You address questions like: 'What kinds of solutions have been developed for this problem?' 'What effect did they have?' 'What other solutions are available for this problem?' 'Is there a better solution?'
- **Aim 4: Implementation** This type of research aims at active intervention. It is also known as 'action' research. You ask questions like: 'How can a designed solution be put into practice?' 'What are the other possibilities?' 'What could the function of the researcher be in this process?' 'At what points in the process of change should the researcher intervene?'
- **Aim 5: Evaluation** This type of research not only aims at active intervention, but also at revision of the design if the proposed solution was not successful. You ask questions like: 'How effective has the proposed implementation been?' 'Does the chosen implementation create additional problems?'

A research project can focus on just one of these research aims. For example, if you aim at researching questions of implementation, then you leave the design problem and the problem of definition to others. These 'others' might be other researchers (thus creating a division of labour between researchers) or the actors themselves. These objectives represent a sort of sequence of research goals/aims. As such, the five aims of research can be grouped together as the five consecutive phases of an ideal research project. Each step accumulates information about the solution to a particular problem and each step provides the input for the next step.

Tension between description and prescription

The biggest challenge for applied research projects, is dealing with the tension which exists between problem and design (Figure A.2). To be more specific: a tension exists between the Reflective Cycle for the researcher and the questions posed by the client. Clients ask researchers to give them an answer to the question 'is this correct?' or 'what am I doing wrong?' The second question which is often put to the researcher is 'how would you do it?' Thirdly, clients ask 'could you come up with alternatives on the basis of the experience of other organisations?' Basically, clients use the same reflective circle of research and research questions as the researcher. But they go in the opposite direction. In the introduction to this Skill Sheet collection this was referred to as the 'adviser's disease'. It boils down to the researcher being too eager to please the customer on short notice, and often deviates the researcher from the basics of good and critical research (➜A1). A good researcher is acutely aware of this tension. Sometimes, aiming at good (basic) research therefore requires a researcher to search for the 'right' customer. Otherwise the tension becomes too great.

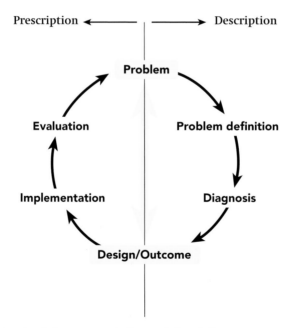

Figure A.2 The tension between prescription and description

Not all steps of the Reflective Cycle need to be performed by the same researcher. This is what forms the labour divisions between the various scientific disciplines. A too rigid division of labour, however, has often resulted in 'sketchy research'. Every researcher should be able to master all elements of the Reflective Cycle. But – depending on your personal preference – not all stages need to be carried out with the same intensity. Neither do all steps have to be sequential: you can begin with an implementation problem, and then ask yourself what the consequences might be of the problem definition by the actors involved. In focusing on implementation problems you can build on the description of the problem offered by other researchers. Building on the work of others is common in large organisations, particularly for strategic management researchers. But you have to be aware that the more you take the choices of others for granted (and refrain from applying the first steps of the circle seriously and systematically), the greater the chance that the results of your research will not address the real problem.

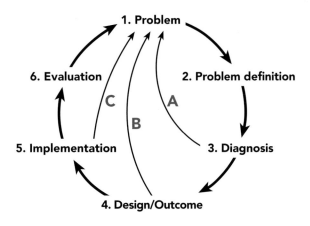

Figure A.3 Reflective cycles for individual researchers

You can go through the cycle in various ways (Figure A.3). Fundamental (basic) researchers often focus their attention primarily on the first and most descriptive steps of research (cycle A). They aim at a better understanding of their research object. Systematically coming to a better understanding is what is known as the *heuristic value* of research. More applied (prescription) oriented researchers place less emphasis on the first two steps and move quickly into the B or C cycles. There are, however, no real shortcuts. Even applied researchers have to try to grasp the problem first. A way to go through these phases of research projects is for instance to build further on existing theory, and check whether it is applicable to the problem at hand.

When you are familiar with the different research aims and the various cycles that you can go through, you can decide what kind of researcher you would like to be. Taking the Reflective Cycle into account, there are five ingredients for a personal profile at your disposal. Table A.3 enables you to decide what your preferred profile looks like, by posing a number of critical questions. If you are inclined to answer the question(s) in the affirmative, include this element in your profile.

Table A.3 What kind of researcher do you want to be: A personal checklist

Personal profile	Critical questions
1 'Conceptualiser'	☐ Do you refuse to take the problem definition of the actor who commissioned the research as given?
	☐ Are you interested in research problems in general?
2 'Diagnost'	☐ Are you interested in finding out the real source of the problem you are addressing?
	☐ Do you want to go beyond the level of analysis of the actors directly involved?
	☐ Do you prefer to do research independent of your research object?
3 'Designer'	☐ Are you interested in designing scenarios to tackle the problem at hand?
	☐ Are you interested in designing solutions for a (perceived) problem?
4 'Implementer'	☐ Do you want to intervene in the research object?
	☐ Are you interested in designing acceptable and feasible solutions?
5 'Involved evaluator'	☐ Do you want to be committed to the organisation that you do research for?
	☐ Do you want to become an active internal lobbyist for the solutions proposed?

A good researcher has an affinity with, and knowledge of all five research functions. You will probably answer many questions in the affirmative. But to avoid losing your way due to a lack of priorities, you will have to specify your preference for a limited number of research profiles. Your priority aims can change from research question to research question (➔A9, A10).

If your research profile looks like:

▪ **1,2**,3,4,5:	you want to be a 'basic' researcher!
▪ 1,2,**3,4**,5:	you want to be an 'applied action' researcher.
▪ 1,2,**3,4,5**:	you want to be a 'critical action' researcher.
▪ **1**,-,3,4,**5**:	you want to be... yes... what do you want to become?
▪ **1,2,3,4,5**:	you lack (research) priorities.
▪ -,-,-,-,-:	you have a problem!

When the problem at hand has never been addressed, when it might require 'heterodox' knowledge, because no appropriate theoretical frameworks are available or easy accessible empirical data is lacking, a researcher might get stuck in the first phase of the Reflective Cycle. Kersbergen (2007) proposes a *'Reflective Cycle of creativity'* (Figure A.4) which basically provides a shortcut out of the problem definition phase in the Reflective Cycle of research (➲the A cycle in Skill Sheet A3). Creativity and creative problem-solving tend to go through three general stages: a problem formulation, a diverging and a converging phase (Cameron, 2005, Parker with Stone, 2003).

The problem formulation phase (which includes some form of diagnosis) is followed by an intentional 'diverging phase' in which divergent thinking is stimulated – i.e. as many different ideas as possible are generated. This resembles the brainstorming technique required for effective meetings (➲G8) and writing processes (➲E1). The diverging phase is followed by a 'converging' phase – selection of ideas and the capacity to realize them. People who control the diverging phase, but do not control the converging phase are considered crazy. People who do master the converging phase are often regarded as intelligent inventors or even geniuses. The converging phase requires insight, imagination, prudence and support, before useful ideas can eventually be implemented. Insight is needed to realize the potential of an idea. Imagination is needed to further develop an idea and tackle the problems by going through the Reflective Cycle of creativity again, until the idea is sufficiently developed. Because people – including researchers – tend to resist change, creative ideas are not easily accepted.

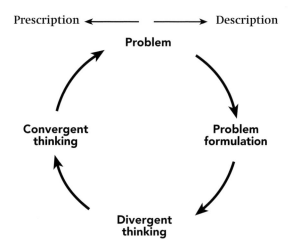

Figure A.4 *Reflective Cycle of Creativity*

Divergent thinking can be part of a person's character, but can also be stimulated through a number of techniques. Basically these techniques 'shock' the mind into identifying new perspectives. There are a number of techniques available that are relevant for research as well as management (cf. Parker with Stone, 2005; Kersbergen, 2007; De Bono, 1992; Van Tulder, 2006). Table A.4 lists some of these techniques. The Skills Sheets website gives more detailed information on some of these techniques. Most of these techniques can be employed individually, but are also well suited for group processes (which makes them particularly appropriate for management problems). After creative new paths of research or unexpected new methods of research have been triggered by these techniques, the 'convergent thinking' phase basically applies the usual selection techniques to redefine the problem and come to a new specification of the research project (➡A5).

Table A.4 Techniques to enhance Divergent Thinking

Blue Sky Thinking	Imagine (dream) the perfect solution without regard for barriers or opposition
Distortion and negation	Select part of a problem, brainstorm on ways in which it can be distorted (made bigger, smaller, reversed). An alternative is negation in which key elements of the problem are denied, followed by the question (amongst others) 'what would happen if this did not exist?'
Assumption busting	What are the underlying assumptions of a proposed solution and try to bust them
Word association	Come to intuitive associations (immediate response, making connections without logical thought) to key words related to the problem
Analogies or Metaphors	▪ Direct Analogy: what are similarities and differences between, for example, the problem and a tree? ▪ Superhero Analogy: what would Spider-Man/George Bush do about my problem? ▪ Personal analogy: can I identify myself with the problematic situation or person?
Mind Mapping	Draw the problem in the centre of a sheet of paper; draw trunks around this problem that represent connected ideas (main and subsidiary ideas) and try to draw connections between these ideas;
Visualization	In addition to mind mapping there are a large number of other visualisation techniques: concept visualization; data visualization; compound visualization; strategy visualization [⊕➡www.skillsheets.com for more links]
Brainwriting	Write all your ideas on a specific problem on post-its; post them on the table or a board; brainwriting is found to be more effective in creating ideas than brainstorming because it evades negative group interactions (Paulus and Yang, 2000).
Bisociation	Combine two ideas or thoughts to develop something new (follows often after brainwriting or mind mapping)

Six thinking hats	Forcing yourself to switch from one thinking approach to another: neutral (white), emotional (red), logical (black), happy (yellow), creative (green), synthesis (blue) (cf. De Bono, 1992)
Write a storyline	What would the 'story' of your research project look like?
Invent a title	Can you come up with a catchy (working) title that not only will attract the attention of the audience when you finish the research, but will also keep you motivated (because you have not yet started the research).
Find alternative images on the problem	■ Advertisement text/images ■ Cartoons ■ Pictures
Get subjective statements	■ Read biographies of some of the key players (how did they perceive the problem) ■ Look at the website of the players to see how they portray the issue (both in pictures and in text) ■ Ask for transcripts of speeches at the Public Affairs department
Organise an exploratory seminar or a lecture	Invite the person(s) who you were not able to get a personal interview with; preferably ask for some 'out of the box' thinking.

[⊕➔www.skillsheets.com]

Research projects are very difficult to manage. Firstly, there is continuous tension between problem and problem definition over time. The greater your understanding of the problem, the more likely it is that you would like to alter your research question. In the course of a research project you will also gain further insight into the resources available, which could cause you to alter your question. At the start of a project you do not know what to look for. At the end you know what you *should have* looked for! Secondly, research time is always limited. These limitations create continuous tension between the preferred and the feasible outcome of your research. Thirdly, your personal research aims and capabilities change in the course of time and they vie for priority. In group research projects this tension will be greater still. It is important to be aware of the *phases* that a research project could go through, *before* you start a research project.

Research steps

There are at least sixteen known steps. Table A.5 gives you an overview, with brief explanations. You can systematically check during the research process what phase of the process you are in and what you could do. Research can be a very chaotic process, resulting from the complexity of many research topics. However, chaos often occurs because of bad planning, limited experience of doing research and the poor discipline of the researchers. Chaos in the initial phase of a project is not necessarily a bad thing. On the contrary, it can help you to formulate an interesting and relevant question. Chaos at the end of a research process is deadly. Researchers should therefore take the following general rules into consideration if they want to 'survive' a research project:

Rule #1: Consider each step of Table A.5, even for the smallest research projects. If you do not follow all of the steps, be aware of the risks you are taking.

Rule #2: Take sufficient time to formulate an interesting question or hypothesis, which will then *motivate* you throughout the whole research project (➔A9).

Rule #3: In addition, take the time to develop a solid feasibility study, and think of the design of the envisaged research project. Assessing the feasibility of research is most important when you work in groups. After going through this phase, try to adhere to your research question and timing, as much as possible (➔A6).

Rule #4: of 'overstretch' during the research process. If you change your research question during the course of the research project, as a rule do not add topics but make the research precise and limitative. Only alter the question at the appropriate time (step four or nine). Be aware that the function of many of the instrumental skills changes during the course of a project.

Phase A: preparation
Putting the aforementioned rules into practice has the following effects on the timing of your research. Usually, half of the time you spend on your research project is focused on reflection, planning and conceptual clarification (Phase A):
- *reflection* (steps 1-3) takes 5 percent of your time (if the research is a group project, do not employ a division of labour during this phase);
- *incremental development* (steps 4-8) of the research proposal takes at least 25 percent of your time (take your time!). This phase only allows a minor division of labour);
- *conceptual specification* (step 9) takes about 20 percent of your time (if you have sufficiently prepared for this step, during the previous steps).

Phase B: implementation
During the first nine steps you can begin making appointments for interviews or for gaining access to libraries (step 10), because this usually takes considerable time. In phase B you can focus on:
- *data collection* (steps 10-11) which takes approximately 40 percent of your time;
- *finalisation* (steps 12-16) which takes at least 10 percent of your time.

When you plan, always work backwards from the ultimate deadline. Leave sufficient time at the end of the project, to present a decent report. When ninety percent of your research time has past **stop** whatever you are doing and focus on the last four steps. At least three days in a project lasting thirty days, should be left free at the end to deal with the final steps even if you have not done all of the research as planned. Otherwise you run the risk of suffering from the following rule, which often applies to research timing:

> **The first ninety percent of a project takes ninety percent of the time, the last ten percent takes the other ninety percent.**

Table A.5 Research Steps

1 Needs		A	☐ Specify your research needs/problems, or those of your client
2 Aim	↓		☐ Specify your research aims: a. Personal (➲A3); b. Topical. Formulate a problem definition and an initial research question. What outcome and impact do you want the research to have?
3 Time	↓		☐ Specify the time available for the research project (➲B8): a. In weeks/days/hours; b. What other obligations do you have during the project? Consider layout and language style (who is your audience?). Designate an editor. (➲G12)

4 Feasibility	↓		☐ Make a feasibility study of the topic and planned methodology (⊕A6, A8). Is it 'researchable' considering available resources and your own capacity/time? Revise the initial question (⊕A9). Decide upon method(s). Stick with them.
5 Question	↓		☐ Develop a question hierarchy: a logical sequence of research (sub)questions, which also contribute to the contents of your research report. Specify the concrete end product of your research (⊕A2).
6 Linkages	↓		☐ Link each (sub)question to a preferred method. Write a rough introduction.
7 Labour Division	↓		☐ If you work in a group: what would be a useful division of labour for the remaining steps? Create sufficient overlap in your labour division.
8 Budgets	↓		☐ Specify the 'budgets' available: ☐ **Time budget.** Set clear deadlines. Specify time modules (⊕B8, B10, B11); ☐ **Page budget.** Clarify the importance of each part in your end product; ☐ **Social budget.** What networks (of informants) are you in (⊕G2)? ☐ **Financial budget.** In case of a commercial product; if this budget is not approved, you will probably have to stop the project; ☐ **Energy budget.** Make clear what your ambition is and how much energy you (and your group members) would like to put in the project.
9 Theory	↓		☐ Finish the conceptual/theoretical part as soon as possible. The main content of your feasibility study has dealt with this already. Elaborate on paper, do not keep it in your head! This elaboration will probably trigger further specifications of your research question and the concepts used when collecting data.
10 Data	↓	**B**	☐ Only now do you come to the part where you collect primary data, do interviews and so forth. Specify a further labour division if you are part of a group.
11 Analysis	↓		☐ Write down the results of your empirical search. Analyse and interpret them.
12 Conclusion	↓		☐ Always repeat your research question(s), draw conclusions (⊕E5).
13 Summary	↓		☐ Write an 'executive summary', this should be approximately one page long.
14 Preface	↓		☐ Write your preface and rewrite your introduction. Reveal all of the analytical and methodological choices that you have made! (⊕A1)
15 Layout	↓		☐ Finalise the layout of your report (⊕E16).
16 Letter	↓		☐ Send a well written letter to the person/organisation who commissioned the research project (also teachers), outlining the status of the report [⊕ ⊕www.skillsheets.com].

An assessment of the 'researchability' of a research project is one of the most important phases in doing research (➔A5). A feasibility study needs to be done *before* you formulate your (detailed) research question, do interviews and the like. Research projects without a solid feasibility study are bound to fail in many respects:

1 *failed answers:* you will not find an answer to your original research question – for instance because the data are not available – and will start to 'improvise' along the way;
2 *failed questions:* you will probably have to change your research question because you could not find the appropriate empirical data (not available or respondents that were unwilling to provide it);
3 *failed time frame:* the whole project will take you more time than anticipated (or had available);
4 *failed skill assessment:* it will take you even more time because you did not antici-pate what additional skills you needed to acquire to succeed;
5 *failed ambitions:* you or your team members (in case of a joint research project) become free-riders because you did not (in advance) properly discuss whether ambitions and abilities match.

The most important aim of a feasibility study is – in a relatively short period of time – to reveal the kind of (re)sources available and how difficult/easy it is to use them. A feasibility study is usually added to the research design and the research proposal, and reveals the methodology that you will be using to tackle the research question. Often, the feasibility study will cause you to revise your initial research question. The feasibility study for a large research project can take considerable time. For an M.A. thesis, for instance, expect to take at least one week to do a feasi-bility study of your initial research question(s). You go through the whole Reflective Cycle in order to check what kinds of resources are available for each stage of the Reflective Cycle (➔A3).

Three main categories of resources to consider in a feasibility study are personal resources, secondary sources – relating primarily to literature – and primary resources.

1 Personal resources
Begin by specifying your own (or your group's) resources:
- *Time:* how much time is available? Be very honest in this personal assessment. List all of your obligations (including your social obligations) and only then spec-ify what time is left for the research project.
- *Intellectual:* what is your experience in the topic and in doing this kind of research?
- *Social:* who do you know who you could contact to help you with the research? (➔G2).

- *Financial:* do you have an opportunity to hire assistants; what is your budget for making photocopies, or for travelling?
- *Ambition:* your ambition level defines the 'energy' resources available for a project; do you go for a 'pass' only, or are you only satisfied with a 'distinction'; this question is particularly relevant in a group research project, because the group members might have diverging ambition levels; specify beforehand what you will do in case of free-rider behaviour in the group (➔G10).

2 Secondary resources

Find out what kind of literature is available on the topic. This is called secondary data. Make a distinction between theoretical and empirical literature. Theoretical literature will be more important in the first phases of your research project, because it can put your research question in a wider perspective. The empirical literature (or the lack of it) will be more important later on. Assessing the availability of these categories separately will enable you to plan more realistically. There are at least six techniques for assessing the availability of literature:

- **Specify a list of keywords and synonyms** that might cover your research question(s). This is one of the most vital parts of the feasibility study. You start with an intuitive list of keywords and then – throughout the feasibility study – add relevant words and concepts that you have found in the literature. Ask specialists about their keywords in your area of research. Most scientific journals specify keywords. So if you have been able to pin down your topic in these keywords, it becomes much easier to find all the relevant literature. Continuously update and upgrade this list throughout the whole research. Thinking of the keywords of your research project also helps in understanding your research object (as part of the problem definition). A focused list can still consist of ten or more keywords.

- Use the **Snowball method**: start from a basic source, usually a book, and search through the list of references for other relevant sources. The biggest disadvantage of the snowball method is that the reference could relate to sources which have been published years before.

- In order to overcome the latter problem, you can also use a *reversed snowball method*. For this method you should make use of the (Social) **Science Citation Indexes**. These indexes are available in many libraries, and will tell you if your basic source has been used subsequently by other authors. The chance that they tackle the same topics is considerable.

- Find out whether there is a **bibliography** available for your research topic. Bibliographies can be added as a separate annex to a book, they can also be the subject of a specialised article that covers the most important articles in a particular area (according to the compiler of the bibliography). When you find a bibliography you should ask yourself: (1) what was the basis of selection; (2) what languages does the bibliography cover; (3) what period is covered by the bibliography; (4) what kind of publications are included; (5) did the authors aim for comprehension or is the bibliography selective; (6) is it an annotated bibliography or not? On the basis of these questions you can get a good impression of the usefulness of the bibliography.

■ Find the **meta-study** that is bound to have been written on (part of) your research topic. Meta-studies have become increasingly popular in most sciences. They give a concise assessment of the content of all the articles written on a particular topic in the most relevant (top) scientific journals. Meta-studies help you in finding out what the 'scientific community' thinks of a particular topic, what research methods have been used, whether there have been any biases in the existing knowledge, and what areas for further research (theoretically as well as empirically) have been identified. The latter forms a great help in deciding what your particular research 'niche' should be. Meta-studies also prevent you from stating the obvious on your research topic.

■ Make use of **reference books**. By using these books you can find out whether the subject of your research relates to a major debate in the scientific discipline. You can get the same information when you consult your old text books. Re-reading some of the books which you have been studying in previous years, can help your understanding of a problem area. Moreover, these books are available in your personal library and therefore easy to obtain. Make good use of indexes (➔C1, C5).

3 Primary resources

Making use of primary resources means that you collect information from the original sources. You should at least consider the availability of two sources of primary information:

■ *Your own observations through participation* in an organisation, and direct interaction with your research 'objects'. Your feasibility study should include an assessment of the following:
  • Can I get to the position in an organisation in which I can gather the relevant information?
  • How much time will I have? How systematically can I elaborate on research activities?
  • What additional information do I need to gather, in order to check my observations?

■ *Interviews and/or questionnaires.* In the feasibility study you should ask yourself:
  • Who do I need to consult to make the interview or questionnaire representative?
  • How can I approach them?

- When should I approach respondents during the research project? For what purpose?

During a feasibility study it can be very useful to interview a few people who are directly involved in your research topic. However, do not try to get detailed empirical information. Your research question may still change, which will mean that the information collected in this interview is no longer useful. The information might even become a burden in the final stages of your research, because you will try to use it even when the information does not 'fit' into your research design. The main function of an interview, in this phase, is to check the feasibility of your research by:

- finding out whether your research question is also used by others;
- getting new ideas, perhaps adding 'sub'questions or hypotheses to your initial question;
- getting suggestions for further reading or where to obtain the relevant information;
- seeking the possibility of sponsorship (perhaps leading to additional questions).

Table A.6 Exemplary final checklist for a feasibility study

Resources	Availability			Consequences for the research question(s) and project organisation
	good	mediocre	insufficient	
1 Personal				
2 Secondary				
3 Primary				

There are many different research strategies. Basically, research aims at describing and explaining (Berkeley Thomas, 2004: 14). On how best to describe and explain, however, substantial debate exists – which will probably only stop when people decide that there is no need for research anymore. In this debate, scientific 'schools' often tend to stress the choice for a research strategy as an 'either/or' dichotomy: you are theoretical or empirical, qualitative or quantitative, descriptive or prescriptive oriented. On the question what constitutes the 'scientific method', generations of scientists have fought fierce battles. This happened in particular in the social sciences where it is much more difficult – if not impossible – to separate the object of research from the subject (i.e. the researcher). Each research strategy and 'school of thought' has its own advantages and disadvantages.

This Skill Sheet identifies [1] the most commonly employed research strategies and discusses some of their advantages and disadvantages and [2] delineates a possible synthesis. Figure A.7 positions these research strategies around the Reflective Cycle in order to help you identify their prime orientation. This categorisation, however, should be used with considerable care: it does not mean that each of the strategies under one category is related (e.g. inductive research is always applied by 'subjectivist' scholars), nor that these research strategies by any means 'only' connect to this part of the Reflective Cycle.

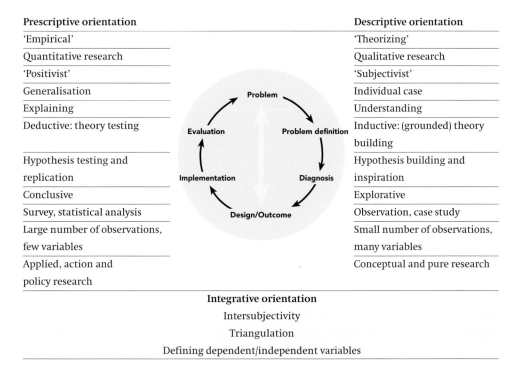

Prescriptive orientation		Descriptive orientation
'Empirical'		'Theorizing'
Quantitative research		Qualitative research
'Positivist'		'Subjectivist'
Generalisation		Individual case
Explaining		Understanding
Deductive: theory testing		Inductive: (grounded) theory building
Hypothesis testing and replication		Hypothesis building and inspiration
Conclusive		Explorative
Survey, statistical analysis		Observation, case study
Large number of observations, few variables		Small number of observations, many variables
Applied, action and policy research		Conceptual and pure research

Integrative orientation

Intersubjectivity

Triangulation

Defining dependent/independent variables

Figure A.7 Research orientations

1 Dimensions of Research Strategies

Theoretical – empirical   'Theory' is an important, but not well understood word. To many students, 'theory' is synonymous with 'abstract', 'vague' or even 'difficult'. However, the basic aim of a theory is to explain something in a systematic manner. This often boils down to a model which tries to identify the most relevant variables, complete with causal maps in which the (expected) nature of the most important relationships is specified. Good theory not only helps you explain and understand better, but enables also better predictions: what would you expect under comparable conditions to happen? Theory-building is needed in case you have observations but no good explanations. Theory-testing is feasible in case you have sophisticated explanations but no data. The controversy between theoretical (abstract) and empirical (practical) research is often artificial. Nothing as practical as a good theory.

In natural sciences, the prerequisite for a good theory is its predictive value: if the experiment you have conducted to test a theory does not lead to the same outcome every time, you might have to adjust your theoretical model. In social sciences, the prerequisite for good theory is its 'heuristic value': the ability to ask the right questions and explain phenomena. The more systematic the explanations, the better the theory. Sophisticated explanations (combined with solid empirical testing) can have a higher predictive value, but the number of intervening variables that have not been included in the original model and that can change the outcome of processes remains substantial. Some social scientists, therefore, prefer to speak of 'approaches' rather than of 'theories'.

Positivist – Subjectivist   The 'positivist' approach to research (Burns, 2000) aims at developing more or less 'objective' knowledge. This ambition stems in particular from the natural sciences in which researchers can abstain from their object of research, and manipulate it at will (experimentation). The 'subjectivist' approach to research acknowledges much more the unique character of social phenomena, the impossibility of separation of research from research object and the difficulty of obtaining sufficiently large numbers of observations to enable any type of really quantitative measurement. The most radical 'subjectivist' research orientation departs from the notion that all knowledge is subjective and that therefore any argument counts.

Explorative – conclusive   An explorative strategy is often used when you are not clear on the nature of your research object and do not know what the existing (scientific) knowledge is on the topic. Explorative research on the basis of field work and descriptive case-studies can lead to new models and theories. In that case it is called 'grounded theory'. An explorative strategy, however, is more generally applied by researchers that want to get to grips with existing insights into a particular area. These insights can be both theoretical – which requires solid literature study – as empirical – observations on a number of cases for instance. Explorative research is primarily qualitative and inductive in nature. In practice, studies are often called 'explorative' as an excuse for not having taken the time to consult relevant previous studies. An excellent ambition for explorative research is the formulation of hypotheses. Explorative research is basically inductive.

Conclusive research strategies can be adopted if you are better acquainted with the research object and with the existing literature. Conclusive research is easier when you already have a set of hypotheses that can be tested, and a number of variables that you can measure. Conclusive strategies tend to stress the deductive and quantitative side of research more. Table A.7 can help you decide whether to use an explorative or conclusive research strategy.

Table A.7 Explorative – conclusive research

When to use exploratory research...	When to use conclusive research...
☐ To obtain background information when you know nothing about a research area	☐ To define relevant groups, for example customers
☐ To define a problem more specifically to use for further (conclusive) research	☐ To estimate how many people show a certain behaviour
☐ To explore the field of new products or services	☐ To count the frequency of particular events
☐ To clarify behavioural patterns, opinions, etc.	☐ To measure changes over time
☐ To understand behaviours and attitudes in order to analyze quantitative data analysis	☐ To come to predictions
☐ To explore topics that are not articulated easily by individuals	
☐ To discover unknown relationships between variables	

Source: based on Malhotra and Birks, 2003

Pure-Applied research Pure and fundamental research focuses more on the theoretical challenges of a particular intellectual area. It can be completely unrelated to the practical side of research. Often pure research is aimed at further elaborating (theoretical) concepts and building more sophisticated (more systematic, more elaborate) models. The basic inspiration for pure research comes from the researchers themselves. Applied research on the other hand focuses more on the practical challenges of actors. The basic inspiration for applied research comes from the 'customer' of the knowledge: policy-makers, managers, interest groups. This often leads to the idea that pure research is 'independent' and applied research is 'dependent'. But this leaves unnoticed that sophisticated applied research can certainly profit from the insights gained through pure research and vice versa. Good applied research always builds on concepts developed in fundamental research. In practice, researchers sometimes call themselves 'applied', implying that they do not need 'theory' or do not require to have a solid understanding of the relevant scientific literature in the area.

2 Synthesis: Triangulation

Often researchers in a project choose a combination of strategies – depending on the nature of the problem, your personal research skills and research ambitions (⊕A3) and the available resources (⊕A6). In most studies, multiple methods and even multiple research approaches are needed to do justice to the problem at hand. This represents the tension between problem and design/outcome (as indicated by the vertical arrow in Figure A.7). It requires an integrative research orientation that aims at improving confidence in the validity of the data, the used concepts and methods. This represents the third orientation out of the dilemmas of either the positivist or subjectivist approach: inter-subjectivity and triangulation. Inter-subjectivity as a research strategy implies that the researcher is looking for support from groups of peers for a particular method or theory. Triangulation further specifies this strategy by searching for multiple methods to obtain data (methodological triangulation), sampling data at different times, places and from different people (data triangulation), using multiple observers (investigator triangulation) and using different theories (theory triangulation) (Berkeley Thomas, 2004:23).

Triangulation poses the challenge of finding the right balance between the strengths and weaknesses of each research orientation. The prescriptive orientation faces the challenge of generalization: to what extent are the few (measurable) variables representative for larger phenomena or for the same phenomenon under different circumstances; to what extent can the specific advice generated for a particular customer also be given to other customers? This is the issue of verification. Descriptive research strategies face the problem of specificity: to what extent can the developed concepts be measured and tested; to what extent do these concepts mean the same to different people? This is the issue of validation (⊕A16).

A final challenge for triangulation is posed by the correct use of statistical techniques. In modern society there often is not a lack of data. But there is a lack of *meaningful* data. Statistical and data-driven research often suffers from the problem of 'conclusions in search of a problem', whereas theoretical research often suffers from the problem of 'conclusions in search of support'. In the first option, researchers often invest substantial time in 'rationalisations' for found correlations, whereas in the second approach the danger of 'statistical manipulation' looms large. Or in a different phrasing: What I want to know I cannot measure, what I can measure I do not want to know. The decision whether you can make use of statistical techniques as part of your research strategy depends on the following considerations (cf. Newton, Rudestam, 1999):
- **Identification of variables**: can you distinguish between '**dependent**' and '**independent**' variables? The dependent variable is what you want to know; the independent variable constitutes the explanation (or explanatory variables); research aims at establishing the effect of an independent on a dependent variable.
- **The nature of the variables**: Variables can be discrete or continuous. [1] **Discrete variables** classify a phenomenon into categories. They can be either [a] nominal or [b] ordinal. The former does not specify any ranking, the second gives some

indication of 'greater' or 'less', without however specifying the exact magnitude of the ranking. Both measures require the ability to categorize into mutually exclusive and exhaustive categories (ibid, 1999: 124). [2] **Continuous variables** classify phenomena into measurable categories. This measure can be based on either an [a] interval or a [b] ratio scale. An interval scale makes it possible to determine the exact distance between categories (for instance temperature, calendar dates, or the answers in a survey on a 5-point scale ranging from 'not at all' to 'completely'). A ratio scale specifies a 'zero point' and makes it possible to measure the relative distance between categories (for instance length, weight, most physical scales). Another type of variable is the **dummy variable** which is also referred to as 'binary variable' because it is either coded 1 to indicate the presence of a variable or 0 to indicate the absence of an attribute.

• The existence and nature of the **control variables** (sometimes referred to as covariates). Is it possible to remove or control for specific variables before examining the effect of an independent on a dependent variable? The more control variables you are able to include in your model, the more sophisticated it becomes.

It is beyond the scope of this Skill Sheets collection to explain statistical techniques in more detail. For more information you can, for instance, refer to Newton and Rudestam (1999). For excellent overviews of the way statistics and maths can be abused, see for instance Dewdney (1993) and the classical 'how to lie with Statistics' from Darrell Huff (1954).

'There are three kinds of lies: lies, damned lies and statistics'—Disraeli

Choosing an appropriate method – let alone a combination of multiple methods (➲A7) – for research projects is extremely difficult. A methodology defines the *methods, procedures, and techniques that are used to collect and analyze information.* Methods are appropriate if they increase the reliability and validity of the research project. This Skill Sheet lists the advantages and disadvantages of five of the most commonly used methods:

1 Experiments
2 Surveys
3 Case studies
4 Desk research
5 In-depth interviews

When you choose any of these methods in your research project, consider the following caveat: the correct use and implementation of each method requires considerable expertise and preparation; consult skilled researchers and read specialised books on how to use these methods correctly.

1 **Experiments** are often used to detect a causal relationship between variables, by changing the independent variable (when I change A, what will happen to B?). Experiments are performed in a controlled environment (often a closed room or an IT environment). Experiments enable groups to be split up. One group will be exposed to a particular stimulus whereas the other group (the test group) will not. The advantage of experiments is that it is a good way of showing the existence of causal relationships with human research subjects (internal validity). Experiments are therefore often used for medical and psychological research (addressing 'how' and 'why' questions ➲A9). The external validity of experiments, however, can be rather low. The subjects of the research operate in an environment that is artificial, which might influence the research results considerably (Verschuren & Doorewaard, 2000).

2 **Surveys** are giving structured questionnaires to a sample of a population. Questions can be asked verbally, written or via Internet (web-based surveys). Surveys enable researchers to accumulate quantitative data for often qualitative questions. Surveys ask for the perception of respondents of particular issues. Surveys require a large number of respondents in order to be representative. The exact number of respondents required and the nature of the questions depends on the type of research and the statistical techniques envisioned. Important advantages of surveys are that there is no direct involvement between the researcher and the respondent, that a wide range of subjects can be covered, that control questions can be formulated to check for the internal validity of the survey and that a large number of respondents can be addressed at the same time. The use of statistical analysis can increase the external validity of the research as well. Disad-

vantages of surveys are that questions often remain multi-interpretable, a lack of depth because of the limited preparedness of respondents to fill out lengthy questionnaires, and the inclination of respondents to give 'socially acceptable' answers. Surveys can manipulate respondents in a specific direction.

3 **Case studies** are particularly appropriate to gain insights into real-life events. Case studies are best used when a 'how' or 'why' question is posed, and the researcher can have no or almost no control over the behavioural event (Yin, 2003). Case studies make it possible to take more qualitative variables of interest into account than with surveys or experiments. Case studies are conducted on the location of the subject(s) to be studied. The advantage of case studies is that more in-depth knowledge on a particular organisation or phenomenon can be obtained. Next, due to the direct interaction between researcher and subjects (in case of participatory observation) the chance that the research results will be easier to accept is greater. A clear disadvantage is the loss of external validity of the results. Making generalisations is hard to come up with. However, the latter depends on the selection criteria for the case study. If the case is selected on the basis of its representativeness for a particular issue or problem, generalisations can be made more easily. Furthermore, on the basis of comparable selection criteria, one can decide for a few cases. If each case study can then be compared systematically on the basis of the same framework, the method gains in external validity as well. A minimum of three case studies is generally considered to be appropriate (See Yin, 2003).

4 **Desk research** is based on using previous research done by other researchers and/or the information that you can directly retrieve from the Internet or from the library. Archive research also belongs to this category. You do not have any interaction with the research subject, so there are hardly any time restrictions to doing desk research. The Internet age makes desk research a particularly tempting way of doing research. However, a major disadvantage of this indirect research method is that the reliability of the information obtained can be quite low (➔A16). Using secondary material requires solid and critical reading skills in order to identify particular biases in your sources (➔C series) and control for its reliability.

Fortunately, journalists, scientists and organisations use a number of principles to guarantee quality. In order to understand what sources of information you could prefer for your desk research, consider Table A.8. It lists a number of the most common principles that are applied by particular groups of people to ensure particular levels of quality. The distinction between a 'normal' scientific journal and a 'top' scientific journal, for instance, is the application of the 'double blind referee' principle. This requires that an article is judged by at least three independent referees. In this process neither the referees nor the author(s) know each other's identity. This procedure is intended to create the highest degree of discretion, quality assurance and independence. It is basically a 'peer review' procedure, and not objective. It is based on the principle of inter-subjectivity, but with the guarantee that – due to the anonymity of all involved – favouritism and groupthink can be kept to a minimum. Therefore scientists tend to favour scientific publications over journalistic products (that nevertheless are also based on specific quality principles, such as the 'hear both sides' principle).

Table A.8 Reliability Principles

Principle	Where Applied
1 Hear both sides	Journalism (quality journals)
2 Check and double-check	Always find at least two sources for one allegation: investigative journalism
3 Triple check	Advise when using Internet as a source
4 Peer review	Science, legal professions
5 Double-blind referees	Scientific publications with top-ambitions
6 Self-regulation, sanctions, arbitrage and appeal procedures	Associations of job groups (bar association, medical professions)
7 Accreditation	Universities, associations, press agencies
8 Statutes/charters	International etiquette for organisations and professional groups
9 Editorial committee/board	Scientific journals
10 Committee/board of recommendation	Scientific journals, research groups, conferences, non-profit organisations, book series
11 Transparency (as a legal provision)	Annual reports, complaint procedures

5 **In-depth interviews** as a research methodology have characteristics (including advantages and disadvantages) that are comparable to those of the case study method. Interviews, however, have more functions. First they can be excellent means of checking whether your research approach is solid or not. Interviewing a few 'experts' in a particular area can help you validate your research questions. This is also referred to as the 'Delphi method'. Secondly, pilot interviews can help you rephrase a questionnaire before you send it to a large number of people. Thirdly, in-depth interviews can give you vital information in case of a 'small numbers' game. In that case it is feasible to talk to all the actors involved. The disadvantages of in-depth interviews are that only a limited number of interviews are feasible, it will take a lot of time to get in touch with the relevant respondents (who might then not be willing to give the interview), and that often you have to promise confidentiality of the interview (➲D series, for more information).

One of the most difficult skills to master is how to formulate a relevant, clear and feasible research question. The preparation of an 'appropriate' question always creates considerable problems during the early stages of a research project. But once chosen, the research question decisively influences the rest of the research project. Choosing the appropriate question does not mean knowing the answer beforehand. On the contrary, it should enable you to *come up* with a relevant answer. *Never* start your practical research without a clear question or set of questions. If you do begin without a clear question, in particular when you apply a set model in practice, you run the risk of formulating 'a solution in search of a problem'. Consultants or econometricians are often reproached for doing this, i.e. departing from idealised (best-practice) or highly formalised models. When the 'real world' does not act according to the model it is likely to be treated as a *deviation* from the ideal rather than an indication of reality. In order to reduce the risk of you coming up with a question that you cannot, should not or need not answer, consider the following six suggestions. Skill Sheet A10 further specifies how to formulate the actual question.

1 When you are in the process of formulating a research question, you will always be torn between two extremes: **What do I want to know** ↔ **What can I know?** As a basic rule begin with the more *qualitative research question*: what do I want to know? Only when you have specified what you would like or need to know, can you consider what (quantitative) data might help you to answer the main research question.

> **'Most of the things you can measure aren't interesting (...) most of what's interesting you can not measure'—Marcia Angell**

2 Take your research *time frame* into account. The shorter the time available:
- the more your first question should also be your final question;
- the more modest your research question should be;
- the more you will have to build your question on what others have specified as 'good questions for further research' in their research (read the conclusions of other studies).

3 Your research question should enable you to be *critical and creative* (➔A1) otherwise the research project will always suffer from a lack of social relevance. If a research project is not worth doing, it is not worth doing well. Consider the following five sets of critical 'W' questions when you contemplate your research questions:

- **What** is the problem?
  - **What** are the causes?
  - **What** are the consequences?
- **Why** is this a relevant problem?
  - **Why** should I tackle this problem?
  - **Why** have others (not) tackled this problem?
- **Whom** does the problem relate to?
  - **Who** do I want the research to address?
  - **Who** would be interested in my research?
- **Where** does the problem exist?
- **When** does the problem appear in particular?

4 Compile a *list of keywords* (➔A6) that you think best cover your research topic. Most keywords will be included in your research question(s). Specifying keywords has at least two functions: it helps you to focus on the most important research topics that you address. It also makes it easier to find relevant sources in the library or in databases, under these keywords. Once you have carried out a number of research projects you will become experienced in this skill. An important side-effect of this is that you will also become acquainted with the advantages *and* drawbacks of reference lists used by libraries and databases (➔C5). Some keywords specify the scientific area (for instance political sciences, regional economics) you aim to do research in. They can be left out of the main research question, but can be important in your search strategy for data in libraries.

5 Decide beforehand what you consider to be the *clearest value (added)* of your research. The practical relevance of a research project often lies in one summary, one table, a figure and a line of argument. Unfortunately for most researchers, research reports are rarely read in detail. Be aware of this and use it to increase the added value of your research by focusing on one concrete end-product. Be modest. It will also help you to focus on the most important part of your research and prevent intellectual 'overstretch'. Specify what you want to produce with your research *in any case*:

☐ a. an overview; ☐ d. a line of argument;
☐ b. a table; ☐ e. ...
☐ c. a graph;

6 What kind of research question do you yourself prefer to read? Look at some other research projects. What question did you like most:
- one that stimulated your mind and caught your attention?
- one that you could more or less answer yourself immediately?
- one that related to a theoretical problem in the literature?
- one that related to a practical problem of individual actors?
- another type of research question...

If you have a clear preference for one kind of question, should you not formulate your own research questions in the same manner (➔A3, A10)?

A research question states the objective of your research. It does not have to be formulated in one sentence, sometimes more sentences (a question hierarchy) are also appropriate. There are two decisions you have to make when designing a research question: (A) whether you formulate a question or a hypothesis, and (B) whether you ask a single question or a number of (sub) questions.

1 Formulating a question or a hypothesis

Questions are often flexible and invite general answers, while hypotheses are more restrictive and force you to be more precise in your answer. Questions will be more appropriate in the earlier phases of your research or if you do not know much about a topic. Hypotheses will be very useful in later phases of a research project once you have finished your theoretical framework (step 9, ➔A5), and you are better acquainted with the research topic at hand. Whether you ask questions or formulate hypotheses also depends on the type of research that you have decided to do (➔A7).

- Avoid using general and descriptive questions or hypotheses. For example, consider the following question: 'What semiconductors strategy is used by the management at Philips?' This question only vaguely specifies the research objective. Such a research question invites an 'interpretative description', i.e. writing down as much information as you can find on a topic. While you are writing you make interpretations. If you do not know anything about the company, about its strategies and about semi-conductors, a question which leads to inductive research can be very appropriate. But this state of total ignorance is not often the case. An appropriate research question should allow you to use the experience of other researchers *and* set clear *limits* for one's own research endeavour. For example, the question could be rephrased as: 'How does the strategy of Philips in the area of semiconductors relate to the strategy of its most important competitors?' This question is still rather general, but it already begins to specify the grounds on which you would like to interpret the company's strategy. You could also ask: 'Semiconductors are considered the core technology of micro-electronics. Why did the management of Philips sell its semiconductor subsidiary in 2006?' Formulating appropriate questions always requires a basic knowledge of the topic.
- As a researcher you are supposed to reduce complexity in your research project. But it will be problematic for you to reduce the complexity of a topic *before* you have asked all the relevant qualitative questions. In that case, you are engaging in research 'politics': you apply the art of the feasible (politics) as opposed to the art of the optimal and effective (science). It is inevitable that you make choices or assumptions when you specify your research questions, but do not make these choices too early in your research project. Make the choice process part of your research.
- If you have more knowledge of the research area – or in case you want to test theories or replicate the empirical results of previous research – you can begin for-

mulating a research *hypothesis* immediately. The question quoted above could for instance be reformulated as the following hypothesis: 'Because of the financial difficulties Philips ran into in the 1990-1995 period, it had to lower its investments in semiconductors, even when its managers were aware of the very strategic value of semiconductors for the rest of its electronics business.' A hypothesis that is too general or too simplistic does little to help you focus your research. Often, the first phase of a large research project will result in the research questions being reformed into research hypotheses.

- Hypotheses can also be formulated to get to easier 'falsification'. Falsification is a principle of appropriate research which is applied particularly in natural sciences. If the researcher finds one example which rejects (falsifies) the hypothesis, you should reject the whole theory on which the hypothesis is based. In social sciences, however, the falsification principle is not always appropriate. You have to live with the following paradox that is caused by the lack of distance between study object and subject (you, the researcher): the more convincing you make an argument and present a prediction, the more likely it is that your prediction will never materialise. Your clients will either act or react to this prediction, and in doing so change the course of events. Paradoxically therefore, the success of a social scientist can sometimes be judged in terms of the limited predictive value of his or her theories!

- **Tip 1**: Read your research question or hypothesis aloud, and ask yourself whether you would dare to do that in public! Do you think that you could come up with an instant answer? Would you be interested in the answer to this particular question? If you hesitate: reconsider your question or rephrase the question/hypothesis!

- **Tip 2**: Do not use long sentences in your research questions. Do not try to include everything in one phrase.
  Make several phrases. Use direct and active phrasing. Use *specifications*: relate the problem to the region/country/firm/person/time that you want to address. Read it aloud again, and if the question does not 'flow', break it up into at least two sentences.

'Keep it as simple as possible, but not simpler'—Albert Einstein

2 The function of a question hierarchy

When you use shorter sentences and specify your research topic in your research question, you will often end up with a number of questions instead of one single question. Your first question should always state the basic problem that has lead to your research project. You then phrase subsidiary questions which break down the original question into more specific ones. This is a so-called 'question hierarchy' (Emory, Cooper, 1991:77). A question hierarchy generally runs:

- from general to specific;
- from more theoretical to empirical questions;
- from questions related to secondary sources to questions which need primary data ($\oplus$A6).

- **Tip 3**: If you base your research on a hierarchy of questions, ask the questions *in a logical sequence*. As a rule, begin by looking at the theoretical and conceptual elaboration of the problem. Only then can you complete further description and analysis. When you are aware of the function of conceptual and theoretical clarification *before* you start with empirical testing, reflect this in the contents of your essay or thesis. The sequence of your question hierarchy is also the sequence of your research report.

- **Tip 4**: Try to think of a *'catchy title'* which covers your basic research question. It will help you to focus your attention on the basic research question. It will also encourage you to finish this project. Your research question and title should motivate at least one person: yourself! And if you are motivated by the question this will probably motivate others. Make your leading question so clear and simple that you can easily reproduce it, whenever it is required. Researchers, who only come up with a title in the final stages of their research project, often also have difficulty in formulating a clear research question. There seems to be a direct correlation between formulating vague titles and carrying out vague research. But do not be mislead: a clear title is never a sufficient condition for good and clear research!

Question to a well-known researcher: Why do you seem to have knowledge of so many research topics? Answer: 'I don't. But that is not necessary either. By formulating a strict definition of a problem, a strict research question leading to a systematic approach, you can make statements in areas in which you not necessarily have to be a specialist.'

Source: De Volkskrant (Dutch daily newspaper), October 20th, 1993

With almost every research project the material quickly 'piles up', forming a mountain of paper or of overlapping electronic files which can be discouraging. For paper as well as electronic information, you have to design an efficient and logical storage system. If not, you will have major problems in retrieving relevant material for your project. Additionally, even if you 'survive' the project stage for which you collected the information you may never be able (or willing) to use the material again for further research. This Skill Sheet identifies four principles to help you to organise your files.

Principle #1: Categorise

Think about the areas of your research interest. Consider whether you are interested in them for a specific research project or whether you have a more general interest in them. Start with organising files in terms of your general interests. Create a sufficient number of files. The initial overcapacity you create is bound to disappear in due course. You can choose any area you like, but to begin with it is helpful to organise your files into three reference areas:

- Topics: what kind of articles do you read regularly in the newspapers? Which topics do you like to keep track of on a regular basis, for example, topics related to functional areas in Business Administration. You could link the material that you collect to the courses that you are attending, and use it for writing essays and case studies.
- Actors: do you have a favourite company or business area? Are you primarily interested in a particular ministry or one type of organisation? By creating a separate file it is easy to store relevant material over a longer period of time.
- Countries: some countries are more popular than others. You will be inclined to collect information on the same country, but it will be spread around the other files/piles at random and thus becomes impossible to reassemble. Choose your favourite country or region (European Union, Southeast Asia) and create files accordingly.

Principle #2: Be selective

It is not a problem to create and fill files. But to raise the user-value of your files you should be selective when deciding what to include. Collect and store only those sources that are difficult to get in libraries, which might not re-appear on the Internet or which you consider to be basic reading for your general interests. In case you want to store hard copies, it is good to have the following sources readily available:

- **Copies of articles** from newspapers and magazines that you subscribe to, which you cannot obtain from libraries or are not allowed to copy information from. Use a personal code to note the sources of the information. For example: 'FT/23/1/08' meaning: 'Financial Times, 23 January 2008'. Do this as soon as you cut out the article. If you do not do this immediately you will not remember the exact dates, and you certainly will not be motivated to compile this data if a long period of time elapses. File according to the date of the source, the most recent sources should be on top and the older ones underneath.

- **Chapters of books** that you consider to be important. Write the basic bibliographical data on your copy (⊕E12). As a general rule: do not make copies of whole books. Copies of entire books give many people the impression that they have collected something relevant, but the thicker the book and the longer the time it takes to copy it, the less people seem to be inclined to read the material. Furthermore, it is a waste of time, money and paper.
- **Original sources**: white papers, transcripts of speeches by managers or politicians.

Principle #3: Register bigger sources seperately

Create a separate system of paper or electronic 'index cards', on which you note the full bibliographical information of your larger sources, in particular books and scientific articles. Specialised software is available for this purpose. Paper or electronic, what you choose is a matter of experiment and deciding what suits you best (⊕C5). If you use this regularly and systematically you will have no problem in compiling bibliographies for the papers you write.

Principle #4: Process the information in time

Only file those sources which you have read – at least superficially. There are several reasons for this principle:

- If you have read it, you know what you have. You are unaware of what you have if you just filed it.
- Some sources can be thrown away immediately because their content is not relevant.
- When you read paper sources, preferably make notes on the paper or article. Consequently, it becomes easier to find the relevant paragraphs if you go through it at a later stage. The larger the pile of unspecified/unread material that you collect, the more discouraging it is even to begin using it!
- It is easier to decide where to file the source once you have scanned or read it. You may even decide to make copies of very important sources and file them twice.

This Skill Sheet explains some of the 'silent' rules that apply to doing research. A major problem when carrying out research is getting people to devote time to provide input for your research. Often, the people who you need information from are also the people with the least time. To put it simply, the basic question that they ask themselves is: **what do I get in return for my collaboration?** This question for a 'fair deal' is rarely stated explicitly, but it will severely affect the feasibility of your search. This dimension in research projects has always been relevant, but with the upcoming of the 'bargaining society' (➔part I: The Challenge) its importance can no longer be ignored.

Because it is not common to offer money in return for time and input in research, the conduct of relevant research resembles one of the oldest forms of economic activity in which two actors trade without using money as a means of exchange. This economic activity is known as barter. Your own trade position involves knowledge, which is contained in research reports, interview elaboration, references to interesting literature or it can even involve the exchange of hearsay. The quality and the extensiveness of the information that you receive from other actors, critically depends on your knowledge of the unspoken rules and norms of research barter. This Skill Sheet presents some of these rules together with suggestions on how to handle them in an effective manner (➔G6).

1 **Fairness**   Always take care of fair terms of trade: ask yourself how you can establish equilibrium in the relationship.

2 **Stakes**   Specify what is at stake (➔A3), so that your (potential) barter partner can form an opinion about whether he/she shares your interest in the topic, and the aims of the research. Specifying the stakes requires:
   • that when writing a letter, you include a short description of the research questions and intended users of the report;
   • that before you call someone, you prepare a short introduction in which you state what the aims of your research are and why you think this particular person is important for your research.

3 **Time**   Always make clear how much time it will take to assist you with your research. If you ask for an interview or if you send a questionnaire, state the approximate amount of time that it will take. Your time reference shows that you have considered the effort required from your informant, and supports your status as a serious researcher.

4 **Return**   The more you give, the more you can ask of your barter partner. So, always make clear (also for yourself) what you give your informant in return for their efforts. If you have nothing to offer at the moment (for example, if you have just begun your university education), be creative when inventing a fair reward!

- The minimum return, which you must always offer, is sending the end result of your endeavour: the research report. Do this explicitly and spontaneously. People expect you to do so!
- You can send your informant a written section which has already been completed. Receiving a draft text, often gives people the 'thrill' of being able to read manuscripts which have not yet been published! Using this important psychological factor is more successful when the research project includes many people. A detailed description of the contents of your research might also do the 'trick'.
- Think twice before you promise to send the transcript of your interview; the transcript might become subject to a bargaining process afterwards where the respondent can force you to change unwanted formulations, even if he/she has in fact stated that (➔D6).
- Compile tables with information about other companies, actors or phenomena in which the organisation of your informant is also included. In your research, work towards producing these kinds of overviews (➔E6). Such an overview makes it easier for your barter partner to check whether the information on the organisation is correct or not. It also gives some insight into the nature of your research and the information already collected. A table suggests that the research is already in progress and informs the respondent that you have only asked for the information to complement existing knowledge, and that you are not at the beginning of a research project. A table also specifies more clearly what you want from your respondent. People will be reluctant to give you information when it is not clear what you want.

5 **Abstain from...** posing open-ended questions that clearly indicate that you do not have sufficient knowledge about the topic. This also gives the impression that you have not done your homework. Examples are: 'could you send me any relevant material on...'; or: 'can you complete this questionnaire...' (followed by ten pages of mainly open questions,); or: 'could you tell me what the people at your department are doing on this topic...'. Open-ended questions like these are **forbidden** in real barter for two equally important reasons. Firstly you will get very few answers. Secondly you are not able to control the quality and direction of the answers. So even if you receive information, it might be useless (➔D4).

If an informant, a 'colleague' researcher/student, or someone who you closely collaborate with is under the impression that you do not respect the unspoken rules of barter, the willingness to collaborate immediately declines. You cannot build good research on relations in which you primarily extract information from the other party. If the declining willingness to collaborate remains part of an unconscious process, you both lose valuable time (➔G1, G10).

Also apply the barter principle to yourself when you provide input to others for research. Make a list of people who also apply the principles of barter towards you: over a longer period of time they will remain the hard and stable core of your personal network of research relationships.

A13 Online Databases

The rise of the Internet and online databases has made access to information much *easier* and *location independent*. Some databases are freely accessible but suffer from little maintenance and independence. Public organisations have a lot of information available online, but this information is not always without bias. Most of the time a licence is needed to gain access to the really interesting databases. Educational and research institutions often have direct access to all types of databases under a licence agreement, which students, professors and researchers can use. The challenge is therefore not the *availability* of data sources, but to select the *relevant* sources and their appropriate use. This requires that you (1) understand the strengths and weaknesses of online databases (Table A13a); (2) are familiar with their characteristics and (3) are able to use the database at the right time of a research project.

1 Strengths and Weaknesses

Table A.13a Strengths and weaknesses of online databases

'Strengths'	'Weaknesses'
• Multi-topic search (matching parameters) is easier;	• Few public (cheap) and reliable databases available;
• Forces researcher to think through the research question before starting a particular quest;	• Sophisticated databases are often expensive;
• Complements library sources (taps many more sources systematically);	• Bias for English language sources;
• Once a search has been executed, it can easily be repeated and/or updated;	• Often no inexpensive texts available, only abstracts;
• Quick search on keywords is possible.	• Database producers often have a vested interest in maintaining traditional divisions in disciplines;
	• Complex protocols and procedures, lack of standards;
	• Possibilities for 'browsing' (making accidental discoveries) are more limited;
	• Databases have a delay (see below).

2 Characteristics
- *Level of knowledge* – There is a continuum ranging from more applied to more theoretical knowledge; the following order of databases exists: *Internet, paper databases, thesis databases, specialist journal databases, e-reference books (encyclopaedia, reference books), (e-)learning books, academic journals, (e-)research reports and dissertations.*
- *Restrictions* – Publishers sometimes have strategic reasons to create a certain

delay. Delays range from one month to two years. In that case, track down the required article in other databases or try to find a hard copy of the journal.

- *Archive databases* – Most databases only contain current information (up to five years old). Some databases contain an archive that stores information for up to ten years or even longer (ABI/Inform / Science Direct). Special archive databases exist to ensure that no important historic information is lost (JStore contains academic journals of five years and older).
- *Quality characteristics of articles and journals* – The scientific value of articles can be measured by the status of the journal. Special databases exist in which 'impact factors' of journals can be found (for example, ISI Journal Citation Reports). International research institutions all have their own list of preferred journals (see for instance: www.erim.eur.nl).

3 Steps in research projects and appropriate databases
Step 1: Orientation

In the first phase of a research project you can use existing literature to see your research project 'through the eyes' of previous researchers. Diverse types of databases are available to help you in your literature search: encyclopaedia, introductions and textbooks. Some universities have databanks of all PhD dissertations and Master's Theses. 'To Google around' can be useful in this phase, but do so with a *critical* attitude (➲A14, A15)

Step 2: Define Qualitative Keywords

Qualitative online databases offer the possibility – through using keywords (➲D4) – to identify whether a research project is relevant and feasible. Define a hierarchy of important keywords and synonyms. If you start and the number of 'hits' is big, you know you are in a very topical research area. Read a few key articles that you have found, and then come up with perhaps other synonyms that you see are relevant for your particular research project. Databases of scientific articles (Table A.13b lists some of the most common) only present a selection of articles and/or journals. Most universities only have a selection, there is only approximately 30% overlap in these databases, and there is still no 'mother' databank that integrates them all. So in case you want to get a good overview of the kind of scientific articles that contain your keyword, you should preferably **consult them all**.

Table A.13b Qualitative databases

Available information	Name
Current events	Business papers, Reuters database
ICT	Gartner
Scientific Articles	ABI/Inform, Business Source Premier, EmeraldFulltext, Springer, Science Direct
Research reports	WoPEC, SSRN

Step 3: Define Quantitative challenges

Whether you use quantitative data in your research project depends first on the nature of your question, but also on the availability and reliability of quantitative databases. If sufficiently reliable and proficient data exist on a topic, try to include that in your research. Quantitative databases (see Table A13c for the most common) are often more costly and you should pay more attention to the way they collect their information. Quantitative databases are notorious for the errors they contain. Even small typing errors can influence your search tremendously.

Table A.13c Quantitative databases

Available information	Name of quantitative database
Business and stock market information	Thomson databases, AnnualReports.info, Datastream
Statistics	Financial Times
Macro-economic information	Source OECD, Economist, FED, ECB, Government sites

- Remember: a 'search' hardly ever delivers the preferred results in one 'go'. Most of the time the information is not specific enough or an 'information-overload' occurs. Change your search assignment in order to improve your search results and repeat your search (➲A14).

Always feel free to ask the librarian for help in your search process. That is their job and most of the time they are quite happy to assist you.

The first option to search the Internet more efficiently is through a search engine. The most popular search engines at the moment are Google, Yahoo, Altavista and MSN. Search engines are not neutral tools. They select information and it is therefore as important to know *how* they work as it is to know *what* the quality of the journal is that you read.

1 General concept of a search engine

A search engine generally consists of three parts (Google online, 2004; Startpagina online, 2004):
- The *spider* – the spider is the program that actually searches through the Internet, downloads the pages it finds, and follows the links on the pages.
- The *database* – the websites that are found, are stored in the database, the index. In this index, pages are stored alphabetically, by search term.
- The *user-interface* – the user-interface, which is the actual search engine you find on the website then searches through this database, in order to find websites relevant to your search terms.

2 Steps in the search process

The more specific your search, the bigger the chance is that the search engine will provide you with interesting links for your research. In general, a number of steps can be identified, when using a search engine (Google online, 2004):
- *Know* what you want to find and select your search terms carefully.
- Do the *right* search. This means you have to use appropriate keywords. These keywords should be as specific as possible. For example, when you want to find something about Nike, use "Nike" as search term, not "a sports brand".
- *Narrow* down your search. By using more than one keyword, you can narrow down the amount of relevant results. So use 'Nike shoes' if you want to find information about the shoes made by Nike. You can also narrow down your search by excluding certain words. This can be done by using *Boolean logic*. If you want to find something about Nike shoes, but not for indoor, you could try Nike shoes NOT indoor (the Boolean AND is used automatically by Google). This can also be done by using the Advanced Search function. The third important way of narrowing down your search is by the use of quotation marks. If you search on "George W Bush" it will only give results in which the complete sentence appears. Make use of the search abbreviations AND/OR/BUT/NOT. The search abbreviations could make your search easier. Make them part of your standard operating procedures.

3 Search results

To find the results that are valuable for you, it is important to know how the results are ranked. Google's website reports that it ranks the hits by *relevance* and *importance*. More than hundred different factors determine a website's relevance in the Google search engine. Besides this relevance issue, Google takes the importance of the website into account. The number of links to a certain website determines the importance within Google's search engine, and by which sites link to a certain website. So, the list of search results is compiled of websites that are relevant to your search terms, in order of importance. Be aware of a possible *bias* in the search results, although Google's website reports that they do not sell placement in results. It is proven that the listing of results can be influenced to a considerable extent. Note also that for example users in China will not find a large number of items, because Google has applied a form of self-censorship in order to be accepted by the Chinese authorities.

So the result that has the most value for you is not automatically the first result that Google presents. What you can do about this is to *narrow* down your search again by using the function of 'searching within the results'. This function allows you to add a new search term to exclude pages which are not relevant anymore.

4 Critical use of search engines

Because everybody can publish work on the Internet, the issue of reliability becomes more important. In general, people will not necessarily reveal sources on their website. Search engine policies are not always as transparent as you would wish. Take the following things into account when using a search engine:

- By searching for more than one source, the probability that something you found is true increases.
- Be aware that many links have a commercial objective. Most of the times the commercial and free hits are separated.
- Be aware that people could make their website foolproof.
- Be aware of the 'Google principle', websites with a large number of cross-links will be put higher on the list. Alternative search engines exist were the ranking of websites is supervised by real people.
- The two line description under the Google hit might not be representative of its contents (the Google search engine draws these lines directly from the original website). Alternative search engines are available that show a snapshot of the whole website.
- The Google search engine particularly has problems giving you relevant hits in case of multi-interpretable words. Other search engines (like Quintura.com or KartOO.com) provide alternatives by presenting so called Tagclouds or diagrams that show a range of concepts related to your search word, after which you can further specify your search.

Some search engines on the Internet are starting to offer certain options and claim to be meta-search engines, i.e. searching into different search engines at the same time (for example mamma.com).

Always make use of *more* than one search engine, because every search engine gives *another output* to your search request.

[⊕➔www.skillsheets.com]

In 1982 the Internet was born. It took until 1993 for the first commercial ventures to be established on the Internet (Griffiths, 2004; Living Internet, 2004). Nowadays, the Internet is freely accessible for almost everybody in the developed world, but the information overload is enormous and its reliability not that obvious. The strengths and weaknesses of the Internet as a source of (research) information are listed in Table A.15.

Table A.15 Strengths and weaknesses of the Internet

'Strengths'	'Weaknesses'
• Up to date, recent information	• Overdose/overkill of information (especially when using search engines)
• Additional information, which is not available elsewhere	• Besides overlap, there are also gaps: Internet is chaotic and unsystematic
• Fast means of communication: the wiki-society (quick correction of mistakes through peers)	• Finding relevant information may be complicated
• Easy way to get in contact with people/ organizations	• Information may not be up to date (no regular updating of information; links out of order)
• Contact is often informal	• Availability (information can be removed from a site or payment may suddenly be required)
• Easy way to get information on a particular subject (discussion lists, chat boxes)	• Relevance is often unclear
• Links provide easy access to other sites	• Reliability can be doubtful: it depends on the source (who provides the information and why); in the wiki-formula it is increasingly difficult to exclude vandals and manipulation
• Democratic: no major barriers to entry	• Wiki volunteers may be biased in their interest and ideas
• May give good insight into the way organisations would like to present themselves	• Bias for actual information and against historic information
• Cheap	• English dominance of search engines and main users.
• Environmentally-friendly	• No clear rules about copyright
• More fun	

Source: based on Kolk (1997)

The strength of the Internet makes it a very useful source of information. However, the weaknesses are sizeable as well. Because Internet is freely accessible to almost everyone, its information overload is enormous and its reliability open for discussion. As a basic rule, consider the Internet as a not a very reliable source. If you visit a website, you have to make sure that it is a reliable source. What can you do to check the reliability of an Internet source?

- Check the website's name and reputation (government website or company website)
- Check the publisher's name
- Check the suffix of an URL (.com/.org/.tv/.gov)
- Check when the website was updated for the last time
- Check several other sources to increase the reliability of your source
- Check the number of visitors to the website
- When referring to an Internet source in your writing always refer to the date you visited the website (it might have disappeared in the meantime) (⊕Series E)
- Visit your university library and ask the librarians whether a certain website is reliable or not.
- Consult your classmates/professor/(peer)lecturer for the latest developments on the Internet sources.
- Always make references of Internet sources in footnotes and endnotes the moment you make use of this particular source in your analysis
- As a 'rule of thumb' check what you find on the Internet **three times**. Investigative journalists **double-check**, but because Internet is notoriously unreliable (see below), you have to at least do one additional **re-check** (⊕A8, A16). If there are no supportive sources for what you have found you should be very careful in using the Internet as the source.
- Use Wikipedia (the Internet encyclopaedia) prudently (see box).

Rules for using Wikipedia

Wikipedia is a free Internet encyclopaedia that exists since 2000. The formula of Wikipedia is that everybody can contribute and edit 'lemmas'. Wikipedia is an open network construction with only a handful permanent staff (5 in 2007) and a large number of active contributors (around 75,000 in 2007). This creates a very flexible and exponentially growing source of information. In 2007 the website attracted more than 40 million visitors. More and more students use Wikipedia as a convenient source for their research. It is particularly useful for getting a quick overview of the definitions of concepts, the most important scientific schools that are engaged in it and basic data and references to research topics.

The reliability of Wikipedia, however, is point of serious debate: the open formula makes it possible in principle to manipulate the lemmas, and add or delete information. Contributors are anonymous, so it is difficult to track the reliability of the source. The information on Wikipedia is often given without reference to the original source. Besides, the Wiki platforms are dominated by specific participants groups: young males between 18 and 40 who primarily contribute on their own interests. Women and older men are underrepresented as contributors. Nevertheless, research published in *Nature* (2005, 438, 900–901) compared articles from the Encyclopaedia Britannica with related articles in the English language from Wikipedia and found on average three mistakes or inaccuracies with the former versus four mistakes and inaccuracies with the latter. That is not a bad score. The research of *Nature*, however, triggered major controversy. For instance, it focused only on articles in the exact sciences, which is an area dominated by (young) men and generally easier to validate for reliability than social sciences topics.

In response to the obvious deficiencies of Wikipedia, volunteers in a number of countries are supervising 'their' Wikipedia to check for vandals and manipulation. But also competing formulae have developed (for instance Citizendium) which uses more strict quality criteria, formulated and checked by experts, and demands all contributors to reveal their own name. These initiatives will not likely stop the increasing use made of Wikipedia as a source for students and researchers. To be practical, therefore, apply the following 'rules' when you do consult Wikipedia:

- Use it as an excellent and easy **first step** in research
- **Never** use it as a reference in your research (➔A1, E12; your writing should be reproducible and Wikis can change overnight)
- **Always** find another source that confirms the information you retrieved from Wikipedia
- Remain **suspicious** of the reliability of the Wiki you use (besides, this is a general rule you can apply also to other encyclopaedias)

Certainly with websites you use often, it is advisable to collect the Internet Uniform Resource Locator (URL). This is the unique address of the website. You can save the information on your computer or you can print the specific information off the website. You will have to save this information, because if you are accused of *plagiarism* (➔E2) you must be able to provide the source of your information. The rate of circulation of websites is very high and many websites disappear into the mysterious landscape of the electronic highway. If somebody wants to carry out a check of your sources, it is very useful to have a copy of the document you used on your computer or in printed form. The validity of your research decreases if you are unable to provide the source to somebody who uses your bibliography.

The site www.archive.org allows you to search for old websites. It is a digital library. Their 'Wayback Machine' could help recover your lost URLs.

[⊕➔www.skillsheets.com]

Validation is the process of checking the reliability of something. Verification is the process of checking whether a specific statement has sufficient predictive or explanatory value. But there is also a more social and interactive side to this 'checking process' which belongs more to the realm of research as a barter process (➔A12). This social dimension of evaluation techniques is the particular topic of this Skill Sheet.

One of the principles of reliable journalism is *listening to both sides of the argument* (➔A8) This principle is particularly relevant in research when gathering information at the micro/individual level of analysis. In research you should complement the principle of hearing both sides with that of *check and recheck*. In social sciences, research deals with the management of doubt (➔A1). Hearing both sides, and checking and rechecking your information are all part of a process which is intended to make your (subjective) impressions shared by others and complemented by other information. As it is almost impossible to develop *objective* knowledge that is shared by everyone, most social scientists aim at developing knowledge that can be shared by many. Building science on the basis of shared knowledge is also known as the principle of *inter-subjectivity* and *validation*. It has been part of a fierce methodological and epistemological debate (➔A7). This Skill Sheet offers a few simple tips which will help you to work towards establishing *inter-subjectivity* as a researcher in a practical and pragmatic way. Applying these tips should help you to improve your research output.

1 Create a pool or network of informants

With multi-disciplinary subjects in particular there are several areas which you will know little about, but which are also interesting and even vital. Therefore your research skills should also include the ability to seek the appropriate advice from those who are better informed.

- Let lawyers check your legal wording, let engineers check your knowledge of technology, let a group of specialists in an area check whether the wording of your questionnaire is multi-interpretable.
- However, **never** send them a preliminary draft which is still in need of considerable re-working. If you use your advisers as correctors, they will be much less willing to act as your adviser with regards to content.
- Do not hesitate to call your adviser, or ask for a short interview in order to check information which you are unsure of. The more work you have done yourself on a particular research topic, the more willing people will be to talk to you.
- Always compile a precise list of the people to whom you have sent material. The larger your pool of informants is, the more problematic it becomes to remember exactly what you have sent to whom and at what time.

- Create a separate file labelled 'correspondence' (in addition to your other files; ⊕A11) in which you collect all of the letters you have received from your informants and copies of the letters you have sent to them.

These points should enable you to create a network of informants that comprises relatively equal partnerships. As long as the partners are more or less equal, the network can be sustained and your research projects can profit from the knowledge of many other 'brains' (⊕A12).

2 Check the way you present your information.

The principle of inter-subjectivity can also be used to determine if the information that you present is understood in the way that you intended (⊕B13). Use the following principles:

- If you write in a foreign language, have the paper checked by a native speaker, even if you consider yourself to be fluent in that language.
- Let some of your peers proofread the manuscript. Make it clear that you realise that progress is mainly established in science through mutual criticism, and the accumulation of knowledge through clear and open interaction of ideas and insights. If you get the impression that your peers are not reading your texts, ask them why.
- If you prepare an oral research presentation (⊕F1) ask someone to listen to it. Make sure this person listens to you from the perspective of your intended audience.

Sometimes it can be an asset to ask an uninformed person (layman) to proofread your text or act as the audience for a presentation. A layman in particular can tell you if the structure and the logic of your arguments are correct.

Series B Study and Self-Management

The Reflective Cycle of Lifelong Learning

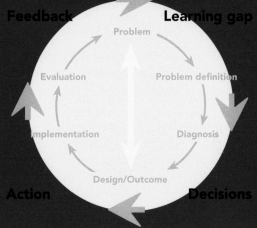

Feedback
Learning gap
Problem
Evaluation
Problem definition
Implementation
Diagnosis
Design/Outcome
Action
Decisions

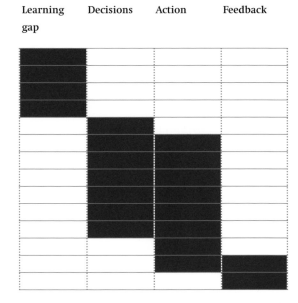

	Learning gap	Decisions	Action	Feedback
B1 Principles of Virtuous/Lifelong Learning	■			
B2 Self-diagnosis: Attitude	■			
B3 What does the Teacher want?	■			
B4 Learning Report and Contract	■			
B5 Study Strategies and Learning Styles		■	■	
B6 Memory and Mind Maps		■	■	
B7 Concentration		■	■	
B8 Good Time Management		■	■	
B9 Procrastination		■	■	
B10 Study Planning: Week		■	■	
B11 Study Planning: Semester		■	■	
B12 Health and Energy Balance			■	
B13 Generating/Receiving Feedback			■	■
B14 Learning Contract II: Peer Feedback				■

Study and Self-management Skill Levels

Level 1
- ○ Learning to digest knowledge: basic principles of 'learning to learn'
- ○ Systematic and active learning attitude, aimed at an academic study
- ○ Rough version of 'learning reports/contract': first assessment of weaknesses and strengths is given
- ○ Feedback aimed at understanding what the teacher wants
- ○ Effective time management (only) possible under pressure
- ○ Understand what an 'integrative approach' to skills means

Level 2
- ○ Development of 'learning to learn' in practice
- ○ Start to decide on what is an interesting 'portfolio' of knowledge topics
- ○ More sophisticated version of learning reports; linking weaknesses and strengths
- ○ Feedback aimed at balancing the interests of teachers and students (own weaknesses and strengths)
- ○ Time management balances study and other activities
- ○ Be aware and able to link simple skills

Level 3
- ○ Knowledge accumulation to generate further learning
- ○ Assertive attitude to come to an integrated approach of the object of knowledge
- ○ Learning report links strengths/weaknesses to opportunities/threats and implementation
- ○ Feedback actively organised by the students themselves
- ○ Effective time management is self-reinforcing
- ○ Students are able to analytically and practically link more complicated skills

Level 4
- ○ Mastery of principles of lifelong learning
- ○ Self-management of feedback and regular update of learning reports (for self-feedback and input for peer feedback)
- ○ Volunteering to provide and receive coaching (example: become tutor)
- ○ Effective time management remains a topic of continuous learning and feedback

Self-management and study skills are the most individual skills to develop. It is your responsibility to develop them, which does not mean that you should forgo the support of tutors or peers. The most important yardstick for measuring your performance in self-management and study skills is their effect on the other skills in the Skill Circle. It takes considerable time and critical self-diagnosis to develop self-management and study skills. They are a mixture of input and output categories. Also, your aims and priorities change over time, as you reach higher levels of understanding and skill proficiency (⊕The Format, part I). The challenge of lifelong (self-managed) learning is to continuously trigger cycles of so-called generative or 'double-loop' learning (Parker with Stone, 2003). This requires that you be prepared to go through the following reflective sequence:

(1) Problem definition: what is the learning phase you are in, and what are the related problems of developing skills? You try to become aware of your '**learning gap**' (⊕B4) by identifying the difference between where you are (zero measurement) and where you or your tutors/teachers want you to be (in a particular period of time). It also requires that you are able to question old models of learning and self-management.
(2) Diagnosis and design: define the skills that you want to develop in particular (**decision**) and try to identify different perspectives (advantages and disadvantages) of the available approaches. Set realistic goals. Write a learning contract and learning updates on a regular basis.
(3) Implementation: translate your goals into realistic actions (**action**). Make realistic plans per week and per semester. Test the development of your skills by looking at your *output*: the way that you give a presentation, sit an exam, write, reach decisions, and – most importantly – the way that you carry out research and deal with relevant problems.
(4) Evaluation: Search for different types of **feedback** at different stages in your personal development.

Five basic principles apply that you should *always* take into account when you want to make your study activities part of a continuous and virtuous learning cycle.

---

1   Assume responsibility for your own learning

2   Be active and intra-preneurial

3   Dare to put yourself in the discomfort zone

4   Create your own learning environment – participate in extra-curricular activities

5   Generate as much relevant feedback as possible: get a coach or tutor

1 Assume responsibility for your own learning

Awareness of learning gaps is only relevant if you assume responsibility for your own learning (cf. Payne, Whittaker, 2006) and are able to work on them systematically in a more or less 'professional' style. The following dimensions are relevant:

- **The importance of motivation**. Ask yourself why **you** want to study this subject (⊕A3). Without clear intrinsic motivation, i.e. based on your own wishes and interests, all your activities will become much more laborious. If your motivation for studying is primarily extrinsic (wish of parents, job perspective), it will be more difficult to *remain* motivated.
- **The need for an active attitude**. Motivation is necessary, but this alone is not sufficient for you to be able to study successfully. Your attitude is also important (⊕B2). Adopt an *active and continuous learning attitude*. Aim at collecting and producing material and interpretations yourself. But know at the same time that trying to further develop the work of others (⊕A1) and revealing your sources (⊕E1, E2, E11) are two of the most important scientific attitudes. Go through the Reflective Cycle systematically (⊕A3) when you diagnose your own problems. Be active when you attend lectures (⊕D7).
- **Awareness of automatisms**. Most human behaviour is based on (unaware) automatisms that are conditioned by past experiences and genetic factors (Tiggelaar, 2005). Most of your habits – whether good or bad, whether intelligent or non-sensical – are the result of these automatisms. In order to change anything, you should become aware of these automatisms.
- **The challenges of the hyperkinetic society**. Multi-tasking, an abundance of information sources, rapid media, all have increased the risk of superficial and chaotic thinking (Hallowell, 2005). This so called 'hyperkinetic society' (⊕The Challenge, part I) affects the brain. In order to take up responsibility for your own learning, you have to develop a solid awareness of the challenges of this type of society.
- **Plan backwards**. Developing skills requires long-term planning. You should be capable of analysing your progress in (combinations of) the different skills, by defining the skill profile that you want to achieve *by the end* of an activity – for instance a course. Look at the study guide for clues. Then, *plan backwards*. Aim at an annual mission definition for your skill development. Make an agreement with yourself which also leaves room for flexible time management in the short term (⊕B9). Realise that skill priorities will change over time.
- **Learning reports**. Systematically analyse your progress in the development of skills (⊕B4). Set new goals for each year. Organise feedback on your learning report either from peers in a self-managed study group, the course adviser, or from one of the teachers (⊕B13).

2 Be active and intra-preneurial

The university creates all sorts of opportunities, provided you make an active effort. See it not only as a project for which you need a number of managerial (professional) skills, but also as one that requires a stimulating portfolio of intra-curricular activities to keep you motivated. Because you operate inside an organisation, the choice you make can be identified as 'intrapreneurial' skill.

◆ **Choose a portfolio of intra-curricular activities**   Try to invest your prime time each semester in:
  • **classes**: what kind of classes should have priority? (see below);
  • **writing activities**: what kind of written products do you work on most ? (see below);
  • **management activities**: become an assistant, active in organising or a peer-teacher;
  • **literature**: 'classics' that you want to read completely, publications by teachers;
  • **journals and magazines**: which ones do you want to read regularly and when? (➲C4);
  • **teachers**: who would you like to know better or receive feedback from: if you know what you want, teachers are always more receptive to your requests for support;
  • **organisations and topics** that you want to know more about: organise your files accordingly (➲A11).

Lacking a purposeful portfolio of activities is the biggest threat for effective self-management.

◆ **Base your choice of classes for each semester on** (cf.Light, 1992):
  • **class size**: choose at least one class that has a small number of participants (1) stimulates class involvement, (2) increases the time spent on course work, and (3) increases your satisfaction;
  • **level**: do not choose only introductory and core courses. Try to gain experience in advanced work in a specific field: it also helps you to make better choices in the next phase of your study;
  • **language**: join classes that are taught in a foreign language. Try to work on at least one foreign language consistently during your studies.

◆ **Create a writing portfolio: write regularly!**   Writing requires practice. Choose a motto: let no day pass without having written a few lines *('Nulla dies sine linea')*. Write in a logbook every day, write an article, a summary, a letter with an argument or do any other structured writing activity. Applying this motto helps prevent one of the biggest enemies of self-management: inertia.

3 Dare to put yourself in the discomfort zone
The only way to go through the learning cycle (➲The Format, part I) is by making yourself acutely aware of your incompetencies (see Figure B.1). The angle of your learning paths is strongly influenced by your ability and willingness to actively

bring yourself into this 'discomfort zone'. Without sufficient investment, your learning path will be much less steep and consequently the outcome of your efforts, much less rewarding. So take risks and learn from mistakes made and the feedback received. Evade academic opportunism and overly calculating behaviour. Think of studying as a business opportunity: in case you dedicate sufficient time and effort to it, the rewards (return on investment) will be bigger as well. The outcome of a project is always related to the size of your efforts.

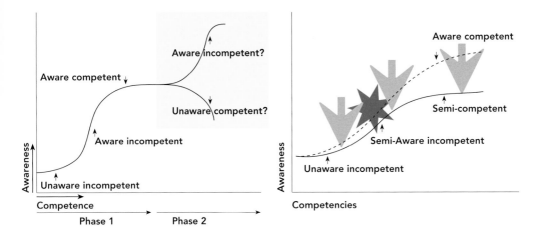

Figure B.1 *Two ways to go through the Learning Cycle*

4 Create your own learning environment

Creating an own learning environment does not only make you less dependent on the quality of the institution at which you work or study, but it also boosts your learning cycle – even when the project you engage in, fails. Two activities in particular are relevant: small study groups and extra-curricular activities.

■ **Create small groups.** If you work in a small group (of four to six people) you learn significantly more than if you work alone. The payoff in terms of self-learning is not so much in achievements (grades), but in involvement, enthusiasm, and the pursuit of topics to a more advanced level (Light, 1990:70). You learn how to cope with free-riders, groupthink (⊕G10), and the importance of constructive criticism (⊕D1, G9). Group work should be creative and challenging, encourage you to 'stretch yourself'. Stimulating group work is bound to affect the quality of your learning and your motivation. This is reinforced if you also become a peer-teacher (⊕G9).
■ **Engage in extra-curricular activities.** Research done at Harvard University shows that there is no negative correlation between the level of involvement in extra-curricular activities and grades (Light, 1990:44). Even students that do a lot of extra-curricular activities do not achieve different grades than those who pri-

marily focus on attending classes and writing the required essays. There is an important bonus for getting involved in activities other than course work: your satisfaction increases tremendously (ibid, 1990:41). Get involved in extra-curricular activities, organise this around academic work.

'Product/result oriented socialising is more important than just socialising' (Light, 1992:8).

5 Generate as much relevant feedback as possible

It is impossible to learn without feedback. But not all feedback is relevant and timely. You have to learn how to give yourself feedback (➔B4, G9), what attitude you can best adopt when receiving feedback (➔B13) and how you can best generate feedback from teachers and tutors (➔B13) and from your own peers (➔B14).

People can have one of a variety of different attitudes towards self-management and learning. Not all of these attitudes are functional or appropriate at particular stages in the education. This Skill Sheet helps you to identify important components of your attitude (individual and in groups) and the kind of synthesis that you could try to achieve.

1 Individual attitude: the dependent and independent learner

The attitude of a student towards the educational institutes and the teacher as its most important representative, constitutes the first dimension for self-diagnosis. Most institutes expect substantial independence of students in their learning. The extent to which the student expects support and encouragement from the institute and its teachers, defines whether learning can be self-disciplined and motivated or requires substantial external stimuli. Students can be 'dependent' and 'independent' learners. Payne and Whittaker (2006) have made the following Table (Table B.2a) to enable students to decipher their learning style. The dependent learner and independent learner are shown as separate states, but individual students can show combinations of both attitudes.

Table B.2a The dependent learner and the independent learner

Dependent learner	Independent learner
Learner wants:	*Learner anticipates:*
• Structured learning experiences	• Complex problems for which there is no single correct solution
• Tutor to take responsibility for the learning experience	• Extensive self-paced, independent study
• Tutor-centred approach	• Student-centred approach
• Rewards	• Encouragement
• Support	• Judgement-free support
• Intellectual stimulation from studies	• Experimentation
• Reinforcement	• Free to explore and make mistakes
• Esteem	
Learner wants lecturer/tutor to be:	*Learner wants lecturer/tutor to be:*
• A subject expert	• A facilitator
• An authority figure	• A guide
• An instructor	**and to:**
and to:	• Negotiate
• Lecture/talk	• Encourage
• Assess/check	• Develop
• Examine/test	• Motivate
• Design and direct the learning experience	• Consult

• Control	• Listen
• Lead/direct	• Evaluate
• Instruct	• Act as a resource
• Encourage	• Provide feedback on request
	• Delegate

Source: Payne and Whittaker, 2006:11

2 Group attitude: 'I' vs. 'Other'

Simone Schenk distinguishes between two styles in the way that students process information when working on a group assignment: an orientation primarily towards oneself ('I-orientation' comparable to the independent orientation vis-à-vis the teacher) and towards others (comparable to the dependent orientation). Table B.2b outlines the characteristics.

Table B.2b 'I' and 'other' orientation characteristics

An 'I-oriented' group member...	An 'other-oriented' group member...
▪ takes his/her own ideas, opinions, concepts and questions as a point of reference for learning;	▪ takes ideas, opinions, concepts and questions of others as point of reference for learning. The 'other', however, has to be acknowledged as an 'authority';
▪ likes to discuss, critically analyse situations and statements. Likes to criticise the ideas of others;	▪ likes to absorb and accumulate knowledge;
▪ talks and interrupts frequently in group discussions; regularly comes up with new/creative ideas and viewpoints;	▪ is a good listener and tries to analyse information in a detailed and thorough manner;
▪ has more problems with the detailed and concise elaboration of assignments, with revealing sources and checking information.	▪ often chooses one approach in group processes and sticks to that. Faces problems with unstructured discussions and is eager to know what the assignment is.

In groups, both attitudes can be functional. Groups composed of *only one type* of participant face specific problems. If there are only 'other-oriented' members, groups lack sufficient 'critical' attitude and the capability to handle assignments effectively. If there are only 'I-oriented' members, groups lack sufficient 'thoroughness', and indecisive discussions could occur. The group is more likely to run out of time. Assignments will often be completed hurriedly, without thorough argumentation.

Generally, however, study groups are often made up of both types of people allowing for the two learning styles to complement each other. But this situation creates additional conflicts due to misconceptions:

▪ The image that the I-orientated group members have of the Other-orientated members: *'They only want to do the assignment by the book, they don't show initiative and have no tolerance of criticism.'*

■ The image that the Other-orientated group members have of the I-oriented members: *'They think that they are excellent, they keep talking, but are doing nothing and criticise everything.'*

It is important to understand the possible functionality of each attitude for group work. In doing this, conflicts between the two attitudes can be prevented and maximum use can be made of each attitude. Table B.2c presents a simple diagnostic tool that can help you to identify the personal attitude of each group member. A number of questions are listed. They can be divided into four categories: (**A**) *if* you participate in a discussion, (**B**) *how* you participate in a discussion, (**C**) *how* you relate to a teacher/tutor, and (**D**) *how* you study in general. If you have mainly answered 'yes' to the 'other-oriented' questions **or** to the 'I-oriented' column, your profile is clear for the moment: you are either a more dependent or a more independent group member.

Table B.2c A simple checklist to discover your group attitude

		'I'	'Other'	blank
A	I want to say something in the group but only when I have studied the assignment closely; I do not want to get into lengthy discussions.		yes	no
A	I regularly interrupt the group discussion process, because I usually have many ideas during the meeting.	yes		no
B	I find it hard to criticise the ideas of others who are more experienced than I am. They know more than I do.		yes	no
B	I am critical towards the ideas of others, even if they are more experienced than I am.	yes		no
C	I believe that there should be a chairperson in the group and I don't think that I am capable of taking that position.		yes	no
C	I don't see the function of a chairperson for this group.	yes		no
D	If I am doing a project I want to know exactly what the teacher wants and expects of the group.		yes	no
D	If I am doing a project I am primarily interested in what I want and what the teacher's intentions are.	yes		no

3 Change process: Creating an individual synthesis?

The more you progress through your course or in the hierarchy of an organisation, the more you might strive for a synthesis of the 'I' (independent) and the 'other' (dependent) orientation. The more people in a group themselves combine the two orientations, the less likely conflicts will appear – or when they appear, they are more easily solved. To further characterise this behavioural synthesis, a second distinction between attitudes that is used frequently comes to mind:

between submissive, aggressive and assertive behaviour. Table B.2d lists some typical verbal and physical expressions of these categories.

Table B.2d Three attitudes and their (non) verbal characteristics

	Submissive *(dependent/other-orientated)*	Aggressive *(independent/ I-orientation)*	Assertive *(interdependent)*
Verbal	■ 'I'm sorry to take up your valuable time, but...'	■ 'Do it or else!'	■ 'I believe that... what do you think?'
	■ 'Would you mind if...'	■ 'That's stupid.'	■ 'I would like to...'
	■ 'It's only my opinion...'	■ 'Surely, you don't believe that.'	■ 'What can we do to resolve this problem?'
	■ 'Well, if you say so...'	■ 'It's nothing to do with me...	
		■ it's all your fault.'	
Non-verbal	■ hesitant voice at low pitch;	■ use of strident, firm and sarcastic tone of voice;	■ steady and medium pitched tone of voice;
	■ avoiding eye contact;	■ rapid delivery;	■ even pace of delivery;
	■ moving around nervously, possibly wringing hands, hunching shoulders, keeping arms crossed for protection.	■ dominate the other with a hard stare;	■ firm eye contact, without being threatening;
		■ gestures like pointing fingers and thumping the table.	■ body posture relaxed, but controlled.

The combination of an individual assertive attitude which recognises the interdependence of group work is the best guarantee for virtuous learning in groups. Assertive behaviour is exhibited by those who respect the right of other people to express their ideas, feelings and needs, while at the same time, believing that they too have the right to express and pursue such matters. Being assertive has clear advantages:

■ your own achievements and potential will be recognised earlier and probably also rewarded;

■ a growing feeling of personal value will be developed;

■ recognition of responsibility for your ideas, feelings and needs by others and yourself;

■ less energy and time is wasted trying to find out what other people are doing (or not).

By Simone Schenk

Teachers often give assignments in order to stimulate you to digest information in a particular manner. They thereby use terms like 'understanding', 'perception', 'critical', and 'application'. But these terms are often interpreted differently by the recipients (Schenk, 1986). Understanding what the teacher or tutor wants, also helps you to better understand what you want personally.

To grasp the way you are supposed to digest and elaborate information, first try to find clear definitions of these terms and the appropriate methods of study. Then, you have to check whether your interpretation matches the teacher's expectation. This Skill Sheet lists a number of the frequently heard interpretations of each of the abovementioned terms. Each interpretation has different consequences for the way you should digest information and prepare for exams.

> General rule: always ask the teacher for (written) clarification of the learning targets.

1 Understanding: interpretations

- You just read the text, without having to stop every time you do not understand a word or a technical term. A more detailed understanding would cost too much mental energy.
- You are able to sense intuitively the meaning of a text, without being able to explain it in detail. By using examples you can understand what is meant, but be careful: a cow is an animal, but an animal need not be a cow (➔C6).
- You can follow what the author of a text means, without being able to apply this approach to a new topic.

2 Perception: interpretations

- You can identify the message per paragraph. Your perception of the main lines helps you to grasp the structure of the whole text. The more 'previous knowledge' you have, the less energy goes into studying.
- You can (re)construct the implicit premises of the author(s), for example, the political preference, or the vision regarding companies and organisations. This kind of perception can be created by using existing political/social/psychological frameworks of reference to ask questions about the material presented.
- You are capable of formulating comparable argumentation and/or you are able to identify fallacies in the author's argumentation (➔C8). Such perception can only be achieved if you have studied the argumentation in some detail. Otherwise, you run the risk of criticising mainly partial elements of the argumentation with too much of your own interpretation.

3 Critical: interpretations

- A teacher may expect you to compare for instance three different approaches dealing with a particular topic. You are supposed to critically assess points where the authors agree and disagree.
- You are supposed to come up with a balanced judgement. You can not copy someone else's statements. You are expected to assess the 'pros' and 'cons' as a relative outsider, master the topic and only then formulate a critical judgement of the approaches.
- You should make explicit the implicit criticism of one author of another author. You must check whether criticism is mainly focused on partial elements, and whether conclusions have been drawn too quickly or are one-dimensional. You have to consider what kind of 'understanding' and 'perception' is at the basis of the observed criticism.

4 Application: interpretations

- As with a cookery book, you follow the recipes step-by-step. Each example is then compared with the related theory/model.
- You use a theory or a model to generate questions about reality. Theories and models in social sciences can not be identified as 'true' or 'false', but as more or less applicable to a particular problem (➔A7).
- You investigate under what practical circumstances you can identify a theory or model, by making their premises explicit. You can look at the background of the author in terms of personal background (political, country, class, company, year) or scientific 'school'.

During your education, you are constantly moving in a continuum, from 'what does the other person think' to 'what do I think'. Monitor your own activities constantly. Do you too often critically assess parts of a text that you are reading? If so you may run the risk of not grasping the structure of the argumentation and coming to misleading conclusions. If you do not look at the background information about the author, you run the risk of not actively digesting the text (➔C2). If you prepare for an exam it is relevant to know whether the teacher is aiming at (and testing on) understanding, critical perceptions and/or applications. Old exam questions can come in handy, certainly if the teacher is prepared to explain the intentions behind the past questions.

5 Exercise

Use Table B.3 as an aid to assessing the intentions of the teacher. The first column contains a number of possible assignments given by the teacher. The second column refers to possible interpretations of 'understanding', 'perception', 'critical', and 'application'. These interpretations can then be used to decide which kind of study method should be used to comply with the intention of the assignment/-teacher. When filling in the third column you confront two aspects of intentions for studying: what you want to do, and what the teacher wants you to do. You will see immediately where discrepancies lie between your preferred style of studying and the teacher's demands. Talk about this problem with your teacher. Many teachers are often open to changes, once they are confronted by serious and dedicated participants (⊕The Challenge, part I).

Table B.3 What does the teacher want and what do I want?

What does the teacher want?	Possible interpretations	What do I want/what should I do?
Multiple-choice exam with knowledge questions	Memorise facts, depart from understanding and perception	
Multiple-choice exam with case questions	Compare and apply theories/-models	
Open exam questions, knowledge	Memorise and repeat facts by using understanding/perception	
Open exam questions, understanding and application	It is essential to argue answers on the basis of facts	
Essay, theoretical topic	Analyse on the basis of understanding/perception	
Essay, practical topic	Theoretical underpinning	
Expects understanding	Text parts, (between) paragraphs	
Expects perception	Texts, between texts or own text construction	
Expects criticism	Approach of renowned theorists or your own input	
Expects applications	From understanding, perception or criticism	

The learning report is one of the main instruments for applying the principles of self-managed learning (➔B1). The learning report can function as a 'learning contract' with yourself, once you are able to move from a mere description of your strengths and weaknesses to a sophisticated and realistic implementation. The word 'contract' should not be taken too literally, but it is important that you be serious about reaching your learning objectives.

When drafting a learning report and contract, ask yourself five reflective questions:

1 Where am I now? (problem definition)
2 What is my problem? (diagnosis)
3 Where do I want to go? (output/design)
4 How can I get there? (implementation)
5 How do I want to test my progress? (evaluation)

These questions offer you a more or less systematic insight and perspective into tackling your own skill deficiencies. Even going through the questions in the Reflective Cycle in a general manner can affect your learning considerably. The learning contract consists of two parts: a *learning report* and the actual *learning 'contract'*. The first part serves as the input for the second part. In the learning report you look at what you have learned in the past and identify what you still have to learn. On the website [⊕➔www.skillsheets.com] you can find a 'strengths/weaknesses' form for each of the skills, to perform this part of the analysis. In the *learning contract*, you ask yourself where you want to go, how you want to get there, and how you plan to test or measure your progress. Table B.4 lists these questions and the operationalisation to choose.

Two yardsticks can be used to measure your skill performance:
(1) an *absolute yardstick* of skill formation, by comparing your skill level to the norms contained in the whole collection of Skill Sheets; use the Skill Level assessments at the start of every Skill Series to assess your approximate **skill level**;
(2) a *relative yardstick* where you compare your skill level with the skill profile of your teaching institute or organisation; this requires that you for instance know what the teacher wants (➔B3).

You can select one of these alternatives in order to look at your progress. The most rewarding exercise is when you look at both yardsticks at the same time and try go through the consequences of using them for you personally.

Table B.4 Five basic questions to develop a learning contract

Reflective moment	Leading question	Operationalisation
	Learning report...	
1 Problem definition	*Where am I now?*	1. Strengths and weaknesses analysis: per skill [⊕➔www.skillsheets.com]. 2. What is my **Skill level** per Skill (➔intros to Series A-G). 3. Which **Skill Profile** is the teaching institute aiming at, or required for your job or organisation (if available)? How close are you to reaching that profile?
2 Diagnosis	*What is my problem?*	1. Which clear deficiencies still exist in my abilities (major weaknesses)? 2. More specific: how well do I perform regarding the **five principles of self-managed learning** (➔B1) and the **eight principles of good research** (➔A1)?
	...as the input for a learning contract	
3 Output/design	*Where do I want to go?*	**State a mission definition for the next year.** Write a few lines or invent a motto that can motivate you for the coming year. Always assign priority to tackling deficiencies in your minimum skills. Make priorities in which you favour writing and research skills (as your core skills).
4 Implementation	*How can I get there?*	**Define a portfolio of activities** (➔B1). Make a distinction between curricular and extra-curricular activities. Which attitude and study style is required (➔B2). Specify a *realistic* plan for the semester (➔B10, B11).
5 Evaluation	*How can I test my progress?*	**Specify a strategy to generate feed-back.** Define the output aim, and the way that you would like to get feedback from peers, teachers, or others, *systematically* (➔B13).

One of the integrating models of the Skill Sheets collection is Kolb's learning cycle (1984). 'Studying' is the art of individual learning in particular through reading books and articles, and listening to lectures. Most of the time the goal seems to be the exam, but in reality of course the exam only functions as a means to check whether you have accumulated sufficient enough knowledge and insights. So reading and listening constitutes a very important source of experience for students. The prime object of your experience, thereby is training and developing your brain. This Skill Sheet considers the basic functions of the brain, how they relate to various learning styles and what implications that might have, for instance, for preparing an exam.

1 The dynamic brain

Traditionally, people tend to look at the brain as a static entity that was created in the first 18 months after birth and that gets 'filled' like a very large cabinet (or a computer with a mega-memory) with experience in the rest of the life. Recent research seems to indicate that the brain is much more dynamic. In interaction with the environment and on the basis of other experiences the brain constantly changes. Particular parts of the brain grow, whereas other parts become used less frequently, depending on the way you use and train your brain. Specific hemispheres in your brain are dedicated to specific functions. The right hemisphere is often focused on more creative functions like spatial awareness, identifying colours, imagination. The left hemisphere of the brain is dedicated to more logical and analytical functions. But both sides intimately interact and it has been shown that for many activities many parts of the brain are used at the same time. Finally, when you grow older, your brain functions might become slower, but your ability to learn does not necessarily diminish – provided you sustain exercises and keep a good energy balance, i.e. sleep and eat well (➔B12).

2 Experience-based learning

Using and sustaining your brain in an active manner contributes not only to your learning, but also to your whole well-being. An approach that links learning and study to the various functions of the brain is the 'experience-based learning theory'. This can also be dubbed 'biology learning'. Zull (2002) portrays both in the following picture (figure B.5). Ideally speaking, learning presents a cycle that moves from concrete experience (CE, in this case studying text books), via reflective observation (RO, making efficient notes), through abstract conceptualisations and hypotheses (AC, e.g. understanding of the text) to active testing or experimentation (AT, the exam or generating feedback). Effective learning therefore also necessitates that different parts of the brain are developed and trained.

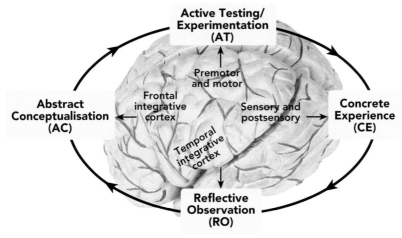

Source: based on Zull, 2002

Figure B.5 Experiential learning cycle and regions of the cerebral cortex

3 Learning styles

Learning Style Inventory (LSI) research (Kolb, 1984) has identified four dominant dynamic learning approaches: diverging, assimilating, converging and accommodating.

1 **Diverging style**: CE and RO are dominant. The style is divergent because people with these learning abilities perform better in situations that call for the generation of ideas, such as in brainstorming sessions. However, as regards studying, this particular style creates considerable tensions, because the person will find it more difficult to concentrate on concrete texts and learn them for an exam. These people often adopt an **undirected learning** style (Vermunt, 1998), which relates to their general ambivalence to engaging in advanced scientific studies. In studies people with the diverging style prefer to work in groups, listening with an open mind and receiving personalized feedback. Studying for an exam probably requires external coaching.

2 **Assimilating style**: AC and RO are dominant. People with these capabilities are good at understanding a large variety of information, which they can put into concise logical form. This type of person is more interested in ideas than in practical value. For study situations, they prefer reading, lectures and exploring analytical models. Their learning style is often **'meaning-directed'** (Vermunt, 1998). This makes them often rather critical as regards multiple-choice exams which do not do justice to the complexities of the literature. Studying for an exam is best organized individually.

3 **Converging style**: AC and AT are dominant. People with these abilities are best at finding practical uses for ideas and theories. They are solution-oriented and aimed at answering questions of others. A converging learning style is often

found with people that prefer technical tasks and problems rather than social and interpersonal issues and therefore can often be found in natural sciences and the medical studies. This type of person is inclined to prefer a **reproduction-directed** learning style, which makes them the perfect candidate for big exams, but also for experimentation situations which require – often under controlled conditions – testing new ideas, simulations, laboratory assignments and practical application. Studying for an exam, can best be organized in a laboratory-like setting.

4 **Accommodating style:** CE and AT are dominant. People with this learning style learn easiest from 'hands-on' experience. The enjoy carrying out plans, act on 'gut' feelings, and rely on people for their information rather than on their own analysis. As a learning style, this type adopts an **application-directed** approach to studying. The accommodating style is particularly equipped for action-oriented careers such as marketing or sales. In study, people with the accommodating learning style prefer to work with others to get assignments done. Studying for an exam is therefore best organized in a study group.

In summary, Table B.5 summerizes the most important characteristics of each learning style and gives you advice on how best to approach an exam, if you have one of these learning styles.

Table B.5 Studying for exams: what style fits you?

Learning approach	Part of brain	Learning style	How to approach an exam
Diverging	CE and RO	Undirected	Get a coach/tutor
Assimilating	AC and RO	Meaning	Individually
Converging	AC and AT	Reproduction	Laboratory and experimental
Accommodating	CE and AT	Application	Study group

With a contribution by Simone Schenk

Why do you have problems remembering the material that you have studied? The answer to this question requires that you understand the distinction between (1) Short-Term Memory (STM), (2) Medium-Term Memory (STM) and (3) the Long-Term Memory (LTM). Mastering your STM will help you in studying material more efficiently. Mastering your MTM will help you to create a feasible week plan (➾B10) and learn how to efficiently spend your time in the days before an exam. Mastering your LTM will help you to develop a more feasible plan for the semester (➾B11) and engage in a more continuous (virtuous) cycle of learning and relearning. In particular for your MTM and LTM a number of techniques are available, such as Mind Mapping.

1 Short-Term Memory (STM)

When you read a sentence the words are initially stored in your Short-Term Memory (STM). The STM contains approximately seven units. In case a sentence is easy to read, like 'the cat was sitting in a tree and looked lazily at a bird on one of the branches', there is no problem in reading the sentence in one effort without much strain. The first part of the sentence is automatically transferred into an image by the STM, which leaves sufficient space in the memory to grasp the second part of the sentence as well. Difficulties appear when you read a complex sentence with many new technical terms, subordinate clauses or insertions. This is the case with many academic texts (➾C series). Your STM reaches saturation point, but there is not yet a part of the sentence that can be made into an image which can be transferred to other parts of your memory and which create the possibility to read through without a great deal of effort (on 'autopilot').

If the first part of a complex sentence gets transferred to other parts of the memory without a clear image, by the end of the sentence you will have lost what you have read at the beginning. To illustrate this, try to read the next sentence at the same speed as you read the sentence about 'the cat...': 'Alternatively the memory readout potential may reflect the initial events of a "motor" nature as the cat prepares to make one response or the other.' Unless you are very knowledgeable about physiology, you will not be able to read this sentence on your 'autopilot'. When you reread the sentence, trying hard to understand the message, you will notice that it is necessary to pause after each part of the sentence while you actively try to create an image of the contents of that part. You need to be aware of this process, otherwise you will not realise that the STM is automatically transferred to other parts of your memory. The more energy the STM takes, the less energy is left for other activities like finding the differences between theories or identifying an argumentation structure (➾C6). Or put the other way around: the more energy you take to engage in other activities during the day (➾B12) the more difficult it becomes to use your STM efficiently.

2 Medium-Term Memory (MTM)

When you study *new* books and/or theories, and you understand what you read, the information is transferred from the STM to the Medium-Term Memory (MTM). The MTM can hold approximately three days of knowledge accumulated. If you continue to study after those three days, without processing the accumulated knowledge, memory problems arise. On day four the knowledge of day one will transfer to other parts of your memory unnoticed, from where you might not be able to retrieve the information. This storing mechanism was not particularly relevant to you at secondary school, because the amount of completely new information that was tested at once could generally have been studied/learned within a period of three days (➲B8). Furthermore, most of the material was covered in advance, which considerably lessened the novelty of any topic to be studied. At many secondary schools automatic repetition is built-in. Students could forget everything after an exam or a vacation, because the teacher very often started to repeat information which had been covered before the exam/holiday. At university, however, most of the material is not explained in class. The number of exams can be large in relatively short periods of time. But more importantly: the number of pages to be studied for each exam will often be very high. The usual method of studying, so successful in secondary school ('filling your MTM'), will prove to be inadequate when you have to learn large quantities of material.

Immediate Exam Preparation

Many students use their MTM incorrectly in the immediate period preceding an exam. This happens in particular when they want to study **new material**. This information is automatically stored in your MTM, which might get saturated and can not be used for repetition of already studied material. For instance, in case you have already digested (studied and repeated) 80% of the material, studying the remaining 20% one day before the exam, might substitute that information for the 80%. What can you do, then? Primarily repetition and understanding. A few days prior to an exam you can use your MTM to learn by heart particular kinds of detailed information that are tested regularly, but that you yourself might not find particularly relevant. What you consider relevant depends on your learning style (➲B5). You might for instance find it much more important to know where you can find the information than to reproduce it. For an exam this attitude contains considerable risks, since you are supposed to reproduce substantial amounts of information and are not sure what level of detail the teacher might ask (➲B3). Under these circumstances you make more active use of your MTM. As long as you know where to find those details in your memory while you do the exam, you do not have to store them permanently in your memory. For example, when you are studying tax law it might be useful to know that there are different types of taxes, the amount and the approximate applicability of those taxes to different income levels. A few days before the exam you should memorise the exact data on all the different income levels by repeating the figures a number of times. The more you have been able to figure out a system for the material that you have been studying – for instance in the form of a Mind Map - the more knowledge can be transferred to other parts of your memory. Therefore, there will be more unoccupied space left in your MTM for details like names, technical terms, figures, exact historical dates. Moreover, a large number of exams in a short period of time (common practice at many universities) presents the student with a substantial assault on the physical condition; especially in the case of studying from early in the morning to late at night for a number of consecutive weeks. The more time you have during the exam period to do short repetition exercises *and* get a good night's sleep, the bigger the chance that you will stay fit, even for the last exam.

3 Long-Term Memory (LTM)

The Long-Term Memory (LTM) can be compared to a library with three departments.

- The *first department* consists of books that are shelved in the sequence in which they enter. When the shelves are full, one moves to another department. There is no structure and no catalogue. During your education, this type of storage is equivalent to reading paragraph after paragraph, trying to figure out the main arguments, after which all of these arguments are learned by heart. Later, only by accident will you be able to retrieve this information in your memory. During an exam or at any other moment, you will know that you 'know something' related to a question, but you will be unable to remember it exactly.

- In the *second department* the books are categorised by topics but the structure remains relatively loose, while a catalogue is still missing. The compartments contain only the names of the topics. While you are studying, using this department of a virtual library means that you try to find the main argument in a chapter or section. You memorise a combination of the main lines. When asked about them during an exam you have to go into the labyrinth of compartments which only contain an indication of topics, thus created in your memory. If someone helps you to the right compartment, for example by posing pre-structured and/or multiple choice questions in the exam, your search process can be easier.

- In the *third department* the topics are neatly organised into groups, while a catalogue is available that can help you to choose on the basis of subjects/topics. While you are studying, filling this department of your library means that you create an image and an overview of the topic, for example by comparing approaches. Which related arguments exist, why do two researchers disagree, what kind of questions create a deeper understanding of the material? By studying actively at this level of understanding, you create a catalogue which enables you to retrieve the accumulated knowledge in later stages.

Mind Mapping and Memorising techniques

1 **Mind mapping**

The Mind map technique is used in a wide variety of areas, but its prime application can still be found in memorising through correct classifications and visualisation. It is a form of 'radiant thinking' (Buzan with Buzan, 2006) which builds on the working of the brain by drawing and mapping information through networks of interconnected keywords – in much the same vein as neurons in the brain interconnect information. Using keywords instead of whole sentences – after which they are organised in hierarchies – is the most effective way of memorising and storing information (Kersbergen, 2007). Some books (cf. Parker with Stone, 2003) even use 'bookmaps' to help students understand and memorise their texts better. Big companies like Boeing or BP also increasingly make use of Mind Maps (Buzan with Buzan, 2006). Note-taking using mind maps is an increasingly common technique. Additionally 'speed-learning' is becoming popular. This technique combines Mind mapping with speed reading (⊕C11). Four characteristics define a Mind Map:

- The subject or central theme is in the middle of the map
- The branches connected to this central subject are the main themes
- The further you are away from the central theme, the less important the information is to the central theme
- All the branches are identified by keywords or key notes. The branches take the form of a neural structure.

2 Skimming

Many students create problems because they – unknowingly – study mainly with their MTM. At secondary school knowledge was automatically transferred to the STM. The teacher performed an important function in this process by structuring and repeating material. At university you have to do this yourself by including time for repetition in your weekly schedule every third day, and by allowing time to digest the material. Even with completely new material you start by asking yourself questions on the basis of the book's contents (⊕C3) for example. Skim through the book, look at the source: note technical terms, headings and tables and figures. By being inquisitive, you activate your LTM, particularly the third department. When you begin to read in detail, keep the original questions in mind. At the end of each paragraph, summarise what you have read, think about new questions, which contributes to the expansion of the catalogue in your third department. Ask yourself whether there are other theories, what presumptions there might be with this approach and what other applications could be relevant. These activities do not have to take much time and your interest could grow.

3 SQ3R

The SQ3R technique is an active reading approach to store the information in the Medium and Long-Term memory. It specifies the five steps students can go through when reading a text: (1) Survey (getting a general idea of the content), (2) Question (ask what a text is about: who, what , when, where, why and how), (3) Read (while marking keywords), (4) Recite or Recall (try to recall what has been read e.g. on the basis of mind maps), (5) Review (flip through the text and check whether all questions from step 2 have been addressed).

4 Note-taking

Two approaches to note-taking can be adopted: linear and pattern notes. When reading a book, they can serve as memory aids. When used as a technique during an interview (⊕D3) they serve as the most important input for the interview transcript and ultimately the research report. Linear note-taking can focus on (1) quotes, (2) summary (in your own words) or (3) outline (main structure). Depending on the aim of the notes, all three techniques can be combined. Outlines can also be drawn as a pattern. The more you do this applying a graphical Mind Map, the more you might consider using a specialised technique: Mind Map Organic Study Technique (MMost).

[⊕⊕www.skillsheets.com for more detailed information on these techniques, examples and exercises]

By Simone Schenk

There are two factors that affect your ability to concentrate: (1) physical and (2) mental factors.

1 Physical factors
■ **Shifts during the day**

Some people are at their best immediately after waking up from a good night's sleep. Others are slow starters and work best in the afternoon. A third group can only concentrate well in the evening and/or at night. Find out for yourself which part of the day you feel fittest in. Plan the activities that require your highest level of concentration at those times.

Optimal concentration is needed for texts that are difficult to read (lengthy sentences; other language). You will need less concentration to do calculations linked to theories that were explained sufficiently. Repeating information by reading/listening/writing, which has to be learned by heart (names, dates) is also possible when you are physically tired. Appropriate moments can be immediately before diner (a moment that most people experience a dip in concentration anyway), before you go to sleep or while you are travelling.

■ **Stimulants: coffee, alcohol, nicotine**
- Coffee is a stimulant. Everyone has an absorption limit, however. If you pass that limit, you become overly concentrated and your adrenaline level becomes high. You may feel pleasantly active, but the energy is going to other parts of your body, not to your brain.
- Alcohol stays in your body longer than you realise. For example, if you stay out drinking beer until 4.00 am your blood will still contain a substantial amount of alcohol when you wake up at 10.00 am. After a night out, take the morning off. Spend the rest of the day on low concentration activities like making calculations or repetition.
- Nicotine is also a physical stimulant, which initially calms your mental activities. If you are addicted to nicotine you will notice that the withdrawal symptoms wither away with the first cigarettes that you smoke, after which you can relax. If you use cigarettes to help you concentrate, and if you smoke regularly, you could easily pass a limit that creates the same problems as drinking coffee.

■ **Time, topic and performance**

Figure B.7 shows the correlation between concentration performance and time. Until you reach time T, investing in an activity can lead to an acceptable performance. After passing T, the performance drops quickly. The 'timing' of time T is affected by the following factors:

- In the case of a difficult text or a new text or topic, the T moves further to the left.
- The more limited the knowledge of a topic, the further T moves to the left.
- If a text is clearly structured, the T moves further to the right.
- The more experience you have with a topic, the further T moves to the right.

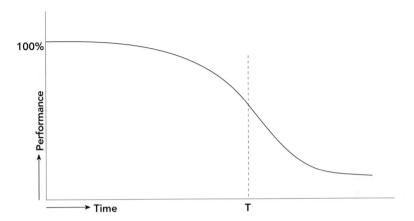

Figure B.7 Performance and studying time

Once you pass time T your efforts are no longer in relation to your performance. A break is necessary. Do not use your brain during the break. Do not enter into a difficult debate or have a 'heavy' telephone conversation. The same also applies to tv-zapping. This is not a very relaxing activity. They require the same or comparable amounts of concentration as you need when studying. You can eat an apple or any other type of food that contains 'slow sugars' (your brain uses a relatively high amount of sugar), do some shopping, go for a run, clean up your room, listen to music on your iPod. If you are functioning well and well-fed (➔B12), a break of fifteen minutes should be enough for you to begin concentrating again.

Beginners (starting a new course) can manage this pattern for three times one hour in a row (➔B10). After that a longer break is necessary. So, when you begin a new course, starting to study intensely shortly before an exam will not work. When compared to your performance in secondary school, time T is located much further to the left, this is also because most study material has not yet been covered in class. Many students realize this only after their first exam period.

2 Mental factors
■ The problems of others

Freshman students in particular face concentration difficulties. They have to think about the situation at home or are concerned with the problems of their (new) friends. Breaking ties and taking more responsibility for yourself is part of 'growing up'. You will also find that the more difficult an assignment is, the more you have problems in isolating yourself from the problems of others:

unconsciously you try to evade the responsibility of facing this particular problem by telling yourself that other problems (of your friends) are perhaps more important. This can be called escape behaviour (➔B8: coping with excuses). Try to dedicate your *prime concentration time* during the day, to the most important activity (studying for an exam, writing a difficult analysis).

- **Your own problems**

  As long as you are busy with other students with which you cooperate – for example in a group assignment – it is relatively easy to concentrate. They will force you to keep your mind on the subject. As soon as you sit alone at your desk to study, other thoughts vie for your attention (➔B9). Many students who have experienced delays in their course said that they started 'worrying' the moment they sat down to study. A good alternative is therefore to create a small study group which creates mutual control, for example by making exam questions together, or going to the library to study together (➔B1). Libraries offer fewer distractions. If you make good appointments with your group of friends for the times that you can get together to have lunch or a coffee break, you create some rules for (mild) mutual control. This advice often works better for 'other' than for 'I-oriented' students (➔B2).

Exercise

Keep track, for a while, of the development of your concentration. How intense is your concentration at various periods during the day? Is there a correlation between time and performance with different types of courses? Try to compare your experiences from secondary school with your present experience. An interesting way to check your concentration level is to close your book at the end of every paragraph or page, and repeat aloud what you just read.

Three general principles help you to manage your time as effectively as possible: (1) gap: identify your most important 'time wasters', (2) decision: work in modules, and (3) action: cope with excuses.

1 Identify your most important 'time wasters'

Bad time management occurs when you cannot handle a number of 'time wasters'. Time wasters are *related* and are often cumulative. Identification should create the precondition under which you can work on tackling your time wasters in the most effective way possible. The box helps you to identify your main 'time wasters'.

Time wasters: a checklist

☝ ⏱ 👎	No **goals/aims** or they are unclear; no set **priorities** or changing priorities.
☝ ⏱ 👎	Unrealistic or no **taxation of time**.
☝ ⏱ 👎	Trying to do too much at the same time (**fragmentation of activities**).
☝ ⏱ 👎	Not being **assertive**, not being able to say 'no'.
☝ ⏱ 👎	**Bad organisation of work, study and private life** and their interaction over time.
☝ ⏱ 👎	Capability of keeping an appropriate **diary**.
☝ ⏱ 👎	You always **postpone** things.
☝ ⏱ 👎	Lacking **personal efficiency** in the organisation of files, diary and/or desk.
☝ ⏱ 👎	You are not capable of **preventing problems** from appearing.
☝ ⏱ 👎	You have no insight into your '**most productive hours**' during the day.

☝ (not at all), ⏱ (a little), 👎 (a lot).

> Lack of time represents lack of priorities.

2 Identify and work in modules

The most prevalent time wasters relate to a lack of aim, priorities and an unwillingness to set deadlines. To tackle this problem, try to work in modules of (a multitude of) three hours: periods of time that can include clear and manageable aims. When you practice working in modules:

- you create a *time focus* in your work, which makes it possible to abstain from other activities during that time period;
- you use the (short, medium and long-term) *memory capacity* in your brain effectively (➡B6);
- you create a feeling of *satisfaction* if you have been able to use the time well, which gives you an opportunity to relax after the set time. Often researchers doing complex research continue without allowing themselves to rest from time to time;

- you allow your *progress over time to be 'measured'* and it is possible to check whether you are now able to carry out a task in a shorter period of time than before;
- this enables you to *employ better planning* in the future.

Four types of modules can be distinguished:
- **Simple/small.** When you have a relatively simple job to do (case, letter, studying a text), define your module in **hours**, with a maximum of three hours. Find out what your peak hours are during the day, and focus the most important intellectual activities during those hours. Organise repetitive work at other times.
- **More complex: Writing.** When you have a more complex task to do, but it is based on material that you have available (simple essay, press release, memo), define a module in terms of one day, i.e. 2/3 modules of three hours.
- **More complex: Writing and searching.** When the work requires research activities in libraries (complex essay, internship report), define your module in terms of **two to three days**, i.e. six to nine modules of three hours. You might be surprised by the amount of information you can digest and the activities that you can employ in three 'concentrated' working days (⊕C5, C11).
- **Complex: Research.** When the research requires a variety of different activities over a considerable period of time (Bachelor's and Master's thesis, Ph.D. thesis) your time management becomes different and even more difficult to control. First, define your modules into *functional activities* (interviewing, reading or collecting the information). Secondly, plan modules of ultimately **one week**, i.e. two modules of three days. For example, try to plan interviews in one particular week so that your other work is not disturbed due to the execution of an interview.

One week seems to be the longest period of time that you can work in a more or less concentrated way on a single topic. If you have planned long modules, also plan *breaks* in which you do not allow yourself to do anything connected with the topic.

3 Avoid distractions: cope with excuses

Experienced time managers of research projects will tell you that during each module, a number of very logical excuses appear related to the contents of the work, which can distract you from your work and thus make your time planning fail:
- There is always reason to doubt whether you have *included all of the relevant sources*.
- There is always reason to think that *someone else* has written your argument already.
- It is always possible to come up with another *research topic which is far more interesting and/or relevant* than the topic(s) that you are presently dealing with.

- You have had the *experience, in the past,* that you could do the work in a shorter period of time, so you might do something else now (watch television, for example) and catch up later.

> Ask yourself: *Do I manage my time or do I let time manage me?*
>
> Could this be your statement? *I know that I have time, but I don't know where to find it at the moment...*

The above rationalisations support *natural 'escape behaviour'* which almost every researcher, student, manager and writer has. However, identifying these excuses is only part of the solution. If you are not able to **discipline** yourself you will not only lose considerable time but in the end you might not be able to finish the research, reading or the writing at all. This may then interrupt all of your other activities and negatively affect your enthusiasm for doing research and studying.

4 Practical tips: a checklist

- **Do it now.** The golden rule of the Personal Efficiency Programme (PEP) developed by the American Institute for Business Technology is: **DO IT NOW** (Financial Times, 4 March, 1992). When you apply this rule, you: (1) only deal with things once and save time that way; (2) have fewer distractions and can concentrate better; (3) catch problems while they are small and (4) you will not have to worry about wasting time explaining to people why you have not done something.
- **Clean up your desk**. A messy desk is not necessarily a sign of hard work. An advisory bureau (Priority Management) came to the conclusion that many people waste up to three hours a week finding things on their desk. (De Volkskrant, 28 December 1994). Disorganised desks in general not only create time problems, but also additional stress (⊕C5).
- **Do the most important tasks during your most productive hours**: for instance it is not realistic to plan serious brain activity straight after a heavy meal.

A personal Efficiency Programme

Two tips are included in the Personal Efficiency Programme (PEP) philosophy that you could 'do now' are worthwhile noting:

- *Clear out all your drawers and files.* Ask yourself: have I ever used it and do I really expect to use it? If I throw it away, and unexpectedly need it, will I be able to get another copy?
- *Set up two trays on your desk: In and Out.* Plan how and when you are going to deal with incoming and outgoing messages.

- **Use your diary smartly.** Most people note all their appointments in their diary, but they do not include time for study or preparation for groups and other work. Study time then easily becomes a marginal (rest) activity and de facto loses priority. This also relates to (not) noting the amount of time that you need to travel from one place to another.
- **Separate private from work.** If you find it difficult to make a clear distinction between work and private life, you will allow too many other people to waste your time. If you allow friends to come and visit you while you are studying or doing a research project, this will create major lapses in concentration. Consider studying as a 'job' (➔B1). Make effective use of breaks.

Procrastination is *the avoidance of doing a task that needs to be accomplished.*[1] This is a 'disease' everybody falls victim to. William Knaus estimated that 90% of university students procrastinate. Of these students, 25% are chronic procrastinators and they are usually the ones who end up dropping out.[2]

Generally six stages can be distinguished in the 'procrastination process' (cf. Burka and Yuen, 1983; Ellis and Knaus, 1970):

1 You want to achieve something that you and others value and respect – *'I've got to start.'*
2 You delay, thinking of advantages of starting later – *'I'll do it tomorrow when I have less to do.'*
3 You delay more, becoming self-critical – *'I should have started sooner'* –and/or self-excusing – *'I really couldn't have left the party early last night, my best friends were there.'*
4 You delay even more, until finally the task has to be done, usually hastily – *'Just get it done any old way'* – or you just don't have time – *'I can't do this!'*
5 You berate yourself – *'There is something wrong with me'* – and swear never to procrastinate again and/or you discount the importance of the task – *'It doesn't matter.'*
6 You repeat the process with the next task again, as if it were an addiction or compulsion.[3]

The general conclusion is that procrastination can lead to feelings of guilt, inadequacy and self-doubt among students.

'Most people spend more time and energy going around problems than in trying to solve them.'—Henry Ford

Why do students procrastinate?
- **Poor Time Management**; procrastination means not managing time wisely. You may be uncertain of your priorities, goals and objectives. You may also be overwhelmed by the task.
- **Difficulty Concentrating**; when you sit at your desk you find yourself daydreaming, staring into space, looking at pictures of your boyfriend/girlfriend, etc., instead of doing the task at hand. Your environment is distracting and noisy. You keep running back and forth for equipment such as pencils or a dictionary.
- **Finding the task boring**.
- **Personal problems**; for example, financial difficulties or problems with your boyfriend/girlfriend.

---

[1] http://ub-counseling.buffalo.edu/stressprocrast.shtml, consulted 25 May 2006

[2] http://ub-counseling.buffalo.edu/stressprocrast.shtml, consulted 25 May 2006

[3] http://mentalhelp.net/psyhelp/chap4/chap4r.htm, consulted 10 January 2007

- **Fear and Anxiety**; you may be overwhelmed with the task and afraid of getting a failing grade. As a result, you spend a great deal of time worrying about your upcoming exams, papers and projects, rather than completing them.
- **Negative Beliefs** such as; *'I cannot succeed in anything'* and *'I lack the necessary skills to perform this'*.
- **Unrealistic Expectations** and Perfectionism; you may believe that you **must** read everything ever written on a subject before you can begin to write your paper or you may think that you haven't done the best you possibly could do.
- **Fear of Failure**; you may think that if you don't get an 'A', you are a failure. Or that if you fail an exam, you, as a person, are a failure, rather than that you are a perfectly ok person who has failed an exam.[4]

Table B.9 Do's and don'ts of Procrastination

Do 👍	Don't 👎
Find out how often you procrastinate and what the main reasons are.	Study in a messy or noisy place.
Specify goals for your life; what do you want to achieve? Try to incorporate them in the short term. Use the SMART method (see box next page).	Hate yourself if things don't go well.
Divide a hard assignment in small tasks.	Keep on working without taking some breaks.
Keep your biological clock in mind, if you study best in the evening, plan the hardest study topics for the evening.	Study without deadlines.
'Chunking': divide your time into blocks of 90 minutes (➡B8). Use one block for hard study, take a break and use the next block for easier things.	Postpone the 'tiresome' tasks. Start with them, otherwise they remain haunting in your mind. Therefore costing a lot more energy.

Exercise to discover your procrastination

1 One good exercise to check for yourself whether you procrastinate, is to keep a diary of what you have *really done* after receiving an assignment. Do so for two weeks.
2 Every night when you go to bed, write down in your diary and specify your occupations for each half an hour. As there is no one else checking you, you can be totally honest. Also when you, for example, have been watching television the whole day.
3 Than after one week re-read your diary, think about it and go on with the diary for one more week.
4 After that week once again re-read your diary and then start really analyzing your activities of the last 2 weeks. Question yourself: *'Do I see any procrastination?'* and if so: *'What caused it?'*.

[4] http://ub-counseling.buffalo.edu/stressprocrast.shtml, consulted 25 May 2006

The S.M.A.R.T. method

Setting realistic goals is vital for anyone who wants to evade procrastination. This necessitates that you are able and willing to (1) set a particular goal, (2) take action on this, (3) be flexible if you find out that you approach a goal ineffectively, (4) invest in your psychological and physical condition. The S.M.A.R.T. method specifies the criteria for setting obtainable goals:

S = Specific and Simple

M = Measurable and Meaningful

A = As if now, Achievable

R = Realistic and Responsible/ecological

T = Timed, toward what you want

Exercise in preventing a lack of time for important assignments

Write down on a sheet of paper the six most important tasks for the next day. Put the most important task on number 1 and the least important on number 6. The next day start with number 1, complete it and than go on to number 2 and so on. You will not have to worry if you don't finish all six, since you wouldn't finish anyway without the list. But now you have at least fulfilled the most important ones (Van den Brandhof, 1998).

Procrastination at second glance...

Abrahamson and Freedman (2006) show that there are also advantages to untidiness, hoarding and procrastination. They stress that the 'tidiness lobby' – exemplified for instance by corporate 'clean desk' policies and tidiness coaches – comes at a price: high cost of maintenance, increased (social) control and squeezing of creativity. Procrastination on the other hand can spur creativity and under some circumstances can be more appropriate even for very operational tasks. For instance, the authors describe how the US Marine Corps never makes detailed plans in advance. Leaving important aspects of an operation to the last minute reduces the risk of wasting time on things that ultimately might prove to be unimportant.

[⊕➔www.skillsheets.com; for useful websites]

Contribution by Simone Schenk

Drafting a weekly study plan has two advantages:
- You become more aware of the amount of time that you have spent on 'doing nothing' (→B9), thereby creating an awareness of how you should plan your study time more effectively.
- You create a 'weapon' or an argument to say 'no' to non-planned activities or to cope with excuses (→B8), by learning how to assess the time necessary for your studies.

1 Schedule your week
- **Make a schedule** in which you include all seven days of the week, list the hours and mark daily modules (morning, afternoon, evening). The schedule on the next page is an example.
- Write down all of the **activities** that you have to do (eating, shopping, sleeping, including the time to travel). If you need a lot of travelling time for example, you can plan to do 'repetition' exercises during those periods.
- Write down all of the **classes and working groups** that you would like to attend. Sometimes, you might even organise a division of labour with other students in attending particular classes, whilst you prioritise reading, understanding and applying the literature.

2 Identify modules
- Once every **three days**, schedule time for preparation of classes, doing assignments and repetition of material that you have already studied (→B6).
- Leave at least **one to two modules** free each week for sports, and important extra-curricular activities (→B1).
- Remember that you can only study effectively for **two to three hours** in a row (including short breaks of about fifteen minutes) if you have to digest new material. Use the breaks in between the modules to go shopping, clean your house or prepare food. Also include these 'lighter' moments in your schedule. This should stop you from doing these (easier) things first, and have your (more difficult) study activities come second.
- Leave **two modules in reserve**. Create latitude in your planning in order to cope with assignments and other work that might take more time.
- **Distribute** the material that you have to study in that week over the hours available. If you need to prepare for an exam, make sure that you include time for repetition in your schedule.

3 Specify rewards
- Make sure that there are **positive stimuli** for keeping to your schedule. Give yourself rewards when you achieve specific aims: finishing reading a chapter, writing a number of pages, preparing a class. Plan **flexible rewards**, i.e. rewards

that you can give to yourself, but that do not imply additional obligations. Going to the cinema would be a proper reward, *unless* you make an appointment with one of your friends a few days in advance. In this case, you might not have achieved your aim, but nevertheless feel obliged to go to the cinema rather than enter into a long discussion with your friend about the reason why you can not go. In the first scenario you can still ask a friend to accompany you, but only *after* you have really reached your aim for that day. The most flexible rewards, though, are the ones that you can do alone: watching a television programme, jogging.

■ Make a clear distinction between your **study and private activities**. Consider studying to be business, to which you have to dedicate sufficient time and that needs to give sufficient return on investment. If you mix up study and private too much, it also becomes more difficult to specify the magnitude of the reward (➲B1).

If you have finalised your schedule for the week, you will see that the direct and indirect study activities will take you much more than a normal working week of forty hours. Part of the reason for this is that the total amount of hours planned for studying in most countries, has to be spent in a much shorter period than a whole year. For example, students are supposed to spend around 1700 hours studying per year in most countries. The yearly study burden, however, is not distributed over 52 weeks (which would amount to 32.5 hours per week study activities) but over 32 weeks, which amounts to 52 hours per week studying. Learn how to deal with these temporary peaks in your study activities, either by spreading a number of your activities over the 'holiday' period and/or concentrating most of your social activities in the longer periods of relative rest.

Table B.10 Example week planning

	Morning	Afternoon	Evening
Monday	9-10	14-15	19-20
	10-11	15-16	20-21
	11-12	16-17	21-22
	12-13	17-18	22-23
Tuesday	9-10	14-15	19-20
	10-11	15-16	20-21
	11-12	16-17	21-22
	12-13	17-18	22-23
Wednesday	9-10	14-15	19-20
	10-11	15-16	20-21
	11-12	16-17	21-22
	12-13	17-18	22-23
Thursday	9-10	14-15	19-20
	10-11	15-16	20-21
	11-12	16-17	21-22
	12-13	17-18	22-23
Friday	9-10	14-15	19-20
	10-11	15-16	20-21
	11-12	16-17	21-22
	12-13	17-18	22-23
Saturday	9-10	14-15	19-20
	10-11	15-16	20-21
	11-12	16-17	21-22
	12-13	17-18	22-23
Sunday	9-10	14-15	19-20
	10-11	15-16	20-21
	11-12	16-17	21-22
	12-13	17-18	22-23

[⊕➔www.skillsheets.com]

Drafting a (rough) plan for a semester is much more difficult than drafting a week plan. It is needed, however, for at least two reasons:

- it prevents an accumulation of activities at the *wrong time*, which can lessen the time available for important courses and other activities;
- it enables you to include feedback sessions at the *right times*, and to adjust your priorities.

1 Identify your portfolio of major activities

■ **List all of the courses** that you plan to attend in the semester. Try to find out *at the beginning of the semester* what the requirements for each course look like: reading requirements (literature: number of pages), exam dates and contents (multiple choice, open book), writing requirements (case/essay), other requirements. See the example on the next page. Try to assign a *priority ranking* to the courses on the basis of two criteria: (1) your own interests in this semester, (2) your interests in the next semester, which might prompt you to do a preparatory course this semester. Take into account, in your priority ranking, the consequences on financing your education and the other external requirements that you have to keep track of.

■ **List the extra activities** (if desirable), in particular self-study groups and major extra-curricular activities (for example, teaching assistant job or organisation of a study trip) (⊕B1). Try to ascertain what their impact could be on your time management and the kind of feedback that you would like to create time for.

■ **Always add a list of your personal activities** that you already know will probably have a major impact on your planning: holidays, big celebrations.

2 Plan your time in steps

Take the whole period into consideration. List the months in the semester (probably five) and start **planning backwards** from the deadlines that will appear. There are a number of different deadlines that have different consequences for your planning: related to exams, papers and extra-curricular activities.

■ The consequences of **exam deadlines** are easiest to take into account:
- As a rule: one week before the exam period you should have studied all of the required literature for an exam **and** repeated the material at least once. Remember that if exams are all together in one period (mostly in the last weeks of the semester), it is almost impossible to study new material. Reserve the exam period for short repetition, in order to keep fit during the exam period and use your memory in the correct manner (⊕B6).
- Acquire all the required literature as soon as possible at the start of the semester. Assess the literature for all of the courses: the nature of the books and other literature (heavy, easy to read, link to what you already know) (⊕C3). If the course has not changed much, ask other students who have already attended the course for their experience, in particular on courses that are

considered hard to pass. Test your reading speed with regards to the literature used: take a section of the book at random and check the time it takes you to read and understand the argumentation. Calculate, approximately, the total amount of hours *you personally (not anyone else)* will need to read, understand and repeat the literature. Do not take the official calculations for granted, because they are aimed at an 'average' student, and you are not 'average'!

■ The consequences of **deadlines for papers and essays** are more difficult to assess, because writing a paper always requires several skills at the same time, often including mastering group dynamics, which can easily lead to general time management problems (⊕B8, B9).

• As a rule: try to have your paper finished a couple of days before the official hand-in date. The last few days are vital for editing, rewriting (⊕A5, G12), and coping with 'unhealthy' group dynamics (⊕G10).

• Make a general calculation of the amount of time that you will have to spend finishing the paper or essay. Plan deadlines for draft versions of your papers that you would like to generate **feedback** on, and specify whether you would like that from other group members or a tutor.

■ The consequences of deadlines for **self-study groups and extra-curricular activities** are the most difficult to assess. The result then often becomes that these activities are squeezed and are not organised at all. For that reason you should also set clear intermediate deadlines for them. Plan deadlines when you want to generate **feedback**.

If you have carried out the instructions included in the above points, you can try to spread the hours required for each activity over the whole semester. Plan to work on many parallel activities each week (but with varying intensities, and *never* at the same time). Do not plan to spend a whole week on one course.

3 Carry out checks

Hang your semester (and week) schedule above your desk. Mark deadlines clearly. Every two weeks, check whether you are sticking to the plan. Which courses are more intensive than you thought initially, which ones are easier, which essay did you spend too much time on (because you became enthusiastic or you found it more challenging), in which courses would you like to invest more time in order to get better grades? Remember the following 'rule of thumb' with regards to time spent on grades: if x time spent results in a '6', 2x is required to get a '7' and 3x an '8'! Some courses and activities will require more time than the official norm, for example, if you lack previous knowledge. If you discover that courses and activities that you did not prioritise, nevertheless take up much more time than initially planned, you should consider skipping these activities!

It sounds like a no-brainer, but unhealthy eating, drinking and sleeping habits are amongst the clearest factors causing even smart people to seriously underperform (Hallowell, 2005). Moreover, bad sanitation and eating habits are amongst the most important factors leading to social exclusion. In neuropsychological research it has increasingly been acknowledged that the health of the brain is crucially dependent on these factors. The brain is in particular dependent on glucose for energy. The brain functions better if the blood glucose level is held relatively stable. This can be enhanced when you avoid consuming simple, sugary carbohydrates (such as pastries, white bread, but also alcohol). Consuming protein-rich food and complex carbohydrates (such as fruits, whole grains vegetables) provides positive stimulants for your concentration level (⊕B7). Multivitamins also contribute to a healthy functioning of the brain. The brain also functions much better if you get sufficient sleep. The exact amount of sleeping time can differ per person, but a good rule of thumb is that 'you're getting enough sleep if you can wake up without an alarm clock' (Hallowel, 2005: 33). It has been found (Hallowell, 2005) that a disturbed energy balance creates a bundle of problems: from impaired decision-making and reduced creativity to reckless behaviour and even paranoia.

1 Sustaining healthy habits

Students might hope that unhealthy habits will not have an immediate effect on their energy level as in the case of much older people. But that is only partly true. Lack of sleep, of good food and regular exercise always contributes to underperformance. So, even if a student is able to get a sufficient grade at an exam, this might be less than otherwise would have been achieved with a healthier and energetic physical condition. Unhealthy habits and lack of energy can have the following creeping effects: (1) undertaking too many activities at the same time, (2) with not enough commitment due to low energy levels per activity, (3) leads to underperformance in more complex areas (in particular research and study), (4) which leads to low self-esteem and (5) a lack of motivation to perform well in these activities, which (6) spurs the motivation to engage in more superficial activities (like drinking and going out), (7) which in turn leads to underperformance, etc. This process in fact mirrors the 'neurotic spiral' as it was identified in Part I (⊕The Format).

Principles of good Energy Management

1. Watch what you eat. Avoid simple, sugary carbohydrates, moderate your intake of alcohol, add protein, stick to complex carbohydrates (vegetables, whole grains, fruit)

2. Exercise at least 30 minutes at least every other day (it produces an array of chemicals that the brain needs: endorphins, serotonin, dopamine, epinephrine and norepinephrine amongst others). The time you invest in exercise will be more than compensated by improved productivity

3. Take a daily multivitamin and an omega-3 fatty acid supplement

4. Moderate your intake of alcohol (it kills brain cells and accelerates the development of memory loss)

5 Get adequate sleep:
- Stop eating two or three hours before you go to sleep.
- Don't drink alcohol or coffee containing caffeine before you go to bed.
- Try to avoid sleeping during the day, you will sleep deeper during the night.
- Create regularity: go to bed and wake up around the same time every day. Having a long lie-in out or staying up late disturbs your biological clock.
- Sleep in a clean bed with a good mattress.
- Make sure the climate in your bedroom is cool, well ventilated and calm.
- Try to avoid using your bedroom as working or living room, if this is not possible make a division between different functions by using a room divider, for example.

Sources: Hallowell (2005) and NHG (2000)

2 Sustaining a healthy working environment

A second factor that influences the energetic well-being of students is the material they use. Increasingly this implies working with computers. Since students work most intensely with computers, they are particularly affected by such modern day diseases as Repetitive Strain Injury (RSI). Research at the University of Utrecht showed that around 40 percent of the students in 2004 already had RSI problems. RSI is caused by a variety of factors such as (1) sitting in the same position for a prolonged period of time, (2) repeated movements (mouse), (3) high concentration and stress levels (→B7), (4) lack of balance between work/study and private. The best remedy to RSI is engaging in good energy management and respecting some basic ergonomic principles. Your computer screen and chair are important factors in the latter (see box).

Ergonomic Principles

1 The Right screen:
   - top of the screen should be at eye level;
   - screen is in front of you
   - the distance to the screen is adapted to the size of the screen and the letter type that is used
   - TFT (LCD screen that uses thin film transistor (TFT) technology) screens should be preferred over CRT (cathode-ray tube) screens
2 The Right Chair:
   - Seat: adaptable to different persons, flat, wide enough and with enough room for the legs
   - Arm-rest: important support and adaptable to different persons
   - Back-rest: high-back and adaptable

Source: Peereboom et al (2003) and Hedge (2003)

It is impossible to learn without feedback. Generating and receiving feedback in particular from your teachers, tutors and coaches is an intricate process that involves substantial social intelligence. Whether their feedback is effective and on time, depends to a large extent on your own attitude and on the way you approach them. This Skill Sheet explains how best to generate and receive relevant feedback from teachers and tutors.

1 Generating appropriate and preventing avoidable feedback

Teachers and tutors are supposed to provide feedback. But the way you treat them in this process determines to a large extent whether they will give you committed and substantial feedback or only 'do their job'. This is particularly relevant when the tutor supervises your Bachelor's or Master's thesis. You will probably have more than one meeting with your supervisor. Negative interaction is triggered when you generate 'avoidable feedback'. This happens in particular when the tutor gets a paper without any indication of its status. In response to the feedback the student replies: 'yes, I know and realise that; but, I didn't have time to do that'. The tutor will feel awkward – to say the least – in this situation. Most of the reading time that was spent in getting through this paper was in fact in vain, because the student would have written a better version anyway! The enthusiasm of the tutor for this thesis project is bound to decline. To generate appropriate and prevent avoidable feedback from a tutor, apply the following rules of engagement:

- Agree on the *way* that you both prefer to give and receive feedback and corrections before you start the tutoring project; this includes a specification of the level of detail, but also of the concrete symbols for correction used (➔C12).
- Understand that good feedback requires hard work from the tutor, which warrants a *good barter* relationship (➔A12).
- Do not leave it up to the reader to find the *weak spots*. State them, and ask for feedback on your real problems. It is a waste of time if you ask feedback on points that you are already aware of.
- Always include a *note* with your paper stating:
  - the status of the paper (x-th draft, passages and methodologies that you have had problems with);
  - what kind of advice and feedback you would like to have.
- Always hand in *previous versions of the paper*, with the remarks from the tutor written on them. Reading becomes more efficient, because not everything needs to be read again.
- If you hand in a text which has been altered (i.e. a consecutive draft of a text that the reader has already read) *use a marker* or lines in the margin to indicate the new parts.
- Always make a *back-up copy*. Never give anybody (including the tutor) the original.
- Finally, do not use your tutor as corrector for language or style problems.

2 Receiving feedback

Receiving feedback requires quite a different attitude than giving feedback (⊙G9). The feedback given represents the *perception* of the other. Perceptions and interpretations of other people, however, are important to take into account. For instance, if the reader of your work or the audience of your lecture does not understand what you mean, you have a problem. A not very functional attitude towards your audience would be to start explaining (again) what you had been trying to say or write. A defensive reaction from the feedback-taker discourages the feedback-giver from saying more. Optimally learning from feedback requires that you concentrate on the information you get, not that you enter into a discussion. In case you do not agree or do not understand what the other means, ask for clarification, do not enter into a discussion. Apply the following four principles when receiving feedback (cf. Oomkes, 1992):

1 Consider feedback as a chance to learn and not as a (personal) attack
2 Do not defend yourself: and do not explain
   a Never reply with 'yes, but'
   b Never start explaining why you did something
   c Do not interrupt the feedback-giver
3 Ask for clarification if you do not understand something
4 Always thank the feedback-giver for the effort

Representation and Dress-code

The process of generating feedback is influenced by appearance and the way in which people make themselves identifiable to their communication partner. A non-professional outlook generally tends to trigger 'casual' feedback as well. The way you dress (silently) influences the perception of the other, but – maybe more important in case you aim at triggering feedback - communicates the way you perceive the other as well. Different organizations have different dress-codes, but always make sure that you 'dress to the occasion'. You can 'dress for success', 'over-dress' or 'under-dress'. Make sure in any case that you limit the chance that you will receive overly critical feedback because of the way you look or behave.

[⊕⊙www.skillsheets.com for more tips]

Writing an appropriate learning contract is an exercise in argumentation and systematic examination through the Reflective Cycle. A learning contract is primarily a contract with yourself (➲B4). But feedback by one of your 'peers' (members of your year group) on this contract can give an extra check on your own analysis. Peer feedback can often be more useful than feedback from a 'senior' – who is often incapable of showing empathy and understanding for your position and argumentation. Giving feedback on a learning contract is not a simple affair. A learning contract is a very personal document. Comments on that can easily be taken as criticism on you as a person. That should of course not be the intention. Peer feedback should be aimed at helping you to sharpen the process of self-reflection by giving you an impression of the extent to which a reader thinks that the draft contract you have written could be a realistic guide through actual future learning processes.

Your peer is invited to look along seven dimensions at your learning contract. They deal with your **assessment and diagnosis of your own starting situation** and the question whether you have been capable (according to your peer) to specify **an appropriate, credible and feasible implementation trajectory**. Peer feedback on the learning contract should be businesslike, to-the-point and without major personal connotations (even if you are asked to give a quick 'score'). It tests the capacity of both parties to handle feedback in a constructive manner. Poorly formulated and superficial feedback on a learning contract is probably more damaging than a badly formulated and superficial learning contract!

Seven dimensions

- **Starting position**
  1 Detailed and relevant explanation of **past experiences**? Including how these past experiences reflected strengths and weaknesses.
- **Diagnosis**
  2 Nuanced and balanced assessment of strengths and weaknesses (not only weaknesses but also strengths and vice versa); extensive or superficial? Sufficient description of interchange between strengths and weaknesses as well as how they affect learning?
  3 Good and systematic elaboration: A. concrete observations; B. all five steps specified; C. all seven skills covered?
  4 Writing style: good, average, bad (writing a personal report requires other writing skills than writing a report; additionally important is how objectively you can report on yourself). How coherently and cohesively is the content expressed in the learning contract?
- **Implementation/future**
  5 **Realistic implementation**: expectations are not too low or too high; aims are concrete and verifiable. Reasonable timeframe suggested for the implementation?

6 **Social** implementation conditions: does the contract specify who is needed to work with or to create favourable conditions for implementation? If so, will working with this person or creating these favourable conditions actually facilitate the implementation process?

7 **Consistent** implementation: combined with your strengths and weaknesses (to what extent are observable strengths reinforced and weaknesses solved? Does the solution include foreseeable impacts upon the student's weaknesses as well as his/her strengths?)

Table B.14 Scoring Sheet Peer Feedback (Learning Contract)

		Score	Suggestions for Improvements/Observations
1 History			
2 Balance			
3 Systematic	A		
	B		
	C		
4 Style			
5 Realistic			
6 Social			
7 Consistent			

Scoring on a scale from 1 to 5

1 unclear or without any substance, needs major revision

2 vague or without enough depth

3 satisfactory, revision suggested

4 clear and substantial

5 an excellent and enlightening self reflection

[⊕➔www.skillsheets.com for a feedback form]

Series C Reading

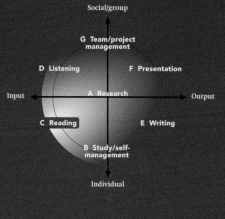

Social/group

G Team/project management

D Listening   F Presentation

Input — A Research — Output

C Reading   E Writing

B Study/self-management

Individual

The Reflective Cycle of Active Reading

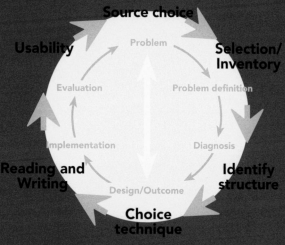

Source choice

Usability

Problem

Selection/ Inventory

Evaluation

Problem definition

Implementation

Diagnosis

Reading and Writing

Design/Outcome

Identify structure

Choice technique

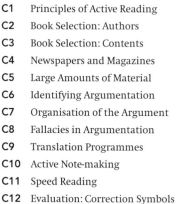

	Principles of Active Reading
C1	Principles of Active Reading
C2	Book Selection: Authors
C3	Book Selection: Contents
C4	Newspapers and Magazines
C5	Large Amounts of Material
C6	Identifying Argumentation
C7	Organisation of the Argument
C8	Fallacies in Argumentation
C9	Translation Programmes
C10	Active Note-making
C11	Speed Reading
C12	Evaluation: Correction Symbols

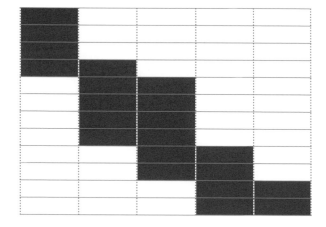

	Selection/ Inventory	Identify structure	Choice technique	Reading & Writing	Usability
C1	■				
C2	■				
C3	■				
C4	■	■			
C5		■	■	■	
C6		■	■		
C7		■	■		
C8		■	■		
C9			■	■	
C10				■	
C11				■	■
C12				■	■

Reading Skill Levels

Level 1

o Reading is reproduction and memorizing-oriented as preparation for exam
o Re-active
o Acquire an attitude to consult relevant pubic media regularly and systematically
o Textbook-oriented (only read what is required)
o Aimed at recognising and reconstructing argumentation
o Slow reading speed

Level 2

o Reading is aimed at understanding as input for exams and short papers
o (Re)Active
o Consult the appropriate popular scientific literature for a project and exams
o Textbook and popular scientific literature-oriented
o Aimed at identifying good and bad argumentation (including fallacies in argumentation)
o High reading speed of popular text, slow for scientific literature

Level 3

o Reading is aimed at gathering and finding relevant information and as input for further research
o Active
o Consult relevant top scientific journals in research projects
o Aimed at understanding why particular argumentation fallacies develop
o Knowledge of the editorial formula of most important sources
o As input for own argumentation
o Scanning skills are optimised and reading speed for scientific texts is increasing to high

Level 4

o Reading is aimed at gathering relevant information for the present position (effective reading of organisational writings, media as well as relevant scientific literature)
o Pro-active attitude: continuously searching for relevant new media
o Continuous training of speed reading skills

Active reading first requires the choice for the most appropriate source (no brainless reading of everything that is available) that can be linked to the issue at hand; after which you come to a selection of what you want to know, which is aided by your identification of structures and argumentation in the read material. Even if you have to read for an exam – which basically implies that you cannot select the literature yourself – active reading is a prerequisite for effective studying (➲B5, B6). Active reading always is accompanied by writing at the same time, either as notes for the exam or directly as input for the paper you write (never read only to read), after which you evaluate what you have read and come to the choice of further sources.

---

1   Effective reading is selective (in sources and in contents)
2   Think: understand the background of the sources you read
3   Analyse: identify the argumentation structure before you start to read
4   Effective reading is always active
5   Master different reading techniques for different purposes
6   Master the technique of intelligent note-making while reading
7   Effective reading is input for social activities

1 Source choice and selection

Every student, manager and researcher spends an immense amount of time going through piles of literature and other written sources. They should be able to keep track of relevant articles, newspapers, books and reports on a more or less permanent basis. It is impossible to read everything that is published even on relatively limited areas of research. Effective reading, therefore, requires *selection* of sources. Making good use of libraries and databases is a vital prerequisite for informed selections. International journals and magazines are also important sources of information. Knowledge of the most relevant journals and their methods for gathering news is important for making an informed selection in this area. The first Skill Sheets (➲C2-5) in this series complement the information on this selection process in the A-series (➲A4, A6).

2 Identify structures

Effective reading always necessitates that you have an idea about *why* you read the material (➲A9, A10). Effective reading requires a *selective* approach to the contents of written material. It is very often not necessary to read a book or an article from 'cover to cover', but how should one select the relevant parts? A good insight into the structure of a book, or the nature of an article, can considerably shorten the reading time and can still give sufficient input for a research project or help you in understanding the exam reading better. In the early phases of your reading (level 1), it is particularly difficult to identify inappropriate argumentation or badly written articles and books. Fortunately, reading is something you can do at your own pace, at times that suit you best, and with repetition (if needed). Reading, therefore, remains a skill that is easiest to train and still the best input for study, writing, presentations and management. The second set of Skill Sheets (➔C6-8) in this series will provide help in identifying both basic and misleading argumentation structures.

> Scientists who only have their wisdom out of books, should be placed on a bookshelf—Wolfgang Eschker

3 Combine techniques of reading and writing

Because your reading can serve so many simultaneous aims and functions, different reading methods need to be mastered. Reading itself often seems to function as a substitute for own independent thinking. In this case, reading is aimed primarily at reproducing or memorising other people's arguments. Reading without processing the information at the same time is not very effective. The same is true in case you prepare for an exam: you underutilise the potential of your brain when you read passively (➔B5, B7). You have to work out routines to actively digest what you are reading. Reading and then thinking about what you have read should always be combined, in order to increase your understanding, and ultimately increase the degree to which you can apply and remember what you have read. It is best to do this in written form.

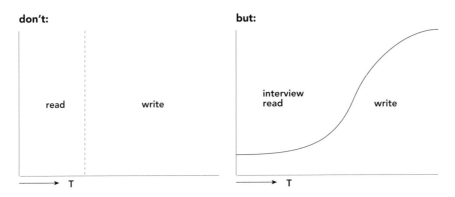

Concrete reading and writing techniques include the skill of active note-making (➔C10), using translation programs (➔C9) and speed reading (➔C11).

4 Reading as a social activity

Reading can rarely be the only source of information for research, study and the development of your ideas. Reading only becomes effective when it is combined with other group experiences. One way of using reading as an input for joint research projects or as feedback technique, is by effectively making notes in the work of others (➔C12).

As part of your education your teacher will often present you with a number of books you are expected to read from cover to cover. In this case it is nevertheless important to grasp the background of the author(s). In general, authors with a good reputation in an area write more influential books – although their writing might not be a particularly easy read. In later phases of your training, the selection of a book by your tutor is almost always inspired by the relative importance of the author in a particular scientific discipline. In research practice you have to select the books yourself, but reading them from cover to cover will rarely be necessary. The most important reading skill is to be able to identify and *select* those (parts of) books that are most useful to you. This Skill Sheet helps you to identify a number of characteristics you should look for *before* deciding to use a book. It looks in particular at information that you can obtain quickly, simply by looking closely at the status of the author(s) and the nature of the text (monograph, textbook, edited volume, reader) and a number of other sources of information generally revealed in books (endorsements, colophons).

1 Monographs

A monograph is an original 'scholarly' text, usually on a single topic. The text is intended to contribute to a specific scientific area, by either introducing new concepts and theories, bringing together new evidence or both.

- Do you already know the authors? What do you know of their *academic status*? If you do not know much about the author(s): what does the book itself reveal about their background and research expertise? Look in the bibliography to see what kind of publications the author(s) find relevant. Do they appeal to you?
- If there is more than one original author: is the book a joint effort or has one of the authors had more influence on the text? Look at the *sequence of authors* (see box). Does the most important author appeal to you?

Author's sequence or sequential authors?

The order in which the names of the authors are printed on the cover, provides information on the relative importance of each of the authors for this particular publication. Since reading requires that you are knowledgeable about the status of the authors, this kind of information is important. Co-authors of magazine and newspaper articles sometimes alternate the sequence of their names. But this practice is rarely used for books. In the case of a normal alphabetical sequence, it is likely that the authors have both given equal input (⊕A12). In the case of a non-alphabetical sequence, the first author is likely to have provided more input than the following authors. This observation becomes more difficult when one of the author's names includes a prefix ('Van', 'De'). You should know whether the authors use the English or American alphabetical notation (⊕E-series; website). Check this by looking at the author's index or the bibliography in the same book. If an American style of notation is used, a book written by 'Kaplinski and De Manchini' for example, indicates that the first author has done the most work on the book. In the British style of notation, this particular sequence would merely be following the normal alphabet, implying that both authors are equally important or that the first author has done the most. The latter you will probably never know.

2 Textbooks and readers

Textbooks are written for educational purposes. The book is intended to provide the reader (often students and practitioners) with a solid overview of the state-of-affairs in a particular area. Textbooks provide a manual of instruction. Textbooks are often accompanied by exercises, exam questions and handy summaries. The value of textbooks lies in their use as teaching instruments. In case textbooks contain many reprints of original texts, they become more of a reader.

- *Status*: check whether the author of the textbook is also a leading author in a particular scientific area (you can check that by looking in the bibliography, for instance); if that is the case the textbook might be aimed at illustrating the usefulness of the author's scientific work and the 'textbook' might in fact be more of a monograph. This happens in particular when the book departs from an original monograph and contains reprints of supportive literature.
- *Institutional background*: check the affiliation of the author(s). Because textbooks are teaching instruments, it is probable that the textbook has been developed first for that particular institute. Is this an educational system or university you can relate to? One of the most important problems with textbooks is that they might have been written for a different audience (for instance an American textbook for a European audience). The affiliation of the author could reveal that.

3 Edited volumes

Edited volumes are also usually monographs intended to bring the intelligence of a number of scholars on a specific topic together. Edited volumes can often be considered as 'intermediary' products in an ongoing scientific debate. Because it often takes less time to publish an edited volume than a special issue of a scientific journal, edited volumes can contain more recent material. Integrated books (monographs) often represent more final products.

- How do the editors or the people who compile the books *announce* themselves on the cover: with a clear statement about their function as editors or not? If the editors are not very clear about their role – for example, when the cover does not state 'eds' or 'compiled by'- think carefully before making use of the book.
- What do you know about the *status of the editors and the authors* in the book? Consider whether a list has been included in the book which also reveals the background of the contributors. Do you know their background? Does the background seem appropriate for the topic at hand? Is it clear what the origins of the book are (conference, research project)? Conference books are often much less focused than books that are the result of a joint research project. They sometimes include relatively weak articles, put into the book for various (political, personal, sponsor-oriented) reasons. In the case of a *reader*, do you know what the exact status of the texts is? Are they summaries of articles, a selection of the original articles or something else? If the reader includes articles that have been

selected by the editors: do they reveal their selection basis; is the shortened text sanctioned by the author? If the status of the texts is not really clear, the user should seriously consider checking the original source and use the reader primarily as a starting point for reading about a particular topic.

■ Consider the *user-friendliness* of the text. Has the editor tried to create value added for the reader or is the book primarily a collection of unrelated texts? One way to check the user-friendliness is by checking whether there is one integrated bibliography and an extensive index.

4 Endorsements

Endorsements are used by the publishers as a *marketing tool* for the book. They only include quotes from people who recommend the book, not by those who criticise the book. They are usually printed on the back of the book. By reading the endorsements intelligently you can get information quickly on the following aspects:

■ the *contents* of the book: often little summaries are included in the endorsements;

■ on the *status* of the book: if the endorsers are respected figures within the particular area that the book concerns, it will probably be interesting;

■ the *history* of the book: if the endorsements include quotes from magazines in which the book has been reviewed, the book has already had a favourable reception. This kind of endorsement can only be included in consecutive prints. The more prestigious the magazines (➲C4), the greater the chance that the book will be interesting and useful;

■ the *author's networks*: if the endorsers are also among the people who are acknowledged in the preface, the endorsements have probably been organised by the authors themselves. Do you know whether the author (accidentally) also works as a consultant for any of the companies listed?;

■ on the *audience* at which the book is aimed: do the endorsements primarily come from academics or are business people and politicians also included in support of the book? Which type of audience appeals to your own research aims and ambitions (➲A3)?

5 Colophons

Colophons and copyright provisions can offer interesting additional information on the background of the author(s), in particular whether the book has really been written by the name(s) on the cover.

The revealing information contained in colophons

One of the most influential books of the 1990s is the book written by James P. Womack, Daniel T. Jones and Daniel Roos (1990) *The Machine That Changed the World* (published simultaneously by three publishing houses). It has been a very prestigious book and from its inception intended to be a cash success. Womack, Jones and Roos are the names included on the cover. The same names are also included in the socket text: explaining their background and their position at prestigious universities. However, when you look at the Copyright (small print on the back of the title page) a fourth name pops up: Donna Sammons Carpenter. 'Who's that?' No reader knows who she is. Her name is not mentioned in the acknowledgements of the three official authors. She is not included in the bibliography or in the index. The most likely solution to this mystery is: Mrs Sammons Carpenter is a 'ghostwriter' of (a part of) the book.

Using ghostwriters in academic texts is not really new. But it is, nevertheless, a cause for concern as the reader does not really know who is accountable for the text – the official authors or a ghostwriter. Accountability and reliability are important in academic practice. From the publisher's point of view it is understandable. It is better to have a running text which sells than a very academic text that does not sell. Many authors have come across active copy editors who rephrased a lot of the manuscript. When the influence of ghostwriters becomes so great that they share part of the copyright, this is an indication that marketing criteria might have prevailed over scientific criteria like reliability.

It is much more common for business people and politicians to have 'their' books and policy documents written by ghostwriters. Be aware of the credibility of 'autobiographies' in particular. Did the person in fact write his/her own autobiography? A politician like Winston Churchill is a renowned exception to the ghostwriter rule. He wrote his books himself and even received the Nobel price for literature for his collected work.

[⊕➔www.skillsheets.com, for a quick book selection scan]

You are standing in a bookshop. You have a favourable impression of the status of the author(s) who wrote the book that you are holding (➔C2). Should you buy the book? The answer to this question depends not only on your financial situation, but also on two additional aspects of the book. Firstly, what is the background of the publisher and what could the reason be for publishing the book? Secondly, your decision depends on a quick assessment of the structure of the book and its arguments.

1 The publisher and the publication

- Is the publisher one of the large *international publishing houses*? Do you know the reputation of the publisher in the area that the book concerns? Look at the places in which the text has been published: the colophon states whether the text has been published in several countries simultaneously. International publishing houses often have very strict referee procedures for books. As a rule, nine out of ten manuscripts, which are sent to these publishing houses, are rejected. This does not necessarily mean that the manuscript was not interesting. It could indicate that the topic was not considered suitable for an international audience.

- In the case of a *local publisher*: consider what the portfolio of the publisher contains. Does the publisher specialise in particular books? Does this book fit into this portfolio? In this case one could assume that the publisher knows whether the book would relate to a market demand. The publisher will probably have good referees as well, thus increasing the reliability of the book.

- About the *price of the book*: if the book is competitively priced (other books with the same number of pages and comparable printing quality are more expensive), it is likely that it has been printed in high volume. High printing volumes are an indication of the trust of the publisher in the author(s).

- Do you know if this book has been published in *hardback, paperback* or both? If the book has only been published in hardback, with a high price, you can be reasonably certain that the publisher is aiming, primarily, at the 'library market'. Libraries buy most of their books from publishers no matter what topic and often regardless of the cost – but with some limit. The (closed) library market thus creates a minimum scale of sales for which hardback books can be produced with limited risk. The additional volumes to be sold on the open market can be relatively modest. Aiming primarily at the library market is an indication that the publisher has limited trust in the book. Very often one can see that the contents of the hardback book have been delivered 'camera-ready' by the layout of tables and figures. Again, this is an indication of a more limited selection basis by the publisher.

- *Additional editions*? A book which gets a second or consecutive print, could be considered to be relatively successful. However, a consecutive print can also indicate that the first print was only in limited volume. Hardback books released by European publishing houses are usually of limited volume. The United States' market is bigger and more coherent, and the volumes required to break-even on hard-back books by American publishers are easier to obtain, even with the first edition.

■ *Package deal?* Is the publisher publishing the book because the author has promised to put it on the 'required reading' list of a course? Many publishing houses (in particular local publishing houses) publish academic books only when the author guarantees that a minimum number of copies will be sold. If the author agrees, the publisher easily breaks-even with this publication, and will probably be less critical about the contents of the book. In the jargon of publishers such a book is called a 'printing order'.

2 The book's contents

■ Define the status of the book as (a) monograph, (b) textbook, (c) edited volume (➍C2). Consider whether this approach suits your needs.

■ Look at the titles and the *table of contents.* What do you already know about the topic? What would you like to know about the topic? Do you think you can anticipate that the analytical focus of the author correlates positively with your areas of interest?

■ *Get an impression of the kind of sources that the book is based on* in order to find out how original the analysis is, and how useful it might be for your purposes:
  • If the authors mainly use secondary sources, the main function of the analysis will be in reinterpretation and theory building.
  • If many primary sources are revealed, the valued-added of the book could be empirical, presenting new data. But does this data really add to your existing knowledge?

■ Most importantly: *get an idea of the reliability of the sources* (and of the book):
  • If the authors use a very limited number of sources, it may indicate that the work is primarily conceptual, very creative, but it could also indicate plagiarism (see below for further indicators)!
  • If the sources are not revealed adequately (➍E12), i.e. many quotes or tables and figures have been included without a proper source, the book will be useless for serious scientific use, because it is unreliable and difficult to check. The author is prone to plagiarism (➍E2).
  • Other indicators of an inadequate revelation of sources include:
    ○ use of information obtained during interviews without really explaining how they were held (➍E11);
    ○ entire sections that are referred to by one source only (mentioned at the beginning of the section: 'this section is primarily based on...');
    ○ inconsistent or insufficient references, indicate that the author may not have been very precise in the research project either.

■ Skim through the tables and figures for *originality and reliability.* Assess the tables and figures: do they include recent data? Are they functional (➍E14)? Are most of the tables based on other sources – implying that the study is primarily a reinterpretation of existing material? Does the study include any new tables and figures – showing more interesting empirical data?

- Look at the *index*. How well developed is the index? Are many keywords familiar to you? If you are working on a concrete research project or essay, compare the index with your own list of keywords (➡A6, E5). Check one of the keywords and assess the text it refers to. The more keywords that are of interest to you, the more reading the entire book becomes an option.
- Consider the *bibliography*:
  - If you are familiar with the topic: what sources did you expect; were your expectations fulfilled?
  - If you are unfamiliar: check publisher's reputation, and the number of promising sources.
- *Skim through the opening sections and the conclusions.* In particular, read the first and the last lines of the book: (**1**) what is the nature of the first line: introductory, a question, a clear observation?; (**2**) what is the nature of the last line: popularising, pathetic, clear and compact; (**3**) do the first and the last lines relate to each other: is the last line an answer to the first line, or is there no relation at all?

[⊕➡www.skillsheets.com for a quick book selection scan]

C4 Newspapers and Magazines

It is impossible to read all of the articles published in newspapers and magazines, even those concerning a limited area of research. Therefore, be selective in your choice of periodicals. When you subscribe to a periodical or systematically go through the articles in a specific newspaper or magazine check the *reliability of the source*. In the case of newspapers you will have to consider: the editorial policy, the selection criteria for publications, the sources of information for specific journalists, and the nature of the press agencies used. In the case of a scientific magazine your main question will be: are the articles screened by referees and what procedure is used? Knowing the background of magazines is just as critical a skill as revealing your sources (➔E11, E12). But it is not easy. Magazines and newspapers do not regularly reveal their background themselves. For example, most newspapers have Style Guides but they are rarely available to the public. This Skill Sheet helps you to become more knowledgeable about the backgrounds of magazines and newspapers, and is intended to motivate you to systematically collect background information about the magazines/newspapers that you consider most relevant. This is yet another way of checking sources.

1 Understanding the editorial policy

When you want to make the best use of magazines and journals, you should take some time to *understand* the editorial policy for the particular source. The editorial policy relates to what audience the journal wants to reach and by what kind of news coverage. Check whether information about this policy has been included in the colophon. Check whether there is a 'Style Guide' that gives more details on the policy. You can get a good impression of the editorial ambitions of magazines by looking at the titles of the articles. But, never assume that the headings of the articles in newspapers represent the contents, because they can be misleading. Headings in newspapers are often made by people other than the actual writer of the article.

Do you know the editorial policy of the magazines you read?

The most influential magazine in the world is the British weekly *The Economist*. Most decision-makers in the world have a subscription to this magazine. *The Economist* was first published in 1843. In the mid 1990s it had more than half a million subscribers. The appeal of the articles is particularly big because Economist journalists use a very strong debating style. The magazine has an unusual editorial policy. Firstly, all the articles are written anonymously. Secondly, the arguments all have the same style. According to the (internal) Economist Style Guide one of the basic rules for the writers is: 'first simplify, then exaggerate'. Or in the words of the editor of the journal: the formula of the magazine is 'three parts factual description and one part strongly held opinion or argumentative analysis.' Finally, since its inception the main, unwritten, aim of *The Economist* has been that 'everything has to give way for the free market' and 'free trade'. *The Economist* was launched to campaign for free trade and all forms of liberty. One could suspect that any argument that runs against this ideology will not be published in the magazine. Nevertheless, many readers consider *The Economist* to be one of the most independent and 'unbiased' magazines in the world.

Sources: Frankfurter Algemeine Zeitung, 2 September 1995; De Volkskrant, 13 March 1993, The Economist, 1 April 2006

2 Sources of information and the focus of the magazine

The deciding factor for defining the quality of a journal and newspaper is where it gets its information from, and whether the journalists themselves are facilitated to do their own fact-finding. Do you know where the journalists get their information from? Are all articles written in the style of an interview, or are there more analytical articles? Does your newspaper take 'investigative journalism' seriously?

Most of the free newspapers (provided at railway stations) primarily get their information from press agencies. Do you know where these agencies get their information from and how reliable they are? The box shows that different press agencies focus on different regions. Their experience in a particular region supports their reliability as a source. Many magazines and newspapers still take a typical regional or national perspective. You have to be aware of this 'bias'. It is, for example, troublesome to rely on American oriented sources *(Business Week or Fortune)* when you want to consider developments in French industry.

International press agencies: do you know the meaning and background of abbreviations?

Reuters: English press agency (London, good source for financial news and news from former British colonies in Asia). **AFP**: Agence France Presse (French, very good for news from France and previous French colonies in Africa). **AP**: Associated Press (USA, extensive network of correspondents). **DPA**: Deutsche Presse-Agentur (Germany, good source for news about Germany and Eastern Europe). **KNA**: Kyodo News Agency (Japan, primarily news on Japan). **IPS**: Intern Press Service (Third World press agency set up to tackle the news monopoly of the western press agencies).

---

3 Additional criteria for assessing the reliability of a newspaper

If you would like to check the reliability of your source further, consider the following aspects:

- How does the newspaper deal with *rectification*: wholeheartedly or reluctantly/small print?
- Who writes *guest columns*: is the magazine able to get to the core of the decision-makers? Are guest columns filled primarily by academics or more marginal observers? Is there a balance in the opinion pages between the contributions of officials and informed observers?
- What is the *nature of the 'editorial'*? Take a close look, over a longer period of time, and compare the editorials from different newspapers. This could reveal the 'ideology' of the journal or editors.

4 Referee procedures in scientific magazines

The selection of a scientific magazine depends on the topics that it deals with. If a magazine offers two or more interesting articles in each publication, it becomes a good choice for selection. The selection criteria and procedures used by the scientific magazine itself, however, give the best indication of the reliability of the magazine. The most strict referee procedure is the so called 'double blind' procedure. Each contribution is submitted anonymously by the editor and given to a sufficiently large number of knowledgeable referees. Their comments are also given anonymously. If the referees offer positive advice, the writer is invited to include the changes proposed by the (anonymous) referees (⊕A8, A12).

The stricter the magazine's selection criteria are, the more reliable it becomes as a source. Referee procedures also form the most important yardstick in compiling the official ranking of academic magazines. 'A' (or 'primary') magazines use the strictest referee procedures – double-blind referees – whereas 'C' or 'D' magazines are less strict – an editor that accepts or rejects the article. Do not ignore magazines because they have a lower position in the ranking. Their content can be just as relevant as that of higher ranked magazines, depending on your research needs.

[⊕⊕www.skillsheets.com for a quick magazine scan]

Reading can serve a variety of purposes at the same time, which leads to different ways of assimilating the material. If you are preparing for an exam you have to rely on the simplest reading technique: you aim at understanding and memorising the material. Memorising is basically a study skill (⊕B6). If you are writing a review your main aim is to formulate a critical analysis and an opinion about the contents of a single source (⊕E-series and website). However, if reading is to serve your core research skill you are trying to find an answer to a particular question. In that case your reading aims will be broader, spread over a large number of sources. Your aims become more varied and reading therefore more difficult to manage. Now consider the following: you are preparing to write a paper or part of a thesis and you have been lucky enough to find a lot of material on your subject. Then the problem arises: how to get the most important information from the pile of paper in front of you? This Skill Sheet specifies one particularly useful technique that can help you to manage this investigation in an effective way.

1 Specify the aim of your search

■ **Link** the aim of your reading with the most appropriate manner for digesting it (Table C.5)

Table C.5 Linking Aims and Manners

Reading aim	Reading/Digesting manner
1 To get a *first impression* of the topics discussed and the composition of the source	Orientation, familiarising
2 To gain some insight into the way the main argument is elaborated	Broad
3 To find an answer to a particular question	Searching
4 To understand the main points and details of the sources	Thorough, memorising
5 To form an opinion on the contents of the source	Critical analysis and judgement

■ **Prepare the structure of your argument**
You can only get the right things out of the material if you know what to look for. The structure (table of contents) of your paper is the 'net' with which you are going to fish for the relevant points from your reading. Of course, the first draft will be provisional (⊕A5). Prepare the basic structure by using keywords (⊕E1, E6). If you want to read effectively, you must always begin by writing!

2 Decide upon the style of your search

■ **Start with the pieces that seem most promising**
You want to improve your knowledge of the topic in the shortest time possible. Start, therefore, with those texts that provide you with the richest 'harvest'. Do not read everything (including more marginal texts) immediately.

■ **Do not lose time by reading texts from beginning to end**
If you know what you are looking for, you can go through the texts relatively

quickly and select the items that are relevant. First, skim through the text and identify the most interesting sections and arguments (⊕C6). Read and mark them carefully (⊕C10). Finally, return to those parts you want to 'conserve' by taking notes.

3 Create favourable conditions

- **Avoid distraction**
  When reading, you should not have all of the unread material in front of you. It can be discouraging or may distract you from the text that you are actually look-ing at (⊕B7, B12). Separate the books that you have already checked from those that you still have to read. Store the material that you have gone through in a way that enables you to find the individual texts easily (⊕A11). Make piles of material or notes according to the sections of your paper or chapters.

4 Use simple techniques

- **Make notes on post cards**
  Use postcard-sized cards/papers for notes. If you do not know the structure of what you are going to write, you will waste time by making too many or not enough notes and finally abandon the system altogether. This is part of the 'storming phase' of powerful writing (⊕E1). If you have planned the structure you know in which part of the paper a specific argument, idea, fact, or citation can be used.

  Number the different sections and write the relevant number together with a *keyword* at the top of the card. Add a summary of the idea and an abbreviation of the text (name of the author, page). This will enable you to find the original text quickly, when needed. Add the exact place to be sure that you are able to find it. Considerable time is lost in the final phase when you cannot finish the footnotes because you do not remember exactly which sources you used.

- **Organise the cards to follow your argument**
  You can make the writing process less complicated by arranging the cards in the order that you use them in the text – cards that will be used several times should be stored under the issue to be addressed first. You will only need to link the ideas on the different cards. Just 'jump' from one card to the next.

5 Create a clear focus

- **Allocate a 'page budget' before beginning to write**
  Before you start writing, allocate the total space of your paper under the differ-ent headings and subheadings of your table of contents. Distribute the text as evenly as possible.

- **Do not leave the writing to the end**
  Alternate between reading and writing (⊕C1). Many ideas will only come once you begin to write. Therefore, do not postpone writing for too long. Use your 'prime idea' for writing and the rest for all auxiliary activities. Do not waste prime time – your most productive time during the day (⊕B6-8) – for reading or organisational matters.

Reading actively and intelligently requires understanding. Understanding requires the ability to identify argumentation structures. If you cannot identify single argumentation structures, it is impossible to judge the validity of the overall structure of a text. This Skill Sheet presents a number of the most common argumentation structures: description, prescription, induction, deduction, causal reasoning, ex-post, ex-ante reasoning, and the use of analogies and metaphors. They often relate to a particular research strategy (➲A7). The identification of these argumentation structures is often complex because several types of argumentation are used *at the same time*. Many argumentation structures also overlap. Understanding argumentation requires that the reader be capable of deciding whether the author has achieved a proper *balance* between the various argumentation structures. This Skill Sheet, firstly, explains the characteristics of recurring argumentation structures (➲E6). Secondly, some pointers have been included to help you decide whether an author has achieved a balance between various argumentation structures in terms of their relative importance and their sequence. This Skill Sheet presents argumentation structures in six dyadic pairs for which the problem of finding a balance in the text seems to be of particular relevance.

I Description	Prescription
Deals with the question 'what is'.	Deals with the question 'what should be'.

Many research texts combine descriptive and prescriptive argumentation. But a solid text makes very clear distinctions between description and prescription. Prescription (or: design) is generally *preceded* by, and based on, description (or: problem definition and diagnosis; ➲A2). 'Mere' description should be treated with suspicion. The suggestion is that a description is more less 'objective'. Each description, however, has an (implicit) framework of reference. Has the author made this framework of reference and the problem definition sufficiently explicit (➲A3)? If description and prescription are mixed, the argumentation will be unconvincing. Be aware that such an argumentation structure could also indicate a poorly developed analytical framework.

II Induction	Deduction
A number of specific observations are used to reach a general conclusion. Ask the following questions to figure out whether one could speak of 'proper' induction: Are the number of observations sufficient? Are they representative? Are the observations reliable and, in case of experiments, properly conducted? Has the conclusion been carefully formulated (that is: only that is concluded what can be proven from the observations)?	A general observation is used to reach conclusions (or consequences) for a specific case. Ask yourself the following questions: Is the generalisation with which the argumentation starts (*premise major*: 'All men are mortal') valid? Does the specific observation (*premise minor*: 'Socrates is a man') that is elaborated fit into the category that is deduced from the general observation? Does the conclusion of the specific case only relate to the observation ('Socrates is mortal')? This kind of deductive reasoning is called Syllogism. (➲C8)

Inductive reasoning is very common in statistical research. Problems often arise from the (re)presentation of the selection, and from the usefulness of the accumulated observations. Deductive reasoning is often found in more macro-oriented sciences or in longer established scientific disciplines, in which research is often meant to gain further acceptance or denial of previously established theories. In general, induction precedes deduction: from empirical observations general theories are/have been constructed, which are then tested on the basis of further specific observations. If the specific observations that inductively lead to generalised observations, are used to illustrate specific observations in the next phase of research, the argumentation runs in a circle and becomes *tautological*. It is always very important for a reader to assess the origins of the induction that lead to the generalisation, even if a research project explicitly uses a deductive argumentation structure. Check the empirical background of the induction. Especially in 'how to' texts, it is important to know the background of the generalisation (➔C8). It is always important to check whether induction and deduction are based on clear and reliable principles.

III Causes	**Consequences**
You are interested in 'why' you see particular phenomena appear. If x happens, z will have caused this. The argumentation is past and explanation-oriented.	You are primarily interested in 'what' the outcome of particular observations is: if *x* happens, *y* will be the result. The argumentation focuses on the future and extrapolations.

Causal reasoning is a specification of inductive and deductive reasoning. A causal relationship in a deductive argumentation departs from a general statement and reaches two kinds of conclusions: (1) the anticipation of a consequence, (2) the reconstruction of a cause. A causal relationship, in an inductive argumentation, focuses on a number of individual observations and the way they relate in terms of causes and consequences. The generalisation of these observations constitutes the final causal relationship. For example, consider the following two observations: the sea is blue when the sky is blue, the sea turns grey when the sky is cloudy. Probable causality: the colour of the sea is caused by the condition of the sky. Always check closely which variables are included and which variables are excluded (*ceteris paribus* provision) from the argumentation. Also, decide whether the yardstick for assessing (*benchmarking*) the outcome of the comparison is appropriate. A normal sequence of argumentation first considers causes before going to consequences. Beware of argumentation structures in which the same causes are supposed to lead to the same consequences even under different circumstances. Also, be very critical when confronted with reasoning in *trends or paradigms*: they are presented as an 'objective' reality (which often they are not) that has comparable consequences for social actors under all circumstances.

IV Analogies	**Metaphors**
The argumentation shows that there is a resemblance between what is observed and other observations. For example you look in the past ('history repeats itself') or in another country to find analogies.	Relate an observation from a known phenomenon but from a completely different background. 'Economics is like a football match'.

An analogy can never really be proven, because the circumstances are never the same. Therefore, when reading analogies pay close attention to the indicators that are specified to make the analogy convincing. Argumentation which uses metaphors can also never be proven. The prime function of both metaphors and analogies is therefore to find additional observations and questions which may bring fresh insight into the topic (*heuristic function*). Analogies are generally more concrete than metaphors and are therefore easier to check. Scientific texts, with many analogies, are often more appropriate than texts with many metaphors (also in the style of writing). Neither metaphors nor analogies can substitute direct reasoning as the basis for observable phenomena (inductive and/or deductive causalities). Check whether the author has found a balance between illustrations and clarification (through analogies and metaphors) and direct argumentation.

V In favour	Against
What supports a particular observation? If an author aims primarily at supportive or explanatory observations the argumentation becomes *apologetic*.	What denies a particular observation? If an author only lists counter-arguments, the text is aimed at *criticism*.

If a text only reveals argumentation in favour or against a particular observation, the reader is faced with an unbalanced argumentation structure. If the author has only made superficial reference to counter-arguments, the argumentation remains weak. There is no particular sequence for presenting arguments in favour or against a theory. For example, it is not a good idea to begin a research text by stating what it is *not about*. It may even be a sign of either intellectual laziness, or of insecurity. It is a sign of good argumentation when a writer tries to take argumentation in favour and against seriously and is willing and capable of 'playing the devil's advocate' when necessary. The more convincing the representation of arguments in favour and against, the more convincing the ultimate conclusions will be. If the research methodology has not been well developed, implying that ex-ante (expectations) and ex-post (conclusions) are revealed and balanced, the danger of *(ex-post) rationalisation* increases: presenting something as reasonable which is not reasonable.

VI Necessary conditions	Sufficient conditions
To have outcome x, condition y should be favourable.	If condition y is favourable, outcome x will appear.

A common sequence of argumentation is first to look at 'necessary' conditions and then to consider whether they are also 'sufficient'. Balanced argumentation and research always considers both conditions (➲E6, A7).

(➲C8 includes a check list for identifying 'misleading arguments')

Understanding a text requires the ability to identify specific argumentation structures (➾C6). But, argumentation structures in turn are made more intelligible by the way they are organised in a logical and transparent way in the overall text. The better you are able to quickly grasp argumentation structures, the better you can make use of, or reject, texts. It also serves as an input to formulate and organise your own writings better (➾E3-6). Three phases in your reading process lead to different assessments: (1) before, (2) during and (3) after reading.

> Clear writers, like clear fountains, do not seem so deep as they are; the turbid look the most profound.—W.S. Landor

1   Before close reading: identify the organisation of the text

The structure of good analytical writing is predictable. You should be able to get a reasonable idea of the nature of the argumentation *before you start studying a text in detail*. If a writer has followed the general principles used for scientific texts (➾E6) the text has a structure that is *intended* to represent the main idea of the argumentation. The structure will be hierarchical or pyramidal and relatively easy to identify.

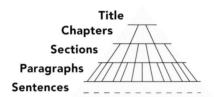

- The central theme is often included in the *(sub)title*.
  Have you ever really looked closely at the title of a text? Take a minute to look at the title, and think about the kind information you get in relation to (1) your own interests, (2) the nature of the question addressed by the author, (3) the nature of the argumentation developed in the text. Titles reveal a lot about the intentions of the author.
- Supporting themes make up the *chapters and sections*.
  In the *introduction* you will find a description of the problem that is addressed and the sequence in which the analysis is presented. Each chapter or section presents further introductions to these themes and refers back to the ones mentioned previously.
- The detailed components of the argumentation make up each *paragraph* in a (sub)section.
  Each paragraph will include only one thought, proof or evidence in support of the general argumentation.

- Often the author has also added (*sub*)*headings* to help you to keep track of the argumentation.
- Finally, the text and sentences include many additional supportive tools to help you to find the structure of the argumentation:
  - signal words or numerical signs: 1,2,3; 1.1, 1.2, 1.3; A, B; or 'firstly, secondly';
  - typographical signs: in particular *italics* or <u>underlines</u> are added to place an emphasis.
- Conclusions are announced as such and include a summary of the argumentation and the way the evidence has been collected (inductive or deductive) to arrive at the conclusion.

If an author has used this kind of organisation it is relatively easy to decide whether this line of reasoning appeals to you and/or fits into your own research aims. If you understand the basic structure well, it is also far easier to *memorise* the text if you read it in preparation for an exam (➲B3, B6).

2 After preliminary reading

If after intense (preliminary) investigation, you cannot find a structure in the argumentation, seriously consider abandoning the text altogether. If the author is not able to make the argument clear to you, why should you invest time trying to 'understand' what the author evidently did not understand! If you cannot decipher a clear structure it is the responsibility – and thus the problem – of the writer, not the reader. If you still begin to read the text, much time will be spent trying to ascertain what the author 'might have meant'. You should not reproach yourself immediately for not being able to grasp the essence of an argument even if the author is well-known. If in doubt, consult other people who have read the same book. You may be surprised how often they share your opinion. Most of the time there are many other books you can consult, so only read the (parts of) texts that are useful to you.

3 After thorough reading: overall assessment

Use the following scoring list (Table C.7) to come to a balanced overall assessment of an author's argumentation. For 'good argumentation' it is not sufficient simply to have a clear structure for the text, three other categories should also be respected: succinctness, simplicity and precision. Everyone would prefer to read texts that include argumentations that score 'good' in all four categories. But the reality is different and argumentations often include bad and good parts.

Table C.7 Argumentation scoring list

	Good	Mediocre	Bad
Clarity (clear structure; balanced argumentation)			
Succinctness (condensed structure and sentences; no argumentation 'tricks')			
Simplicity (adequate phrasing, short sentences when necessary; no suggestive words)			
Precision (sources are clear, data is relevant and sufficient)			

Beware of simplistic (not: simple) argumentation. Simplistic argumentation is misleading most of the time. In that case they become 'fallacies': arguments that are demonstrably flawed in their logic or form. But fallacies are not always easy for the reader to identify. In going through a text carefully you may not be aware of a number of argumentation 'tricks' that are used by authors. Deciding whether or not to abandon reading a text can only be done once you manage to think about the arguments in the context of the whole text or book. Skill Sheet C6 provided an overview of specific argumentation structures. Table C.8 lists the various categories of fallacies, how to identify them, why the particular fallacy might have occurred, and the possible consequences for the serious reader.

Table C.8 The nature of fallacies

Categories	Example/indication	Reason of author and consequences for the reader
1 Prescription gets mixed with description	In the middle of a text (not clearly separated) you read, for example, 'The growth of turnover has been lower than ever. This should not be accepted...' Prescription or undue normative statements are often also recognisable from the use of qualifications such as 'fantastic' or 'bad' (➲E9).	The author is too eager to give advice; has not gone through the whole reflective cycle (➲A2, A3); has not made a clear distinction between analysis and advice. If this happens too often you can skip reading the text.
2 Reversible causalities	■ You read a text stating: 'if not C then D', but you can easily also state: 'if not D then C' (for example, after adding a number of intervening variables). ■ Post-hoc reasoning: suggests that C causes D *because* D comes after C in time.	The author is presenting quasi exactness. Time sequence is never a sufficient condition for causality. Argumentation structure should be denied. Abandon the text or broaden the analytical perspective to the intervening variables that are not included in the model.
3 Improper induction	The author has not explained or insufficiently explained what the (re)presentation of the observations is and how they are used to reach general conclusions. No counter-examples are included. The author makes use of popular wisdom or stereotypes to prove something: 'like father, like son'.	The author is either emotionally involved in the topic or suffers from mind-idleness. Some examples or individual observations may be useful, but the conclusions should be ignored.

4 **Improper deduction**	■ *Abusive syllogism*: inferior argumentation appears particularly when there are incomplete or improper syllogisms: major premise: All politicians are not to be trusted; minor premise (John is a politician); conclusion: John is not to be trusted. The major premise in this sequence represents an improper generalisation (induction) which makes the whole argument false. ■ *Disjunctive deduction*: 'if-if' or 'either-or' reasoning: one of the premises is presented as a dilemma, a choice between two mutually excluding alternatives. If one possibility is not applicable, the other one must be. Inferior argumentation, in this context, is, for example: 'either he is on time, or something terrible has happened. He is not in time, so...'. A much used argumentation trick in politics also puts the choice between improper or poorly specified alternatives: 'Clinton or Chaos'; 'Either victory or death'.	Inferior reasoning. Because vital information (one of the premises) is withheld from the reader, the author is manipulating the reader. Reasoning as well as conclusions are wrong, and should therefore be refuted. It is difficult though, to counter this type of argumentation, because it is not intended to be part of a scientific debate. Argumentation should not be taken seriously (although the interest constellation behind the saying should!).
5 **Reason by improper analogy**	Analogies can never be sufficient proof for an argument, but they can present an element of likelihood and have a heuristic value. Analogies, like metaphors become improper when they are presented as the sole proof.	Use the analogy as a stimulus for further thinking. Do not debate the conclusion. It is built on improper reasoning.
6 **Rationalisation**	Writers who master the basics of argumentation (➔E6) always explain how they have come to a particular selection of examples, theories, and analogies. If you read selection criteria like: 'these categories are not elaborated because they were not relevant to the rest of the research' you might be confronted with an improper *(ex-post)* rationalisation of the research methodology. This kind of rationalisation, then, is bound to appear in the argumentation itself.	The author(s) have probably not systematically developed their research methodology or argumentation. Their selection is based on unspecified or ex-post reasoning. The 'evidence' presented in the text should be treated with great caution.

Translation or dictionary programmes can be useful when reading or writing a text in a foreign language. But they contain a number of problems that you should be aware of.

1 Between simple word replacement and translation programmes

There are automatic translation and simple word replacement dictionary programmes. Dictionary programmes – often marketed as 'translators' – simply replace each word by its equivalent in another language. Dictionaries, however, can not really qualify as language translators. What is meant by automatic translation is a process that involves some context and grammatical analysis. The depth and quality of such programmes varies widely. There are free programmes available on the internet (such as Babelfish) while the more sophisticated ones are for sale.

Though frequently coarse and erroneous, automatic translation is useful in a number of ways:

- *It gives a rough idea of what the text is about.* This is particularly helpful when you are doing research on the web and find a document in a foreign language. Automatic translation will tell you quickly whether or not the document is worth looking at in detail. Though the text may not be translated perfectly, simpler things such as tables will also be translated and these facts and figures can reveal interesting information.
- *It serves as a basis for a human translator.* This saves a lot of time, though there is a risk that the human translator will produce low-quality translations.
- Lastly, an author can use automatic translation as an *extra check for clarity and grammatical correctness* of the own text. Translation errors can indicate problems in the original text, such as complicated grammatical structures. If a translation programme cannot correctly process a piece of text, this could for instance be due to features in the original language that will make it difficult for a human reader to understand it as well.

As translation programmes improve, more complicated texts can be translated. As for now, automatically generated text can never be relied on completely.

2 Tips for using translation programmes effectively

- Separate your text into *small short pieces of text.* Translating short texts separately is faster than translating a large text. The downfall is that the translation programme might not be able to make proper use of context.
- *Use normal language.* Avoid proverbs and idioms, dialects, slang or technical terms.
- *Say things directly*, be succinct and literal, and avoid hidden humour and sarcasm.
- *Write short and simple sentences.*
- *Write words and phrases in full form*, avoid abbreviations and do not leave out words that you might think are unnecessary, such as 'that, which or who'.
- *Use words that have specific meanings* instead of words with several meanings. For

example words ending with the suffix 'ing' can be ambiguous, like playing, which can be a noun or an adjective.

- Make sure ambiguous words have *suitable contexts* that translation programmes can pick up.
- Use a *spellchecker* and check your *grammar*. Standard *punctuation* is very important; end every sentence with a period or question mark. Parentheses, hyphens, dashes, etc. can cause problems with any translation programme.
- *Avoid special characters or symbols*, these can often cause confusion for any translation programme.

C10 Active Note-making

The way to handle a text depends on the aim of your reading (➔C1, C5). Actively going through (parts of) a text always requires that you make notes. This Skill Sheet describes the most commonly (ab)used note-making techniques.

1 Underlining

Printed texts are not sacred, so *underline* important sentences and sections, even in expensive hardback books (except those from libraries!). You increase the intensity and speed (➔C11) with which you read a text.

- Do not underline everything. If you force yourself to be selective you will be able to understand the argument more clearly. Also, do not underline full sentences, rather underline words or groups of words.
- Only underline once you have read the whole paragraph. If you underline while you read, you could end up underlining everything. Restricting the use of underlining also increases your understanding of the message in the text.
- Should you underline with a pencil or a pen? A pencil has the advantage that you can rub it out afterwards. But: if you know that what you underline with a pen cannot be erased, you will probably be more selective.
- The same principle can be used to decide whether lines made with a ruler are preferable to (less time-consuming) those made freehand: the more accurate the underlining is, the more time it takes, and therefore the more you will be inclined to be selective. So it may be advisable to use a ruler and write with a pen.
- If you prefer you can use a *marker*. Remember, however, that the marks fade away and are sometimes difficult to photocopy.

2 Use the margins

- Indicate the number of arguments used by numbering the different components: 1, 2, 3.
- Write a *question mark* in the margin if you do not immediately understand the argument. If the text contains many question marks, you should ask yourself the reason why you did not understand large parts of the text. Remember that this is often because the text itself has been badly written and argued (➔C7, C8).
- Write an *exclamation mark* in the margin if you find a phrase particularly relevant. Interestingly enough, you may think differently of this passage later: sometimes exclamation marks can even become question marks or *vice versa*.
- Get used to writing *codes* in the margins which refer to your *research topics*. For example: the part of this text which includes information on active reading skills would be given the code 'SS-C10' in the margin.
- A text that you think may be interesting for *someone else* could be marked by a vertical line in the margin, together with the first name or initials of the person.
- Other remarks can also be written in the margins. Try to make them legible so that they can serve their purpose: as input for further digestion and use of the text.

Actively reading the newspaper?

- On an empty table, with enough space to spread out the newspaper;
- With a pen within reach to mark the articles, and immediately write the date and source if you want to keep the article;
- With sharp scissors also within reach, to cut out the article. An alternative is to use a specially designed knife, which only cuts through one newspaper page so that you can leave the paper lying on the table. Check what is on the back of the clip.

3 Use small cards

Note down important quotes and/or ideas, which you get from reading the book, *immediately* on a small card. This will slow down your reading tempo. But if you wait until you have finished the text and then make your notes you will need to go through the sections again and not many people are prepared to do that.

4 Make active summaries in the form of a table

Do not make a summary of the whole book if you do not need one. Only summarise those parts (on cards or on your computer) that you need for your own topic (➲C11). A well-tried and more active method is to summarise what you have read in a table. This helps you to identify the most important characteristics of the analysis (the vertical and horizontal axes of the table). Filling it in immediately enables you to identify the analytical *gaps* left by the author. Often, compiling a table helps you to add your own observations to the boxes, or even extend it to include other characteristics (more rows or columns). The table can immediately transform your summary into an independent piece of interpretation/analysis.

5 Make active summaries in the form of diagrams and Mind Maps

In a diagram or Mind Map (➲B6), you try to reproduce the arguments of the author.

- Identify the key concepts.
- Try to find the relationships between these key concepts.
- Make a graphical representation of these relationships. You increase the clarity if you can do the following:
  - draw a *hierarchy* of key concepts if appropriate;
  - make a distinction between independent and dependent variables (always check whether this causality can not also be turned around; ➲C8);
  - print important key concepts bigger or bold;
  - draw clear and one-directional arrows between the variables; if you have too many two directional arrows, the picture becomes too complex and its distinctive nature too limited.
- Good diagrams are not easy to draw. Make a first attempt straight away, but be prepared to redraw the diagram several times.
- When you have finished reading you can think about making *two diagrams*: one which mirrors what is in the text; the other which leaves the concepts in the same spot in the presentation, but adds questions marks and perhaps additional

arrows representing your own ideas. Printed next to each other, these two diagrams offer an instant insight into the more questionable parts of the author's argumentation.

Reading is a daily and very time-consuming activity. Most people have never really reflected on their own reading skills, since this is a basic skill that you have learned at a relatively early age. After that age, your reading pace quickens primarily because you are more experienced in reading rather than that you have improved your technique. Quantity, however, rarely triggers quality. This Skill Sheet discusses a number of characteristics and techniques to improve your reading speed. Speed reading works on the premise that your brain processes pictures and not words (Turley, 1989). But always remember the first rule of speed reading: the quickest read is once you have been able to select out *irrelevant* material; that takes no time and always beats brainless speed reading (⊕C2-4).

1 Slow and quick reading

The average reading speed is around 230 words per minute. But most people are capable of reading at least as fast as 500 words per minute. They are 'held back' by *bad reading habits*. Slow readers also generally read with poor comprehension (Fry, 1963). This is because reading and understanding a complex sentence requires the reader to hold the information in their short term memory (⊕B6). By reading slowly it becomes *harder* for the reader to keep the information in the memory, and therefore harder to understand. It is accepted that slow readers can actually increase their comprehension by learning to read faster – until a certain limit (Bell, 2001). Conversely, of course, poor comprehension can also explain for slow reading. Everybody has the experience that slow reading in a foreign language is the necessary start of a learning curve. The same applies to a new area of research or another scientific discipline: you start off with slowly going through texts, trying to identify the most important concepts, and if needed looking them up in dictionaries or glossaries. After you have mastered these phases, your reading speed will increase automatically. So slow reading is not always a bad thing. On the contrary, it represents a very functional phase in research and learning (⊕The Challenge, Part I). 'Comprehension is achieved by reading neither too fast nor too slow' (Coady, 1979). Once you are more acquainted with a language or an intellectual area, improving the quality of your reading is never a bad thing. That is what speed reading is basically about.

2 Technical causes of slow reading

There are different kinds of technical causes for slow reading. The method of reading will influence the causes of slow reading. If we abstain from the content argument, presented above, major causes include (University of Texas Learning Center, 2002):
- We reread words.
- We tend to read everything the same way regardless of what it is and why it is being read.
- We fail to become involved with the material being read, to interact with the author and to anticipate his next thought(s) or his conclusions.

- The 'recovery time' from one line to the next is often slow.
- We sub-vocalise (hear words in our heads) which limits our reading to the speed of speech.
- We read every word (60% of the words are structure words as opposed to content words).
- Notice that there are also individual variables that lead to slow reading such as intelligence, motivation, lack of vocabulary, comprehension levels, physiological and psychological traits. So never consider speed reading techniques as a panacea for your slow reading or – even worse – your lack of comprehension.

3 Effective speed reading

First pay attention to the environment in which you read. It is important to have a dedicated area for studying with basic attributes such as adequate lighting, proper ventilation, decent sized desk and good seating. This room should prefer-able not include a TV, stereo, other people and telephones, which will lead to dis-traction (⊖B series). Secondly, some pointers can be given on how you could try to speed up your reading speed in Table C.11.

Table C.11 Do's and don'ts of speed reading

'Do's'	'Don'ts'
• Force yourself continuously to read a bit faster	• Do not 'mouth' the words while trying to read yourself
• Find a quiet environment, make sure nothing and nobody can distract you	• Do not read along with your finger on the side of the page
• Set reasonable goals, to read a certain amount of pages in e.g. 30 min.	• Do not fear to lose comprehension of the text while reading
• Track the main idea of each paragraph. This can be done by reading for ideas and concepts, not for isolated words	• Do not pay attention to every word specifically
• Relax your eyes (close your eyes for a few seconds and open them wide)	• Reading from paper goes faster than reading of a screen
• Try to memorize what you have read after each part of a book (chapter/section)	• Never read back

Source: Speed reading online (2004)

There is no one best way to actually read texts. It is often suggested that you have to move your eyes diagonally over a text. But there are other speed reading meth-ods as well. Below a number of them are shown. You should try to find out which method best suits you (see: www.utexas.edu/student/utlc/handouts/512.html).

	1. Move your eyes diagonally.
	2. Read the words at the beginning and at the end of each line.
	3. Read the words in the middle of each line.

Besides all speed reading tricks there will always be a difference of reading between people caused by different intelligence levels, motivation, interests and vocabulary.

[⊕➔www.skillsheets.com for more information]

Reading tends to be an individual and input-oriented activity. But reading can also become part of a social activity if it is used as a feedback or evaluation technique. Here, the general rules of peer-teaching and giving effective feedback apply (⊃G9). Active reading also implies active note-making. Note-making becomes feedback to the writer of the text (including yourself) once you are able to make clear corrections in the text. This Skill Sheet lists a number of principles to apply when you correct a text. You can make two types of corrections:

1 *passive* corrections are used to indicate which phrases are unclear/wrong and need work, leaving it up to the writer to come up with corrections;
2 *active* corrections are used when the reader takes time to think of concrete alternatives for the specific piece of text. This process is far more laborious than passive corrections and thus requires considerable commitment and time from the reader.

Rule #1: When you work with a group of your peers you should *always* adopt the most active type of correction. In peer groups there are no leaders or followers. Everybody is responsible for the final text, which also requires that everybody show commitment to reading all of the texts thoroughly.

Rule #2: When you work as a tutor specify the amount of time you have available to make corrections and – consequently – what kind of corrections the writer of the text can expect from you. In general, tutors will make much more limited corrections, because the ultimate responsibility for the text lies with the individual writer, not with the tutor.

Rule #3: Leave wide enough margins at the left and right of the text and a line spacing of 1.5 or more. This facilitates clear corrections. Try to make corrections in the margin *legible*.

Rule #4: Always *combine* correction marks in the text with marks in the margin. The marks in the margin should make it impossible for the writer to overlook the correction marks in the text, and because the margins contain more space, the marks can be more elaborate.

There are two types of symbols used by proofreaders. The first are official standard symbols as specified by the British Standard Institution, which were adopted by the International Standards Organisation (ISO 5776:1983) and by most publishing houses. These symbols are used for relatively small *editorial* corrections. The most frequently used symbols are summarised in Table C.12a. The second type of symbol deals with the content of the text and is more personal. Each tutor develops own symbols. Table C.12b shows a number of these qualitative symbols, which might be used by you and/or your corrector/reader. Make sure that writer and corrector agree upon the exact meaning of these symbols.

Table C.12a Standard editorial symbols

Instruction	Mark in text	Mark in margin
insert in text the matter indicated in the margin	⅄	new matter followed by ⅄
substitute character or (part of) word	(through characters or words)	new character or word delete (when no words are given)
close up, no space	link words	
correction to be ignored	under character to remain	
insert space between words	between words affected	
insert space between lines	between lines to be separated	
transpose letters or words	round matter to be transposed	
insert character(s)		followed by new character(s)
insert additional character(s) (alternative marks)	F ꝑ ꞵ 7 ꝫ	F ꝑ ꞵ 7 ꝫ followed by new character
run on (no new paragraph)		
start new paragraph		
start sentence on new line	before sentence to be moved	
move to the right	before matter to be moved	
move to the left	after matter to be moved	

Table C.12b Qualitative correction symbols (on contents)

Instruction	Mark in text	Mark in margin
No running sentence. Rephrase!	under sentence	
Paragraph difficult to understand, rephrase/rethink.		
What do you mean? Are you sure? Rethink!		?
I do not think this is correct, leave out or formulate anew.		? ?
No or unclear source, reveal your source(s)!		⟨ SOURCE ⟩
Same words are used too often, reword!	on the same page	

Series D Listening

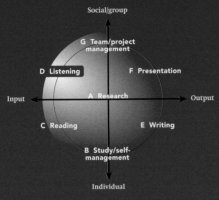

Social/group

G Team/project management

D Listening   F Presentation

Input   A Research   Output

C Reading   E Writing

B Study/self-management

Individual

The Reflective Cycle of Constructive Listening

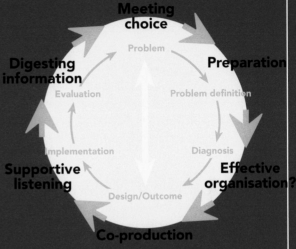

Meeting choice

Problem

Digesting information

Preparation

Evaluation   Problem definition

Implementation   Diagnosis

Supportive listening

Effective organisation?

Design/Outcome

Co-production

	Preparation	Effective organisation	Co-production and supportive listening	Digesting
D1 Principles of Constructive Listening	■			
D2 Preparing Interviews	■	■		
D3 Managing Interviews		■	■	
D4 Asking Questions			■	
D5 Body Language			■	
D6 Processing Interviews			■	■
D7 Attending Lectures			■	■
D8 Listening for Feedback				■

Listening Skill Levels

Level 1

o Relatively passive, consumption and teacher-oriented
o Increased concentration level to cope with longer lectures
o Limited preparation for classes and the background of the courses
o Limited understanding of the background of the teacher
o Capable of conducting a simple (closed) interview

Level 2

o More active. Understanding that listening is a form of 'co-producing'
o Sufficiently good concentration level to benefit from longer lectures
o Good preparation and understanding of the background of courses
o Modest linking of listening and own presentation skills
o Capable of conducting and digesting a more open interview

Level 3

o Always active; aimed at own questions and research projects
o Joint preparation of classes (leading, for instance, to other type of lectures)
o Listening is systematically used as input for own writing and presentation skills and research
o Capable of designing, conducting and digesting interviews and other means of oral input
o Immediately identifying debate tricks, argumentation fallacies and the like

Level 4

o Constructive listening in order to serve as input for effective collaboration and management
o Listening as real-time input for effective decision making and debate/dialogue
o Interview skills are applied in job interviews too

Always treat your respondent with respect. Do not send a preliminary first draft of your report to a person who you want to interview, unless you believe that it is more or less complete. Often, researchers try to use the interviewee as a sort of 'corrector'. They send a draft that has a number of blank spaces, spelling errors and inconsistent argumentation. *Nobody* appreciates this, even if you state that it is only a first draft. You will lose the goodwill of the interviewee very quickly. This can often apply to your academic supervisor as well (➔B2). *Do not experiment with this rule.*

2 Specific preparation: setting the scene

- **Background**. Consider the background of your respondent:
  - Do you know what your respondent's (interest) position is in the organisation;
  - Specify why this particular person is important for your interview.
  If you do not know about his/her background, allow some time during the interview to ask the respondent to explain this.
- **Objectives**. Set your interview objectives. Link them to the stage of the research that you are in (see above). Write down your objectives in short statements.
  - State your possible 'biases', 'hopes', 'fears' and expectations regarding the interview. Doing this should enable you to avoid 'reductive listening' (➔D3, G4)
  - Think about how you could establish a 'barter' system for the interview: how can you compensate for the time that your respondent has 'lost'? (➔A12)
- **Impression**. Think about the impression that you want to make in order to obtain information that you need. Decide on the style and/or 'tone' of the interview:
  - friendly and inquisitive: you want to know his/her answers/opinion;
  - searching: asking your respondent to become actively involved in your search process;
  - confrontational, posing or assertive: if you check your information by challenging the interviewee to disclose interesting information, be prepared for a debate or even an argument instead of an interview.
- **Introduction**. Prepare a brief introduction about the research questions and the reason for the interview. It should not last longer than two to three minutes. If you are unable to do this, there is something wrong with your research question or with your presentation skills. Compose the introduction by using a few key-words, this will ensure that your presentation is spontaneous. Do not learn it by heart. This will lessen your ability to improvise. Formulating a good introduction will give you the appearance of being well prepared. You should also agree upon *the amount of time approximately available* for the interview during the introduction. The actual duration of the interview is often open to last-minute changes. Be prepared to be flexible.
- **Interviewers**. Limit *the number of people* conducting the interview. When more than one person conducts an interview, be aware of the risk that the interviewee may have the feeling of being 'cross examined'. Furthermore, unstructured questions can be contradictory which gives a bad impression of the group. If you carry out an interview with two or more people first ascertain: (1) who will be

the main person asking the questions, giving the introduction and finishing the interview, (2) who is responsible for elaborating notes (everyone takes notes as a rule, but only one person should take more time to elaborate them).

■ **Contact**. *Contact the person* either in writing or by phone (➔E series, website): repeat the aims of your research and the reason why you would like the interview. If you yourself do not already have a reputation in your chosen field, always try to offer the name of a referee: who advised you to contact this person. Confirm the date of the interview, supply a contact address in case the interviewee needs to cancel the interview.

3 Specific preparation on content

■ Take notes. Work on your ability to take *notes while carrying out the interview*. You will become a more active listener (➔D1, D6). Taking notes allows you to revert back to points that the interviewee has made previously, during the interview.

■ No tape recorder! Taking notes is better than using *a tape recorder*. It is extremely important for the interviewee to have trust in the interviewer. When you use a tape recorder, even if you have asked for permission, you will never know if your respondent withheld information that would otherwise have been given. You ask the interviewee to trust you when you use a tape recorder. The interviewee does not know your background and will never be really sure that you will not to use the tapes for (1) literal quotations, or (2) for other goals, possibly in a classroom or with friends ('listen how ignorant this guy is...').

■ Questions. Prepare a checklist. Working from a *pre-set list of questions* can be very useful and ensures a minimum number of relevant answers. But respect three rules: (1) never make the list too long, (2) leave enough room to elaborate on specific points that prove interesting during the interview, (3) *designate priorities* i.e. decide which questions you really want to have an answer to.

The interviewer is responsible for procuring the necessary information during the time allowed for the interview. The organisation that you choose, the kind of introduction that you compose, the way in which you use your diary and the way in which you utilise the time available, can all be considered to be active listening skills. This Skill Sheet lists the various phases of an interview and provides a checklist for organisational points, which, when followed, will ensure that the interview is as effective as possible. When the interview begins you will do most of the talking, so be brief. During the interview your talking/listening ratio will be approximately 20:80, whereas at the end of the interview the amount of time that you talk will increase again.

1 At the start of the interview

Create a positive atmosphere. This does not necessarily mean that you should talk about the weather. Briefly outline the aim of the interview (⊕D2). Use five 'W' questions like:

- **Who** are you?
  Use a business card that states your name and the organisation that you are working with. Put the card that you get in return on the table in front of you: it helps you to remember the name of the interviewee.
- **Why** are you here? What are your aims, expectations, context, who advised you to talk to this person?

Always make clear what the reason for the interview is and what the respondent will get in return. Establish an agreement for barter (⊕A12).

- **What** are you going to do with the information? Will you quote or not, how to establish barter? Make explicitly clear that you are not a journalist who has to rely on opinions and statements that can be quoted directly. Literal quotes that concern someone's opinions are rarely proof of anything. When an interviewee provides dates, quote that and refer to the general source. If an interviewee gives you an opinion this can serve as *background* information for yourself, reinforcing particular conclusions. You do not need to be that recent in your coverage. If the interviewee thinks that they may be quoted directly, they could become more cautious and may even refrain from disclosing relevant information (mostly without revealing why). State that you will not quote the person even if they did not ask you not to quote directly. Taking notes instead of using a tape recorder will also increase the degree of trust established between the partners (⊕D2).

- General rule for research interviews: never quote the person that you have interviewed.
- Make the no-quote provision clear as soon as you begin the interview.

■ **How** are you going to conduct the interview? The sequence you propose, whether you have open, closed or semi-structured questions.
■ **When** will the interview will be over? State the amount of time that the interview is going to take. In the event that the interviewee does not have the required amount of time available:
(1) set a new date;
(2) decide on the questions that should take priority together;
(3) or do both 1 and 2.

2 During the interview

■ **First observations**. Write down the name of the respondent, the starting time of the interview and the location. Perhaps also make a few notes of your *first impressions* (handshake, a chaotic desk, body language) of the person you are interviewing. First impressions can – unconsciously – influence your judgement on the person being interviewed. All of the subsequent answers will then be assessed more negatively or positively than is granted. Your interview may become biased. Consider to what extent the first impressions influence your judgement. A good physical appearance, for example, does not necessarily imply that he/she will have interesting opinions.
■ **Name interviewee**. *Repeat the name of the person* regularly during the interview. If you just say 'you', your respondent may think that you have forgotten his/her name. Additional barriers will be created if the person believes this to be the case. But, beware even more of calling someone by the wrong name, this can have a very negative effect. Use the business card as a reminder.
■ **Listening process**
  ■ Beware of *reductive listening*. Every listener modifies what is actually being said to a certain extent. There are many reasons for this kind of 'reductive listening'.

Reasons for reductive listening
○ you do not like the person;
○ the speaker is inconsistent;
○ what is said is not what you want to hear;
○ you like the person but the information given is not relevant;
○ you (dis)like the organisation the person is working with;
○ the person has a high/low position in the organisation;
○ you may find it difficult to concentrate.

- Try not to be judgemental. 'Shut out' motives for reductive listening as much as possible (Guirdham, 1990). Write these impressions down as well.
- Adopt an *active listening posture*: show your interest. Look at the posture and body language of the interviewee and (re)act accordingly (➡E6).

- **Time management**
  - Know where your *priorities* lie:
    - o if you are running over time you should be able to skip less important questions and get to the point;
    - o make a short checklist (➡D2) on your note pad;
    - o *never* confront the interviewee with a shopping list and an uninvolved interviewer.
  - In the case of a *longer interview* (or if the interviewee takes a long time to answer the questions):
    - o summarise the information regularly;
    - o ask the interviewee to either go over a point that you did not understand ('I did not quite understand this...');
    - o or make it clear that you would like to get back to this later on.

- **Questions interviewer**
  - Develop a system for your questioning:
    - o do not ask a long series of 'heavy questions';
    - o alter the intensity of the questioning to allow the interviewee to relax occasionally;
    - o ask *sensible questions* and get used to taking notes while you are listening.
  - Do *not become too personal* during the interview. This will make it difficult to sustain the division of roles and thus obtain interesting information.
  - As a rule, do *not interrupt* the person.
  - Do *not quote other interviewees*: if you gave them the same (non) quoting provision as you did with this interviewee, how will your interview partner be able to trust you?

- **Answers interviewee**
  - *Beware of evasion and vagueness*. Do not give the person the chance to be vague or evasive. Do not move on to the next question, repeat it as long as your question is sufficiently relevant.
  - *Beware of 'socially desirable' answers*: the interviewee tells you what you want to hear (or what he/she *thinks* you want to hear). Overcoming 'socially desirable' answers necessitates that you are knowledgeable about the person and about the topic. Be in a position to say; 'if I understand you correctly...' or 'but on other occasions you have answered differently...'. Uninformed interviewers are more likely to get vague and even misleading answers without being able to do anything about it.

3 Before finishing the interview

- *Go through the list of questions.* Do this openly and tell the interviewee that you are checking to see whether you have missed anything out.
- Ask if your respondent has any other information that could be relevant, but that you did not ask for.
- Present a *short summary* of what you have discussed. List possible appointments and who is responsible for keeping the appointment.
- Tell the respondent *how you will use* the interview and when he/she will get something in return from you (as a reward for the time spent).
- Ask if you can *come back* to any points that on closer observation may not be clear. People rarely refuse, which becomes a good argument if you really have to return.
- *At the end* of the interview ask whether the interviewee knows of any other people who may be able to help you. There are two reasons for this particular timing: (1) the respondent might be more willing to think about this request, (2) the respondent has a better idea about what you want to know.
- Do not forget to *thank the respondent* for his/her time and the information!

To develop an effective questioning style, you already have to know the kind of questions that could be asked. In a real interview situation you often use a combination of many different question categories and styles. Interviewing, therefore, represents a balancing act between the various options that are open to you (categories and styles) and what you can do in case problems occur.

'Blessed are the skilled questioners, for they shall be given mountains of words to ascend. Blessed are the wise questioners, for they shall unlock hidden corridors of knowledge. Blessed are the listening questioners, for they shall gain perspective.'—Halcolm's Evaluation Beatitudes

1 Question categories

The kind of questioning style you adopt depends on the impression and the atmosphere that you would like to create during the interview (➔D2). You should be familiar with the various categories, the drawbacks and the positive aspects, before you select a combination of techniques. Find out what kind of questions you feel comfortable with (Table D.4a). Check whether they are also effective for the purposes of your research.

Table D.4a Basic question categories

Question	Example	Remark/function
■ Open	• 'What do you think about...' • 'Could you tell me a little bit about... • *Reflective/hypothetical:* 'If you were in the following position, what would you do...'	• Invites more elaborate answers and perhaps more relevant (spontaneous) information; • Is more difficult to control; • Use a list of 'priority' questions that *must* be addressed.
■ Closed	• 'Do you consider this measure appropriate for the aims included in the long-term planning' • 'Do you agree with this contract' • *Multiple-choice question:* 'Do you prefer (a), (b) or (c)?'	• The reflective or hypothetical question guides the interviewee's answer, because it specifies the topic. You could also use *comparisons* to achieve the same effect; • Gives you maximum control over the interview, but also more limited flexibility; • Requires considerable knowledge in order to be effective, and can only establish simple 'facts';

		• Can lead to simple 'yes' 'no' answers that represent more the interpretation framework of the interviewer than of the respondent.
■ Suggestive/leading/ rhetorical	• 'Don't you also think that...' • 'Wouldn't you agree that...' • 'I think this is morally wrong. What do you think?' • 'I expect that you are well informed about this topic'	Avoid asking questions in which the answer is implicit in the question ('leading') or in which your opinion is included ('suggestive'). You manipulate your respondent more openly than might be liked. This interview style could have serious effects on the reliability of the answers you get. It may also anger the interviewee.
■ Socratic	• 'Why is this...' • <and if you get an answer you continue> ...why ...why?	Very effective for getting to the causes of a particular phenomena or to the core of a person's opinions. Continue asking the 'why question' until you see that the respondent becomes irritated.
■ Confrontational/ interrogative	• Questions asked in rapid sequence • Questions asked in an aggressive manne • 'Are you withholding information?'	This style could lead to information that otherwise would not be revealed by the respondent. But it could easily become counter-effective if the interviewee becomes annoyed with interviewer/interrogator during or after the interview.
■ Awareness-building	• 'Do you know that...' • 'Are you aware that...'	Used in action research. The question is intended to introduce your respondent to new ideas and new insights. The questioning itself is supposed to lead to action, but is not necessarily 'leading'. Can be very manipulative (see category 3).

2 Questioning style: basic pointers
■ **Short and clear questions**

Do not ask multiple-interpretable questions. In the case of long and complex questions, the interviewee must select the parts of the question that he/she wants to address. This lessens your control over the answer.

Complex questions invite complex answers

- **Avoid the 'laundry list' syndrome**
  Make a checklist for the questions, but leave room for improvisation and real interaction with the respondent. Be aware that the respondent, who is confronted by an interviewer that goes through a detailed checklist, easily loses interest. Always try to be spontaneous and create a good atmosphere for the interview. First ask for information, then for opinions.
- **Do not try to be too clever**
  The simplest comments and questions are often the best. Use phrases like: 'If I understand you correctly...' (this is called: *echoing*), 'I don't understand this yet...'.
- **Never overlook unclear or inadequate answers**
  Repeat the question and/or in a different way. Do not be afraid to ask 'stupid' questions. If you allow vague answers to pass unchallenged, your respondent might continue giving superficial information and the interview will be less useful.
- **Avoid judgemental remarks**
  Do not criticise or make judgmental *remarks* during the conversation. 'I find what you say ridiculous...'. If you do this, your role will change in the interview and make the interviewee 'suddenly' feel observed and analysed. The interviewee becomes more cautious and less co-operative.
  - *Try not to judge* the interviewee in moral terms like 'good/bad', 'fair/unfair', 'positive/negative'.
  - This may also become apparent in your body-language (frowning when you do not approve). The willingness of your interviewee to respond to your questions will reduce.
  - Remember: scientific interviewing requires that you first get the relevant information and only later evaluate it.

Beware of reductive listening (⊕D3)

- **Preconditions for being critical**
  If you want to be *explicit and critical* use one of the following techniques:
  - ask 'do I understand you correctly...?' You repeat the remark and your interviewees are confronted with their own opinion (at least your interpretation of it);
  - ask whether the opinion expressed may change when other variables are added;
  - ask your respondent what would happen if you reverse the same reasoning;
  - depersonalise the question: 'the newspaper revealed...'
- **Pause for thought**
  For example, in the case of laconic – brief, concise – answers use two techniques:
  - pause and wait to see whether he/she would like to expand on the brief reply;
  - repeat the answer, but now with a question mark (echoing).

Echoing Example

'Can you tell me about what you do in your spare time?'; 'Visiting art exhibitions.' **(Pause!)** 'Visiting art exhibitions...?' Now the person may still just say 'yes', but it is more probable that he/she will go into more detail

(cf. Mackenzie, McDonnell, 1985: 20)

■ **Preparing next question**

Should you *prepare the next question while you listen*? This is not really wise to do. You may lose concentration and miss what the interviewee is saying. You will be less able to ask follow-up questions on the answer given. See television interviews for examples where the interviewer simply asks the questions that have been written by an editor. The effect on the interviewee is disastrous. The interview will be 'sub'optimal and probably a waste of time for both parties.

3 Should problems occur...

Problems are bound to occur in most interviews. Table D.4b lists a number of situations that might occur during the interview and suggestions on what you might do.

Table D.4b Problems and Solutions

Problem	Reaction
Respondent is *not telling the truth*	Do not say so, be patient – try to include some control answers and obtain the information from another angle or another source.
Respondent is *talking too much*	Do not intervene too abruptly, try to come back to the original issues, remind the respondent of them and return to another point.
Respondent *questions your legitimacy*	In the event that the respondent questions your legitimacy: stay calm and refer to your contact person, promise secrecy or promise to send the text of the interview for a check.
Respondent *asks your opinion about a question*	Do not be afraid to give it, but do not be too blunt. Not giving your opinion could make you appear less trustworthy and the atmosphere of the interview may be less positive.
Respondent *starts giving answers to later questions*	Let this happen, but keep control over the interview. Redirect the questions back to the original sequence.
Respondent does *not give an answer* to the question	In case it is one of your priority questions, rephrase it and repeat the question as many times as needed to get an answer.

Respondent *takes charge of the interview*	This is a sign that you have been too passive in the interview. Try to regain the initiative by asking direct questions that are directly followed by further questions. Do not give the interviewee breathing space until you have regained the initiative.
Respondent *is not very talkative*	Silence can be caused by many factors. Try to figure out what is the matter and act accordingly: in case of not knowing the answer, give further clarification; in case of not willing to give answers, try to adopt another perspective on the question (for instance by referring to what you already know). Do not fill the silence left by your respondent yourself – you might end up doing an interview with yourself.
Respondent is *hostile*	Show that you understand that the topic or the occasion might be difficult. You can also ask the respondent directly whether he/she would like to proceed another time and finish the interview for the moment.

D5 Body Language

The way people communicate provides an important source of additional information about the contents of their speech. Communication methods do not only refer to presentation techniques, but also to the 'physical attitude' of a person. Posture and specific gestures are also known as non-verbal behaviour or 'body language'. Correctly interpreting body language, therefore, also constitutes a listening skill. During lectures, body language adds meaning to the spoken word; with interviews and in group interactions it is even possible to gain additional information through the manipulation of the body language of the person you talk with.

The function and meaning of body language can differ from culture to culture. It is not always easy to interpret what you observe. But this does not lessen the importance of body language. A perceptive observer is a more sophisticated listener (Table D.5). A more sophisticated listener will react at the right moment, and can give more appropriate feedback to the presenter. Equally important: if you become a skilled observer you can learn more about your own body language. You will be better able to use and control your own gestures and physical attitude, which fundamentally contributes to your speech and management abilities in general (➔F9).

Table D.5 Interpreting body language

	Possible observations
■ Face/head	Be realistic about what you can deduce from facial expressions: they give a clue as to *what* people are thinking or feeling. It is very difficult to interpret a facial expression. Different people see different things. Facial expressions combined with different body posture can have different meanings. Listeners appreciate it most when the presenter appears relaxed and smiles occasionally (not all the time) as an indication that the presenter enjoys lecturing or giving the interview, wants to enter into a discussion and understands the topic.
■ Eyes	If the presenter or respondent does not manage to establish eye contact with you, this might indicate that he/she does not really want/dare to communicate with you. The presenter could be very nervous due to a lack of experience, and/or he/she may not fully understand the topic. People that do not look you in the eye might also just be shy. People that are lying tend to look upwards – for a moment. The function of eye contact, however, really differs per culture. In some cultures it is not considered polite to have direct eye contact. In this case people look down (and certainly not up).
■ Voice	There need not be a direct relationship between voice and personality or contents. But, when speakers raise or lower their voice or put question marks in their wording, you could assume that this is done intentionally. The voice, in this case, is intended to support and reinforce the message. Statements that end with a higher tone (question mark) suggest that the person is not very sure of the topic or the argument.

■ Hands	Standing or sitting with folded arms, hands held tightly, or in the pockets, in principle always creates distance from the audience. It can be a sign of disdain, of insecurity, or both. A presenter who places his/her hands in front of the mouth shows insecurity. This may also be true for 'big gestures'.
■ Feet	If the presenter crosses his/her feet or moves them regularly in an uncoordinated manner, this signals insecurity.
■ Clothing	Clothing and accessories provide the most information about the impression that people want to make. It shows part of their personality, but not necessarily the most important part (➲B13). Be careful with your inferences.
■ Posture	Guirdham (1990) points out that body movements indicate how *strongly* people feel something. Presenters who pace anxiously in front of the audience are not thought to be very convincing. But presenters who rarely move, with blocked shoulders, have to add a variety of facial expressions and hand movements. Otherwise they show that they do not really want to 'reach' the audience.

When interacting with a smaller group of people, body language can give you vital information regarding their thoughts about the meeting, and the degree to which they accept what you are saying. The more there is at stake (interviews, decision-making meetings) the more important body language becomes. Controlling your body language is particularly important when there is only a small space between each of the participants. Each person has a sort of 'territory' that you intrude upon if you come within touching distance of someone else. Be aware of this. The less you control your body language, the more your gestures will be seen as an 'intrusion'. This intrusion will immediately (often unintentionally) lessen their willingness to engage in an open discussion with you. This holds true even in cultures that are more tactile, i.e. in which the physical distance between people is generally small and people touch each other more regularly.

Interpreting and manipulating gestures

The body language of the people who you speak to, or bargain with, gives you an indication as to whether the discussion is going in a positive or negative direction:

- **Negative**. Everyone knows that there are many gestures that you can use to make clear that you are *not really interested*: looking out of the window, feet on the table, head bent, and so forth. Consider carefully how the person who you are talking to responds to changes in your behaviour: for example when you change your tone, or address the person more directly, or when you ask a different type of question. Train yourself to distinguish between the body language associated with being physically tired and that associated with being tired of a discussion. If you are unsure, check by asking, for example, if the person 'has had a bad night'. This question is acceptable and gives information on how to interpret the body language of the other.
- **Positive**. Not many people are aware of the function body language can also have for the *confirmation* of an opinion. When the person you are talking to adopts the same gestures as you (arms crossed, position of the head and/or upper body).

Copying behaviour can be seen as a confirmation of your position even if your conversation partner is actually saying something else. In order to check who is copying whose body language, change your posture in a subtle way (change the position of your hands) and see whether the other person does the same. If conversation partners copy your body language you can be quite sure that you are trusted and even liked *or* that they are also aware of the positive function of body language. In the case of the latter you are playing a different bargaining game. Be aware of this possibility, otherwise you may think that different rules apply.

Interpreting and manipulating positions

The place that people choose in a room or at a table gives you an indication about the role(s) that they would like to play. Observe who takes the position at the head of the table, who waits until everyone else is seated, and so forth. If you know people for a longer period of time, you will notice that they often sit in the same chair or next to the same person. But as with the observations mentioned above, people who are aware of the signals you give by the position you take in a room, may also intentionally take another position, in order to influence the other participants or the meeting. The chairperson who does not sit at the head of the table is probably trying to alter status and become less 'visible', in order to make other participants more active and involved. Try to check during the conversation whether the initial impression (of leadership respectively of lower status) was really accurate or just body language intended to influence the discussion.

Problem solving

If you meet the same group often, and would like to break through established role patterns, it may be worthwhile to ask the participants to change their position in the room regularly. Swapping seats in a room can help create a 'fresh' perspective and contribute to solving inter-personal conflicts (⊕G2, G8, G11)

Processing the information that you gather in an interview is part and parcel of constructive listening skills. An interview is only finished *after* you have written up the notes that you took. Seven principles guide this process.

Seven principles for successfully processing interviews

1 Get skilled in making reproducible notes and abbreviations while listening
2 Conduct and process interviews in the language of the interviewee
3 Quickly write a first account of the interview
4 Check for reductive listening after the interview
5 Be disciplined when writing up a sequence of interviews
6 In principle, do not send your transcript to your respondents
7 Send a thank-you note

1 Make reproducible notes while listening

Making notes while conducting an interview requires a lot of practice. You should be able to concentrate on what is being said while you are writing. The use of abbreviations is often necessary in order not to be writing all the time. Get used to a number of abbreviations and symbols in order to be able to decipher different types of notes (➔C10):

■ Use special codes (for example, ✻, #) in the margin indicating that this is your opinion – not the interviewee's.
■ If the respondent makes an interesting remark, use quotation marks when you register it. However, do not quote the respondent literally in your research report. The quotation marks should serve to indicate the relevance of the information to you at a later point in time.
■ You might wish to write your commentary in your mother tongue if you conduct an interview in a foreign language (in order to clearly distinguish your own notes from the transcript of the interview in the original language).
■ Indicate immediately, in your notes, when you find a remark important or perhaps questionable. If you do this clearly, it will be easier to return to this point before finishing the interview.

2 Conduct and process interviews in the language of the interviewee

If you conduct an interview in a foreign language, write the notes *in the language* of the interview. People who have insufficient practice and in particular insufficient knowledge of the written language may hesitate to do this. Written language is always more difficult to master than the spoken word. But since you are the only person reading it afterwards, perfect spelling is not necessary. If you are unsure about the spelling of a word use *phonetic spelling* and later reconstruct the original wording. It will increase the pace of the interview. Respondents appreciate speed in interviews the most. The alternative is much less appealing.

If you translate everything as you write, the following can happen:

- It will be far more *difficult to grasp the meaning* of what is said. You will find it very difficult to concentrate on what the respondent is saying and to ask relevant questions.
- Furthermore, you *do not have enough time* to take in everything which is said. Too much time is spent on the translation.
- You will never be sure that what you have written is actually what was said or is the result of a *translation error*. This is especially true with words that can be interpreted in a variety of different ways and that you may have misunderstood during the interview. If you have not written down the original word, you will be unable to discover the mistake.

3 Quickly write a (first) account of the interview

If you take notes during an interview it is important to write up those notes as soon as possible afterwards. If you wait too long it may be difficult for example to read your handwriting and/or understand the notes correctly (was this my own commentary or something that the respondent actually said?). Immediately after the interview try to find a place nearby where you can write up the first draft of your notes. Go through them and rewrite those passages that are difficult to read. Make a clear distinction between your own commentary and what you have heard from the interviewee. Work through the following points:

- **Assign importance**. Indicate which passages are of particular importance. Underline them with a coloured pen so that when you read the interview your attention will immediately focus on these parts.
- **Identify your own commentary**. Go through the codes in the margins and make sure that they are clear. Add additional commentary if you think that it is appropriate.
- **List material received**. Always make a separate list of the material (books, articles, brochures) that you have received. Soon you will not know which sources you collected yourself, and which ones were supplied by the respondent. The more generous the respondent has been, the more the same will be expected of you according to the principles of barter (➔A12).
- **Formulate conclusions**. Make a short decision list. You could use a separate box in which you note:
  (a) what you promised to do;
  (b) what other appointments you have made;
  (c) a number of other conclusions that you would like to make instantly.
- **Specify your impressions**. Write down some of your immediate impressions regarding the effectiveness of the interview, and give yourself feedback on the effectiveness of your interviewing style.

4 Check for reductive listening after the interview

A good interviewer is aware of reductive listening (➔D3). It can seriously limit the effectiveness of an interview. In handling this problem, use the reflective circle (➔A3): first analyse possible reasons for reductive listening (preferably before the interview), then put these out of your mind during the interview, in order to give the respondent the chance to offer information without biases entering your mind while you are listening. This information can be evaluated once the interview is over. When you elaborate the interview, evaluate *ex-ante* and list additional judgements that might have popped up during the interview (➔D3). Confront your observations with what you have really heard and try to be more objective when assessing the information.

5 Be disciplined when writing up a sequence of interviews

- Never wait long before writing up your interview notes in a presentable, typed format. Respecting this rule becomes more critical when you do a sequence of interviews in a short period of time. Always write up the notes on the *day* of the interview.
- If you let two or three days pass by, you will probably experience difficulty reading your own handwriting or you will be unable to remember all of the things that you have not written down. But if you had rewritten the notes immediately you would have been able to remember these things without difficulty.
- After several days, other impressions and information, which you receive from other people, begin to mix with your interview results, creating an enormous problems in identifying from whom you received the information.
- Writing up the notes during a trip gives you the satisfaction of having your report finished before – or on the same day as – your arrival. Once you come back to your own country, it is far more difficult to write up the notes because your familiar surroundings will create new distracting demands. You will have told the story of your trip several times already.

Writing down what you have already presented to people is repetitious, boring and therefore creates motivation problems.

6 In principle, do not send your interview transcript to your respondent

It seems polite, but it is rarely of any use to send the actual transcript that you made during the interview to your respondent. Your research is seldom aimed at quoting people, but the respondent might – on second thought – want to correct the researcher for the wrong reasons. For instance for political reasons (slip of the tongue) or because the statement on paper looks stronger than when spoken. The correction process consequently can become part of a bargaining process rather than a simple 'checking' process. The researcher could then be forced to change the text even when the transcript adequately covers what has been discussed, and even when the alterations do not change the function of the interview for the final research (➔D2). This is a waste of time for both people. Remember that each answer that is misunderstood will always remain your responsibility. As a researcher you can never blame the interviewee as a journalist can.

7 Send a thank-you note

As soon as you have written up the interview, write a thank-you note to the interviewee. Clarify what they can expect (when will the report be finished and sent to them). If you have additional questions, put them in this letter. In principle, always send the results of your completed research work to the persons you have interviewed and ask for feedback.

Attending lectures is often the only way to get information on particular subjects, or be able to interact with well-known (thus rarely available) people. Attending lectures requires a particular kind of constructive listening skills. The basic attitude is that you take responsibility for the outcome of the lecture: by asking questions, through appropriate preparation and an active listening posture. You get out of a lecture what you put into it. The listener is always 'co-producer'. If you are unaware of this process many lectures will be a waste of time. If you have difficulties to concentrate for the duration of a presentation (e.g. if you are prone to daydream) train yourself to prolong your listening skills. Lapses in your concentration are not necessarily caused by the lecturer. Your concentration increases when you follow seven rules: (1) properly prepare mentally, (2) read in advance, (3) be actively involved, (4) adopt an active posture, (5) ask questions and (6) always evaluate.

> **The more 'actively' you attend a lecture – the more you are 'involved' in the lecture – the greater the benefit to you. Work on being a 'co-producer' during lectures.**

1 Prepare mentally

Always prepare yourself for the lecture. At the beginning of a lecture (or a series of lectures) ask questions such as: what can I expect: what will probably be the main points of the lecture? What do I know already? Particularly important: what do I want to know? Even ask this question if you are required to attend a lecture as part of a course, for example. There will always be some topics that are of more interest to you than others. You have to prepare to identify them in time. Asking these questions will only take a few minutes, once you have taken your seat to concentrate on them. Remember: you are going to spend a few hours that you could otherwise have spent going to the theatre or studying the literature! *Write down what you want to know* on top of your notebook, and check whether these questions are addressed regularly, and if they are answered by the lecturer.

2 Read in advance

In order to prepare yourself properly for the lecture, read the required literature for the session. It is as simple as that! In the event of a guest lecturer you should try to read an article that he/she has written, or an interview with him/her. Most of the time this information is given to you by the organisers beforehand. Many students complain that they do not have time to read all of the literature. This could be an indication of a high reading burden, but could also indicate that you are not managing your time properly (➔B8). Try to find out which reason is more important. In any case, skim read the literature in preparation for the lecture (➔C11). Otherwise, it could be a waste of time going to the presentation. You will be unable to make a distinction between new findings and summaries of previous literature. Being unprepared makes it more difficult to engage in intelligent discussions. You will be afraid to ask questions, so you remain silent and in doing so also influence the nature of the lecture. If you do not read the literature, the willingness of the teacher to enter into a debate with you will rapidly diminish.

When should you consider *not* attending a lecture?
- When you have more difficulty processing information that is given verbally than written information.
- When you think that the lecturer is not able to communicate well.
- When the approach chosen by the lecturer is vague and abstract.
- When the lecturer does not appear to be sufficiently informed him/herself.
- When the lecturer merely reproduces a written text.
- When the lecturer progresses too quickly and makes it impossible to think about the information received.
- When the lecture proceeds too slowly, making it tiring to follow.
- When you are not able to influence the lecturer's speed so that it corresponds to your needs.
- When the auditorium is not suitable for the sessions and no other rooms are available.
- When little or no time has been allowed for discussion or clarification questions.

Source: Junne, 1976:20

3 Be actively involved

Get used to listening and taking notes simultaneously (➲C10, D6). If possible ask during or after the session whether the transparencies or slides are available. But continue to take detailed notes even if you have the transparencies. Your concentration will inevitably lapse if you do not take active responsibility for digesting the information by documenting your thoughts, questions and criticisms at the same time. Do not take the organisation of the lecture for granted. If you think that an alternative method of organisation could increase the effectiveness of the lecture, say so. It is useless to spend time on boring listening (and presentation) exercises.

4 Adopt an active listening posture

If you want to be actively involved in a lecture, there should not be a big distance between you and the lecturer. Therefore, sit as close as possible to the front of the room. You will not only show your interest, but you will also give the lecturer the chance to keep you interested by addressing you more directly and/or responding to your body language. The way you sit has two effects: (1) it affects the way that you listen, (2) it indicates your level of interest to the lecturer. Both effects are often mutually reinforcing. If you do not sit upright your concentration will easily lapse, and because you look disinterested the lecturer will see this and also become less interested, which in turn reinforces your impression of disinterest. Increase your concentration. Do not sit on the edge of your chair or lean backwards.

5 Ask questions

Be prepared to ask the lecturer questions. Your concentration increases because of the adrenaline running through your veins. Make sure, however, that this physical reaction does not affect your ability to listen to what is actually being said (⊕D4). Asking the person next to you a short question should not be a problem either. It could even show the lecturer that you are paying attention to what is being said. If you begin a long conversation with your neighbour, the message to the lecturer is more one of disinterest. Think for a minute what this attitude might do to the lecturer's motivation. Constructive listening implies that you are capable and willing to put yourself in the place of the lecturer. Think, for instance, about the dilemma that the lecturer faces when mixed signals come from the audience (which is often the case): one part is leaning back and talking to each other, while the other is paying attention and making notes. Should the lecturer only address the section of the audience which is actively involved (running the risk of increasing the rumour) or explicitly addressing the uninterested section (running the risk of boring the interested listener)? Try to establish a positive interaction with the rest of the audience as well as with the lecturer.

6 Always evaluate: the one-minute paper

Take one minute at the end of the lecture to consider (1) what you have learned, (2) what you did not like, and (3) what you have missed in the lecture. Think about what you expected and what you learned. This technique is known as the *'one-minute paper'*. Following lengthy research on how to increase the effectiveness of the teaching system, Harvard University started to ask students to write a short paper in the last minute of the lecture (Light, 1990: 36). In this paper students can express their opinion on the lectures offered, and give suggestions for improvements. By writing a one-minute paper after every lecture, students develop a routine of systematic and prompt evaluation on the content of the lecture. It increases their awareness immensely. The papers can be handed to the lecturer anonymously, who then gets an excellent, and immediate, evaluation of the lecture with sometimes surprising suggestions. The Harvard papers do not have a standard format – other than the time restraint of one minute. The one-minute paper sheet, shown below, does have a standard format to serve as an example. A short checklist for the didactic and rhetorical qualities of the presenter has been added in order to make the paper more useful for the teacher. The introduction to the F-series explains the categories (logos, ethos, pathos) listed.

The one-minute paper

(1) What is the big point I learned in class today?

_____

_____

_____

(2) What is the main, unanswered question I leave class with today? _____

_____

_____

_____

Presenter's rhetorical qualities

	Good	Mediocre	Bad
Logos			
Ethos			
Pathos			

Listening and observing in a systematic way can be used as input for a variety of feedback aims. It can be an input for the evaluation of presentation skills. It can be used to receive feedback either individually or from a group. Listening can in a particular way also function as input for your own argumentation and writing skills.

1 Listening to give constructive feedback

Constructive communication is 'owned', not 'disowned' (Whetten et al., 2004: 248). It requires that individuals that engage in giving feedback do this as involved persons with an own opinion ('I think'), rather than as an uninvolved 'judges' with a statement ('we think', 'it is') (⊕G9). Owned communication is assertive communication (⊕B2). It focuses on the problem (an effective presentation, for instance), not on the person. The art of giving constructive feedback to others requires that one is capable of listening and observing in a systematic and constructive way. Systematically listening to a lecture also provides input for your own presentation skills. Constructive feedback always consists first of a number of more or less neutral observations, followed by a personal assessment of the effectiveness of the message. For your observations, you can use very detailed analysis schemes, but basically you (1) try to figure out whether you could distinguish a clear opening, argument and conclusions, and (2) whether that was supported by verbal and non-verbal behaviour as well as the effective use of tools. For your personal assessment you ask yourself: is it clear what the presenter wanted to get across, did it raise my interest, and was I inspired by the presentation [⊕⊕.skillsheets.com for an analysis form].

2 Constructive listening to feedback of others

The art of receiving feedback requires a specific intellectual attitude (⊕B13). But it also requires a particular listening attitude. If you adopt a non-constructive listening attitude towards your feedback givers, you might discourage them to be completely honest and/or to give you feedback again. The following listening pointers apply to receiving oral feedback:

o   keep calm, listen carefully and concentrated;
o   do not interrupt the person offering the feedback;
o   always make notes (in order to show the feedback giver that you are serious);
o   adopt an active listening posture (lean forward to show that you are interested; look open and receptive to the feedback);
o   do not act defensively (do not say 'yes... but'); never become angry at the person giving the feedback; do not take it personally;
o   concentrate on the words that are being said, instead of on the way that they are being said, or on (your perception of) any hidden messages;
o   summarize the feedback in your own words;
o   when confronted with negative feedback, try to get the person to specify and make concrete;
o   always welcome serious feedback, and always thank the feedback giver afterwards.

3 Listening to constructive group discussions on your writing

A productive method for discussing a paper that you have written is to organise a group session and let the members of the group talk about the paper. They should discuss what they would do if they were responsible for the text. The author is 'forced' to listen and can not express defensive and rationalisation behaviour. If the author could actively participate in the discussion, the feedback from the group would be affected, often negatively. If the actual author of the paper is only able to respond at the end of the session, the whole session may become more positive and more output oriented. The writer must be patient. This is often very difficult. But it can also be very rewarding, because the other participants have much more room to come up with interesting suggestions.

4 Listening to yourself

You will often get new ideas, especially during a discussion. Sometimes these ideas will be triggered by listening to other people, but it can also happen that you 'hear yourself' saying something that you have not previously thought about. There is no reason to assume that you have internalised such an argument the moment you use it. Do not hesitate to say to the person(s) who you are speaking to: 'this is an interesting thought, I'd better write it down immediately!' If you do not do this, there is a considerable chance that you will not be able to remember your own argument, not even within half an hour after the discussion took place.

Constructive listening is taking responsibility for the outcome of communication processes. Even in case you are only listening to a lecturer you influence the mode of communication and ultimately the extent to which you can benefit from the lecture. The same is true for interviewing as part of a research project. Whereas listening in general serves as an input for your own learning, applying the principles of constructive listening considerably increases the effectiveness of your efforts. This pertains in particular to more social activities like management and presentations. Management research has shown that effective listening is the single most important skill in becoming a good manager (Whetten et al., 2004: 251).

1 Always prepare: you always get out of your listening what you put into it
2 Really listen, do not judge or interrupt: keep an open mind
3 Beware of your co-producer status in the speech of another
4 Time your questions well
4 Supportive listening: show empathy, concentration and interest
6 Become skilled in listening and note-taking at the same time
7 Notice the importance of posture and non-verbal communication: show an active posture yourself
8 Be prepared to give feedback and do not immediately come with solutions
9 Always digest the information immediately after the meeting

1 The preconditions for constructive listening

People are able to listen at the rate of 500 words a minute, while speaking at a normal rate only constitutes 125 words a minute. This explains why people can communicate with more people at the same time. Many people's occupations necessitate a great deal of listening. Executive managers, for example, spend around half of their time listening (Keefe, 1971: 10). While passively listening to one speaker, however, a person can concentrate on average for only a few minutes. There are other problems related to listening skills. In the bargaining society people tend to think of their own arguments during the time they are supposed to listen to someone else. This negatively affects their listening absorption capacity. People are often more focussed on what they are saying than on what they are hearing in return (Lewis and Graham, 2003). Multitasking in addition also seriously lowers the absorptive (listening) capacity of people. An often heard complaint therefore is that people 'do not listen anymore'. The first principle for constructive communication therefore is that you are aware of the importance of listening and start creating the preconditions for effective listening. This requires solid preparation (⊕D2), and a real focus on concentrated listening with an open mind and a minimum of judgement (⊕D3, D7).

We were given two ears but only one mouth. This is because God knew that listening was twice as hard as talking—CASAA Student Activity Source book

2 Listening as Co-production

The amount of time that most people can listen effectively depends as much on the presentation and speaking skills of the 'sender' of a message (⊕F-series) as on the listening skills of the individual 'receiver'. Constructive listening is the opposite of reductive listening and requires 'co-production' of the spoken word in at least two ways.

- By asking *questions* at the right (or wrong) time listeners can influence the direction of the speaker so that it becomes more (or less) useful for themselves. Listeners make clear what their level of understanding is or what they would like to hear by the kind of questions they ask. The presenter in turn can produce a more customer-oriented speech.
- The listener's *body language* presents the speaker with positive or negative feedback signals, which are also bound to influence the spoken word. Effective interpersonal communication develops when there is 'congruence' in both verbal and non-verbal communication (Whetten et al., 2004: 238).

Effective listening in interviews, conversations and in lectures ultimately depends upon the ability to ask appropriate questions. Many people – in particular in bigger audiences – are very hesitant to ask questions, because they fear that they might look foolish. The fear of asking a 'stupid' question is present in all of us.

A Dutch proverb states: 'one fool can ask more questions than one hundred wise men can answer'. But a Chinese aphorism states: 'who asks a question might look like a fool for five minutes, those who do not ask might remain fools for the rest of their lives'.

Few listeners are aware of their 'co-producer' status nor do they actively work on it. On the basis of social interaction –mainly by making use of focused questions – you can increase the relevance of the information given. Co-produced listening becomes 'constructive communication' in case the listener can show sufficient empathy so that the other is feeling understood. The two invest in a conversation and thereby in each other (Harris, 1997). Constructive listening skills are the building blocks for effective communication, even amongst rivals. The second set of principles for constructive listening therefore relates to the way you behave in a meeting: by showing empathy, applying an appropriate and active listening posture (⊕D5), and by asking questions in an appropriate manner and at the appropriate time (⊕D4).

3 Listening as a technique: balancing listening and writing

Constructive listening skills require substantial practical experience in efficiently registering the information received. For example by taking notes during a conversation, which in turn can lead to better questions and improve the conversation. Taking notes also keeps the listener active and prolongs the span of concentration. The ability to balance listening and writing skills is particularly relevant when carrying out interviews. Interviewing involves talking and listening at the appropriate time: at the start of an interview you talk more (20% listening, 80% talking), whereas when the interview really begins to develop you should listen more (80% listening, 20% posing questions). Afterwards, the effectiveness of your listening skills is shown by the written interpretation of what you have heard. Taking minutes in a meeting could also be considered to be a specialised listening skill, but since this is part of a decision-making process, minute-taking will be treated as a management skill (➔G8). The third set of constructive listening therefore consists of your technical skills in efficiently digesting the information during and immediately after the meeting, while using it as input for further research (➔D6) by yourself or for others (➔D8).

D2 Preparing Interviews

Personal interviews, as opposed to questionnaires (➔A8), are an excellent way of getting primary information or help you with your research outline and methodology. Interviewing means listening. Gaining the appropriate information is dependent on the questions that you ask, the aims that you set for the interview and the degree to which you can control the circumstances under which the interview is carried out. This Skill Sheet reveals the different functions that interviews can have in the various phases of a research project and how to prepare an interview.

1 Stages of functionality in interviews

Researchers often carry out interviews with the wrong people and during an inappropriate stage of their research project. If you are in the process of completing your research, it is not very functional to speak with a 'generalist' who brings up a variety of additional questions which broaden the focus of the research. Generalists may also be found in the higher levels of an organisation. It can be more useful to talk to middle-managers, who may be just as well informed on a particular topic, but, even more importantly, may have more time available. In the initial phase of your research, however, generalists can be extremely helpful. Make a *distinction* between the different phases of your research planning and the nature of the interviews (➔A5):

- During the design phase, at the *beginning* of your research project:
  - Find out whether your particular research question is shared by others: if you hear from your respondent that there are more people working on the same research question, the feasibility of your research will be bigger (➔A6) due to the increased number of potential interviewees and additional sources.
  - Develop new ideas, add a hypothesis to your original idea.
  - Try to find further reading, or where to obtain relevant information.
  - Look for sponsorship possibilities (which will perhaps lead to additional questions).
- As you carry out the research:
  - Get the information that you require; make sure that this information cannot be obtained through publicly available sources!
  - Find out the names of the people who can give you a precise answer to your particular question.
- *After you have written your report*, but before printing or publication:
  - Check the way that you have presented and interpreted the information (➔A16).

Series E Writing

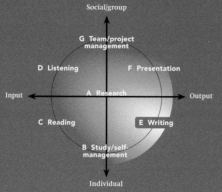

The Reflective Cycle of Writing with Power

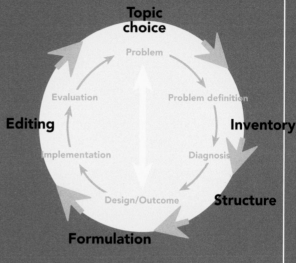

	Inventory	Structure	Formulation	Editing
E1 Principles of Powerful Writing	■			
E2 Plagiarism	■			
E3 Reporting: Opening Parts	■	■		
E4 Reporting: Main Body		■		
E5 Reporting: Final Parts		■	■	
E6 Argumentation		■	■	
E7 Rewriting		■	■	
E8 Style: Common Errors			■	
E9 Style: Phrasing Problems			■	
E10 Spelling: Common Errors			■	
E11 Quoting and Paraphrasing			■	
E12 References			■	
E13 Abbreviations and Acronyms			■	■
E14 Tables, Figures and Boxes				■
E15 Bibliography				■
E16 Layout				■

Writing Skill Levels

Level 1
- Writing simple texts with acceptable argumentation
- The writing *process* is key (formulation gets most attention)
- Essay-oriented
- Sources are not systematically revealed
- Link between reading, self-management and writing: learning how to come to a well structured piece

Level 2
- Writing a solid line of argument, based on a clear question, in an acceptable amount of time.
- The *argumentation* is key (structure gets most attention)
- Group Research becomes paper and case study-oriented
- Most sources are revealed and importance of listing sources is understood
- Growing attention for layout and solid editing

Level 3
- Writing a publishable text, based on clear questions or hypotheses
- The sophistication of the *product* and its *contents* are key (all phases get equal attention)
- Individual research paper-oriented
- All sources are systematically revealed
- Increased proficiency in English writing (as the lingua franca of science)

Level 4
- Writing applicable texts for specific audiences
- The *impact* of the writing is key (all phases are important, but often in a much shorter time span)
- Individual policy paper-oriented
- Sources need not always be revealed (for instance to protect an 'inside' source). However, the writer understands very well the need for utmost integrity and solid writing skills

Writing should be aimed at having an effect on the reader. In this case the principles of 'writing with power' apply (Elbow, 1981). Before you start writing you should have an idea of the output you are aiming for, and the problem that you are addressing. If you have decided what your end-product will be, what part of that end-product (in the case of a bigger piece such as a thesis) you are working on, and the audience you aim at, you develop the text in four consecutive phases: (1) inventory, (2) structure, (3) formulation and (4) editing. Writing with power is a dialectical process in which you alternate between writing and (re)reading, argumentation and editing, searching and synthesizing. According to the rules of 'writing with power' each of the four phases takes approximately the same time. Only when you take sufficient (relative) time for each of these phases can your writings become powerful. This is independent of the time at your disposal. The principles of powerful writing apply equally for a one hour column, as for a one year thesis. The same rules apply for writing a joint paper, but with group papers each phase creates a different group dynamism that requires additional project management skills (➔G1, G7).

---

1   Think! Sloppy writing is the result of sloppy thinking

2   Powerful writing is rewriting, good rewriting is rereading

3   Take sufficient time for sufficient brainstorming

4   Be consistent: whatever referencing method, layout or writing style you use, use it consistently

5   Powerful writing requires managing the different roles in the writing process: inventor, researcher, writer, editor

6   The occasion defines the most appropriate writing form

7   Avoiding plagiarism is only possible if you understand what it is and why it is bad for you

8   Always reveal your sources

9   If your reader does not understand you, you have a problem: easy reading is hard writing

10 Mastering writing skills is nothing without contents, mastering contents without writing skills is not adequate either

1 Inventory (brainstorming)

Powerful writing first necessitates a *brainstorming* session with yourself. You *write down everything that comes into your mind* and that you have collected during preparatory research: ideas, quotes, statements and so forth. If you use a word processor, you should enter the information and ideas into your computer without looking at the style, logic, readability or the layout. The function of this phase is to provide space to write down everything that comes to mind regarding the problem. If you do this, this phase can become very creative. However, be aware of plagiarism in particular in this phase of your writing process. Always reveal the sources, always add quotation marks if you copy-paste a text (➔E2). Sloppy referencing leads to sloppy thinking, which in turn probably leads to sloppy argumentation and writing. It will in any case lead to sloppy science.

2 Structure (norming)

Secondly, powerful writing requires that you *read and judge* what you have written. Which arguments are good and which not so good; what is missing; what structure should your argument best adopt. The more structured you have worked during the inventory phase the easier this phase becomes. On the other hand, if you had had a strong brainstorming session in the first phase you may have come up with a number of comments that may destroy your original argumentation. Allow for these kinds of changes at this stage. If you work on a computer, print out the results of your brainstorming and cut the paper into pieces. Add numbers, or question marks. Do not work without a printout, because you lose the overview if you only have texts on your computer screen. With texts on paper it is easier to make notes and throw them away once you have finished. Whatever futurologists say, powerful writing – certainly as part of a research project – will probably never become a really 'paperless' affair.

The minimum requirements of academic writing

Mastering basic grammar is a minimum requirement without which communication becomes very difficult. The most basic academic writing skill is the systematic and correct *use and revelation of sources*: using references, (⊕E12) avoiding plagiarism (⊕E2), making good use of quotations and paraphrases (⊕E11), explaining abbreviations (⊕E13), making decent figures and tables (⊕E14), and compiling solid bibliographies (⊕E15). These skills are *minimum requirements* – nothing more, nothing less. Mastering them is only the start of writing a scientific report (an essay, a thesis), as mastering grammar is only the start of writing a novel. People have good reason to boast the *integrity* of a writer if information is presented as if it were entirely 'new' thoughts and data. Novelty is the (implicit) suggestion when you write without proper references. Use the following rule of thumb: on average 80-90% of what you write has already been thought of by other people. If you do not properly refer to the sources used, you can be reproached for *plagiarism*. But what is more important is that you lose track of your own intellectual learning process (⊕E2, E11). A reader who is confronted with writing that does not comply with these minimum writing requirements, will consider this a sign of sloppy thinking and therefore will not take the results very seriously (⊕A1).

3 Formulation (performing)

Thirdly, focus on writing once more. But writing now becomes for the most part *rewriting*. You have a clearer idea of your argument and the contributory parts. It is recommended that you leave the notes that you have made in the inventory phase and begin formulating the text again from scratch. You will find that your brainstorm notes are rarely written in a consistent style. It is often easier to write down the sentences anew than to enter into a laborious editing process with hastily written sentences. Therefore, the rewriting largely takes place in your head and is based on the notes on the paper. You will have to formulate many new pieces of text during this phase. Your brainstorm argumentation always contains gaps.

Aim at sentences of eighteen words, on average. Make the sentences that include the most important information as short as possible (below the average length). Sentences that contain additional information can be longer.

Much more than in the case of a novel, writing skills for research are a craft that almost everybody can (and should) learn. If you respect the minimum requirements incorporated in these and other series of the Skill Sheets collection you need not be brilliant in your way of expression to still be effective in the transmission of your message. Like in story-writing, however, be aware that easy reading is hard writing (Ernest Hemingway). Many students also often seem to forget that they write to be read. Observing the way that many scholars write you may wonder whether they would like to be read at all.

4 Editing

Lastly, you have now got a more or less structured argument, and the first attempt to put it into reasonable written language. Make a printout. This version can be considered your *first draft*. You can start rewriting the text itself in this phase, but this requires yet another state of mind. You must be able to read the text as if it were written by someone else. Because of the separation between the phases this is less difficult than it seems. In the previous phase you were 'someone else' because you aimed at a different product. Now you are the editor of the text. An editor checks the text in terms of at least three aspects: (1) logic, (2) readability and spelling and (3) layout. A good editor will not be impressed by the 'darlings' of the writer if they do not contribute to these aspects. Editing the text can take several rounds of reading and rewriting, of rereading and rewriting. But the basic structure of your argument and paper will probably not be altered. Otherwise the various phases become mixed up, and you run the risk of creating a (mental) state of chaos. It will no longer matter how many times you rewrite the text: your end-product will remain weak.

- Writing means: reading critically as if it were someone else who wrote the text.
- Writing with power means: kill your darlings!
- Writing with computers means: using the [delete] command.

Powerful Writing Formats

Powerful writing critically depends on your ability to match the content and style of the message with the intended audience and the occasion. Choosing an appropriate format for your writing therefore requires that you have a good understanding of what you (can) aim at in relation to the particular strengths and weaknesses of the format. The most common writing formats and their functions are:

o **Summaries and book reviews** (as an input, for instance, for your literature study)
o **Essays** (how to write a good and influential essay)
o **Letters and Faxes** (how to communicate efficiently what you want)
o **Letter of application/CV** (in order to get a job)
o **Internship/trainee reports** (how to check whether your internship has been effective for you and for the organisation)
o **Thesis proposals** (how to write a proposal that is not only informative for your supervisor, but also helps you in focusing on the main line of your thesis during the writing process)
o **Internet** (what kind of 'netiquette' should you adopt to communicate effectively)
o **Press releases** (how to efficiently get the gist of a message across on one page)
o **Policy Memo** (how to effectively support or trigger a decision-making process)

Each of these formats is further elaborated and supplemented with concrete tips on the Skill Sheets website [⊕➔www.skillsheets.com]

Plagiarism is an increasingly serious phenomenon in all parts of society. It is best to acknowledge that only a relatively small part of the ideas that you express in your writings are your own 'inventions'. Good researchers make active use of the information of others. Critical and independent thinking (as an important aspect of scientific behaviour) begins with a critical *awareness* of the sources you use and refer to (➔E11, E12). You should *not* be discouraged to incorporate the concepts of others into your thinking. On the contrary, you must refer to the proper sources in the correct manner. There is a famous saying that *'we are all dwarfs, but we can stand on the shoulders of giants'*. This means that we can only hope to add a small contribution to already existing knowledge accumulated by the intellectual giants before us. So you will take over ideas and quotes from a large number of people and sources. Plagiarism, therefore, is not the act of taking over the work of others. Plagiarism in general is a matter of incorrect quotations and paraphrasing (➔E11). There are easy techniques to remedy that problem. Tutors often find out that students are often not particularly aware of what plagiarism in fact is. This Skill Sheet explains what plagiarism is (and what it's not), what its causes are and how you can evade committing plagiarism.

1 What *is* plagiarism?

Texts written by others are not your texts. It sounds simple, but many persons do think this is not the case. These persons use your text or somebody else's to compose a report and 'forget' to refer to your text. It means pieces of text are copied and used without notice of the author, or are not referred to in a proper way. If that is the case, you can be accused of *plagiarism*. A number of examples of plagiarism are mentioned in the box below.

Plagiarism is:
- Copying somebody else's paper and delivering it as your own paper.
- Literally copying large parts of somebody else's text, with **or** without a proper reference.
- Literally copying of a paragraph or sentence of somebody else's text without quotes, with **or** without references.
- Copying of a sentence or paragraph, but changing some words, with **or** without references.
- Writing down a paragraph or sentence, while it is not clear whether it is your own work or somebody else's (for example, quotes are there, but just belonging to a part of the quoted text).
- Copying somebody else's text with incorrect sources (source is not traceable, source is false).

Source: Hand-out Jeroen Van Wijk

---

2 What is *not* plagiarism?

A number of examples can be given, in which cases it is **not** plagiarism:
• Writing down common knowledge; knowledge that is generally accepted.

- Quoting of quantitative data (graphics and tables). The source must be placed directly below the graphic or table.
- Quoting a number of sentences from another author put in brackets and directly followed by a correct (fully and directly traceable) reference (⊕E11).
- Paraphrasing: writing down an argument in your own words, your opinion, or a conclusion of another author, followed by a reference (⊕E11).

3 *Causes* of plagiarism

Plagiarism arises often because of simple carelessness, and sometimes through intentional deceit. Plagiarism through carelessness is foolish because you deprive yourself of the satisfaction of developing your own thoughts (you are unaware of the difference between your own and someone else's thoughts). Intentional deceit is not only wrong, but an intelligent reader often identifies this easily. Furthermore, a number of other causes for plagiarism exist:

- It has become very easy to use somebody else's text: computers, the Internet, scanners, speech conversion. The chance that somebody is caught is still small. But more anti-plagiarism measures are developed and introduced in the market. Furthermore, universities and commercial firms are developing programs to fight plagiarism. These universities/firms have created certain software programs that could be of help in the fight against plagiarism. Many anti-plagiarism software programs are available.
- Many online firms offer papers, summaries, and redaction support, against payment.
- Students/managers/consultants do not know precisely (or do not want to know) what is allowed or not.

> Another help could be the WayBackMachine on the website www.archive.org, which can trace many old websites (when somebody states that the source was real).

4 How to *avoid* plagiarism?

- Re-state the main story line of somebody else's paper in your own words. Do not watch the original text while typing. This is called paraphrasing.
- Quote or paraphrase never more than a brief paragraph (around ten to fifteen lines).
- Always include correct references.
- If you have found the perfect text, collect a number of the same texts and write your own text about the comparisons and differences.
- Do not make yourself responsible for judgements of others (or the bad sources others might have used and that you have probably have not checked).
- Do not accept any excuses to commit plagiarism. Such excuses do not exist.

> When you begin to quote other peoples' ideas *correctly,* you create a *justifiable use of sources.*

E3 Reporting: Opening Parts

Each report consists of three more or less 'standard' parts: the opening, the middle (main body) and the closing parts. This Skill Sheet specifies eleven components that could be included at the beginning of a report. Table E.3a makes a distinction between minimum requirements (components that should always be included) and optional requirements. For further illustrations and inspiration on layout and contents of other optional categories you can always use the books published by renowned publishing houses in your bookcase.

Table E.3a Components opening part report

Minimum requirement	Optional
1 Title Page	1a Copyright provisions
2 Table of contents	1b Dedication (for...)
3 Preface/acknowledgement	2a List of Figures/Tables*
4 Introduction	2b Foreword (written by someone else)
	2c Executive summary*
	3a List of abbreviations*
	3b Notes on contributors

* Optional, but strongly recommended

1 A title page (of a research report) includes:

- a clear and informative title; a descriptive subtitle: not more than 14-15 words in total;
- full name of the author(s), in principle in alphabetical sequence (➔C2);
- place and date (Month and Year) of publication;
- name of the supervisor(s);
- institutional affiliation: name and address.

2 A table of contents includes:

- a typographical formula revealing the *structure* of the report: clear distinctions between parts, chapters, sections and subsections by means of bold, underlining, italics, capitals, or whatever you think is appropriate;
- all introductory components following the table of contents; with page indication (Roman);
- all 'Part' titles in capital letters and bold print (**PART I**; **PART II**); with page indication (Arabic);
- all chapter titles and sections that are numbered; page numbers (subsections do not need numbers);
- all closing components: Epilogue, Appendix, Bibliography, Index; with continued page indication.

Executive summary

An executive summary should give the reader a quick and clear overview of the contents of the report. The reader should be able, on the basis of reading the summary, to decide whether or not it would be interesting to read the report completely. Executive summaries should *not* be over two pages long.

3 A Preface/Acknowledgement includes:

- a short explanation stating *why* this particular research was of interest to you;
- a brief reference to the scientific discourse that relates to this piece of work. Refer to the institute that you are working/studying at, and the approaches you have benefited from most;
- a list of the *people* you have co-operated with or obtained information from. List *all* of the people who have helped you. Not doing this gives the impression that you might not know where (or whom) you got the information from, i.e. of sloppy research. The only reason *not* to include the names of respondents is because of reasons of privacy, which is rare. Keep track of all the people (including secretarial and administrative staff) who have helped you;
- a 'thank you' line for your supervisor (in the case of a thesis)? Umberto Eco (1977) is clear about this: no, do not do it, because your supervisor did only what he/she was supposed to do. Eco is right **(1)** if the thesis still has to be graded, and **(2)** you only mention the name *qualitate qua*. But if the support of your supervisor has been particularly helpful and/or exceptional with regards the general practice, including the name of the supervisor shows that you are capable of appreciating good feedback;
- phrasing in the 'I' form. Do not use 'we' (*pluralis majestatis*) if you are sole writer. This is the only place where you can be really personal. The 'I' form is optional, you can abstain from using it;
- your name, place and Month/Year indication at the end of the preface (in italics).

If it is a *shorter article* the acknowledgements are covered in the opening footnotes that also include information: (1) on your own background, and (2) gives credit to the people who have helped you with the article. Be careful not to forget people who have proofread your article and made valuable comments. You will lose their support very quickly if you do not do this (➔A12). Never forget to thank anonymous referees when they have looked at your manuscript. Serious refereeing of articles takes considerable time.

4 An Introduction includes:

- your basic *research question* and research aims (➔A2, A3, A9, A10). Make sure your question is not interwoven in a long piece of text. State the question, put a box around it, write it in italics, or use an 'indent';
- a longer explanation of the (scientific) discourse that forms the *background of your question*;

- an explanation of the *methodology* that you have used for the research, and why you have used this;
- an outline of the *parts/chapters* of your work. Explaining how these parts *relate to each other* and *why you have chosen this sequence*. The latter is often missing from introductions and obscures the argumentation – the logic – of the paper. You also provide a clear guide for the reader as to what your paper is all about;
- *guidance* for different types of readers (if you aim at different audiences);
- **no** announcement of a conclusion/summary at the end of the chapter. That there will be a conclusion is self-evident (➡E5).
- a statement concerning *all of the relevant choices* that you have made during your research project (➡A1).
- not necessarily all of the *definitions* that you use. Listings of definitions make an introduction hard reading. Definitions are part of your research strategy, so include separate sections in which you make an *well-founded choice* in definition. The introduction always explains the most important choices of the project.

Never forget a *good opening line*. It should (1) characterise your research, and (2) its occasion, as well as (3) stimulate the reader to start reading.

5 Layout opening components

Table E.3b shows the sequence of the opening parts of reports. Of the four minimum requirements in each report, the sequence is more or less set. In some cases acknowledgements come before the table of contents, but this is rare. The sequence of the optional elements is also very common, but here more variations do appear (except for the position of the copyright provision and the dedications). Sometimes a preface is called introduction or foreword, but in general the basic functional sequence holds.

Table E.3b Opening components for a research report

Minimum requirements (always include)	Optional
1 Title page (**no** page nos) ⊕	1a Copyright provisions (**no** page nos)
	1b Dedication (for...; **no** page nos)
2 Table of contents (page nos: optional) ⊕	2a List of Figures/Tables (page nos: optional)
	2b Foreword (written by someone else; page nos: optional)
	2c Executive summary (with page nos)
3 Preface/acknowledgement (page nos: yes) ⊕	3a List of abbreviations/acronyms (with page nos)
	3b Notes on contributors (with page nos)
4 Introduction (Arabic page nos)	

Nos = numbers (plural abbreviation; ➡E13)

Use lower case Roman numerals (i, ii, ix, xv) as page numbers, beginning with the title page until the introduction. From the introduction onwards use Arabic numerals. Start *revealing* the Roman numerals from the table of contents/preface onwards.

Always start page numbering (and chapters) on a right-hand side page.

This Skill Sheet specifies the principles of user-friendliness of research reports. It explains how that principle boils down to a preferred contents of each of the consecutive parts of a text or report: chapters, (sub) sections, and (sub) paragraphs.

1 User-friendliness = readability

When you write a paper pay attention to the 'user-friendliness' of your effort. A readable text includes the following elements:

○ Firstly, state what your main *message* is and make clear the way you want to *elaborate* this message.

○ Always organise a text according to an *increasing degree of specificity*: (1) chapter, consisting of (2) (sub) sections, which are composed of (3) paragraphs. The contents of chapters, sections and paragraphs are always built up as a logical pyramid (◉C7). In case your structure is well organised, you do not have to announce every section separately. It follows 'logically' from the previous one.

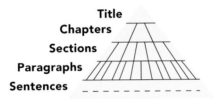

○ Assist the reader from time to time, with strategically positioned *summaries*, and with an intelligent use of *headings*. Do not assume that a reader will understand your message when you use a vague structure or composition. The common reaction of readers, towards misleading or vague structures, is to think that the writer (you) probably does not know what they are talking about. In short, ensure the **clarity** of your writing.

2 Purposeful chapters and sections

Make it clear to the reader what you think the function of the section is. Always do this in the introduction to the section or chapter. Even within a chapter, a short introduction can be very useful when you move to an additional issue. For each longer section or chapter you should:

○ refer to the *contents of the last section*;

○ state what is discussed in the section itself. Try to summarise in a sequence of points: 'firstly, in this section the issue of ... is tackled, secondly... thirdly...';

○ make clear *why you have chosen this particular sequence*. What is the *internal cohesion* of your choice? What is the relation to the general question or hypothesis of the paper? Repeat the question;

○ think about a *'catchy' first line* that attracts the attention of the reader. You could also use a quote. The quote could be anything, but should also be referred to in the text (◉E11), otherwise it will be meaningless.

Rule #1: Each separate chapter and section should be introduced with a short statement about what you are going to say.

3 Conclusive chapter and sections

The conclusion of a chapter or section is just as important as the introduction.

o Always give a brief summary of a chapter and a longer section (exceeding approximately three pages).

o *Never add material/information to the presentation in your concluding statement.* It is not sensible to add new material in your conclusion. If you do this, you have not given proper thought to the composition of your paper. The reader will notice.

o Think about the nature of your *last line*. Your last line can reveal much about your character as a writer and researcher: question mark, exclamation mark, mystic, factual, a 'peter out' line (that is: a very vague remark). Think about the impression that you want to give the reader when they reach the end of your paper (➔C3).

Rule #2: Each separate chapter and most sections should end with a conclusion.

4 Paragraphs

o Paragraphs are not sections.

o A paragraph indicates a *separate element* in your text. Each paragraph should contain not more than one theme. The key remark on this theme should be placed in a prominent place: either the first/second or last sentence of the paragraph.

o Focused opening lines enable readers to grasp your message quickly.

This Skill Sheet discusses the aims, sequence and contents of the final parts of a report. Table E.5 shows the minimum and optional parts you might consider including.

Table E.5 Concluding parts

Minimum requirement	Optional	Presentation sequence
Conclusion	Epilogue	1 Conclusion
Biography	Glossary	2 Epilogue
	Annexes	3 Glossary
	Index	4 Annexes
		5 Bibliography
		6 Index

1 Conclusion

Conclusions, executive summaries (⊕E3) and prefaces are often the parts of your report that are read most thoroughly.

The conclusion is often read first, without proper knowledge of the rest of the report.

You might think this is not 'how it should be', but it will be of benefit to you if you bear this in mind when writing your conclusion. Therefore, a general conclusion should largely stand on its own feet (⊕E4).

- The conclusion always repeats the research question(s). A general conclusion not only repeats the main research question, but also the sub-questions tackled in the respective chapters.
- After 'refreshing the memory' of the reader with regards to the research question(s) in the conclusion, the writer tries to present a well-argued answer to that question.
- In the final conclusion you should consider carefully what the consequences have been of *flaws* in your research methodology, or other practical research problems, for the validity of your answers.
- A conclusion *never* adds new information!
- The conclusion ends with a good last line.
- Conclusions also specify *recommendations for further research*.

2 Epilogue

An epilogue is mainly used when new information has appeared between the time of finishing the main manuscript and the text going to the publisher or your supervisor. Sometimes a guest writer provides an epilogue instead of a foreword. But, aim at including only meaningful texts containing relevant information on 'what happened after' the research was finalised. Never use an epilogue to enter into a personal debate with somebody, in areas that were not part of your research project. The epilogue preferably only relates to your original research question.

3 Glossary

Glossaries contain concepts and a short description of their meaning. Glossaries therefore are more than mere lists of abbreviations and acronyms (⊕E13). Glossaries are sometimes used as an excuse for not elaborating on the meaning of important concepts in the text. A glossary is not a complement to your text, but merely a checklist of commonly used concepts and definitions. Glossaries are particularly useful in texts containing many discipline-specific terms. The general rule remains therefore: *refrain from composing a glossary*.

If you do include a glossary:
o Try to limit its length.
o Be consistent with the definition in the glossary and your text.

4 Annexes

It is not uncommon for annexes to contain more pages than the main text. An annex can be useful when it comprises data and figures that support the text. Often, however, annexes represent an integral part of the analysis. When this occurs, always include the particular information in the text and not in an annex. The latter forces the reader into a frustrating effort of repeatedly having to turn the pages from annex to text and back again. It is a good idea to summarise relevant annexes in one table or figure. A paper that integrates text, figures and tables in a balanced way, is more appealing to the reader. A multitude of annexes will quickly distract the readers' attention.

You put an explanation, data and tables *in an annex*:
- when the information can be summarised easily in the text;
- when it only contains background information or illustrations for the general analysis;
- when you need to explain the methodology of a specific part of your research in detail. An explanation of the methodology should also include information about your search strategy and about your informants. The latter can be dealt with in a separate annex;
- in the case of questionnaires: *always* include the full questionnaire and all details of the answers (percentages and averages if needed) in an annex.

Rules of thumb for Annexes

- An annex should *stand on its own feet*. Add introductions and explanations to the annex to make the annex accessible to a reader.
- Only compose an annex when you have referred to it in the text. Or to put it another way: once you finish a report, check that all annexes have been referred to. Check that all annexes *are there*. This is obvious, but nevertheless this principle is often forgotten, in particular when you give an intermediary version to a tutor. Referring to an annex in the text, which the reader then searches for in vain, is very irritating.
- Give annexes a number *or* a letter (Annex A, Annex 1). Be consistent. Never mix the two!
- Preferably use the same layout for the annexes and the text. It increases the status of your whole report.
- Limit the number of annexes as much as possible.
- Number the pages of the annexes as ongoing pages of the regular text, so that the reader is able to find the specific annex quickly, and the annexes can be listed in your table of contents.

5 Bibliography

Detailed information on what constitutes and how to compose a bibliography can be found in Skill Sheet E15.

6 Index

An index contains the most important concepts and names, and reveals the location in the text by page number. An index is an important tool for reading a longer text effectively (➲C3, C5). It takes considerable effort to compose an index, although modern word-processing equipment makes it somewhat easier. M.A. or M.B.A. students seldom compile an index for their reports. Nevertheless, a shorter index can sometimes present complementary information to the general contents of your report. It can also be useful for you, as the author, if you think that you will be able to use the report at a later date. Furthermore, writing an index occasionally helps you to consider the keywords that are most relevant to your type of research, and thus helps you to search in libraries for related sources (➲A6). So try it once, even if it is a short report.

E6   Argumentation

This Skill Sheet provides a selection of basic tips and pointers that have proved to be valuable for the *practice of writing* valid and plausible arguments. This Skill Sheet does not focus on the principles of *formal logic*, i.e. the almost mathematical elaboration of the structures of argumentation.

1 Argumentation = dull

It is a pity for researchers who are aspiring novelists, but scientific texts should be transparent, predictable and therefore often relatively 'dull'. You state beforehand *what* you are going to explain to the reader. You specify *how* you are going to explain it: how many aspects, characteristics (for instance: 'the following three arguments can be used in favour of...') and how they can be linked. You then come to explicit **conclusions** and refer back to your line of argument.

2 Characteristics of good and bad argumentation.

Four points that help to identify the interrelated characteristics of 'good' and 'bad' argumentation are listed in Table E.6a. Score your own and others' texts on these characteristics. In case you write a review for feedback using these concepts always helps you in making up your mind on the sophistication of the argumentation.

Table E.6a Good versus Bad argumentation

Good argumentation contains:	Bad argumentation contains:
• clarity	• ambiguity
• succinctness	• lengthiness (too many words)
• simplicity	• unnecessary use of complex vocabulary
• precision	• inaccuracy (sloppy phrasing)

3 Pro and con arguments

Research writing always pertains to and is embedded in wider and critical discussions. Argumentation can then be considered part of an effort to come to conclusions in disputes. Behind every argument there are interests, opinions and discussions. Behind every argument there is a counter-argument. There are always more sides to an argument, so it is better to include them in your own argumentation. A good method of arguing, therefore, is by systematically trying to *list arguments 'in favour' and 'against'* an observation. Try to list equal numbers of arguments both for and against ('pro' and 'con').

- If there are many more convincing arguments in favour of something, this is a strong indication that the overall argument might be true.
- If there are more convincing arguments against the theory, this is a strong indication that you should not support the general observation, design and implementation (➡A5).

- However, always bear in mind that some arguments can be much more important than others. Think carefully about the relative 'weight' of an argument.
- If the number of pros and cons are the same: think about the *conditions* under which favourable or unfavourable arguments may prevail. You could design a new problem definition or could try to come to a synthesis. When the arguments in favour match the arguments against, it is appropriate to talk of a *dilemma*. If you make choices without solid argumentation regarding your reasons for doing this, be aware that you are withdrawing from your position as a researcher and are becoming a politician (➔A3).

Get used to *playing 'devil's advocate'* in your reasoning. You must avoid sloppy argumentation and weak evidence structures. However, do not focus on this attitude *only*. Create a balance in your attitude in order to create a balance in your argumentation (➔C6) and apply the principle of triangulation in your research (➔A7).

4 Schematising your argumentation

It often proves useful to **argue by schematising**. Two relevant techniques are:

- A **table**: specifying columns and rows (different variables and their interrelationships); the empty boxes in the table reveal gaps in your reasoning (➔E14).
- A logic **tree**: revealing your main 'lines' (the tree's branches) of reasoning; reveals parallel arguments, the specificity of particular arguments; and the nature of the interrelations: necessary/sufficient conditions if you dare to elaborate the tree scheme in arrows as well. This technique is also used in Mind Mapping (➔A4; B6).

5 Definitions

Explain the concepts that you use by giving definitions. Definitions should be:

- clear, succinct (short), simple and precise;
- non-circular (definitions in dictionaries are often circular);
- context specific;
- explicit on main points and side issues, and on what the definition does *not* include.

6 Fallacies in argumentation (➔C8)

Fallacies are arguments that are basically flawed. Everybody is prone to fallacies in basic argumentation. Table E.6b presents a checklist of commonly used phrases that can be interpreted as weak argumentation or even fallacies.

Table E.6b Common Fallacies in Argumentation

Fallacies in argumentation	Example
Authority/big names	'As Weber already stated...', or 'I agree with Marx that...'
Normative adjectives:	'exceedingly expensive houses', 'incredible statements', 'honourable major'
Normative assessments	'Everyone knows', 'It is clear', 'It is obvious that', 'Naturally', 'It is a fact'

Clichés	proverbs like 'unknown, unloved'
Stereotypes	('the' Italian, 'the Chinese', 'women', 'men'
Rationalisations	making something or someone look more purposeful afterwards than was the case
Conclusive words	'thus', 'therefore' (➲E9)
Suggestive dots	'but we know better…'
Improper inductions	only generalise examples after proving their representativeness
Improper deductions	apply a general statement to a specific case only when the statement holds true for all cases (which is very unlikely in social sciences)
Improper causality	if X comes *after* Y, it is not necessarily caused by Y *(post-hoc reasoning)*
Tautologies	rephrasing the same argument as if it were additional evidence

6 Strengths and weaknesses

When dealing with the argumentation of others or of a particular scientific area, you could also **list the 'strengths' and 'weaknesses'** of the argumentation. A number of approaches can then get summarised in a qualitative table that lists as many strengths and weaknesses as possible. Specific approaches or arguments rarely include only strong points or weaknesses. So it is better to make an inventory first, and then make a selection from an overall view than on the basis of partial argumentation.

7 Necessary and/or sufficient condition?

A particularly convincing type of argumentation is also created by asking whether something (an indicator, a characteristic) provides *(1) a necessary and/or (2) a sufficient condition* for something else. The following combinations can be explained in the text:

- A is a necessary, but *not* a sufficient condition for B: other inputs are also required, so you must look further in your research project.
- A is a sufficient, but *not* a necessary condition for B: other inputs can create the same outcome.
- A is a necessary *and* sufficient condition for B: this is the strongest type of argumentation you can have in social sciences. With such argumentation you come close to the principle of *verification*.
- A is *neither* a necessary, *nor* a sufficient condition for B: you often use this type of argumentation when you want to criticise the argumentation of someone else, using the strongest possible wording. Such reasoning comes close to the principle of *falsification*.

Argumentation requires discipline, but no thought discipline without language discipline.

[⊕➲www.skillsheets.com for more examples of good and bad argumentation]

Your writing should be clear, succinct, simple and precise (➔E6). In scientific writing, however, you generally deal with complex topics. Adopting the right style immediately is asking the impossible. Your writing style covers the end-product on paper, but also relates to the process of writing itself. Both are closely connected. Your ultimate writing output is critically dependent on the way you manage this process.

Powerful writing requires a particular state of mind...

The late John Kenneth Galbraith was one the most appealing writers in economics. Many may disagree with his observations, but there are few who do not envy his writing style. Once Galbraith said of his writing that it reaches his (much admired) state of 'spontaneity' at about draft number five: 'It was usually on about the fourth day that I put in that note of spontaneity for which I am known' he once admitted (The Economist, May 6th, 2006). Writing is rewriting. Rewriting requires time and is hard work. If you plan to write a paper and have the first draft finished on the last day, your writing is bound to lack spontaneity. Rewriting requires professionalism: that is the dedication to learning from your own mistakes, and developing your abilities (➔B Series). Rewriting requires flexibility and an awareness of the problems facing the reader. Understanding these problems requires you be self-critical. The more you understand the writing process and your own writing habits, the more it becomes possible for you to identify problems when they appear (and that is often!), and find the appropriate solutions. Check the properties in Table E.7 and find out whether vices or virtues dominate your basic attitude to writing.

Table E.7 Vices and virtues in attitudes to writing

Vices (bad properties)	Virtues (good properties)
☐ **Self-satisfaction**: thinking that you have nothing more to learn in terms of your writing	☐ **Self-criticism**: it can always be written differently, and probably also better; you are curious for the commentary and advise of others
☐ **Disdain**: your writing is clear enough, but the reader is too stupid to (1) understand what you mean, (2) assess the value of your thoughts, and (3) work with it	☐ **Empathy**: you try to understand, as much as possible, the expectations, hopes and problems of your readers
☐ **Rigidity**: your present writing habits are OK, you do not need to get advice or change anything	☐ **Professionalism**: writing is a skill that you do not learn easily
☐ **Resistance to working more rationally**: writing is only a matter of creativity, systematic writing has no value added	☐ **Systematic**: you make a plan, talk about it with others, work in consecutive phases, control the quality of the outcome
	☐ **Reflexivity**: you constantly try to gain insight into your own writing habits and the process of writing itself

Source: Steehouder et al., 1992

... which changes over time

Rewriting requires a mental state that is different from the mental state you need when you write something for the first time. Writing requires formulation skills, rewriting requires *reading skills* as well as reformulation skills. Reading the texts written by others, however, is quite different from reading your own. Reading your own texts depends on which phase of the writing process you are in. For the required state of mind, it is therefore best to *separate writing* texts *from reading* as much as possible. In this process, computers can be a very powerful aid, but can also have considerable drawbacks, if you lack the mental state explained above. Two problems can appear:

o if you print out what you wrote, but are impressed by the high quality of printed text from your computer, even if it is only a draft. Many people have difficulty in correcting their own texts (➔C12), but this barrier becomes even higher when the text is of 'printing quality';

o if you work from the screen the mental problem takes a different turn: you lose overview of all the components of your argument. Reading as an input to rewriting requires that you think of your argumentation from a total vision, which can often only be achieved if you lay all your notes next to each other – in order to re-arrange them – in a bigger space than your computer screen can offer . To save paper (and the forest) you might try to decide as early as possible on the structure of your argumentation after which your reading and rewriting process only needs to focus on smaller modules of your report.

It is better to work in consecutive phases than to (re)read and (re)write at the same time.

'Sorry for the long paper. I didn't have time to make it shorter.'

This Skill Sheet does not repeat your grammar lessons. Solving grammar deficiencies is your own responsibility, and should not be left to the goodwill of a university teacher or your colleagues at work. There are, however, a number of problems with writing style that appear time and time again. They cannot really be considered blatant writing errors, but nevertheless create problems in scientific texts. This and the following Skill Sheet (➲E9) list the most common 'style problems'. Many writers are not really aware of these problems, so recognising them is always a big step forward. There are alternatives available.

1 Reification

> **Reification: Attaching personal characteristics to an organisation or institutions.**

When considered superficially, reification represents only an error in style. Often, however, it indicates an error in interpretation as well. By presenting an organisation as a unified whole or a monolithic block, scholars underestimate the possible divergence of opinions within the same organisation. Different departments within IBM often think quite differently about a topic, as is the case with different government departments. So always **try** to *identify* the group or person responsible in an organisation, in order to increase the relevance of your analysis. Unintended reification in any case is a sign of weak methodology and thoughtless choices for specific levels of analysis in your research. Some examples:

Reification	Alternative
'The United States are considering....'	'The President of the United States is considering...'
'Shell thinks it is well equipped to...'	'Shell's management thinks it is well equipped to....'
'The Ministry of Economic Affairs has written a report...'	'The Ministry of Economic Affairs has issued a report...'

2 Passive instead of active phrasing

Writing in the passive is a common problem of style: 'it is being...', 'this is thought of as...'. The passive makes your writing 'heavy'. Many students think this is required to make their papers appear more important. On the contrary, they become difficult to read and only a handful of readers will be impressed by your phrasing. It is often simple to rephrase a passive sentence into a more *active* form. For instance:

Passive form	Active form
The cause of this can be found in...	This is because...
At the present time...	Now...

3 Long instead of short sentences

Science, for many people, implies long and complex sentences. There seems to be a bonus for the social scientist who can formulate the longest sentences. But lengthy sentences are nearly always completely unnecessary and weaken your writing considerably. People who experience difficulty in formulating running sentences should not try to rephrase the sentence. It will inevitably result in lengthier sentences. Most of the time it is possible to make two compact and clear sentences out of one longer one (⊕E1).

| **Get to the point! Writing is the art of leaving out.**

4 Abusing brackets and quotation marks

Texts become heavier when the author puts too many remarks in brackets, or words between quotation marks. The use of brackets weakens the text and makes it open to multiple interpretations by the reader. As a rule you should place as few remarks between brackets as possible, unless it is a functional reference (⊕E12). You should also apply this rule to the use of inverted commas, unless it is functional, for example when using quotes or the introduction of a new concept.
o Try not to have more than two or three remarks in brackets per written page.
o Most statements that have been placed in brackets can be written in a separate sentence.

5 Abuse of footnotes (⊕E11)

Footnotes are often abused as a means to elaborate on certain additional points that were not included in the text. In principle apply the following basic writing rule:

o if it is worth stating, you should include it in the text;
o if it is not worth stating, your comment should have been left out of the paper anyway!

There are exceptions to these rules. You can use footnotes:
o with references to interviews [a list of which can be in an annex];
o when you refer to an internet source [long reference that is not functional in the text];
o when you *aim at different audiences* at the same time.
  For example, if the running text is aimed at an audience with less knowledge,

the footnotes can be intended for a more informed audience, and can give additional information. Implementing this writing strategy is very risky, because you can easily become 'stuck in the middle' and write texts that do not appeal to anybody.

6 Unspecific time indication

It is important that your time indication be phrased in positive and precisely indicated periods. A phrase that begins with 'In the past...' is much to unspecific and can easily be formulated more positively. Always try to use the most specific year indication available. If you write in December and your paper is released in January, the phrase 'last year' suddenly refers to a completely different year. Rephrase your time indication into positive and clearly formulated periods

Vague and unclear	Positive and precise (if possible)
'In the past, measures have been taken to...'	'Measures have been taken to...'
'Lately...'	'Since the beginning of the 21st century...'
'In the last ten years...'	'From 1997 to 2007...'

7 Unclear or ambiguous indications

Do not use	When you mean
America	The United States (of America)
England	The United Kingdom (including England, Scotland, Wales and Northern Ireland)
Holland	The Netherlands (having ten other provinces besides the two Holland provinces)

8 Gender-specific language

Avoid gender-specific language, unless really appropriate in the context of your research. Avoid the use of 'he' (when it could be he or she), either through the use of 'they' or by repeating the noun if possible. Many people write about 'managers' or 'politicians' and in the next sentence refer back to this category with 'he'. The implicit message you give is that all managers and politicians are male. In order to overcome this style problem, writers sometimes state at the beginning of a paper 'with he, I mean he or she'. This is in fact a gender-specific solution to the gender problem and therefore not very elegant. The same goes for the use of 'she' as the general person indication.

Limit your use of he/she phrasing. There are often alternatives.

9 Writing in another language

If you have difficulty writing in your own language, the problems can increase in another language. If you translate your own bad writing into English, for instance, 'the English version simply compounds the confusion and thickens the fog' (Sheila McNab, NRC Handelsblad, 16 January 1990). You can use writing in a foreign language to leapfrog some of your writing deficiencies, but only if you write in the other language without translating from your mother tongue. But you should continually try to refine your native language skills.

Some words and phrases instantly reveal meanings other than those that the writer intended. For example: if you have been lazy when writing your text, if you have not formulated a sound argument, or if your paper was badly organised. The most common words and phrases that fall into this category are listed in Table E.9, together with the commentary an informed (thus critical) reader may have. The conclusion is simple: avoid using these loaded words. Exceptions can support the rule, but there are a large number of alternatives.

Table E.9 The Hidden meaning of phrases

If you write:	A critical reader may think:
'having said this'	...You are writing, not talking...
'Thus...', 'therefore'	...So what? Conclusive words rarely come after a solid argument. They often indicate that the author wanted to stop writing. A logical conclusion does not have to be announced...
'in other words', 'to put it in another way'	...Couldn't you have stated it more clearly in the first place?
'etc.', 'and the like'	...The author means: 'I don't know more' or 'I don't want to think about it further'...
'As stated earlier'	...If you have stated it earlier, why repeat it? If you refer to a previous text in this vague manner you probably did not take the time to look where (even: if) you mentioned it...
'Again'	...Not 'again'!
'It is clear that...'	...Is it?
'It is a fact that...'	...is it?
'This/That is...','The previous is'	...What? Are you referring to the previous sentence, paragraph or chapter? If you want to refer to a preceding sentence or observation, be more specific. Add a subject.
'we' (writing alone)	...A writer with Royal aspirations (*pluralis majestatis*) or an identity problem...
'More later on'	...When? Why later, why not now? If it is logical that it will be dealt with later, why refer to it now?
'I will' (when you announce a chapter or section)	...The author means 'I hope to...'. The introduction was probably written before the rest of the chapter. It is not certain that the announced contents can actually be found in the chapter. Hope is often in vain... but don't take it too personally!
'obvious', 'naturally'	...It will probably be not that obvious and certainly not that natural, otherwise the writer wouldn't have to use these words! If it is obvious, it is obvious...
'In short'	...So before you couldn't formulate your argument in a more concise way?
'...' (end of a sentence)	...What are you suggesting? (➔E6)

'the market', 'the Italians'	...Undue generalisation and induction (➔E6). The author probably has done insufficient specific research...
'fantastic', 'great', 'enormous', 'tremendous'	...such enthusiasm probably covers up weak contents. Highly improper in scientific texts...
'yours truly', 'the under-signed', 'the writer'	...Using old-fashioned words, the author probably has a status problem!

[⊕➔www.skillsheets.com for an analysis form to help you keep track of your own style 'problem children']

This Skill Sheet provides information on a number of (English) spelling errors that occur frequently, in particular: time indication, and numerals.

1 Time indication

Good spelling	Wrong spelling
'twentieth century'	'20th century'
1980s	1980's, '80s, or eighties
2000	'00
'from 1982 to 1996', 'between 1998 and 2001'	'from 1982-1996', 'between 1998-2001'
January, February, March	january, february, march

- You can use a slash (/) to indicate a financial or academic year that covers more than one calendar year: 1998/99.
- You can abbreviate months when used in tables and footnotes, but always use the name of the month and not the number.

2 Numerals

In a running text, the following numbers are preferably *written in words*:

Good spelling	Wrong spelling
One, two, three, ... eighteen, nineteen.	1, 2, 3, ... 18, 19.
Ten, twenty, thirty, ... eighty, ninety.	10, 20, 30, ... 80, 90.
One hundred, two hundred, ... nine hundred.	100, 200, ... 900.
One thousand, two thousand, ... nine thousand.	1.000, 2.000, ... 9.000.
One million, two billion, nine trillion, ...	1.000.000, 2.000.000.000, 9.000.000.000.000, ...

- All *other* numbers can be written in numerals (Arabic notation; examples 45, 875, 1,235).

The following numbers should *not* be written in words:

Subject	Good spelling	Wrong spelling
Sequence of numbers	3 percent, 5 percent, and 8 percent	three percent, five percent, and eight percent
Dates	6 July 2007	six July 2007
Units	50 Hz, 1 Gigabyte	fifty Hz, one gigabyte

Differences between languages appear in particular with regards to punctuation English spelling in general uses a comma as a thousands separator, instead of a point. The majority of non-native writers of English do not do this. They also consequently use a decimal comma instead of the correct decimal point. A comparable problem arises as regards the notation of dates.

Subject	Other languages	English
Numbers	1.856.236,89	1,856,236.89
Dates	9 May 2002: 9/5/02	May 9 2002: 5/9/02

3 Common spelling errors for non-native English speakers

A common spelling error made by non-native English speakers is to link words together or to use a hyphen (-). Undue linking of words is especially a problem for people whose mother tongue is one of the Germanic languages. The word 'Spelling error' is given as an example:

Good spelling	Wrong spelling
Spelling error	Spellingerror, Spelling-error

It is worthwhile noticing, however, that the English language has developed an increasing number of compound words as well. They often have come about through frequent use, such as 'proofread', 'database' or 'keyword' for example. The same is true for hyphenated compounds, when used as an adjective, as in 'time-consuming activity'.

In many languages it is also usual to add capital letters to nouns, or to begin specific meaningful words with a capital letter. You should keep *capitalisation* to a minimum, i.e. write in lower case words like:

Preferred spelling	spelling
government, church, state, party, volume	Government, Church, State, Party, Volume

4 Typos and spell checkers

Typographical errors (typos) are very irritating to a reader when they appear frequently in a text. It distracts the attention of the reader from what you want to say. A few typos could be enough for a reader to question the content of the whole text! If you make use of word-processing equipment, you can also use software that checks the spelling. It does not take much time, and helps you to avoid the most obvious typos. However, it cannot be a substitute for careful proofreading. You must be aware of the fact that the most popular English language spelling programs are in fact American-English. Most non-native English writers mix-up American and British English. Choose the one you are most familiar with and be consistent. Make a list of your common language errors to remind you of your usual inconsistencies [⊕➔www.skillsheets.com for a checklist].

5 Authentic foreign keywords

These words should be included in their original form: put them in italics or underline them, refrain from using quotation marks: *keiretsu* (Japanese business conglomerates) instead of 'keiretsu';

Subject	Good spelling	Wrong spelling
Authentic foreign keywords	*keiretsu*, <u>keiretsu</u>	'keiretsu'

- The first time they appear in the text they should be explained and/or translated.
- This rule does not normally apply to company names.
- Make sure that your spelling remains consistent.

6 Anglicised names

These names ('Munich' for 'München') have to be used consistently throughout the whole text;

Subject	Consistent	Inconsistent
Anglicised names	Munich, Brussels	München, Bruxelles or Brussel

Use the 'search' command in your word-processing software to check for *consistency.*

7 Listing common words

Many writers are often inconsistent in their spelling. The (in)consistency problem becomes greater when you write a collective paper. In order to avoid lengthy and tedious spelling checks at the end of the writing process, start by making a short list of the words that you are likely to use often. Decide upon your preferred spelling. Often, booklets exist that state preferred spelling rules. But since most languages are developing constantly, these rules may not always apply.

Invest in a good *dictionary* for *each* language that you read and write in. *Place* your dictionaries as *near* as possible to your writing desk. Learn to make *active and frequent* use of your dictionaries.

E11 Quotations and Paraphrasing

This Skill Sheet lists the basic principles and some practical tips for the correct use of quotations. Critical and independent thinking begins with critical *awareness* of the sources you use and refer to (➔E12). You should *not* be discouraged from incorporating the concepts of others into your thinking. On the contrary. When you begin to quote other peoples' ideas correctly you create a *scientific routine*. This Skill Sheet discusses three dimensions of correct quotation: (1) the difference between direct quotation (literally taking over somebody's words or writings) and paraphrasing (putting in your own words), (2) how to reproduce quotes in texts, and (3) when and how to add changes to a quote.

1 Direct quotations

○ A few words
When you want to quote a number of words or indicate a topic, put these in single quotation marks (' ').

Type of quotation	Example
A topic	Yesterday, I read the book 'Gulliver's travels'.
A statement included in a sentence	The Director stated that 'higher profits can be expected'.

- Use a comma (,) to separate your own introductory phrase from a quotation of one sentence or less.

○ Short quotations (one to four lines)
Use a colon (:) to introduce smaller quotations.

xxxxxxxxxxxxxxxxxxxxxxxxxxxxxxxxxxxxxxxxxxxxxxxxxxxxxxxxxxxxxxxxxxxxxxxxxxxxxxxx
xxxxxxxxxxxxxxxxxxxxxxxxxxxxxxxxxxxxxxxxxxxxxxxxxxxxxxxxxxxxxxxxx: 'Solutions always lead to new problems, complications and repetitions somewhere else.' (Tenner, 1996:23).
xxxxxxxxxxxxxxxxxxxxxxxxxxxxxxxxxxxxxxxxxxxxxxxxxxxxxxxxxxxxxxxxxxxxxxxxxxxxxxxx
xxxxxxxxxxxxxxxxxxxxxxxxxxxxxxxxxxxxxxxxxxxxxxxxxxxxxxxxxxxxxxxxxxxxxxxxxxxxxxxx

○ Longer quotations (four lines or more)
Longer quotations are usually indented and separated from the main text by a space above and below.
- Some publishers leave out quotation marks for these indented quotes.

xxxxxxxxxxxxxxxxxxxxxxxxxxxxxxxxxxxxxxxxxxxxxxxxxxxxxxxxxxxxxxxxxxxxxxxxxxxxxxxxxxxxx
xxxxxxxxxxxxxxxxxxxxxxxxxxxxxxxxxxxxxxxxxxxxxxxxxxxxxxxxxxxxxxxxxxxxxxxxxxxxxxxxxxxxx

> 'The fastest way to get an engineer to solve a problem is to declare that the problem is unsolv-
> able. No engineer can walk away from an unsolvable problem until it is solved. No illness or
> distraction is sufficient to get the engineer off the case. These types of challenges quickly
> become personal – a battle between the engineer and the laws of nature' (Adams, 1996: 190-91).

xxxxxxxxxxxxxxxxxxxxxxxxxxxxxxxxxxxxxxxxxxxxxxxxxxxxxxxxxxxxxxxxxxxxxxxxxxxxxxxxxxxxx
xxxxxxxxxxxxxxxxxxxxxxxxxxxxxxxxxxxxxxxxxxxxxxxxxxxxxxxxxxxxxxxxxxxxxxxxxxxxxxxxxxxxx

○ **Consecutive quotations**

Although it might seem absolutely clear that quotations, which are closely inter-
spersed in the text, were all taken from the same source, it still remains necessary to indicate the source of each in a separate reference.

---

xxxxxxxxxxxxxxxxxxxxxxxxxxxxxxxxxxxxxxxxxxxxxxxxxxxxxxxxxxxxxxxxxxxxxxxxxxxxxxxxxxxxx
'The level of understanding was quite low' (Katzenstein, 1997:45).
xxxxxxxxxxxxxxxxxxxxxxxxxxxxxxxxxxxxxxxxxxxxxxxxxxxxxxxxxxxxxxxxxxxxxxxxxxxxxxxxxxxxx
xxxxxxxxxxxxxxxxxxxxxxxxxxxxxxxxxxxxxxxxxxxxxxxxxxxxxxxxxxxxxxxxxxxxxxxxxxxx
'In the same vein one can conclude that the future looks bleak' (ibid: 56).
xxxxxxxxxxxxxxxxxxxxxxxxxxxxxxxxxxxxxxxxxxxxxxxxxxxxxxxxxxxxxxxxxxxxxxxxxxxxxxxxxxxxx
xxxxxxxxxxxxxxxxxxxxxxxxxxxxxxxxxxxxxxxxxxxxxxxxxxx: 'nevertheless, we should pay attention to the differences' (ibid).
xxxxxxxxxxxxxxxxxxxxxxxxxxxxxxxxxxxxxxxxxxxxxxxxxxxxxxxxxxxxxxxxxxxxxxxxxxxxxxxxxxxxx
xxxxxxxxxxxxxxxxxxxxxxxxxxxxxxxxxxxxxxxxxxxxxxxxxxxxxxxxxxxxxxxxxxxxxxxxxxxxxxxxxxxxx

2 Paraphrasing

Paraphrasing is almost like quoting: you reproduce substantially the form and
combination of ideas taken from another source, but put it into your own words.
All paraphrases must be identified with their source.

• Referring to the sources is even necessary if, you adopt a line of reasoning, an
idea, a phrase, even a word you heard from someone else if this was really relevant for your argumentation. In the reference – a footnote is most appropriate –
you can state:

Example

'I was first drawn to this line of argument by Mr. X.'

• Should you *paraphrase an argument that has been paraphrased* by someone else?
Abstain from doing this as much as possible and go to the original source.

- *Never*: paraphrase an indirect source while referring to the original source *without* consulting the original source.
- When you paraphrase a *list of points*, the source indication should be included in your introductory sentence before the colon. For example:

Example

'The following arguments support this view (Petersen, 1988: 36):'

But if you add your own points to the list, you should reveal the source *either* with each point, *or* find an alternative way of presentation.

> **Tip from Umberto Eco (1977:198): paraphrasing an argument can best be done without looking at the original text. You preclude plagiarism and you make sure you are able to reproduce the main bearing of the other's argument.**

3 Sources for quotations

o **Secondary sources (readers, textbooks)**

In scientific discourse it is commonplace for authors to refer to other sources to build their own argument. Limit the use of these indirectly revealed sources, for example '(Vernon quoted in Humbert, 1993: 156)'. You refer to the original source that can be another book or article because the writer may not have used the quote correctly.

- In the case of *readers or textbooks* in which excerpts of original texts (i.e. quotes, but without clear indications of what has been left out) are included: always look at the original source in order to find out whether the excerpt is correct. If the complete text has been copied in the reader, you can use the indirect quoting provision noted above.
- It is not recommended to use this quotation: 'Mintzberg comes to the opinion… (Johnson, 1993:78).'

o **Interviews**

It is not appropriate to *quote interviewees* in a research text. You are not a journalist and you will rarely be interested in the statements of individuals. Moreover, it will be much more difficult to get information from your interviewees if they think that they might be quoted.

- If the interviewee wishes to keep a secret identity, nevertheless try to find a way to reveal your source: (1) only refer to the date and the company, institution or the function; (2) list interviewees in an annex (➲E5). Always keep files in which the source of your information is revealed. You must be able to provide the identity of the original sources for your tutor. If your interviewee does not allow this you can not do credible research.

- If you refer to information gathered in an interview, do this in a footnote. Include the exact date of the interview, the place and the interviewee (example: Interview Mr. Brozalski, 26 August 2002, Erasmus University Rotterdam).

Never quote yourself!

4 Changing quotes?
○ **Original spelling**
Do *not change original spelling* in quotes and titles, even if it differs from your own spelling, unless:
- If you want to indicate that material was omitted from a quotation, you should insert parentheses with three dots inside: (...); four dots are used to indicate an omission between sentences. These omissions should never include the essence of the quote!
- If you alter the quotation – for example by changing the verb from a past into a present tense, or by adding your clarification as an editor – you must enclose the changes in square brackets: [ ]. If you clarify something, you should add your initials to the text.

For example: a sentence you might want to quote is:
'scientists are dwarfs, but they can stand on the shoulders of giants' (De Vito, 1992:2).
- Do not quote this as: De Vito (1992) considers scientists as follows: 'scientists are all dwarfs...'
- In version (a) you can quote: De Vito (1992:2) considers 'scientist (...) dwarfs, but they can...'
- In version (b) the sentence could become: According to De Vito (1992:2) 'scientists are [intellectual, RvT] dwarfs, but...'

○ **Double/single quotations**
Depending on your style and spelling (➔E8-10) use *double or single quotation marks*. If you use double quotation marks, a quote within a quote gets single quotation marks and *vice versa*. For example:

'It is noted that each "prospect" can be pursued by...' (Kitsch, 1977: 87).

- In the original source "prospect" might have received single quotation marks.

○ **Add an emphasis**
If you add an emphasis by underlining/italics in a quote, state 'emphasis added' and your initials in the reference. If the original had underlining/italics you add 'author's emphasis' in the reference.

E12 References

As a basic rule, you should *always* refer to the sources that you have used. Revealing sources is not only a principle of scientific soundness, but also of intellectual integrity. When combined with the correct use of a bibliography (➲E15) an appropriate system of references should make it possible to:
- return to the original sources if needed;
- show the reader where you got the information from;
- enter into more fruitful discussions, because other observers might reach different conclusions based on information from the same sources.

This Skill Sheet first clarifies the basic principles of the two most commonly used systems of references:
(1) Harvard Reference System (in the text and in bibliography);
(2) Note Reference System (as footnotes or endnotes).
Three reference styles will be distinguished:
(1) General reference (references to the general meaning of a book or article);
(2) Argument reference (or paraphrasing; references to an argument on a particular page);
(3) References to Internet.

1 Reference systems

○ Harvard Reference system

The Harvard Reference System gives a shortened reference in the text and a full reference in the bibliography. References in the text give you instant information on the source from which you will be able to check the full reference in the bibliography (➲E15). This system is preferred by *almost* all publishers as well as academic readers.

Harvard Reference System	Example
Text reference	(D'Aveni, 1999).
Bibliography	D'Aveni, R., (1999), 'Strategic supremacy through disruption and dominance', *Sloan Management Review*, Vol. 40, No. 3, pp. 95-106.

○ Note Reference System

The Note Reference system gives the reference in a note at the bottom of a page. The footnote indication should always be added after the period or near the word you want the note to refer to: 'bla, bla, bla'[1].

Note Reference System	Example
Note at the bottom of a page or at the end of a text	[1]D'Aveni, R., (1999), 'Strategic supremacy through disruption and dominance', *Sloan Management Review*, Vol. 40, No. 3, pp. 95-106.

- Use footnotes only, when you will use notes as references. Do not use end-notes, because the reader has to turn pages every time.
- Only sparsely use *abbreviated* references, like 'op.cit', 'ibidem' or 'Idem' and only in case the original reference is listed nearby in the text.
- Use footnotes when you have made considerable use of interviews, because the reader will see so many text references he can be distracted.

2 Reference types

o **General reference**

If you only refer to the general message contained in the writing of another person, it is sufficient to mention the author and the year of publication in parentheses at the end of the sentence, followed by a full stop. For example: '(Freeman, 1982).'

Type of source	Text reference
Co-authors	(De Wit and Meyer, 2004).
Three or more authors	(Charbit et al., 1991).
More references	(Freeman, 1982; Kitsch, 1977).
Author's name is already part of your sentence	'According to Kitsch (1977) innovation processes...'
Title book/article already in the text	'Dicken in his Global Shift (1986) writes...'
More sources from the same author	(Marshall, 1912a) and (Marshall 1912b).
More writers with the same family name	(Johnson, J. 1993; Johnson, P., 1993).
Last name includes a prefix, like 'van' or 'von'	(Von Weiszacker, 1992).

Et al.: Latin: et alii (and others).

cf. means 'see' (cf. Morgan, 1984).

Prefix (for example: van, el, von): the bibliographical reference can be different.

You might have to refer to anonymous sources; like:

Type of source	Text reference
Newspaper	(Financial Times, 8 February 2001).
Magazine	(The Economist, 12 January 1999).
Publications of institutes or organisations	(United Nations, 1998).
Annual report	(Heineken, 2002).

- *Newspapers and magazines*: it is better to use the date than the number of the edition in the text.

You might have to refer to *non-original sources*; like:

Type of source	Text reference
Max Weber quoted in paperback of Janssen	(Weber, quoted in Janssen 2001: 198)

- *Bibliography*: in which 'Janssen 2001' is mentioned in the bibliography.

- Do **not add a footnote** to a heading stating: 'most of this section is based on' followed by a particular source. Refer to the source where appropriate in your text. Repeat this as many times as necessary.

○ **Argument reference**
In case you refer to a more specific argument, you should also be more specific in your reference. Include page references that are added after the year of publication with a colon and a space. For instance: (Marshall, 1912a: 43) or (Piore and Sabel, 1984: 34-36).

Sometimes you can omit unneeded zeros or digits in page indications. The notation only changes with the second page indication:

Type of source	Text reference
Pages below 100	(Marshall 1912a: 1-3; 94-95).
Pages above 100	(Piore and Sabel, 1984: 107-8; 617-18; 1002-6).

- Pages above 100: unless the first number is multiple of 100.

○ **Internet references**
- Always reveal the complete source as well as the date you consulted the source! So for instance: www.rsm.nl/dp8/xfhk, consulted on March, 2 2006 [explanation: the site might have disappeared the next day so the date of consulting is important as well].
- When referring to an article that appeared 'online' in a journal or newspaper directly mention the article instead of the complete website address (➲E11, E15).
- If you know who the author is the reference is the same as referring to the author of a book or (paper) article: (Bos, 2002).
- If the author is unknown, you only mention the main internet page and the date the page was last updated: (www.oxfamnovib.com, May 2002).

Articles on the internet (author is known)	Surname author(s), First name (or initials) (year of last update) *Title of article*, URL, Date and year of application website.
	Example: Bos, H. (2002) *Dogs should be on a leach*, www.hondenvriend.nl/artikel/lijn1821.htm, 23 June 2004.
Articles on the Internet (anonymous author)	URL (Year of last update) *Title of the article*, Date and year of application website.
	Example: www.hondenvriend.nl/artikel/lijn1821.htm (2002) *Dogs should be on a leash*, 23 June 2004.
Wikipedia reference	Never! Always search for further supportive material (➲A15)

This Skill Sheet lists a number of generally applicable rules for correctly using abbreviations and acronyms (which are abbreviations that create a word that is easy to pronounce like 'radar' or 'NATO').

1 Abbreviations: when to avoid them
It is important to realize two things when using abbreviations:
- A reader will *not* automatically *know* what you mean by an abbreviation, for example NATO or EU.
- It is better to spell abbreviations *in full* the first time and repeat the abbreviations during a longer text.

■ Abbreviation of a concept or organisation in another language

English	French	Dutch
European Union (EU)	Union Européenne (UE)	Europese Unie (EU)
North Atlantic Treaty Organisation (NATO)	Organisation du Traité de l'Atlantique Nord (OTAN)	Noord Atlantische Verdragsorganisatie (NAVO)
United Nations (UN)	Nations Unies (NU)	Verenigde Naties (VN)

- The meaning of abbreviations can be completely different using different languages.

Different types of abbreviations

Type of Abbreviation	Good spelling (in scientific text)	Wrong spelling (in scientific text)
One word	Query	Qy.
One word	Miss	Ms.
One word	Table, figure, percentage	Tab., Fig. Per cent (%)
Common expression	Pay on delivery	p.o.d.
Common expression	S'il vous plaît	s.v.p.
Foreign name	Saint	St.

- Write the words *in full* in scientific texts.

■ Contracted form

Good spelling (in scientific text)	Wrong spelling (in scientific text)
I am	I'm
She has	She's
He had not	He hadn't

- Do not write in the *contracted form, like I'm, she's or he hadn't* in scientific texts.

■ Latin expressions

Latin expression	Meaning
e.g.	For example
cf.	See (cf. Porter, 1980, pp. 45-67)
Op.cit	Quoted work

- Readers think of different meanings with common abbreviations of Latin expressions in scientific texts.

> A reader will not be able to *remember* the exact meaning of the abbreviation that you have explained on a previous page. *Repeat* the meaning of an abbreviation from time to time.

2 Abbreviations: how to use them correctly

Abbreviations can not possibly be left out of texts all together. Abbreviations add certain efficiency to your reading and writing, which should not be underestimated. Moreover, a number of abbreviations are just as common as words written in full. Therefore, the remainder of this Skill Sheet will state a number of spelling rules for abbreviations that can often be used *without much explanation*.

■ Abbreviated job titles

Some of the most common titles are:

Abbreviation	Meaning
Prof.	Professor
M.Phil	Master of Philosophy
M.Sc.	Master of Science
Ph.D.	Doctor of Philosophy
B.Phil.	Bachelor of Philosophy
M.A.	Master of Arts
M.B.A.	Master of Business Administration

- It is recommended to check national spelling conventions. Rules differ from country to country, but in general job titles get a full stop. Check the following example; the abbreviation of the word 'professor':

English and German	French	Dutch
Prof.	prof	prof.

■ International system of measurement

Abbreviation	Meaning
Kg	kilogram
M	meter
A	Ampère
KWh	kilo Watt hour
Hz	Hertz

- These abbreviations (kg and m) are usually written in lower case. In abbreviations derived from a person's name, the letter referring to that name becomes a capital: Hz (referring to Hertz).

■ Currency indications
In economic literature, the problem of misinterpreted abbreviations often occurs with currency indications. The currency abbreviation should always be *preceded* by the currency indication (example A) and some currencies have *no space* between letter and figure (example B).

Example	Good spelling	Wrong spelling
A	euro 500, yen 10.000	500 euro, 10.000 yen
B	$100, £300	$ 100, £ 300

- If you are not one hundred percent certain that the reader will understand, spell the currency out the first time you use it.

■ Nationally used abbreviations
Use the nationally used abbreviations, if appropriate, even in English texts. For example, it is the following in case of the status of a company in:

Country	Abbreviation
The United States	Inc. (Incorporated)
The United Kingdom	Ltd. (Limited)
Germany	AG (Aktiengesellschaft)
The Netherlands	N.V. (Naamloze Vennootschap)

- These abbreviations are always added *after* the company name.

■ **Abbreviation with or without full stop**
- The full stop is *dropped*:
    - in some languages for personal indications: Mme (French; Madam); but in American English for instance all abbreviations get a full stop (or 'period'): Mr. (Mister).
    - in the international system of measurement: kg, m (see 2.2);
    - unless explicitly chosen by an organisation, most abbreviations do not contain a full stop. Some even start with a capital: Eureka, Esprit (for European collaboration programmes). Others are composed only of capitals, but without a full stop: UN, EU, NATO (see 1.1).
- A full stop is *added*:
    - in abbreviations of names of countries or cities: U.S. (United States), U.K. (United Kingdom), N.Y. (New York), L.A. (Los Angeles);
    - according to convention: 'ed.', 'ch.', 'vol.', 'no.', 'ibid.', 'et al.

Abbreviation (singular)	Abbreviation (plural)	Meaning
Ed.	Eds	Editor(s)
Ch.	Chs	Chapter(s)
Vol.	Vols	Volume(s)
No.	Nos	Number(s)
Ibid.	Does not exist	The same
Et al.	Does not exist	And others (Latin: et alii)

- The full stop disappears again in the *abbreviated plural*: 'eds', 'chs', 'vols', 'nos'.

■ **Economise on space: tables, boxes and figures**
   When you want to economise on space, you can make more use of abbreviations such as '%' in tables, boxes and figures. You have to explain the meaning of the abbreviations close to the table, box or figure (➌E14).

As a rule: avoid using a lot of abbreviations whenever possible; never use an abbreviation *without explaining the meaning.*

Tables, figures and boxes can clarify a text considerably, provided they are used properly. This Skill Sheet discusses the structure and the layout of these three instruments. A table usually consists of columns/rows, a figure is made up of drawings, and a box contains texts.

Table	Figure	Box

Table 6.1 Degrees of internationalisation of Japanese, European and US firms (1980-90)

firms	internationalisation (in)*		
	1980	1985	1990
Shell	50	60	70
IBM	40	45	43+
Toyota	low+	10	13

Sources: UNCTAD, 1993: 45-7; OECD, 1995: 144

Notes: * defined as the ratio of exports:imports:turnover in home market; +1989; + < 5%

Figure 1.4 Population development in Africa, 1600-1940 period

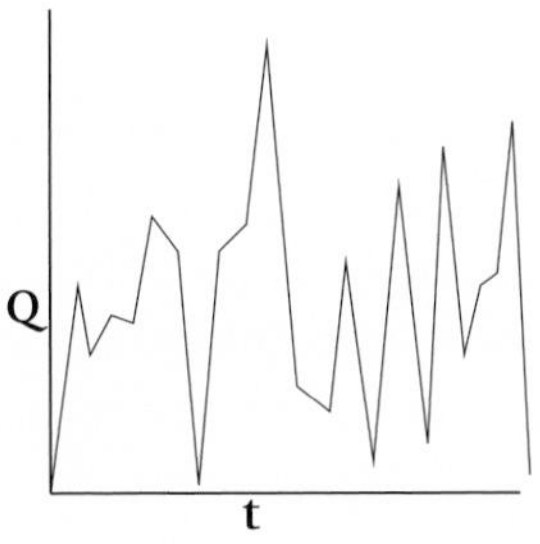

Source: Cantwell, 1960: 3

CIM, a solution in search of a problem

The CIM abbreviation has different meanings, for different groups. Depending on the interests involved, CIM stands for: 'Continually Improving Manufacturing'; 'Computer Interfaced Manufacturing'; 'Creative Implementations in Manufacturing'; 'Change In Manufacturing'; 'Computer Integrated Management'; 'Computer Integrated Manufacturing'.

Source: based on Davis, 1987: 45; Dankbaar, 1989: 20-22

1 Main aspects tables/figures/boxes

A reader should be able to understand a table, figure or box without having to go through the whole text. A reader should always understand three important aspects of tables/figures/boxes: their status, aim and contents.

○ **The status**
Is the information your own invention or taken from somewhere else?
- *Always identify the source accurately*, beneath the table; note 'Source:' followed by an exact reference according to the Harvard reference system without parentheses and without a full stop (for example 'Source: Coase, 1937: 25').
- *No source indication* reveals to the reader that it is your own invention. (⊕E2)

○ **The aim**
This always requires a clear heading/title containing information about:
- the *topic*: in clear, short and unambiguous phrasing;
- the *place* or region: 'European Union', 'Argentina', 'Rome';
- the *timeframe*: applicable for most information in the table/figure (period or year).

○ **The main contents**

What do the columns, the rows, or symbols in the table or figure mean:
use *clear abbreviations* for column and row indicators, or use notes to explain;

- *distinguish* column and row indicators from the other information by using bold, italics or underlining;
- *always* include a *legend* if your figure has arrows and other symbols. The legend is often placed in a separate box to distinguish it from the rest of the figure;
- *under* the table/figure, include *explanations* of the symbols used *in* the table/figure to point at *exceptions* to the information in the title.

> **Basic rule**: Tables / figures / boxes should largely *'speak for themselves'*, but should always be explained and referred to in the text.

The basic rule stated above seems contradictory, but it is not. Figures, tables or boxes are used in support of a text, they can never act as a substitute for well-formulated text and analysis.

Figures, tables and boxes can have various functions: a complement, an illustration, a more detailed elaboration. The function should always be clear from the adjoining text. But the text should concentrate on the analysis and not on lengthy explanations, which means that the figure/table/box should be presented in a way that is largely self-evident.

If the information contained in figure, table or box does not have a function in your analysis, it should not have been included in your text. The practical application of the basic rule can also be elaborated as follows: without any major alterations you have to be able to use the figure/table as a *transparency/slide* for a presentation (➡F5).

2 Qualitative tables

Tables do not need to be quantitative. Tables can also include qualitative information. Useful applications of qualitative tables consist of (1) summarising your own argument; (2) summarising the arguments of others. By using a table format you are organising your information and argumentation along clearly identifiable lines (the rows and columns). Putting your argument in a table increases the clarity of your writing substantially. If you do this *before* you begin your research, it can also improve the clarity of your analysis. This technique is also known as argumentation through schematisation (➡E6).

3 Layout: Tables and figures

- Always spell 'Figure' and 'Table' in *full*. Also do this in the text.
- *Number* tables and figures, preferably by chapter: first number is the chapter, second number the indication of the sequence of the table/figure in the chapter: '1.1', '3.5'; '10.1'. Tables and Figures follow separate sequences. You could have a 'Table 4.3' and a 'Figure 4.3' in the same chapter.

- Always begin the *heading/title* with a *capital letter*. With shorter titles the whole title can be capitalised. This is a matter of taste and preference. Headings/titles should be printed '*bold*'.
- *Full stop*. Do not use a full stop *at the end of items* in a list of tables or figures. Use ';' to mark the difference between separate items in the same category in the table or figure. Do not use a full stop either at the Table or Figure number. Do not use a full stop at the end of the heading, nor at the end of the sources and notes, unless the latter contain an explanatory sentence.
- In the case of a table *always* place the number and description *above* the table. Always place the 'Source(s):' indication *below*. Sometimes, the number and title of figures are placed *below* the image.
- This is done because figures and the like are very often originals drafted by the author. If this is the case, there need not be a source below the figure either. A title *and* a source at the same position is messy.
- Use a *capital letter* for the 'Source' and 'Note' indication.
- Add *explanatory notes* below the Sources. Do not use footnotes. Do not number the notes. It can be confusing because the table already consists of numbers. For a single note use an asterisk (*); for more than one note you can use other signs: °, §; or: you can use letters: a, b, c...
- Make clear what belongs to the Table/Figure and what belongs to the main text. *Insert sufficient space* (preferably two hard returns) between the title and the source/notes and the running text.
- When you *refer to the Table/Figure in the text*, refer by number – 'Table 4.5 illustrates...' – rather than 'the figure on the next page illustrates...' or 'the table following'.
- Be aware of *copyright* provisions when you copy complete tables, pictures or figures!
- Whenever possible *position* the table/figure on the relevant page, i.e. where it is discussed.
- Only use the *landscape* (vertical printing) option if the table has many columns.
- If the table runs onto *another page*, repeat a short title indication. For instance: '*(Table 6.1, continued)*'
- With a thesis, add a list of Tables/Figures after the contents, and before the preface (➔E3).

4 Layout: Boxes

The use of boxes is often aimed at presenting information, which the author could not really find an appropriate place for in the analysis itself, but nevertheless found 'interesting'. Boxes are often (ab)used for this purpose, like lengthy footnotes (➔E11) or annexes (➔E5). When included, boxes:
- should have a clear function in the text;
- often serve illustrative and/or layout purposes (like the boxes in these Skill Sheets);
- should, if appropriate, identify a source that can be placed *in* or *below* the box;
- should preferably be
- not be longer than one page.

The bibliography allows the writer to use shorter references in the text. Your text is then easier to read. It also makes it easier for yourself and the reader to check whether you have considered the most relevant literature on the subject. All your written sources are alphabetically listed in one place and not spread at random over the whole paper. A bibliography requires accurate work during your research. Do not wait until you have finished writing your text.

'Golden' rules of a bibliography

- List your sources *alphabetically and chronologically*.
- Do *not* include sources that you have not referred to in the text.
- Do *not* include works that you have *not* read, in the bibliography. *Never* compete on the *length* of your bibliography. Make sure that the references in the text (➔B11) and your bibliography *match perfectly*.
- In principle, do not split up your bibliography according to sources (articles, books).

No reference in a text without a bibliography; no bibliography at the end of a text without references in the text.—Irene Cieraad

1 Digital administration bibliography

The update of your bibliography is nowadays easier than ever before. Software companies have developed reference programs that support you in building your own digital bibliography. In this way, you can create a *digital administration of your bibliography*. Examples of these reference programs are Endnote, ProCite, and Reference Manager. These programs keep your bibliography automatically up to date during the whole process of writing a report. You will never face those moments at the end of the writing process anymore that you had to look for references that disappeared in the sometimes chaotic process of writing. These programs have some other advantages:

- Abstracts are included in your bibliography. It could be very helpful during a literature scan in the process of writing an essay or a thesis.
- Keywords are included; which helps you to estimate the importance of an article for your research purpose.
- Automatically updates your bibliography to a certain style (Harvard, APA, footnotes, or others; every journal has its own reference system).
- Providers of these programs frequently update their reference style.
- Makes your research effort more efficient. It saves a lot of time at the end of the writing process.
- Well-known libraries, like the American Library of Congress or the British Library automatically have an option to put the reference in your digital bibliography. More and more libraries will add this option to their services.

- Overall, you will never be frustrated anymore, when you need to *compile your final bibliography* once you have completed the paper (when you have returned most of the literature to the library). It is all locked up in your own digital bibliography.

> **Never lose track of your references anymore. Use an online administration program (Endnote, ProCite, or Reference Manager) for your own digital bibliography. [⊕⊙www.skillsheets.com for further information on these programs].**

2 Bibliography: author

A bibliographical reference starts most of the times with the last name of an author. But it sometimes turns out to be different, for example when the author is unknown. Some additional possibilities to help you administrate these bibliographical references:

Situation	Solution for bibliography
Anonymous source	Use title as reference, use 'anonymous', or N.N.
More than one author	Note them *all* in bibliography. Never use 'et al.'
More sources from the same author	Marshal, A. (1912a), ... Marshall, A. (1912b) (⊕B11)

- *Prefix*: (examples: van, von, el, etc.) In references in the text they are stated first. In *European bibliographies* (and libraries) they are placed after the family name. So look under the letter 'W' for a reference to 'Weizacker, von'. In *American bibliographies* (libraries and data bases) you will find 'Von Weizacker' in the authors' register under the letter 'V'.

3 Overview main bibliographical references

The most widely used bibliographical references are summed up in this paragraph. Each box contains the 'theoretical' reference and a 'practical' one. Some specific remarks concerning this reference are added below the box.

– **Books**	Last Name Author(s), First Name (Editor in case of edited volume) (Date) *Title of Book*, Number of Edition (if other than 1st edition), Place of Publication: Publisher, ## pp. (optional).
	Brenner, R. (2001) *The Financial Century: from Turmoils to Triumphs*, Toronto: Stoddard Publishing, 214 pp.

- *Date of publication*: only state the year;
- *Full title* information of publication: title and under title;

- *Essential information on the publisher*: Include always the place of publication and the name of the publisher;
- If you used a translation of a book: never list the original source instead.

– **Article in books**	Last Name Author of Article, First Name (Date) 'Title of Article', in:
– **Essay in books**	Name Book Editor (ed.) *Title of Main Book*, Number of Edition, Place of
– **Chapter in books**	Publication: Publisher, pp. #-#.
	Ismail, M.N. (1999) Foreign firms and national technological upgrading: the electronics industry in Malaysia, in: K.S. Jomo, Greg Felker and Rajah Rasiah (eds) *Industrial Technology Development in Malaysia: Industry and firm studies*, London and New York: Routledge, pp. 21-37.

- *Date of publication*: give more specific information: edition, number, month.
- *Full title* information of publication: add the full title of the book.
- Articles, essays or chapters in a book: *do state* 'in:...'.

– **Article in paper**	Last name Author(s), First Name (Date) Title of Article, *Name Paper*,
– **Article in journal**	Place of Publication: (Publisher, pp. #-#).
	Hall, W. (14 August 2002) Credit Suisse loss worse than expected, *The Financial Times*, New York.

- Do not include *newspapers* as an entry in your list. If you want to, make a separate list of the journals and newspapers that you have made use of.
- Articles in a newspaper or journal *do not state*: 'in:...';
- Do *not* include anonymous sources taken from the press.

– **Article in periodical**	Last Name of Author(s), First Name (Date) 'Title of Article', *Title of Periodical* # (Date of Volume or Issue): pp. #-#.
	D'Aveni, R. (1999) 'Strategic Supremacy Through Disruption and Dominance', *Sloan Management Review*, Vol. 40, No. 3, pp. 95-106.

- The *exact page references* in a *periodical article* are mandatory.
- *Full title* information of publication: add the title of the periodical.

– **Annual report**	Title annual report (Date) Title of article, company name, pp. #-#

Ahold annual report 2001 (April 2002) Financial Highlights, Royal Ahold NV, pp. 2-3

- *Title of article*: Mention the part(s) of the annual report you have used.

– **Internet** – **Internet (author unknown)** – **Email**	Last name of Author(s), First name (date) Title of Article, Online Place of publication, Website visited: (Date), Available WWW: URL address
	Fairley, P. (2002) Wind Power for Pennies, www.technologyreview.com, 30 July 2002
	www.technologyreview.com (2002) 'Wind Power for Pennies', 30 July 2002
	Fairley, P. (2002) Wind Power for Pennies, in: Technology Review, www.technologyreview.com, 30 July 2002
	www.technologyreview.com (2002) Wind Power for Pennies', in: Technology Review', 30 July 2002
	Last name of Sender, First name (date), Title of Email, Name of recipient, date Sender and recipient names and email addresses, title of the email, and the date
	Jaspers, F. (2004), E-communication, Email from H. Quak, hquak@rsm.nl, 11 August 2004

- *Website visited*: it is necessary to include the exact date of the page visit. Web pages change regularly.
- *Uniform Resource Locator (URL)*: the exact address of the Internet reference.
- Always *store* an email message that was used as a reference.

– **Report of an institution** – **Report of a conference**	Last name of Author(s), First name (date) *Title of Report*, Place of Publication: Publisher, pp. #-#
	UNCTAD (2001), *World Investment Report 2001: Promoting Linkages*, Geneva: United Nations Publication

- *Institutional reports* can be listed under the name of the institutional department if the author's name is not given. (Example: Commission of the European Communities (1987) *Report on State Aid*, Brussels: Directorate General IV (Competition Policy).

- *Full title* information of publication: in the case of an *internal paper from an institu-tion*: add the name of the institution.
- *Full title* information of publication: In the case of a *conference paper*: add the title of the conference.

4 Layout bibliography

- When the reference is *longer than one line*, use an indent for the remainder of the reference.
- If one name is used several times, it is sufficient to use: '–'.
- Works by a single author precede works edited by that author; these in turn pre-cede works done in collaboration with others (according to the Chicago Manual of Style, 13th edition).
- Note that a bibliographical entry always refers to the whole source, not to one page number (which is in the text) (➔E12).

Example of a bibliography

Bannan, N. (1981) 'Anglo-Scandinavia structures in Northern England', unpublished M.Phil. thesis, University of Cambridge.

Bickley, A.R. (1990) 'Septimius Severus: the later years', *Antiquity* 24,2: 261-81.

Brenner, R. and Glick, M. (1991) 'The regulation approach: theory and history', *New Left Review* 188: 45-120.

Brödner, P. (1987) Fabrik 2000: *Alternative Entwicklungspfade in die Zukunft der Fabrik*, 2nd edition, Berlin: Edition Sigma.

Buckley, P. and Casson, M. (1991) *The Future of the Multinational Enterprise*, Basingstoke/London: MacMillan.

— (1988) 'A theory of cooperation in international business', in: Contractor, F. and Lorange, P. (eds) *Cooperative Strategies in International Business*, Lexington, MA: Lexington books, pp. 125-147.

Butaney, G., John, E., Smith, M. and Wortzel, L. (1988) 'Distributor power versus manufacturer power: the customer role', *Journal of Marketing* 52, January: 52-63.

Brown, G. (1991) *Roman France*, trans. D. Sheldon, London: Batsford.

Chesnais, F. (1993) 'Globalisation, world oligopoly and some of their implications', in: Humbert, M. (ed.) *The Impact of Globalisation on Europe's Firms and Industries*, London: Pinter Publishers, pp. 12-22.

— (forthcoming) *La Mondialisation du Capital*, Paris: Syros, Alternatives Economiques.

Commission of the European Communities (1987) *Report on State Aid*, Brussels: Directorate General IV (Competition Policy).

De Wit, B., and R. Meyer (2004) *Strategy: Process, Content, Context*, Third edition, Thomson Learning, London.

Van Deth, G.A. (2004) *In Search of Competitive Dynamics in the Management Consulting Industry: Reflecting on McKinsey, Berenschot, and Cap Gemini Ernst & Young*, Master's thesis, Erasmus University, Rotterdam.

E16 Layout

Advanced computer software facilitates the usage of many 'fancy' layout programs – adding colour, changing fonts, presenting three-dimensional tables. Always remember that it is ultimately the contents that count and not their appearance! Weak contents can never be substituted by a good layout. Good contents, however, can easily be ruined by a weak layout. The layout is always instrumental in getting your message across. This Skill Sheet summarizes the minimum layout requirements.

1 One space

A very simple rule, but one which is often forgotten: always *leave only one space margin* after: a full stop (.), a comma (,), a colon (:), a semi-colon (;), a closing quotation mark ('), question marks (?) and exclamation marks (!). *Never leave a space margin in front* of these marks.

2 Italics

Do not hesitate to use *italics* to attract the reader's attention to the most important passages. The reader needs some focal points in the text. Reading long pages of text without any change in the textual 'landscape' is very difficult. Of course, do not put everything in italics.

3 Indents

Use 'indents' intelligently. An indent moves the margin of a whole paragraph to the right/left. It is not very elegant when indents are continued on the following page(s). This gives a very 'shaky' image to the text space. In the final stages of editing your paper, consider the consequences of your layout choices for the whole text.

4 Chapters/sections

o Chapters should always begin on a new page, preferably on an odd page. Sections can begin anywhere, but preferably not at the bottom of a page.
o Never call something a 'chapter' if it is not, for instance when five or less pages of text are called a 'chapter'. The reader is given the impression that you are trying to upgrade the status of your text by giving small parts of your research 'bigger' names than they deserve. The reader might begin to think that the rest of your research is also 'puffed up'. Only use the heading 'chapter' if it is 'a real chapter'. A chapter generally is a separate part of the analysis that amounts to more than five to ten pages.
o Do not call a 'section' by name ('Section 1.8'), but write down the number and/or the heading only.

5 Paragraphs

o Use a 'tab' or one or two spaces before the first lines of a new paragraph. Be consistent throughout your text.

o Avoid having many short paragraphs on one page. The resulting 'notched' page layout presents the reader with a staccato image of your text, and contributes to a rather turbulent state of mind of the reader (➔E8).

o Avoid long paragraphs: longer than one page. Long paragraphs make the layout of your page tedious and unspecific. If you combine this type of page with no bold print or italics, the reader is left without any visual guidance as to the consecutive parts, main issues and side issues. Reading becomes harder because it is difficult to concentrate on such dull looking texts.

6 Position title/headings/figures/tables

Always check that a *title or heading* is *not* positioned at the bottom of a page while the rest of the text is on the following page. This is sometimes called a 'widow' or 'orphan' construction: the title becomes divorced form the adjoining text. This error occurs when people do not check the final version of their paper. The same is true for the last line of a paragraph that has been positioned at the top of a new page. The latter is more difficult to change, but always make an effort. Always perform a final check of your paper for 'widows' and 'orphans'.

Also make sure that your *tables and figures* are on one page. In most word-processing programs there are protection functions that make it impossible for a table or figure to become spread over two pages. Find out how to operate these functions efficiently.

7 Headings and titles

o Formulate **short headings**; avoid headings that exceed one line.

o Headings rarely contain a full sentence: there is **no verb**; there is rarely a punctuation mark (except for ':'); there is no full stop (not after the numerals nor at the end of the heading).

o Formulate **active and direct headings**.

Active and direct heading	Passive and indirect heading
Job security	The various aspects of job security
Indicators of argumentation	The most important indicators in argumentation processes.

o Always use titles and headings as support and guidance for the reader. Never use them as a substitute for your text. Do not refer to the title in your text, by 'this' or 'these' indications.

DON'T:	DO:
• 3.6 Financial selection methods	• 3.6 Financial selection methods
• These methods refer to...	• The second method to select projects is financial...

- o Do **not centre** headings (chapter titles can be the exception).
- o Make headings and titles clearly **distinguishable** from the rest of the text: (1) by using line spaces above and below them, (2) by using bold letters, italics, capital letters (⊕E6).
- o Show the **different levels** of headings (and thus the structure of your text). Two basic variants exist:
  - ▪ stylistic: '**CHAPTER**', 'SUBHEADING', '*sub-subheading*', 'sub-sub-subheading';
  - ▪ numerals: '1 CHAPTER', '1.1 Subheading', '1.1.1 Sub-subheading', '1.1.1.1 sub-sub-subheading'.
  - ▪ You may choose a combination of both variants, for sub-sub-subheadings in particular.
  - ▪ Do not use more than three degrees of subheadings. As a general rule: use subheadings sparingly. Publishers do not like the numbering of subheadings *unless* you use extensive cross-referencing in your text.

8 Clearly structured text

Scientific texts should be relatively predictable and should contain a clear structure. This means that the layout of your text, headings, subheadings and the like should also be relatively simple. If you want to be creative you should focus on the 'peripherals' of your text: (A) the chapter titles and title pages, (B) the page headers or footers, (C) the tables, figures and boxes, and (D) the margins. But even these parts of your paper should remain functional, which is why their design should also follow a number of minimum rules.

Minimum rules	Creative pointers
Number and title of chapter: ■ chapters generally start on odd numbered pages; ■ the first chapter page either does *not* contain a page number or it is positioned at the bottom of the page; ■ the title has the same top margin as first text lines; ■ title letters are bigger than the character you use in the text, but not more than three times the normal text size	☺ put part of the title or the chapter number in a box; ☺ use different fonts; look at layouts in other reports: not every combination is 'tasteful'; a common combination of fonts is the title in Helvetica and the text in Times (New) Roman; ☺ add vertical lines to your title; give the title a different appearance from the text
Page headers or footers: ■ use page headers or footers; never mix the two; ■ the page headings are short and normally do not exceed five words; ■ page headers/footers do not contain a verb (as is the case with headings in the text, ⊕E4); ■ page headers or footers are smaller than the letters in the text and are often in italics or bold to distinguish them from the main text; ■ no page numbers on empty pages	☺ add a running line under or above the heading or footer; ☺ switch odd and even pages with different headers: in general odd pages contain the title of the chapter or part, whereas the even pages can contain the title of (1) the section, (2) the whole report, (3) the author(s); ☺ you can add a logo to the header or footer (see these Skill Sheets, for instance)
Tables, Figures and Boxes: ■ for the basic requirements of tables/figures/boxes: ⊕E14; ■ in the case of tables, many publishers ask their writers *not to add vertical rules*; it makes the table more difficult to read	☺ add shades of grey, shadows and the like; make sure that the grey is not creating reading difficulties; grey shaded text is generally printed **bold** to support their readability; ☺ very decorative: you can use colour print for figures. But do not think that this will impress anybody if the text around this image is still sloppy. On the contrary, the more beautiful the images are, the more badly written surroundings will be noticed
Margins: • use sufficiently broad margins that allow the reader to make notes in the margin; • the margins for your headers and footers should be exactly the same as your main text; • if the width of the left and right margins differ, always have bigger left than right margins	☺ some organisations affix a number to every paragraph in addition to numbering sections and chapters (⊕E6). This makes it easier to edit or refer to a document because you just refer to the paragraph number. Policy documents and legal documents, therefore have numbered paragraphs; ☺ write *keywords* in the margin of paragraphs, as a service to the reader and a further revelation of the structure of your argument; ☺ Use the left and right margins for the page numbers

Series F Presentation

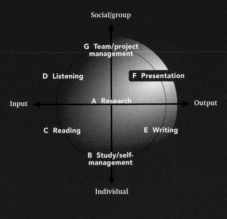

The Reflective Cycle of Effective Presentations

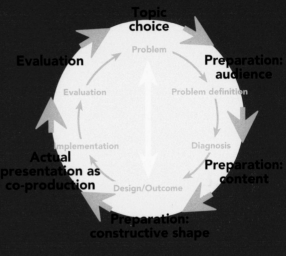

		Preparation: audience and content	Preparation: shape	Actual presentation	Evaluation
F1	Principles of Effective Presentation	■			
F2	Preparation	■	■		
F3	Presentation Formats	■	■		
F4	Presentation Design	■	■		
F5	Design (PowerPoint) Slides	■	■		
F6	Last-minute Presentation Checklist		■	■	
F7	Effective Use of Practical Tools		■	■	
F8	A Balanced Approach to Questioning			■	■
F9	Body Language			■	■
F10	Dealing with Disasters			■	■

Presentation Skill Levels

Level 1

- Based on personal experience
- Aimed at developing your own presentation skills
- Understand the (contextual) advantages and disadvantages of oral presentations
- Physical appearance (body language and intonation) form prime aim of feedback
- Use of simple audio-visual means
- Feedback by teacher or tutor
- Limited ability to receive and use feedback

Level 2

- Based on your group's research
- Aimed at effective knowledge transfer
- Understand the (contextual and content) preconditions for effective presentations
- Effective transfer of knowledge forms prime aim of feedback
- Increasingly sophisticated use of audio-visual means
- Feedback on presentation provided by the own group

Level 3

- Based on your own research
- Aimed at co-producing knowledge
- Ability to organise the preconditions for co-production of knowledge and interaction
- Balance between appropriate body language, content and the use of audio-visual means on the basis of a good understanding of the audience
- Self-organisation of feedback
- Good ability to receive and use feedback
- Understand the criticality of preparation of the presentation, room and support equipment

Level 4

- Based on research and experience
- Aimed at constructive communication and co-producing knowledge
- Action-oriented
- Flexibility in addressing various audiences
- Bargaining over the duration and content *before* the actual presentation to ensure that the presentation and the research is done justice

1   A good presentation can never be a substitute for weak contents, but strong contents can easily be overshadowed by a weak presentation

2   The occasion defines the most appropriate communication form

3   Representation defines the way you want to be looked at

4   Effective presentations balance speaking and listening

5   Effective presentations are always a co-production of speaker and audience

6   Bad presentations do not exist, only bad preparation

7   Failing equipment is never the fault of the organisation

8   Act responsibly: the manipulative power of the word (pathos) is stronger than you think

9   Always try to create the most favourable environment for your presentation

Presentation and writing are both output oriented skills. Their effectiveness depends on the degree to which the sender of the information has an impact on the receiver of the information. Presentation, however, also differs considerably from writing. There are, first of all, clear limitations to the ability of presenters to convince their audience. The capacity of the audience to 'digest' the information offered verbally is much more limited (⊕D Series) than in case of a written text. The audience can not turn the pages back to look at the previous arguments or push any 'repeat' button if the argument is not clear instantly. Interaction with the audience could hinder (because of noise, for example) the presentation. There are important communication barriers in the interaction between a speaker and the audience:

Speaking	*does not necessarily mean*	listening
Listening	*does not necessarily mean*	understanding
Understanding	*does not necessarily mean*	agreeing
Agreeing	*does not necessarily mean*	applying
Applying	*does not necessarily mean*	remembering

Source: Fendrich, 1979: 18

From limitation to opportunity

But, one can also turn the limitation into an advantage. The audience can contribute to the presentation by asking informed questions, or by showing interest (or lack of it), which can stimulate the presenter to continue or change in order to directly tailor the presentation to the needs of the audience. The writing process, on the other hand, is a lonely and indirect activity. Readers will only start providing feedback on a written text a considerable period of time after it was finished. It is difficult to keep motivated with such relatively indirect incentives. The immediate feedback possibilities of presentations can be very stimulating and conducive to developing a good argument. Moreover, presentations (and other forms of communication) provide a considerably wider variety of interaction models, which can increase the impact of the message – provided the presenter is able to link the best presentation mode to the audience. What the most appropriate presentation style is, and whether presenters can apply this, depends as much on their practice as on their intellectual ability to choose appropriate means in preparation. The effectiveness of a presentation critically depends on these abilities. Good content is a necessity, but never a sufficient condition for a good presentation. Luckily, a large number of tools are at the disposal of presenters, but using them effectively requires considerable skill and knowledge of the limitations of their usage. It also requires a willingness to 'set the stage', i.e. to create the most favourable condition for a presentation. That can never be achieved during a presentation, but happens all in the preparation. Behind the scenes is often where effective presentations are constructed, first in solid preparation with respect for the 'design' rules of effective communication (either with or without tools), but secondly also in direct bargaining with the environment. What seem like 'spontaneous' presentations are, often, the result of hard preparation. Easy presenting is hard preparation. In principle there are no bad presentations, only bad preparation.

Respect for rhetoric

If you want people to apply and remember your argumentation, the aim of the presentation can therefore never be to 'solely' transfer information. Giving a presentation is a social activity, so the audience plays a vital role in the 'production' of the knowledge. Presentations only aimed at information transfer underutilize the potential of presentation as a means of interactive communication. For information transfer, writing remains the best tool. This basic idea is supported by the classical Greek theory of rhetoric (box).

Three building blocks for persuasive presentations
- **Logos**: the *force of arguments*, which relates to the contents of the presentation, the line or argument adopted and the evidence that is presented.
- **Ethos**: The *credibility of the person* who is presenting the information, which depends on the authority or the impression given by the person. The more credible a person seems, the more an audience is likely to accept what is said.
- **Pathos**: the degree to which the presentation affects the audience, i.e. whether or not the presentation touches the *emotions*.

Source: ancient Greeks

In the listening skills series (➔D8) the building blocks of rhetoric were already introduced as a feedback aid for presenters. To utilize the potential of presentations to its full capacity, presentations should be an act of *co-production* between the presenter and the audience, a balancing act between the three rhetorical dimensions. Serving one rhetorical dimension without taking the other dimensions into account always leaves a presentation sub-optimal. The combination of the rhetorical characteristics varies from person to person. It depends on position and experience. For example, you could lack *ethos* because you have not yet acquired a reputation in your field, or you have just begun doing a job. To compensate you should work on the impression you make, your arguments and your appeal. Unfortunately, many speakers who *are well known* seem to think that they can economise on the *logos* and even the *pathos* part of their presentation. The result is something that everyone has ample experience of: uninspired, badly formulated and weakly prepared speeches that are only given because of the reputation of the speaker – a waste of time for both the speaker, and the audience. It is also easy to see that there is often more convincing power in speech than in writing. But – as we can learn from studies into mass communication – when pathos prevails, speech can also unleash great manipulative powers. In scientific presentations, the importance of *logos* over the other two rhetorical dimensions should always be respected. But the more *logos* can be combined with *ethos* and *pathos*, the more the effectiveness increases, even of a scientific speech. In all cases, the most effective presentations are always those that combine contents with form. More importantly even, good presentation skills can be acquired and trained, provided one is willing to learn it and organises effective feedback.

The building blocks of effective presentations

Effective presentations basically apply all the rules of constructive communication (⊕D series). They create a balance between speaking and listening. But presenters have better possibilities of creating the right preconditions for constructive communication than in the case of listening. Greater possibilities create greater responsibilities. The presenter can choose a topic, and prepare in advance the most appropriate tools and techniques. Their effectiveness, however, rarely depends on the actual verbal presentation skills of the presenter, but on a host of other dimensions that constitute constructive communication. It depends, (1) on the time allotted to the presentation; time determines preparation (⊕F2). It also depends on a correct assessment of (2) the audience and the setting of the presentation, which largely determine the chosen format (⊕F3), the content (⊕F4) and the design of the supportive tools (⊕F5). The degree of co-production that can be established, finally, depends on the dynamism of the actual meeting. From the perspective of the presenter, this dynamism can be positively influenced by practical last-minute preparation (⊕F6), by taking care of a proper appearance (⊕F7), by adequately dealing with questions (⊕F8), the presenter's body language (⊕F9) and the flexibility with which unexpected or adversarial circumstances are handled (⊕F10).

There is a number of 'checkpoints' that should *always* be taken into consideration when you begin preparing a presentation, i.e. *before* you really set down the design of the presentation. Always consider the following five questions before you start designing any presentation:

1 How *much time* do you need to prepare your *presentation*?
2 Who will be your *audience* and what is the setting?
3 What are (consequently) your aims and what kind of presentation is appropriate and feasible?
4 Which *equipment/tools* can you use in what setting?
5 Do you want to *practise* before?

1 Timing your time

The time it takes you to prepare a presentation depends on:
- the complexity of your topic;
- your experience;
- the type of presentation (for example, a thesis presentation or the presentation of a case).

In general, best assume that a very short presentation will take relatively more preparation time. Ten minutes constitutes a short presentation. Short presentations are the most difficult. When your presentation is longer than half an hour, often relative preparation (preparation/presentation) time decreases again (Figure F.2).

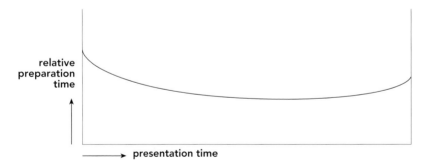

Figure F.2 *The Balance between preparation and presentation time*

Prepare a *time schedule* for your preparation period: use the same principles as with powerful writing (⊕E Series) in general and essay writing [⊕⊖www.skillsheets.com] in specific. Apply the 50/50 principle for effective preparations. Bad presentations often originate in preparations in which too much time is spent on one or two of these principles. In your presentation you are in fact as good as the weakest link of your preparation. For important presentations, plan to have your story ready at least three days before the presentation, allowing some time for practice, feedback by others, second thoughts and alterations.

The 50/50 Principles for effective preparations

☐ Use half of your time to conceptualise your presentation and to decide what it is that you want to say:

- *Inventory* and brainstorming: 30% of your preparation time;
- *Structure* into a very limited number of points: 20% of your preparation time.

☐ Spend the remaining time (fifty percent) on further elaboration of your presentation:

- *Formulation*: of your argument and storyline – on cards, on transparencies/slides or otherwise: 30% of your preparation time;
- *Editing*: if you use visual tools, try to give your presentations an interesting and consistent layout (⊕F5): 20% of your preparation time.

2 Assessing the audience and setting in advance

The effects of different audiences on presentations are quite obvious, but the importance of assessing the audience correctly is often not well understood. A good assessment makes the difference between a presentation in front of 'the' audience (detached) or with 'your' audience (attached and co-producers). A presentation in front of a small audience requires a different approach than a presentation in front of a large audience in a big auditorium. If your audience is well informed you should invest time developing better contents. If your presentation comes at the end of a long succession of other speeches, it is a good idea to spend more time producing an interesting and 'witty' introduction. Once you know who your audience will be, it is relatively easy to think about the consequences for your presentation. A good presenter will always try to get adequate information. Unfortunately, it is not always possible to get the information in time. Make sure, in that case, to arrive earlier and check *before* your presentation what the actual audience and the settings are in order to make some relevant last-minute adjustments to your presentation [or negotiate with the organisers and/or the teachers for optimal conditions for your presentation]. Always take the responsibility in your own hands, never wait for the organisers to come up with instructions. They often have other tasks at the same time that might intervene with your interests. But at the moment of presentation you alone (not the organiser) will suffer from the consequences of bad preparation. In case even last-minute arrangements prove impossible, other techniques are available during your presentation to assess 'your' audience (⊕F6, F10).

Preparation questions for assessing the Personal setting

- **How many** people will you address?
  - Small group: interactive presentations often work best in groups of up to fifteen persons
  - Medium-sized groups: up to 60 people, importance of using tools increases
  - Large groups: above 60 people; importance of simple/concise messages increases
- **Why** are they there?
  - Obligatory (course)
  - Voluntary: did they have to pay to attend?

- – Because of their involvement in the topic
- – Out of interest
- What is the **composition** of your audience?
  - – Demographic characteristics: age, gender, culture
  - – Educational background
- What is the **level of understanding** of the topic of the audience?
  - – Experts (professors) ⊕ focus most on content and information
  - – Fellow students ⊕ focus more on persuasion
  - – General audience (Thesis presentation) ⊕ balance persuasion and content
- What is **their status**: are they decision-makers?
- What is **your status** (in the eyes of the audience)?
  - – What is your **reputation**?
  - – What is your level of credibility (*ethos*) with the audience, i.e. to what extent do you have to explain who you are?
- Who is officially '**in charge**'?
  - – Chairman of the day
  - – The teacher or a tutor
  - – A fellow student
  - – Remember: ultimately you are always in charge of your own presentation
- Will you be the end, or the beginning, of a long **sequence** of presentations?
  - – First presentation of the day: 'wake up call' for most
  - – Second presentation: most focused and active listening posture (provided they did not fall asleep again during the previous presentation)
  - – Third presentation: span of attention will wither away and additional means are needed to keep them involved
  - – Fourth presentation: try to get out of this position (depends a bit on the time of the previous presentations; in case of short presentations, it need not be bad).
  - – Fifth presentation: ask for a break.
- Will your presentation be immediately before, or after, a **break**?
  - – Before a break: understand that you are the only person keeping the audience from getting a break; you don't have to make the presentation shorter – be assertive – but nevertheless assess what this circumstance implies for the effectiveness of your speech
  - – After a break: understand that you are the first to talk to an audience after they had engaged in more active interaction; relate to this
- Who are the **other speakers**?
  - – Same story: establish possible overlap and use this as a linking-pin for your own presentation
  - – Different story: make sure that the audience does not get confused; provide a 'bridge' with the other presentations

3 Prioritize Aims

In deciding upon the most effective type of presentation (⊖F3) you should establish first what you aim at. In order to be effective, presentations can have various aims at the same time, but it is vitally important to establish your **priority aim**:

- transfer information (remember the limitations of presentations for this aim);
- make yourself known to your audience (working on your public profile);
- stimulate your audience into making decisions;
- stimulate the audience into taking some form of action;
- try to please your audience;
- add to the occasion (special occasions like inaugurations and the like);
- trigger questions from the audience (➲F8);
- provoke your audience and trigger them into debate;
- attempt to create active listening and/or learning;
- inspire your audience to start reading the literature;
- other aims?

4 Identify availability of equipment and the setting

Equipment. Presentation tools are very important. They define the shape of the presentation, the nature of the possible interaction and to a large extent therefore also the contents and the effectiveness. The available equipment thus defines the limitations as well as the possibilities of presentations. The decision for the use of particular equipment is therefore also a decision for the design, and consequently for a particular type of presentation (➲F4, F5, F7). Consider whether the following tools and equipment are available at the venue of your presentation. Always check before the actual presentation whether they work:
- ☐ Overhead projectors (to make use of transparencies)
- ☐ Video equipment
- ☐ Beamer (technical personnel on hand to give support?)
- ☐ Clip/flip chart? (markers available?)
- ☐ Whiteboard or blackboard (sufficient markers available?)

Setting. The actual setting of the lecture/presentation room is often as important as the availability of equipment. Often organisations try to match the size of the room with the available equipment, but this is not always the case. Prepare yourself to be active as regards influencing the setting. Some examples:
- ☐ In case of an oversized lecture room: ask participants to come forward to facilitate co-production
- ☐ In case of a chaotically organized meeting room: rearrange the tables so that you can actually talk to each other

Posture. The available equipment and the organisation of the room define what constitutes an optimal use of the equipment. Picture yourself in advance in this setting. What is the most appropriate way to present:
- ☐ Sitting on a chair
- ☐ Standing behind a desk
- ☐ Standing and whole body visible
- ☐ Sitting behind a desk
- ☐ Walking around
- ☐ Sitting on a table (experienced presenters!)

5 Practice and try-out

Depending on your experience (your Presentation Skills level), you may wish to *practise* several times before the 'real' presentation. Take your time for this. Mistakes at the real event cannot be deleted, so taking responsibility for a good presentation requires that you also take responsibility for adequate practice. Be aware, however, that there will always be substantial differences between practice and the actual event (box). This is not necessarily bad.

☐ Mirror, 'fake' audience, 'friendly' audience

- It is recommended to practise your presentation in front of a mirror. You are able to observe yourself, which improves your own attitude/positioning during the final presentation.
- You could also practise your presentation in front of a fake audience: a picture of someone, a poster, a group of teddy bears... whatever works for you. This fake audience will give you the feeling that you are talking to a real one.
- Ask a number of fellow students to listen to your presentation. They can give you decent feedback beforehand, provided they know what kind of feedback you want, and are able to do this systematically (➔D8). A friendly audience makes it easier to make mistakes, a too friendly audience however will not be able to give you the appropriate feedback you need to prepare yourself for the actual presentation. Talk about your expectation before you start the trial presentation. A good way of creating a more realistic try-out environment is by asking your audience to **play roles**: let them imagine the audience or slip into the skin of your most ardent critic; how would they then respond? (And how would you respond in return?)

Noticeable differences between try-outs and the real presentation

1. **Physical**: You are more nervous: the level of adrenaline increases, which can have both positive and negative effects on your presentation (check how this affects you). For instance, your nervousness intervenes directly with your brain activity during presentations, you are less relaxed and less flexible. So do not think that a difficult argument that you dealt with during the try-out, will be easy to reproduce when you present your argument in front of the *real* audience.

2. **Time**: It will always take longer than it did during the try-out. The actual presentation is often at least thirty to forty percent *slower* than the try-out.

3. **Clothing**: You will probably wear different clothes during the actual presentation than those you wore during the try-out. Make sure that the clothes that you wear during the actual presentation are comfortable and that you feel relaxed wearing these clothes.

4. **Interaction**: A presentation might not be as entertaining as it was when you practised: not all jokes or witty phrases will get the reception that you hoped for; other factors can also disturb the presentation and lessen the desired effect. The audience will probably be less friendly and understanding than your friends that attended the try-out. Talk about this in the try-out. Some presenters get really confused with this process and the audience will recognize it. It will result in an audience that does not take you seriously, because they think that you are not telling them your story in a natural way.

5   **Infrastructure**: the supporting tools, equipment and the environment probably differ substan-
    tially from the actual presentation. Preferably practise in a comparable setting with comparable
    tools, but if this is not possible (which it often is not) use your imagination!

☐ Further recommendations

- Do not write down the entire presentation *word for word*. It could deprive you of
  spontaneity in your presentation.
- Do *not* attempt to learn your presentation by heart. It will take away much of the
  spontaneity as well. But do know the general structure by heart. Learning by
  heart may make you more nervous because you will probably forget some of the
  lines, which can easily cause inexperienced speakers to panic.
- If you arrange your first try-out at the last moment you run the risk that this will
  only add to your feeling of uncertainty. Certainly if you discover that there are
  problems: it will no longer be possible to change the presentation, which will
  make you even more *nervous*.

The occasion – in combination with your aim – defines the best presentation strategy and decides whether your presentation can be considered effective. The success of the format depends on the aims of your presentation (⊖F2). Very often you want to serve more aims at the same time. The occasion defines whether a good format is available or whether you run the risk of too many points which is always related to unclear aims and/or bad preparation. The same applies, for instance, to your writing skills (⊖E4). An effective presentation always represents a balancing act between the various formats available to you. This Skill Sheet lists the most common formats of presentations, links that to their aims and gives a number of tips to increase the effectiveness of the format. Three types of presentations can be distinguished:

1 Presentations aimed at the transfer and generation of knowledge
2 Presentations aimed at convincing people
3 Occasional speeches

1 Knowledge-oriented presentations

1a Content presentation

Aims	Share results with your audience and show that you master the topic.
Occasion	Presentations of the business plan, research report to the customer, presentation of your Master's thesis or Ph.D.
Contents	• Introduction: opening line, case, problem definition, illustrative case (⊖F4).
	• Main part: three points maximum.
	• Final part: summary and wrap up line.
Remarks	• Takes between ten and fifteen minutes: you have to cope with the fact that you have to present the results of a long-term research in a relative short time period; do not bargain over the time.
	• Support presentation with around one tool (visualisation is essential for people).
	• Address the person in the audience (relatives?) with the least understanding of the topic (shows you are 'above' the topic), however without annoying the more informed audience (the exam committee).

1b Informative presentation

Aims	Share facts and/or agree upon rules with your audience.
Occasion	First class of a new course, start of a competition.
Contents	• The rules of the game for the course are explained (presence obligatory or not; exact time of the exam; hand-in of assignments). All rules must be clear and unambiguous.

- First make sure that everybody understands these rules ('do you understand them?'; 'do you understand the consequences for you personally?').
- Next, make sure that everybody accepts these rules ('are these fair rules?') and if not, discuss any point of ambiguity directly. Explain the teaching aims and how they relate to the rules in order to explain your perception of their fairness.

Remarks	• It is essential to present all facts and rules as clear as possible. Can be rather dull.
	• Preferably write it all down.
	• Silence and attention is critical; take responsibility for this – because the audience might not be assertive enough – otherwise you will suffer from ambiguity in the rules later on in the project/course.
	• If the rules are not shared by everybody at this stage (or are unclear) you will inevitably run into difficulties later on.
	• Some repetition of the facts and agreements is often necessary.
	• Some serious bargaining can occur in this phase, but be prepared to do that now, otherwise the bargaining will never stop.
	• Do not conclude that people have read everything and have understood it. Check that at the same moment (not later).

1c Introducing a speaker

Aims	Welcoming the speaker; introducing to the audience; creating interest for the speaker and for the topic of the speech.
Occasion	Conference, workshop, class.
Contents	• Welcome speaker and audience: 'good morning/afternoon/evening'.
	• Mention the title and topic of the speech.
	• Give background information about the speaker: position(s), publications, other characteristics.
	• Explain the background of the speaker to the audience: why should they be interested in the topic of the speech and in the speaker?
	• At the end: invite the speaker to take the stand and commence with the speech.
Remarks	• Keep it short: do not attract undue attention to yourself.
	• Do not make remarks on the subject of the speech (the speaker may not be prepared to tackle those aspects), unless you have agreed to do so with the speaker.
	• Prepare beforehand, together with the speaker, the most appropriate introduction.

2 Convincing presentations

2a Persuasive presentation

Aims	Convincing someone of the usefulness of a plan/product.
Occasion	Product presentations (trying to convince customers of the fact that they should use your shampoo), tender bids (x companies are trying to convince you of the fact that their plan is the best for you).
Contents	• Starts with the problem of the client. • Possibly gives information on best-practices (as inspiration for the client and sign of your own competencies). • Presents the solution in the best possible manner (use fancy tools if available).
Remarks	• Points of attention: examine the desires of the client carefully. • Consider what the level of 'seniority' is that the client expects; make sure that you meet this expectation.

2b Recruitment presentation

Aims	Convincing somebody to join your organisation/club/team.
Occasion	Recruitment presentations for the football club or for the student association. Announcement of an activity (congress, outing) for which you want to recruit as many people as possible.
Contents	• Keep it very short (max. 2 minutes). • Use only a few slides or a prepared video. • Make your audience curious and enthusiastic for the association.
Remarks	• Understand your audience: adjust the presentation to what they expect of you. • Think of an appealing past accomplishment of your association. • Be enthusiastic. • Make sure that your presentation is 'wanted' by the teacher whose class you 'barge into' with your recruitment talk. Preferably ask them for an additional endorsement of your association. • Make sure you use the right equipment.

2c Debate

Aims	Convince somebody to share your opinion.
Occasion	Houses of parliament, panels, scientific schools.
Contents	• Deliver a clear and structured statement. • Listen critically. • Quickly analyse the core arguments of your opponent. • Find the weak spots in your opponent's argument. • Construct a counter-argument. • Deliver this in a concise, quick and often witty manner (one-liners).
Remarks	• Part of bargaining society (➔Challenges, Part I), creates sub-optimal outcomes. • Makes clear where differences are, but not necessarily the commonalities. • Can serve as an important phase in deliberations. • Problem with most debates: no real end or conclusions (we agree to disagree) and primarily reiterations of already existing opinions. • Focus is often on the people, not on the problem.

2d Dialogue

Aims	Convince somebody to work on common solutions.
Occasion	Negotiation tables, intra-organisational gatherings, intermediation.
Contents	• Show empathy for the other and for the problem. • Identify (brainstorming) whether you share ideas on the problem and possible solutions. • Focus on the problem not on the people. • Talk about possible solutions and understand the interests of participants. • Find the strong points in your partner's argument. • Construct a possible joint argument.
Remarks	• Dialogue form can often be 'abused' for just informing partners (without interest in their opinion). • Is of increasing importance in solving conflicts, but needs to be made more strategic if real sustainable solutions are the aim (cf. Van Tulder, with Van der Zwart, 2006). • Dilemma with dialogues: too modest ambitions for the problem at hand.

3 Occasional speeches

It happens to everybody: you are expected to give a speech for a 'special occasion'. These occasions can be very important for you as a researcher: an inauguration, a welcome, introducing someone, a table speech for the department. These speeches have a number of characteristics in common. They (**1**) are short, (**2**) do not make use of tools, (**3**) tell people what they would like to hear, (**4**) have to have an appealing opening statement, and (5) follow a very simple structure, which can be memorised easily, or can be written down on one small card.

3a Rendering thanks

Aims	Finalising a speech; showing appreciation for the speaker; including the contents of the actual speech and the response of the audience.
Occasion	Conference, workshop, class.
Contents	• Thank the speaker on behalf of the audience, the board and/or the organisation. • Include the reactions of the audience in your 'thank-you speech'. • Give an appreciative judgement on the previous speech: 'clear argument', 'provocative'. • Show gratitude for the effort of the speaker. If appropriate ask the speaker to come back.
Remarks	• Make notes during the speech. Do not say: 'I will not try to summarise this speech because it was so interesting' (you show the audience that you are a lazy chairperson). • In case a discussion follows the speech, start with a temporary 'thank you', which becomes a final 'thank you' after the discussion has ended. • Do not criticise or present complementary arguments to the speaker (you run the risk of not allowing the speech to end and of starting another debate).

3b Welcoming

Aims	Welcoming people and making them feel comfortable.
Occasion	Any occasion for which you are the master of ceremony or part of the welcoming committee.
Contents	• Explain what the organisation does, and who the organisers are. • Explain who the people in the room are, and why they are present. • Connection between the organisation and the audience: why has this particular location been chosen for this meeting, why are they welcome? • Finish by explaining the organisation, what will happen next and state that you hope it will be an interesting or rewarding meeting.
Remarks	• Do not say you 'anticipate that the meeting will be successful'. You do not know yet, and that is up to the audience. • Keep it brief.

3c Paying tribute

Aims	Giving someone an unforgettable day: pay tribute to the person's special qualities.
Occasion	Wedding, anniversary.

Contents	• Begin with an anecdote in which the special characteristics of the person come to the fore.
	• Elaborate on the reason for the meeting: the tribute to one person.
	• Create a sense of history: 'How long ago did he/she become member of our organisation?'
	• Explain the importance to the organisation: 'what would we have been without you?'
	• Elaborate on the positive characteristics of the person. It is possible to reveal less positive characteristics as long as it is humorous.
	• Relation of audience to the person addressed: is his/her party also their party?
	• Then the speech becomes directly aimed at the person:
	  – 'you are congratulated on behalf of...';
	  – 'we would like to give you a gift. It is...' (after which it is explained why this present is chosen).
	• After the gift has been presented, propose a toast.

Remarks	• Use the 'we' form in the speech. • Avoid clichés and empty expressions. Prepare the speech well. • Look at the person while you are speaking. • Involve the partner/spouse in the speech. If appropriate give flowers or another gift.

3d Responding to a tribute

Aims	Showing gratitude and appreciation.
Occasion	Wedding, anniversary.
Contents	• Say thank you for what has been said and offered. • What does the gift mean: how and where will it be used? • If appropriate, report the compliments: 'I could not have done this without the help of...' • Finish by offering best wishes for the future.
Remarks	• It is not inappropriate to be emotional, but try keep your emotions under control as much as possible.

3e Inaugural speech

Aims	Presenting yourself as the new functionary.
Occasion	Accepting the chair position, a professorship, a directorship or a ministerial position.
Contents	• Say thank you for the appointment.
	• Show appreciation for the trust that has been placed in you.
	• Show that you are aware of the responsibilities linked to this position.
	• Pay tribute to your predecessor.
	• Explain what you think the job at hand requires, and how you hope to achieve it.
	• Explain what you hope future collaboration with others in the organisation will be like. Ask that they have some understanding and patience with you as a newcomer in the job.
Remarks	• Prepare this speech carefully.
	• Never criticise your predecessor.
	• Do not make demeaning remarks about your colleagues.

3f Table speech

Aims	Entertaining and pleasant during a dinner. Witty speech, preferably with an original view.
Occasion	Wedding, celebration.
Contents	• Explain the reason for the dinner.
	• Tackle remarks made by previous speakers.
	• Emphasise the pleasant nature of the dinner and the occasion.
	• Explain the topic that you would like to address, and reveal the basic structure of your speech.
	• Tell a lot of anecdotes and try to tell as many one-liners as possible.
	• Finish with a casual prediction for the future and a toast.
Remarks	• Write the structure of your speech on a small card.
	• Write a number of appropriate one-liners on another card.
	• If you can: play on the reaction of the audience (this is something you should prepare, i.e. know who your audience will be).

Presentations can be very stimulating and informative as long as a number of general design rules are taken into account. What seems 'spontaneous' in a presentation has very often been the result of careful design and solid preparation. This Skill Sheet explains the most important dimensions of such a design.

1 The time limit

Find out before you start your preparation what the time available is for your presentation. In case you do not know this, design a more flexible format.

2 Presentation type

Ask yourself what type of presentation you are going to give in relation to occasion, the audience and their expectations (⊕F3). What added value for the audience are you aiming at?

3 Start with a 'situation' or problem

Invent a story, relate to a newspaper article, in any case start off with something that your audience personally can relate to. This will attract their attention, and will make it clear that your presentation deals with a problem for which you will come up with some answers. In case the problem is something that the audience is also interested in, you will immediately have the attention of the audience. Make your first presentation slide picture that problem. Why the problem appears, whether it is a problem (for whom) or what can be done about it.

4 A limited number of key points

Only plan to tackle a very *limited* number of key points: preferably two to three.

'There is one problem almost everyone has when preparing a presentation. They try to *include too many points*. When giving a presentation, time is not only the limitation. You are also limited by the capacity of your audience. You can be smooth, calm, make good eye contact, and still try to say too much. (...) In general, if your audience retains *one* key point, you will have done very well. Three is a maximum. People just do not listen very well. Slides help, vivid stories help, but they help emphasize your key points. Do not expand the number of key points you can make. Do not hope for more than three.'—Paul Broholm

5 Define a clear structure: define your 'storyboard'

In order to avoid tackling too many points, a *clear structure* is mandatory.
- Make a hierarchy of points. Think about the most important point(s). What is the message you would like to get across? Why would your audience be interested in this message?
- Do not present long lists of points or ideas, because your audience will *not* retain

all of them (they might end up even not retaining any of them due to presentation overload).

- Only make statements, which reinforce your main point. This requires a strict *selection process*.
- Use a Mind Map to define your structure, and give a graphical presentation of the structure of your presentation (➔B6).

| **If in doubt, leave it out.**

6 Invent oratory highlights

Experienced speech writers of 'great communicators' such as American presidents would advise you to state something that can stick in the memory of your audience. This is part of careful planning and research. This is not about the number of examples you give; they can add to the complexity of the message. In particular specific one-liners or casually mentioned quotes add to the persuasiveness of the message. These are often the least spontaneous parts of a speech. There are excellent quote books and websites available. Make sure, however, that the quote is really appropriate for the occasion and issue at hand.

Minimum requirements for effective speeches

- At least one (memorable) one-liner
- One nice image or metaphor
- One challenging paradox
- One appropriate quote
- With PowerPoint: one illustrative cartoon or visual joke

(Advice from a Presidential speech writer)

7 Plan repetition

- Modest repetition is necessary to reinforce your ideas during the presentation, and to get the message across.
- Repetition keeps the attention of the audience focused.
- Too much repetition can be annoying as well.

8 Always explain consequences of your argument clearly

- Most of the audience is busy following what is being presented. If you do not explain the implications (for them) of what you are saying, they will be confused, and in the end also dissatisfied with your argument.
- Other members of the audience may become distracted 'by trying to think through the implications of what you have said' (Guirdham, 1990: 247). You will also lose their attention.

9 Plan three parts

All research presentations are made up of Three Parts:

- 1 Introduction ➔ state what you want to say (10-15% of the time).
- 2 Main part ➔ make your point/s (75-80% of the time).
- 3 Final part ➔ conclude/summarize what you have said (5-10% of the time).

☐ 1 Introduction	☐ 2 Main part	☐ 3 Conclusion
• General rule: not too long! • Attract attention (joke, provoke). Pose a question that is intriguing for the audience. You should be careful that your joke does not alienate your audience. Tell a story illustrating the problem at hand. • What is the question or the problem you want to address? What is the aim of the presentation? • Definition of the problem and the method you will use to tackle it. • Introduce yourself (background, reason for the research). • Possibly, include a preview to the next speaker. • Why is it of interest to the audience? • Give a survey of your presentation. • Maybe start already with the conclusion as a teaser?	• Make the structure of your presentation explicit. • Keep the general structure as header or border to show 'where' you are in the presentation. • Plan to supply sufficient examples. • Search for graphics, images and cartoons that reinforce your message. • Do not deviate from your problem. • Use the three S's: Structure, Signposts and Summaries.	• Use a separate slide to announce the final part of the presentation. • Keep it short after that announcement. • Make a summary of your key points. • Present your conclusion and/or message, explicitly. • Always think about a final 'blow': a pertinent, catchy, ending that your audience will remember (often a cartoon at the end of a presentation will do the trick).

F5 Design (PowerPoint) Slides

There is an abundance of software programs available to produce very professionally looking slides. Advanced software can only help you with the form of your presentation. It can help you get the message across better, but it can never substitute contents and good argumentation. Good argumentation requires: simplicity, succinctness, clarity and precision (➲E6). This Skill Sheet explores how these principles can be elaborated in a proper design of your presentation slides. All presentation media have advantages but also disadvantages, so it is vital to take these into account in your design and usage of a relatively advanced medium like PowerPoint. Many people tend to use PowerPoint as the solution to all their communication problems. This is certainly incorrect (➲F1).

Advantages PowerPoint	Disadvantages PowerPoint
☐ You can prepare slides at home	☐ You cannot change slides during presentation (in case of PowerPoint)
☐ It is possible to retain eye contact with your audience during the presentation	☐ In semi-dark presentation rooms it is difficult to actually get eye contact with your audience
☐ It is possible to reproduce very complex drawings, sound, pictures and even clips in your presentation	☐ Loss of flexibility: you might have to skip through various slides during your presentation (distracts audience)
☐ Added speed: it is quicker to add information on slides/transparencies than to write it all on a whiteboard	☐ Presenter loses sight of the total presentation (no preview of next slides)
☐ It is possible to 'build up' an argument: by showing one sentence after another	☐ Risk of too much 'movement' in the presentation (distracting)
☐ Students can receive the slides in advance and use them in their preparation for attending the lecture (➲D7)	☐ Speed of the presentation increases, which makes it more difficult to make relevant notes
☐ Presentations are easier to customize for each audience: it is relatively simple to add, change or delete slides	☐ Getting the slides in advance can lower the concentration level of the audience and thus the effectiveness of the meeting (➲D1)
☐ Looks very professional	☐ Abuse of a graphical technique: too many words
☐ It is possible to use colours to add to the content	☐ Presenter makes himself very dependent on the proper working of machines (beamer as well as the computer). Need for contingency plans increases, which increases preparation time (even if it proves not necessary)
☐ Graphical presentation is often an excellent complement to an oral presentation	

1 Simplicity

Never put too much information on one slide, because people *first* start reading, watching and finally *not listening*. Complex tables and figures are not suitable for slides, because they are often difficult for the audience to read. Most of the time, the information included in complex tables or analyses can be *split up* into more 'manageable' parts.

As a rule: do not write more than *seven* words per line and *seven* lines per slide.

2 Succinctness

- Use *keywords*. Do not write down whole sentences on slides, except if you use a separate slide for that and only when strictly necessary (for example, the definition of a concept or the research question of your thesis). This enables you to make a more spontaneous presentation, in which you phrase your argument in the most appropriate style for the occasion, i.e. colloquial speech (a presentation for a group of people, that are meeting one another for the same reason, for example a seminar of the WWF).
- With data, *use rounded figures*: 6.5 instead of 6.349, 10 instead of 9.96. There is one exception to this rule of course: when the added digits matter a lot. For instance in statistical presentations. Try not to show too many of these long equations and figures in your presentation. People do not have the time to read – let alone digest – it anyway. Use the PowerPoint tools to highlight some of the most telling data. For the rest: keep this kind of information in the written material (which could be a hand-out).

3 Clarity

- Use clear letters (*capitals*) that everyone is able to read, even at the back of the room. Preferably use printed letters or write very clearly. The character size you use depends on the size of the room in which you are giving the presentation. Use the following 'rules of thumb':

If the *length/size* of the room is...	...the *character size* should be approximately	Example Times New Roman (letter size)
< 10 meters	5 mm (Times New Roman 10)	10
10-15 meters	10 mm (Times New Roman 15)	15
15-20 meters	15 mm (Times New Roman 20)	20

- The length of the letter size is given in millimetres, because every letter type has a different size). When you use another letter type than *Times New Roman*, it is essential to estimate yourself how big the signs of the slide should be.
- *Do not use too much complex vocabulary*. Do not use professional jargon, unless your

audience is made up of professionals, or you are prepared to explain it in your presentation too. If you think that people will be unfamiliar with the term, and the term adds value, include slides with the definition.

- Include a short header or footer on each slide, stating the topic of the lecture or the part of the presentation you are in. This gives extra information to the audience and keeps their attention focused. Too much information, however, can just as easily distract the audience. Only use short headers or footers.

Many presenters start their presentation with the following sentence: Can the people at the back of the room read the slides? Check this beforehand and make sure it is well prepared.

4 Precision

- If you use research data or other information that someone else compiled, apply the golden rule of Skill Sheet E1 and E2: **always reveal your sources!** A slide without a source suggests that you collected the information yourself. If this is not the case, you are misleading the audience. Merely mentioning that the slide was taken from someone else's work is not enough to do justice to the *intellectual source*. Moreover, information conveyed through visual media is more effective than the spoken word. If you only state your source verbally, it will be more easily forgotten by the audience.
- *Number* your slides, in order to keep everything organised.
- Keep the *layout of your slides consistent*. Try to use only 'standing' ('long'/'portrait') or 'lying' ('wide'/'landscape') slides.

5 Further tips

- *Comics* can be a useful way of communicating your message. You could even wake up your audience! However, you should select them carefully and they should only include a one-topic illustration. If a comic is not relevant or difficult to interpret, leave it out.
- Print a paper *copy* of the original slides. Write your additional remarks on these (numbered) copies and keep them with the slides. These (numbered) sheets form the basis of your presentation. If you want to avoid having to use big pieces of paper, during the presentation, write down the remarks on small (numbered!) cards (cue cards) or print a hand-out for yourself from PowerPoint.
- To increase the impact of your presentation, make a hand-out for the audience of a selection of the most important slides. Hand this to the audience **at the start** of your presentation. Listening becomes reading as well, which increases the effectiveness of the communication (➲D1).
- For important presentations, always produce a set of transparencies that you can use in case the PowerPoint projector fails.

At the actual time of your presentation you face the challenge of getting your message across (➡F1). Often, however, in particular inexperienced presenters forget one or two vital things in the immediate period before the preparation which can seriously damage the effectiveness of the whole presentation. This Skill Sheet helps you to check whether you have thought of these last-minute factors. It should help you in focusing on delivering an excellent speech.

Table F.6 Last-minute Checklist

Up front	☐ appropriate clothing?
	☐ laptop; ☐ cue cards; ☐ food and drinks; ☐ hand-outs; ☐ objects;
	☐ markers
Place of action	☐ class room open and available?
	☐ equipment operational?
	☐ organisation of presentation: room for notes?
	☐ posture: right attitude?
	☐ phrasing: in the mood?
	☐ questions: explain how you would like to deal with that
	☐ time schedule: what will happen if you run over time?
	☐ something goes wrong

1 Up front
1.1 Clothing
Dress appropriately for the occasion. If you dress badly, your audience may conclude that your research could be sloppy as well [⊕➡www.skillsheets.com].

1.2 Take the following tools from home with you:
Slides, laptop and all kinds of devices (electric cords; mouse), cue cards, food, drinks, hand-outs, objects to make clarifications, markers. If your presentation critically depends upon one of these tools make sure you have them in your possession.

2 Place of action
2.1 Always arrive on time
- Check whether the lecture room is open and/or available (no other lecturer for instance). If not, go and look for the person who can open the room for you; this will take time; if you don't have time it will add to your stress.
- Take some time to get a feeling for the surroundings (size of the room and other characteristics) so that you feel relatively comfortable in the room.
- Go to the restroom and check for the last time whether your clothing is still appropriate.

2.2 Check the equipment
- Check that the equipment is working and familiarize yourself with it. If you wait until the audience is already in the room, it will add to your stress.
- Check whether the people at the back of the room will also be able read your slides – walk to the back and observe whether you can read the smallest print on the slides.
- If you need a microphone: make sure that it works.
- Check your laptop and all connections.

2.3 Organisation of presentation
- With longer presentations, it is best to have the presentation structure in a place where everyone can see it: on a sheet of paper on the flip chart, or written on the whiteboard. The audience will then be able to keep track of your progress as you go through the structure. If you use slides, use the general slide regularly to explain where you are in the presentation; keep this slide on a separate pile (or use the side bar of the PowerPoint slide to show the contents of the presentation and where you are at the moment).
- Draw pictures, your outline, that you want to use during your presentation beforehand on the whiteboard. When you do it during your presentation it looks very messy, or you even forget to make the drawings.
- Lay all transparencies, notes, and so on down in front of you in an orderly way. Do not make a complete mess of all your objects! Think of a way of keeping things orderly and making sure that you will not lose anything half-way through your presentation. For example, put everything that you still need on the left, and all the things you have already used on the right.

2.4 Posture
- Try to make contact with the audience immediately. Do not 'hide' behind a desk or overhead projector.
- Adopt a positive and self-assured posture: stand straight, relax by controlling your breathing.
- **What you give is what you get**: a positive attitude can lead to a positive reception from the audience, but a negative attitude almost always leads to a negative reception by the audience!
- Do not be afraid to smile! Be yourself. Show enthusiasm.

2.5 Phrasing
- Greet the audience ('good morning').
- Introduce yourself! You will be surprised how many people forget this.
- In your introduction *never* say: 'I will keep it short' (it is irrelevant and nobody believes you).
- Do not say that you start with a boring overview of facts (the rest of your presentation will also be dull).
- Avoid referring to your 'personal history' ('from my own experience').
- Refrain from using popular words or fillers: 'you know', 'etcetera', 'eh...', 'okay'.

2.6 Questions

- Indicate directly at the beginning of your presentation, whether you want to answer questions during your presentation or at the end (➔F8).

2.7 Time schedule

- Discuss with your audience what your time frame is; make sure that they can anticipate when approximately you are going to stop (it helps you in managing the expectations of the audience properly).
- In case of a set format and if you are running over time, never start negotiating with the chairperson to get more time. Only ask if it is possible to continue. If the chair does not agree, finish your presentation as quickly as possible.
- If your presentation is too short: no problem, people will have more time to ask questions.

[⊕➔www.skillsheets.com for a last-minute checklist]

During presentations, the dosed and balanced usage of tools can tremendously increase the impact of your presentation. Tools can, however, also become a disturbing factor when not managed correctly. This Skill Sheet lists pointers for the practical use of: (1) slides, (2) paper hand-outs, (3) the whiteboard and flip charts, (4) videos/DVDs and (5) perhaps other exotic means.

1 (PowerPoint) Slides

It has been stressed already that PowerPoint slides have many advantages, but also serious drawbacks (➔F5). The drawbacks in particular appear in the practical use of PowerPoint slides. To prevent these from happening, take the following tips into consideration:

1.1 Start presentation

- At the beginning of your presentation make clear to your audience whether you expect them to take notes, or if they can download the slides afterwards.
- Do *not make too many slides* for a short presentation, unless you are very experienced. The continuous action at the projector distracts the audience's attention from what you are saying.
- In case you use overhead transparencies, make sure that there is a table or something else within easy reach of the projector, on which you can place *three piles of slides*: **1.** the ones you will use, **2.** the ones you have used (with the back facing upwards so that you are not disturbed by the text), **3.** slides that you will use again.
- Check where the *cable(s)* for the overhead projector/beamer are lying/hanging. Make sure that you can not trip over them during the presentation. Remember: the fear of tripping over the cables will add to your nervousness/insecurity and thus affect your presentation.

1.2 Specific techniques during presentations

- Do *not cover part(s) of the overhead transparency* during the presentation. It gives the audience the impression that they are being kept in the dark. The audience becomes aware that you are manipulating them by (temporarily) withholding information. Furthermore, most people are not able to routinely cover the correct part of the slide, which can give the presentation an amateurish and more chaotic appearance. Make separate slides in order to 'build up' your statement. **PowerPoint** enables you to cut a slide into pieces; bringing up a sentence upon each click.
- Many overhead projectors have the option, named perforation pins, with which you can position your slides. You can use this option to clarify effects by piling up your slides. You can use this for example with the organisation charts (first internal divisions, next the external divisions and finally the administration). **PowerPoint**: place your laptop in such a position that it is still possible to read the information easily on the slides for yourself and your audience.

- Do not cover part of the slides *yourself!* Make sure you are *not* in front of the screen or covering part of the light source (creating shades on the projection). Use a pen or another object (not your hand) to indicate the main points. You will have to remove your hand, whereas a pen can keep on pointing. If your hand shakes while you are pointing, the projector will also magnify this gesture! **PowerPoint**: use a pen which radiates a red light on the screen.
- Do not *'talk to the projector' or to the computer.* A frequent mistake made by presenters using slides is that they look at the slide on the projector or on their laptop computer, while they present the information. Sometimes this is because of insecurity, which the audience will always notice. You cannot 'hide' behind the projector/computer. Very often, however, talking to the projector/computer is just a case of a bad technique. If you do not look at the audience your presentation will be more difficult to follow. So leave the machine where it is and regularly look at your audience or look at the projection screen.
- Check regularly to see if the audience can read the whole of the slide, i.e. whether you have placed it on the projector correctly. This means that you must glance at the screen from time to time.
- Do not read aloud, *word for word*, what the audience can already read on the screen. There is one exception to this rule, when you for example have placed a slide with a definition. Read the definition slowly for your audience. In this way, the audience gets some time to reflect on the information.
- If you want to focus the audience's attention on what you are saying, turn the projector off. (Use Fn function on a laptop).
- When you use many slides and you want to talk 'around your slides', then it is the best thing to take some distance from the machine or start walking a bit. It takes the attention away from the projector.
- When you do not use many slides, you can turn off the overhead projector or use the Fn or 'b' function on your laptop, which creates a blank projection.
- Every time you project, you have to indicate briefly what is mentioned on the slide for your audience. It is the audience that starts reading anyway. When you start talking right away, they will not listen until they are finished reading, which creates considerable distraction (even with experienced listeners).

2 Paper hand-outs
- Usually, paper hand-outs are used to provide a printed version of the slides of the presentation. They have the advantage that the audience can easier take notes during your presentation and go back if necessary to take additional notes. The disadvantage is that the audience can see in advance what you are going to tell them, which lowers the 'spontaneity' of your presentation (and thus its impact ⊕F1). Furthermore, you might skip slides during the presentation which still appear on paper (in any case a waste of paper). A solution to both issues is to only print a few slides that present the main gist of the presentation (in particular summaries and complex diagrams).

- More radical: use one plain sheet of paper stating the *basics of your presentation*. The audience can always keep track of your argument, but nevertheless also concentrate on the spoken word.
- *Write a number of questions on paper* and leave enough space for the audience to make notes. From time to time, ask the audience to fill in the answers. If they do this you can search for common denominators in the answers. The sheet could also include a graph or a table with some blank spaces to be filled in by the audience.
- More sophisticated hand-outs can invite direct *evaluation*. You can challenge the audience to write down what they think of your presentation. Depending on your expectations, you can even use the answers to the evaluation questions *during* the presentation and go another way, if necessary. At some universities, students are asked to write a *one minute paper* after the lecture to give feedback to the lecturer, but also to increase their own awareness (➔D7, D8).

3 Flip chart, whiteboard/blackboard
- A *flip chart* (a pad of large paper sheets on a stand) is only appropriate for smaller audiences. The flip chart can also be used to build up information or to guide the audience through an argument (and go backwards if necessary). The advantage of a flip chart over a whiteboard/blackboard is that you can write the information down before the presentation. But these are all functions that can also be served by an overhead projector. A flip chart is easier to transport to rooms where there are no whiteboards/blackboards or overhead projectors.
- A *whiteboard* or a *blackboard* is more appropriate for bigger audiences and in temporary support of an argument. You can draw a graph or write down an important point that you want to remain visible for a longer period of time. The whiteboard/blackboard is also useful for revealing the plan for the session or the main parts of the argument even when you use a projector!

Whether you use a flip chart or a whiteboard/blackboard, always respect the following rules:
- Be sure you write *large enough* for everyone to read it.
- Fill the board or the sheet *systematically*. Make sure that the audience can read what you write on the lower parts of the board or the flip chart.
- *Do not speak while you are writing*: it will be difficult to hear you, and you will very likely be standing in front of what you are writing.
- You are standing with your back towards the audience. Make sure that the audience already knows what they have to do, while you are writing (make a remark before you start writing).

4 Video/DVD

Showing a video or DVD can be very useful, as long as it is closely linked to what you want to present. The less time the clip takes, the more impact it has. It can be very effective to begin by presenting a short clip. Do your presentation in such a way that you use some of the images from the tape and ultimately show the tape again. If you are successful, people will view the second showing of the video with 'different eyes'.

But... always be aware of the following drawbacks of tools that are too technical:

- You have to be prepared to *practise* a lot. Unskilled use of technology does more harm than good.
- Presentations with computers are also only a good idea if you fully *master your equipment.*
- A 'slick' use of slides, video and computers may also *distract* the audience's attention from your message. You run the risk of having to compete with your tools for their attention. The aid must be an aid and not the sole carrier of the message!
- Videos are difficult to *integrate*. They can break up the presentation. Bear this in mind. Tailor-made videos – which can be designed especially for your presentation are either very expensive or of poor quality. The latter is as distracting to the audience as a video that is not relevant.

Keep your presentation aids simple, so (technical) problems will be less likely to occur, and the results will be most effective.

5 Exotic tools?

- A *painting or object* can be used as a symbol for a more complex analysis.
- A *sound* or a short piece of music can sometimes say more than a thousand words. If you want to appeal to the emotions of your audience this can be very effective.
- Wear a *T-shirt* with the most important message, or a provocative statement, written on it. Be aware that the audience may look at your T-shirt more than they listen to what you have to say.

Questions during a presentation can considerably improve the effectiveness of your communication, because it stimulates participants to co-produce the presentation. However, badly managed questions can be a disturbing factor as well. In case presenters ask themselves 'rhetorical' questions, they are only interesting if the audience shares these questions. In case people in the audience ask dysfunctional questions it can seriously slow down the pace of the presentation, and even jeopardize the whole presentation. However, in principle questions are the bread and butter of effective presentations, and should therefore be actively pursued by presenters even when one fool can ask more questions than one hundred wise men can answer (➡D1).

1 Questions from the audience during the presentation

Make it clear from the outset whether you think it is a good idea for the audience to ask questions during the presentation. If you expect to be nervous, it is better not to do this. It is much more difficult to control your presentation with questions than without. If you get questions, see point three for how to address them. However always make a distinction between:

- Questions for clarification
- Questions for discussion

In case people have questions for clarification it will help the presentation tremendously if they are allowed to ask them directly the moment they feel the need for this. Otherwise you might 'lose' your audience.

2 Questions to the audience during the presentation

A more controlled way to involve the audience is by asking questions during the presentation. This is the basic philosophy behind the Socratic method used in many American business schools (➡D4): by interrogating the audience – for instance by continuously asking 'why' questions – you can reach to the bottom of a problem. Challenging questions catch the attention of the audience. The specifically challenging question used in the Socratic method puts the student in a clear 'discomfort zone', which has been identified as the best way of starting up your learning cycle (➡B1). But you have to be very careful not to overdo it. They may feel uncomfortable if you pose challenging questions or pick out people in the audience. This is particularly troublesome in European or Asian cultures. Besides, not every issue lends itself for the Socratic questioning method, and not all presentations are in front of students. If you as a presenter prepare a hand-out, which includes information and questions this might be less confronting. You can then have a short break, during the presentation, in which *everyone* in the audience can think about the questions and the hand-out.

Well formulated questions can provoke so called '**unlearning**' by raising your audience's uncertainty level and also the attention for what you are going to say. Look at the following examples (Guirdham, 1990: 246): Instead of entitling your talk 'How advertising works', call it 'So you think you know how advertising works'; instead of 'How to get rich', 'Do you really want to be rich?'

3 Questions after the presentation

If the audience can ask questions after the actual presentation, there are two options to announce as soon as you 'open the floor':

- You want to answer one question at a time;
- You want to collect a number of questions and then give an answer(s).

In both cases address the question(s) as follows:
- Begin by acknowledging the question: 'Thank you for this question', or 'Interesting question'.
- Summarise the question if it is a long one: 'if I understand your question correctly, you want to know...'; or in the case of more questions: 'I think that a number of questions relate to one another' (after which you explain which combinations you think are relevant).
- You reply. If you do not know the answer, say so!
- Try to get confirmation of your answer: 'have I answered your question sufficiently?'

- Practise these techniques beforehand with some other team members/students.

It is often difficult to keep your posture under control during presentations. In a bargaining society, the way in which you express yourself is often as meaningful as what you say. Your body language is part and parcel of an effective presentation. Managing your body language is more difficult if you do not have much experience in presenting in public. In Skill Sheet D5 you can read how you can *observe* body language from the perspective of the audience. In this Skill Sheet a number of situations are described related to specific parts of your body. It will be analysed where these gestures come from, and what they (could) imply. The meaning of your body language is always 'in the eye' of the beholder! In addition, concrete tips will help you to avoid this kind of behaviour either through external help or through your own action (*Avoidance trick*). Finally, it will be shown that a well timed movement with a certain part of your body can also work to your advantage. In this sense, a well-timed movement can become part of your standard presentation procedures. The kind of influence you can exert with this is described in the 'strategy' part. This Skill Sheet treats the following parts of your body: (1) head, (2) eyes, (3) voice, (4) upper body, (5) hands, (6) lower body and (7) feet.

1a Head: downward look

Results	• *Makes you look shy*
	• *You feel insecure*
	• *You get shortage of breath*
Origin	• You are afraid to face the audience
	• You are focusing too much on what to say
	• You are adopting an obsequious attitude
	• You are fearing a judgment
Avoidance tricks	• Choose a clear eye position (focus your eyes in between two persons; you are not forced to look somebody in the eye)
	• Get inspiration from your contents
	• Get a signal from your audience (you have instructed somebody to ask a question)
Strategy	• You want to show your audience that you are thinking
	• You want to get a reaction from your audience

1b Head: upward look

Results	• *The audience thinks you have a dominant/arrogant attitude*
Origin	• You are afraid to face the audience
	• You are feeling insecure
Avoidance tricks	• Choose a clear eye position (focus your eyes in between two persons; you are not forced to look somebody in the eye)
	• Practise your presentation in front of a mirror (for example at home in the bathroom; make sure that nobody is at home!)
	• Get a signal from your audience (you have instructed somebody to give a signal before the real presentation takes place)
Strategy	• Show your authority to the audience (you can only apply authority when you really possess it!)

2 Eyes: one focus point

Results	• *The audience is doubting whether you are talking to them (or to the wall or to somebody outside the room)*
	• *You are not interested in the other part of the audience (you are only looking at the professor)*
Origin	• You are afraid to face the audience
	• You are trying to avoid an information overload
	• You are feeling insecure
Avoidance tricks	• Choose a clear eye position (focus your eyes in between two persons; you are not forced to look somebody in the eye)
	• Put a signal on your cue card (a note with a bright colour)
	• Acknowledge stress signals with the purpose to avoid information overload
Strategy	• Get people silent (focusing on somebody for a long time)
	• Ignore somebody (do not look somebody in the eyes)
	• The presenter has some time to think

3a Voice: monotonous, slow and low

Results	• *You are losing the interest of your audience*
	• *Your audience does not take you seriously anymore*
Origin	• You are having trouble with your own body movements
	• You are feeling stressed
	• You did not prepare your presentation well enough
Avoidance tricks	• Present with an open body (no arms in front of your body; make slow movements with your arms to support an argument)
	• Put a signal on a cue card (note: talk louder!)
	• Make your contents more interesting for your audience
	• Practise your presentation singing in the bathroom (you are forced to talk in another way)
Strategy	• Use it to check whether your audience is still listening more carefully to your presentation

3b Voice: high (in particular at the end of a sentence) and fast

Results	• *You are losing the interest of your audience, while you are saying so much that the audience can not process it anymore (a human being has a limited brain capacity)*
	• *Your audience does not take you seriously anymore (somebody probably does not feel like telling the audience something useful)*
Origin	• You have got a wrong way of breathing
	• You are feeling stressed
Avoidance tricks	• Take a breathing break (give yourself time to relax)
	• Take a moment of silence (about five seconds)
	• Articulating in an exaggerate way (talking slows down automatically; practise this at home!)
Strategy	• Wake up your audience
	• Create a type of tension in the room (what will be said next)

4a Upper body: closed (arms crossed and shoulders tight)

Results	• *Your charisma is insecure*
	• *Lack of discussing power or dull charisma*
Origin	• You are looking for protection
	• You are feeling stressed
Avoidance tricks	• Practise in front of a mirror
	• Get a signal from the audience (waving when it happens; you make an agreement before the presentation)
	• Signal on a cue card
Strategy	• Get rest and control
	• Give the audience a moment to relax

4b Upper body: raised shoulders

Results	• *Your appearance looks shy*
	• *The audience thinks that you are doubting what you are really doing here*
Origin	• Taking a defensive position (you are indicating that it will be nothing anyway)
Avoidance tricks	• Practise in front of a mirror
	• Get a signal from the audience
Strategy	• Help! (you are telling the audience: be nice to me; I have prepared so well for this presentation)

5a Hands: in pockets

Results	• *Uninteresting attitude*
	• *Casually*
Origin	• Get rid of stress
Avoidance tricks	• Use cue cards
	• Take a non clicking object in your hands (for example an eraser)
	• Practise in front of a mirror
Strategy	• Show that you know what you do

5b Hands: extreme movement

Results	• *Restless (you look like a conductor or a stressed weather man)*
	• *Disturbing, because your audience starts observing instead of listening*
Origin	• Get rid of stress
	• Over prepared (you are so focused on your contents, that you start making extreme hand movements)
Avoidance tricks	• Position your arms close to your body
	• Practise in front of a mirror
Strategy	• Underline the importance of an argument

5c Hands: holding on to an object or the desk

Results	• *Restless, disturbing (you are clicking with a pen the whole time)*
Origin	• Get rid of stress
Avoidance tricks	• Take a non clicking object with you
Strategy	• Use cue cards (you can write down a number of catchwords or even your whole presentation on these cards without being disturbing)

6a Lower body: extremely mobile

Results	• *Restless (It looks like you are watching a tennis match)*
	• *Visual overload (Gosh, it is him again!)*
Origin	• Get rid of stress
Avoidance tricks	• You should walk only to another point in the room (only when you are starting another part of your presentation)
Strategy	• Keep in contact with your audience (it has become a bit dull without any movements)
	• Keep your presentation alive (the audience is falling asleep; it is time for a loud walk)

6b Lower body: wiggling

Results	• *Restless (People start writing down how many times you moved)*
	• *Visual overload (The audience only focuses on the wiggling; they do not pay any attention anymore to your presentation contents)*
Origin	• Wrong position
	• Injured (painful muscles/accident/one leg is longer than the other)
	• Get rid of stress
Avoidance tricks	• You walk to another position a few times
Strategy	• Keep in contact with your audience (it has become a bit dull without any movements)

7 Feet: either crossed or at short distance

Results	• *Wiggling*
	• *Possibility to fall down*
Origin	• Get rid of stress
	• Injured (accident/one leg is longer than the other)
Avoidance tricks	• Create some space in between both feet (more flexible in your movements)
	• Bend your knees a bit (more flexible in your movements)
Strategy	• Keep in contact with your audience (it has become a bit dull without any movements)

This Skill Sheet discusses a number of disturbing factors, which you might have to face when presenting. These things can happen? No, in practice these things *will* happen! Experienced presenters can tell you that Murphy's Law almost always applies; so you'd better prepare yourself. In practice students and inexperienced presenters put the blame for a disastrous presentation on these factors, on the equipment, or on other people. As a general rule, keep in mind: you are the only one responsible for either avoiding these things to happen or for dealing with them in an appropriate manner during your presentation! Although the audience might understand for instance that it is not your fault that the equipment breaks down, your presentation will nevertheless be affected and afterwards you will only be judged on the content of the presentation, not on possible excuses for why it failed. This Skill Sheet portrays a number of situations in which you should learn to cope with this type of disturbance. In this way, you can make potentially disturbing situations less problematic for yourself and ultimately also for your audience.

1 Equipment breaks down

Situation	*You have checked all equipment beforehand (➔F2, F6) and everything worked fine. But the over-head projector or the beamer stops functioning half-way through your presentation. A new one is not available.*
Reaction	Make sure that you have a piece of chalk or a whiteboard marker with you. In this way, you can pursue your presentation on the (white)board. Overhead projectors are more reliable than beamers, so make sure you always have some transparencies available when you have prepared something for the beamer/computer.

2 Forgotten object

Situation	*Half-way through your presentation you find out that you have forgotten an essential object or a slide for your presentation.*
Reaction	Explain the audience exactly what happened, but that you will try to explain as good as possible what you intended with the object or the slide (use the board to explain it better).

3 Asking questions (you have clearly explained beforehand that you do not answer questions during your presentation. The following situations can occur:)

Situation	*Somebody asks a very essential question.*
Reaction	When you get signals from your audience that more people face the same problem, you can still decide to discuss this issue.

Situation	Somebody asks a question merely to look interesting.
Reaction	Always react professionally and friendly. If this person remains obtrusive become more explicit in your answers, by stating that the question has nothing to do with the object of your presentation.

Situation	You do not know the answer to a question.
Reaction	Admit that you do not know the answer. You can offer to search for the answer or refer them to somebody who might know the answer.

Situation	Somebody keeps asking a question (again and again) without listening to your answers.
Reaction	Try to remain calm and try to break through this wall of ignorance. If it still does not work, then conclude that you both have a different opinion about this subject (only in this very specific case) and leave it at that.

Situation	You feel that people did not understand your presentation because of the type of questions they ask.
Reaction	You can decide to repeat a piece of your presentation and clarify what exactly it is about. You can also consider giving a short summary of your whole presentation and underlining the main points again.

4 Lost your text

Situation	You prepared your presentation well, but you lost your text in the middle of your presentation.
Reaction	Take a break for ten seconds and try to recover that part of your story. If you do not manage to return to your story within ten seconds, admit that you forgot your text. You take some time to check your notes to recover your presentation. In this way, you clearly explain what you are doing and the audience will take note of this fact. This creates the best chance of pursuing your presentation without large damage.

5 Attitude/Behaviour audience

Situation	The audience is not very silent, moves around, and you get the impression that they do not like your story.
Reaction	Try to get the audience on your side again by making a joke or making an obvious slip or try another way of presenting.

6 Unexpected entrance

Situation	*Somebody is entering the classroom too late.*
Reaction	Stay focused on your audience. Wave this person in with your hand, but do *not* say a word! When you do not react yourself to the person that is late, the larger the chance that your audience remains focused on you instead of on the person that entered the class room late.

7 Comforting moments

Situation	*To feel more comfortable during a presentation, a number of tips may help.*
Reaction	• You can change your slides more *slowly*, so that you create another five seconds of time to think.
	• You can look away from the room for a moment so that you have a number of additional seconds to relax and some extra time to think.
	• You can *drink* something so that you have some additional time to empty your mind.
	• You can *breathe* more deeply so that you create a number of free seconds. You can use these seconds to take some time to relax and think.
	• You can ask a *short question* to somebody in the audience so that you have some time to reconsider the following parts of your presentation.

Series G Team and Project Management

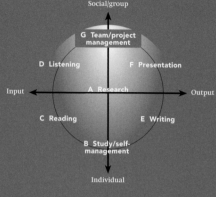

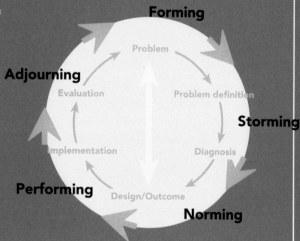

The Reflective Cycle of Effective Project Management

Forming

Problem

Adjourning

Evaluation

Problem definition

Storming

Implementation

Diagnosis

Performing

Design/Outcome

Norming

	Forming	Storming	Norming	Performing	Adjourning
G1 The Principles of Effective Team Management	■				
G2 Forming: Members, Roles and Dependencies	■	■			
G3 Brainstorming		■			
G4 Norming: Tasks and Roles			■		
G5 Decision-making			■		
G6 Basics of Effective Negotiations			■	■	
G7 Group Contract				■	
G8 Effective Meetings				■	
G9 Feedback and Coaching				■	
G10 Unhealthy Group Dynamics					■
G11 Dealing with Conflicts					■
G12 The Final Stage: Tasks and Roles					■

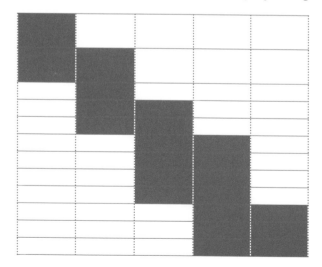

Management Skill Levels

Level 1
o Ability to perform relatively simple organisational assignments
o Supervision, assignment
o Input and simple tasks-oriented
o Understand the basic characteristics of free-rider behaviour and group dynamics
o Giving feedback
o Ability to effectively make use of a tutor

Level 2
o Ability to apply the principles of project management and perform more complex assignments with less detailed briefs
o Formation of group externally induced
o Understand the basics of effective brainstorming and meetings
o Identify free-riders behaviour in others and yourself
o Basic knowledge of meeting and decision-making techniques
o Giving and receiving feedback
o Ability to effectively coach each other

Level 3
o Ability to conduct sophisticated research projects
o Self-management, marginal supervision
o Output-oriented
o Formation of group internally induced (on the basis of joint interests)
o Understand that free-rider behaviour takes different forms throughout the various project stages; take effective action
o Understanding decision-making techniques and how to effectively organise meetings
o Organising feedback
o Ability to effectively make use of a supervisor

Level 4
o Ability to organise and delegate sophisticated projects
o Joint responsibility and team management
o Impact-oriented
o Timely forming and adjourning of project teams (basic principle of effective network management)
o Preventing of free-rider behaviour
o Ability to effectively make use of a coach
o Organising constructive and continuous two-way feedback
o Mastering decision-making techniques

1 Every team is a group, but a group is only rarely a team
2 Effective teams always push themselves up the Team Life Cycle in order to produce high quality results
3 Effective teams thrive on diversity not on conformity
4 Sophisticated management skills are based on the same principles as research and study skills
5 Effective teams manage their internal and external (network) dependencies smartly
6 Team members should be willing to regularly swap roles
7 Team management requires intricate knowledge of constructive negotiation rules (and the willingness to apply them)
8 Every team member is equally responsible for the end-result
9 Dedicate always sufficient time for: (1) open brainstorming and (2) evaluation and peer feedback
10 Become a coach/tutor/peer teacher

1 The need for effective project and team management

Research and study are often organised as a group activity. In order to work effectively on a project as a member of a group, management skills are a mandatory element of a skill profile. Acquiring and applying management skills, however, is more difficult to achieve because they consist of a mixture of input as well as output characteristics. The effectiveness of a 'manager' depends on the behaviour and interests of the group members, and vice versa. Managing a group always represents a balancing act between diverging individual interests, competencies and temperaments. The diversity of a group, however, is almost always a necessary – but not sufficient – condition for success. Groups of 'friends' are notoriously ineffective; groups of people with the same skill profile often clash or end up in apathy. So the fact that groups are often made up of 'colleagues' – people who do not have to like each other in order to collaborate – is not necessarily bad. But collaboration between colleagues requires different skills than when you work with friends. Project groups run into problems when the two identities get mixed up. Or when you aim at acting like friends in a group, whereas a more colleague-like attitude would be more professional *and* effective – a problem that many students face when they collectively try to work on an assignment. Mastering management and study skills – combined in acts of 'doing it yourself' – have greater learning effects than any of the other skills contained in this Skill Sheets collection (box).

What activity best 'sticks' to your memory?
1 doing it yourself (90%);
2 saying it yourself (70%);
3 reading and listening (50%);
4 listening (20%);
5 reading (10%).

Source: Fendrich, 1979: 17

Output-oriented activities such as writing, managing and speaking have the biggest impact on your learning. They require that you do many things yourself, but on the basis of thorough (written) preparation. Research into management skills shows that, to be a good and effective manager, you need many of the basic research-oriented skills (➡A series): flexibility, professionalism, systematic evaluation, open-mindedness, self-criticism. It was found that the good and effective managers share a high 'tolerance for ambiguity': they are challenged by novelty, complexity and sometimes even the insolubility of a project (Whetten et al., 2004: 71). This could be the profile of a dedicated researcher as well. A good manager is research-oriented.

2 The Learning Cycle of team management

All project teams, regardless of task, member characteristics, duration, and circumstances go through comparable stages (Guirdham, 1990): 1) forming: the appropriate team, (2) storming: taking adequate time for brainstorming over possible dimensions (causes as well as consequences) of the project, (3) norming: deciding on the basis of more or less objective 'norms', (4) performing: implementing it, after which (5) the team can be adjourned, provided they performed well. Caproni (2005) calls this the 'Team life cycle'. In fact it shows a strong resemblance to the personal learning cycle (Figure G.1; ➡Format, Part I). Going through the team life cycle effectively indeed requires a learning process form unaware competency to aware competencies. However, the responsibility for this learning cycle is now in the hands of the whole group. A successful cycle thereby represents the movement from 'group' to 'team' (cf. Whetten et al., 2004): (1) in the forming stage, there is a group, but not a team; (2) in the storming phase issues of control are being settled through discussion and dissent – the team starts to develop; (3) in the norming stage individual relationships and norms are being established – consolidating the team; (4) in the performing stages the team reaches maturity and becomes self-directed or self-actualising – the group has become an effective team; (5) in the adjourning stage with successful teams the project has been accomplished – the team can be disbanded (the so-called mourning team) or rejuvenated for a new assignment. Each of these stages creates specific challenges to the group and the individual group members. Effective teams, thus, 'promote the personal growth needs and well-being of team members' (Caproni, 2005: 343).

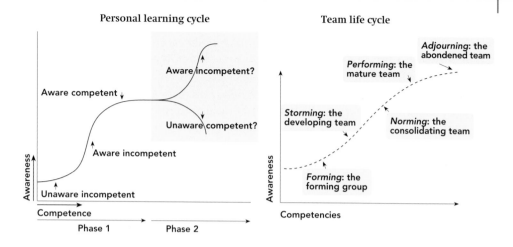

Personal learning cycle

Team life cycle

Figure G.1 Stages of team development

3 Contents and principles

Managing a research or study group is not very different from managing a company. Team skills present, however, a greater bottleneck than the individual skills contained in the Series A-F. The skills, related to the understanding and dealing with people in a concrete project are the most complex of the whole skill circle, because taking responsibility for learning at this side is always a shared activity. The object and subject, input and output of researchers get easily mixed up when they are engaged in group projects. Effective group members change actively and timely between roles like 'leader', 'analyst/thinker' or 'worker'. 'The best horseman is always on his feet', as the saying goes. In research projects, well functioning group members are not only riding ('leader') the horse or standing aside watching and commenting ('analyst/thinker'). They also have to be prepared to take the role of the horse ('worker') occasionally. But chosen at the wrong moment, the role can lead to undesired outcomes.

Effective collaboration in a research group means...

- Giving as well as taking
- Mutual respect
- A commitment to teamwork
- Basic discipline in delivering what is promised by agreed dates
- Not assuming that you are busier than anyone else

Source: Monica Schofield (TuTech Hamburg)

Following the stages of group formation, a number of skills are particularly relevant: (1) assessing the personal traits of team members and team roles in the forming stage (➐G2) and the principles of effective brainstorming in groups in the storming stage (➔G3). For the norming stage a variety of tools are available. Some of them have been chosen for inclusion in the Skill Sheets collection: on what tasks and roles to agree (➔G4), decision-making procedures and effective negotiation (➔G5, G6), and the outline of a group contract (➔G7). As regards performing, the G-series of the Skill Sheets concentrates on models, measures and insights to deal with the dynamism of group processes, either to sustain the virtuous learning cycle (➔G7-9) or effectively deal with problems that might arise (➔G10, G11). Free-rider problems in particular appear in any group – any individual person deserves a 'free-ride' from time to time. But the challenge is not to have it disrupt the virtuous learning cycle. The solution to this particular management problem is relatively simple (➔G10). Finally, projects can only be finished and teams successfully adjourned in case you manage the final stages of the project properly (➔G12).

The formation of the right (project) team critically depends on the interests, strengths and weaknesses, and ambitions of each individual team member. Balanced teams consist of members that share ambitions, but complement each other's skills and knowledge. In effective teams, skills and roles are linked productively. This Skill Sheet helps you to identify your own skill profile in relationship to the roles you are inclined to take in groups. These profiles can serve as a basis for discussion in the group in the 'forming' stage. What personalities are represented in the team, what are their existing internal and external dependencies, and can ambitions be aligned? (1) The Skill profiles present in a group define the *level of ambitions* that you can formulate for a project. (2) The Team Role profiles define the *breadth of the ambition* that is obtainable through the group, (3) the Network and Dependency profile define the *feasibility* of these ambitions.

Step 1: Identify Skill Profiles

To define your individual skill profile you can build upon techniques introduced already in the other Skill Sheets:

- Fill out your personal **learning report**, in particular the strength/weakness assessment of each skill (➔B4);
- Specify you **Skill Level** as regards each of the relevant skills: level 1, 2, 3 or 4. Use the checklist in this book at the start of each Skill Series.
- Define your **research orientation** (➔A3): [1] Conceptualiser, [2] Diagnost, [3] Designer, [4] Implementer, [5] Involved evaluator.
- Identify your personal **Attitude** (➔B2) in general and towards groups in particular.

The best start of a project is when you prepare this before the first session. This is your personal 'zero measurement'. It will help you considerably to (a) understand what you want, and (b) what you can contribute already, whilst enabling you (c) to evaluate better at the end of the project what you have achieved in your personal learning ambitions. Talking about this personal background is also an excellent way of introducing yourself to a new group. A short summary of your filled-out profile makes it possible to make this otherwise very personal assessment more or less 'objective'. After an inventory of these skill profiles the group can assess what kinds of ambitions of a project are feasible.

[⊕➔www.skillsheets.com provides a form]

Step 2: Identify Team Roles

To what extent can individuals with completely different skill profiles effectively work together? Belbin (1993) reasons that differences among team members in fact *enhance* the functioning of the whole group. She defined nine roles that have to be present in a successful team. Every role has its own specific character traits, each role supports another role (Table G.2). Belbin's team role model explains why certain persons can cooperate very well and others less. People normally fulfil more roles in teams, but nobody is good at all roles. There are 'allowable weaknesses' in the skill profiles of team members. In effective teams, team members complement one another. Consequently, frustrations, which arise within every team, can be contained easily, when team members are well aware of the function of differences in the group.

Research amongst business students in 2006, hypothesized a number of relationships between the Belbin categories and the Skill Profiles in the Skill Sheets (Lander and Leliveld, 2006). Table G.2 shows in a simplified manner the results of this research project. Noticeable is in particular the strong skill profile of the implementer. This particular category is often also one of the most outspoken categories in group processes. Coordinators, shapers and resource investigators scored well on every skill. So, for these team roles it can be suggested that they approach most clearly the ambition of this Skill Sheets collection, i.e. an 'integrated' approach in which all skills are related and considered vital for study, research and management. This link has never been researched in detail, so these first research results have to be interpreted with great caution.

- Identify which of Belbin's Team Roles are present in the group
  [⊕⊕www.skillsheets.com provides a form and reference to related websites]
- Link these team roles with the research orientation and skill profile of each team member. Table G.2 links the Belbin roles with expected skill and research profiles. Examine to what extent the expected skill orientation in Table G.2 applies.
  [⊕⊕www.skillsheets.com for references]
- Discuss on the basis of these profiles whether the group has sufficient diversity and complementarity in Team Roles and Skill Profiles to work together on this particular project.

Table G.2 Linking team roles, skill profiles and research ambitions

Belbin Team Role	Characteristics	Research Orientation (⊕A3)	Skill Orientation
1 Coordinator	Mature, confident, a good chairperson. Clarifies goals, promotes decision-making, delegates well.	Process oriented: always takes whole Reflective Cycle into account	High score on all skills. High level of self-management skills.
2 Implementer	Disciplined, reliable, conservative and efficient. Turns ideas into practical action.	Diagnost, designer, implementer	Output-oriented: scores well on presenting and writing, but not on reading and listening.
3 Shaper	Challenging, dynamic, thrives on pressure. The drive and courage to overcome obstacles.	Designer, implementer	High score on all skills. High level of self-management skills.

4 Plant or innovator	Creative, imaginative, unorthodox. Solves diffi-cult problems.	Conceptualiser	Input-oriented. Scores well on reading and reasonable on listening, but badly on presenting and writing.
5 Resource investigator	Extrovert, enthusiastic, communicative. Explores opportunities. Develops contacts.	Diagnost, designer	High score on all skills, High level of self-manage-ment skills.
6 Monitor/ evaluator	Sober, strategic and dis-cerning. Sees all options. Judges accurately.	Involved evaluator	Strong research orienta-tion: Listening, reading and writing oriented
7 Team worker	Co-operative, mild, percep-tive and diplomatic. Lis-tens, builds and averts fric-tion.	Implementer	Process-oriented: listening and self-management ori-ented
8 Completer/ finisher	Painstaking, conscien-tious, anxious. Searches out errors and omissions. Delivers on time.	Implementer, evaluator	Individual and output-ori-ented. Lacks special quali-ties, but is often better reader than writer.
9 Specialist	Single-minded, self start-ing, dedicated. Provides knowledge and skills in rare supply.	Conceptualiser, diagnost	Individual-oriented. Is reader and writer.

Source: based on Belbin (2006), Lander and Leliveld, 2006

Step 3: Network position and dependency relations

In any group or network individuals interact on the basis of skills, team roles, but also on relative power positions. Effective groups respect the *rule of barter* (➔A12). In group processes barter is not necessarily voluntary. So you must be will-ing and capable to 'manage with power' as Jeffrey Pfeffer (1992) calls it. Effectively managing with power requires that you *diagnose* your present relative dependen-cies as well as those of the other group members in the formation stage. This defines the 'room for manoeuvre' for the group in developing *realistic* goals. In par-ticular the shape and nature of the networks amongst the project participants decide whether the group can actually become a 'team' (➔G1). There are two net-work dimensions: the external and the internal networking position.

• **External networks**: whether the group can be effective depends on the extent to which each individual group member is dedicated to the project. In case the group members do not have other contacts and/or networks they operate in, they will be highly motivated to work in this team. This kind of team often gets the work done in the allotted time. But the risk of 'groupthink' (➔G10) looms large. Furthermore, the division of labour that the group agrees upon can become 'solidified' and members get 'stuck' to one skill they originally had a rel-ative advantage in – writing, researching, chairing – even when the project

285

requires other skills. This is the problem of **'closed' networks**. In case the group members have plenty of external contacts, this could seriously affect the internal dynamism. For instance because they will be more opportunistic in their group work, or because they will be more easily distracted (the other networks demand their attention). This is the problem of **'open networks'**. On the other hand, open networks are often more creative and flexible. So both types of networks have positive and negative sides. In the formation stage you should establish the kind of network the group is in, and what the opportunities and threats are. Figure G.2 pictures the two types of networks, their consequences and tips for a hypothetical project team of three people (1, 2 and 3).

Figure G.2 External networks and their consequences

Open Network   **Closed Network**

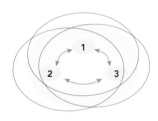

Characteristics:

- No/hardly any overlap in individual social networks
- Research team is 'temporary' coalition
- High degree of opportunism possible
- Relatively low sanctions in networks on 'malperformance' and opportunism (free-riding)

Characteristics:

- High overlap in individual networks (lots of common friends)
- Long-term coalition
- Great loyalty to the group
- High sanctions on 'malperformance' and opportunism (such as free-rider behaviour)

Consequences and tips:

- Be clear about your output ambitions
- Specify individual competencies and roles in more detail
- Define the nature of the internal network interaction very clearly:
  - o decision-making procedures
  - o level of mutual dependencies
  - o responsibilities per group stage (storming, norming, performing, adjourning)
- Define the 'exit' option: when to terminate the project

Consequences and tips:

- Beware of 'groupthink'
- Danger of 'solidified' specialisation and continuation of labour division even when this is not functional or desirable
- Specify in detail the competencies you would like to acquire; plan to change roles during the project or over various projects
- Particularly important phase is 'brainstorming'. Closed groups tend to skip this phase regularly (→G3)
- Define the 'finish' option: when do you consider this particular project finished

- **Internal networks**: external networks have an influence on the way internal networks function. The internal 'room for manoeuvre' is defined by the mutual dependencies created in the project. When commencing with a group project each individual group member should ask themselves the following questions:
  - o How dependent do I want to be on the performance of the group and the activities of the other group members?
  - o How dependent do I want the group to be on my own performance?
  - o How much time does each member have available for the project?
  - o Is there a convergence or a divergence of expectations, skills and preferred dependencies of the participants?

[⊕➔www.skillsheets.com for personal questionnaires]

The 'storming' stage of a project aims at identifying all possible dimensions of a particular problem in order to define the goals and strategy of the team in the most open and creative manner. A well-organised brainstorm helps to redefine individual priorities and sometimes even those of the original project and group goals. The effort is basically input-oriented and informal, but – when executed properly – it creates a solid foundation for more formal and output-oriented stages (the norming and performing stages). The biggest mistake project teams normally make is to rush through the brainstorming stage. Whether or not the group dynamism is positive in the later stages of a project depends as much on the norming stage in which the rules and priorities are defined, as on the storming stage in which ideas are generated and common ambitions are defined. Brainstorming is a reiterative phenomenon, however. It can take place during several stages of a project. This is particularly important when new problems arise. For example, when one of the team members does not perform well, the team can organize a brainstorming session to find solutions for the problem.

Always take sufficient time for brainstorming.

1 Brainstorming phases

One of the most important characteristics of effective brainstorming is that all possibilities and alternatives are considered by the team. Collective brainstorming can add new insights and fresh perspectives to individual brainstorming, which has been introduced as a very good technique for powerful writing (➔E series), creative researching (➔A4) or effective learning through self-management (➔B5). Group members can introduce new perspectives and can challenge the other members to re-think their ideas. In this sense, the risk of missing or forgetting important elements of the problem can be decreased via the group process. Effective brainstorming generally consists of five phases:

- **Generating** ideas – *During this phase it is important that group members give no judgement on the ideas generated. This phase is solely geared towards listing the options, no matter how bizarre or impractical they might seem.*
- **Examining** the list of options – *All the options will be listed, discussed and clustered. Have any options been left out? By clustering options, new insights can be gained insights.*
- **Eliminating** unfeasible ideas – *After further examination and after further clustering, ideas that are not deemed feasible should be eliminated. Ideas that do not apply to the current situation can be considered non-feasible.*
- **Discussing** the remaining options – *The remaining ideas are discussed in a structured manner. For instance, by listing the advantages and disadvantages of each option.*
- **Selecting** one or more options – *After thorough discussion on the advantages and disadvantages of each option, a choice will be made for a limited number of the options (preferably one or two).*

2 Brainstorming strategies

- *Associative brainstorming* – Each individual team member writes down words that are associated with the project's topic. Later on, all individual associations are compared and combined.
- *Process brainstorming about a process* – Each individual team member writes down their concrete idea on the ideal project process (including main subjects, questions, and practical matters). Every individual defines end goals and the steps to achieve this. Later on, all process expectations are compared with each other.
- *Collective verbal brainstorming* – Each team member is invited to 'think out loud' without any restrictions. The chair should guarantee that sufficient time is available, whereas someone writes down all the ideas mentioned. An individual brainstorm is not necessary with this type of brainstorming. Later on, a moderator (or the chair) should come up with observations on what the brainstorm has delivered.

3 Managing the process

From the third step onwards in the brainstorming process – so in the selection and decision-making phase – conflicts can arise within the team. People who push their own interests too much in this phase, decrease the willingness of the other group members to contribute to the joint group project. Take sufficient time in this phase to discuss and specify group aims which are shared or at least accepted by all group members. Take in this stage in particular the basic negotiation and feedback rules into account (➔G6, G9). Applying these rules helps avoid conflict in a team.

Other problems derive from the relatively chaotic process that brainstorming entails. There are two temporary roles that need to be allocated in order to make sure that the brainstorm does not end up in chaos: the 'chair' and the 'secretary' or 'rapporteur' role.

- *The chair* – Brainstorming without a (temporary) chair ends up in chaos. The chair manages the brainstorming session, in particular by making sure that nobody interrupts one another, that no comments are given on the proposed ideas before everybody is given the same opportunity to share their ideas with the group. Furthermore, the chair has to make sure that the brainstorm remains focused on the main subject. Finally, the chair takes the responsibility that something has to come out of the brainstorm. So the chair acts as 'primus inter pares' (first among equals), as the facilitator of the process, not as the decision-maker. The chair can summarize all pros and cons, and propose a decision-making procedure (➔G5).
- *The rapporteur* – The role of the secretary or rapporteur of a brainstorming session depends on the chosen strategy. In particular for collective verbal brainstorming, the role is vital and requires a high degree of integrity. Because many possibilities are mentioned during a brainstorm, nobody except the secretary will be able to remember; so the reporting could be biased (and therefore not accepted in later phases by some of the participants). The secretary therefore does not participate in the brainstorming either, but has the sole task to register.

A good technique is to write all remarks down on the blackboard. The group members then can see whether their remarks are taken seriously. While writing down, the secretary can pose clarification questions, but not participate in the discussion.

One of the most important functions of the norming stage of team development is to reach agreement on *functional* roles and the related tasks for each team member. Functional roles can differ from the personal roles in the *forming* stage (➔G2). The 'coordinator' in Belbin's framework for instance not automatically has to take up the 'chair' position in group meetings. This Skill Sheet lists what is required of the participants to facilitate a virtuous group process *before* the group process starts. In principle, the discussion on these requirements will therefore be part of the first meeting. Agreement is required, first on a common attitude of each team member and secondly on who is going to execute the most important functional tasks/roles during the project: the chair and the minute-taker. Identifying tasks, roles and attitudes in the norming stage, will prevent serious conflicts from appearing during the project. The actual execution of these roles and tasks is part of the performing stage (➔G10).

1 Basics: a common attitude

A group meeting is only effective when a number of negative meeting characteristics (see box) are dealt with by *all* participants. In principle, this can be achieved by two behavioural approaches:
- Strive for positive attitude
- Beware of reductive listening

The seven most negative meetings characteristics

Meeting characteristic	Bothered a lot (%)
Drifting off the subject	83
Poor preparation	77
Questionable effectiveness	74
Lack of concentration	68
Verbosity of participants	62
Length	60
Lack of participation	51

Source: Smart (1974), quoted in Haynes (1988:13)

1.1 Positive attitude as a participants' requirement

Active participation in a discussion creates the best condition for the effectiveness of the meeting itself, but also for your individual learning process. Active participation relates in particular to your attitude as a participant to discussions. There are two types of attitudes: negative and positive.
- **Negative**: means that you are satisfied with being critical, or 'pulling the rug' from beneath someone else. This is generally considered to be a forceful debating technique. But, in fact you are only trying to reinforce a feeling of 'superior-

ity'. The debate largely remains a waste of time for yourself and everybody else in the meeting.

- **Positive**: means that you feel responsible for and involved in the end-result of the discussion. You can be as critical as you like, but at the same time also try to think about alternatives. Positive team members concentrate on the problem not on the person (➔G6).

A positive attitude is generally the most successful. If a meeting heads in the wrong direction, or the chair is unable to lead the discussion, everyone should feel responsible for initiating a discussion on the organisation of the meeting, in order to restore its effectiveness. It is not sufficient to blame one participant for disrupting the discussion or the chair for lack of leadership, once the meeting is over.

> Everyone is responsible for the end result. If the discussion has been boring or unsuccessful, each participant is to blame.

1.2 Beware of reductive listening

As an individual member, or as the chairperson, be particularly aware of the mechanism of *reductive listening*: individual group members are more concerned with 'saying their piece' than with listening to and interacting with what is actually being said in the group. Reductive listening is an error that also occurs in interview situations (➔D3) and in the bargaining society at large (➔the Challenges; part I). It seriously hampers purposeful exchange in meetings, because people are expressing their views rather than contributing to the purpose of the meeting. It constitutes the difference between 'debate' and 'dialogue' (➔F3, G5). The problem can only be tackled in a group when the aims of the discussion are agreed upon first. If this is the case, the chair or any other participants can politely point to the (lack of) relevance of particular contributions to the purpose of the debate, and thus contribute to a more effective and less time-consuming meeting.

2 Process: the two most important tasks

Most people in small groups take up different roles. But even if your group is relatively small (three to five people) *always* appoint a chair or discussion leader. You can decide to do this in a 'revolving' manner, so that every group member becomes chair from time to time, but it is often better to choose one person, who then can also count this to be his/her prime responsibility. The problem with revolving responsibilities is that the task might remain unattended. This is particularly problematic for the chair position. The second important task is the minute taker. This is a particularly important task because it keeps the members to their promises and acts as a sort of 'check' on the effectiveness of the chair. Every group member in principle has the responsibility to act as chair and take minutes, but in day-to-day practice it could be sensible to assign these tasks to two of the group members – the chair for the whole trajectory, the minute taker perhaps per session differently. This all depends on the way you want to organise the team process. Do not complain, for instance, during the process that the team members do not deliver according to what was agreed in the last meeting if you also 'forgot' to make effective notes and communicate that to the others. Do not rely too much on 'natural leaders' in small groups. In bigger teams a number of other functional roles can be distinguished and delegated to individual group members (see Belbin ➔G2), but in particular in smaller teams the chair and the minute taker remain the most important (separate) functions.

Motto: every team member takes responsibility for the whole process.

Implementation: make sure that two functions are always covered: chair and minute taker

Chair function:	Minute taker function:
• *Time management* of the overall meeting and of each separate part; makes sure that each phase of an effective meeting gets sufficient time (in particular brainstorming ➔G3)	• *Memory*: keeping everybody to their appointments
	• *Check*: makes sure that what is discussed leads to clear appointments; checks the chair for doing this
• *Keeping to the issue* (not drifting off the subject)	• *Action*: keeps an overview per action point along the 5Ws: Who, What, Where, Why and When; critically investigates that each member does what is promised
• *Project planning*: keeping the internal planning up to date	
• *People*: making sure that everybody is given a chance to participate in the meeting	• *Informant*: sends action information to non present people
• *Facilitator*: makes sure that the meeting room is available and functional	

Decision-making procedures always figure prominently in group processes, even when there is no formal agreement. The bigger the group, the more formalized decision-making has to become. The smaller the group, the more informal decision-making becomes. But whether formal or informal, managing decision-making procedures effectively is extremely important in the effective management of teams and projects. In teams many decisions have to be made. For instance on (1) the goals, (2) the ways to cooperate, (3) the agenda for the next time, (4) action points, (5) responsibilities, (6) quality of the products, and... of course (7) the decision-making procedure to adopt. Often smaller teams do not discuss this. One reason for this is that talking about decision-making procedures is often considered a sign of distrust. Small groups seem to operate on the basis of 'consensus', but what exactly does that mean? Often informal hierarchies exist in which in fact the agenda is set by a 'leader' who dominates the decision-making (⊕G8). In later phases team processes can run into serious problems, for instance because individual team members do not feel committed to the project for which 'the others' have decided what to do. In the storming and norming stage – when you decide upon the final research question and how to operationalise them – it is particularly important to be more careful about the decision-making process. This Skill Sheet specifies the phases of decision-making – which follow the consecutive steps of the Reflective Cycle – and lists a number of decision-making techniques you can choose from.

1 Phases of decision-making

Decision-making can take up several consecutive meetings. The steps undertaken in effective decision-making processes in principle follow the phases of the Reflective Cycle (⊕A1):

- *Recognise and define the problem* – If the topic has not been prepared by a group member especially assigned to do this, the chairperson should give a (intermediary) problem definition by way of introduction. Diagnose the characteristics of the problem. The chairperson should list the different interests involved or opinions on the topic existing in the group and outside it.
- *Aggregate solutions* – Thinking about solutions can be organised in group meeting in particular by brainstorming or by issuing a report, or installing a committee. This phase should aim, primarily, at descriptions of the preferred situation.
- *Make scenarios* – Make scenarios and anticipate what the consequences could be of the implementation of each scenario. The group can be split into subgroups, which discuss separate scenarios of solutions and present listings of 'strengths' and 'weaknesses'.
- *Selection* – Selection of one scenario and selection of an implementation plan. In the same meeting a particular implementation plan can be chosen and be clearly defined: time frame, responsibilities, resources located. Often, the latter elaboration's can only be presented in the following meeting.
- *Evaluation of the implementation* – Evaluation is only included in the subsequent

meetings, preferably on a regular basis. The input provided during the meeting by a specially assigned evaluator, very often leads to a redefinition of the problem, after which the whole group goes through the circle again, but now at a higher level of (mutual) understanding and with less ad hoc decision-making.

Ineffective decision-makers do not go (or do not dare to go) round the whole cycle. Effective procedures for decision-making create the possibility for individual group members to perform functional roles, and work on the development of a set of common norms and rules that need not be bargained over all the time. Effective decision-making does not necessarily aim at *perfect* solutions to problems. The bargaining process that is needed to reach perfect agreements may lead to nothing. It would have been easier to agree on the 'best available' solution at the start. Non-effective procedures always build on *ad hoc* decision-making, and thus create limited learning experiences for the group as a whole. Individuals may gain, but the overall effect is always less than optimal and not easy to reproduce in a next phase of decision-making.

As with bad presentations (➔F3) or sloppy writing (➔C7, E4) ineffective decision-making procedures have one major drawback: too many points/opinions. In processes involving a group, the variety of opinions is spread around the different participants and the discussion may become a battle for prestige. Therefore, effective decision-making should always leave room to list individual interests (in a brainstorming phase) *before* the discussion about solutions begins. The different interests in the group are often part of the problem.

2 Types of decision-making

The type of decision-making that is chosen in teams can seriously affect the effectiveness of the team. Each has its risks and benefits for the group process. Often various techniques are mixed-up in the representation of a decision: for instance it regularly happens that a decision is said to be taken unanimously, but in fact was taken by consensus; consensus in a meeting where not everybody is present could in fact also imply that the decision was taken by 'majority'. Understanding the meaning of these decision-making techniques is a vital skill for survival in the bargaining society (➔The Challenge, Part I). Knowing how to use various decision-making techniques in practice is a precondition for effective team management. Different decision-making techniques can be functional for different phases in a project. You can choose from the following procedures:

☐ **Unanimity** – everyone is in total agreement; it gives each one group member a 'veto'; unanimity is often applied in cases where it should be absolutely sure that everyone agrees and takes up the responsibility for what has been agreed upon. In project management, unanimity is required when you set the rules of engagement for the group (➔G6) in general and for the way you deal with specific circumstances, like free-riders (➔G10).

☐ **Consensus** – not everyone needs to agree totally, but nobody disagrees with the outcome; this also gives group members a certain veto power, which however is much less used; in group projects consensus is best used with brainstorming

(➔G3) and as normal practice in most meetings (➔G8).

☐ **Sociocratic method** – decision-making by 'consent' is an interesting alternative to the consensus method. The meaning of the word 'consent' is that decisions are made only when no one involved knows of a significant argument against the decision – there are no paramount objections; before that point is reached, each reasoned argument is included in the discussion. All decisions must be made by consent, unless the group agrees to use another method. Because socio-cratic decision-making stresses so much the argumentation skills (➔A10, E6) they can be particularly beneficial in a research setting [⊕➔www.skillsheets.com].

☐ **Majority** – is the normal procedure in 'democratic' processes, but is particularly risky in team projects because a substantial minority may be left out of the solu-tion, and therefore create additional problems in later phases. Majority rule can be applied in case that particular majority is also prepared to execute the task or in case of conflicts (➔G11). Various majority rules are:
   ○ *absolute majority*: half of all group members plus one;
   ○ *ordinary majority*: most of the votes that have actually been submitted (can be much less than the absolute majority and also depends on the quorum agreed for a meeting to be valid);
   ○ *qualified majority*: only two thirds, or three quarters of the votes are sufficient to reach a decision.

☐ **Delegating** – the group delegates the responsibility for the execution of a partic-ular decision to a group or an individual within the group; the more vague the delegation is, the more the decision-making is left to one delegated person. In authoritarian organisations, such a delegate is the leader.

☐ **Others** – there are several other decision-making procedures. They relate, in par-ticular, to the voting procedures that you can adopt:
   ○ by voting in clusters of possible alternatives (in this case the order of the clus-ters is very important, it can be manipulated and can mean that the solution preferred by each group member does not get selected);
   ○ by weighted voting: some participants have more voting power than others;
   ○ by letting each group member communicate in writing.

Negotiation is necessary when members of a group or organisation have different interests but nevertheless try to reach an agreement. This is almost always the case in projects and team management – even if individual group members might perceive this otherwise. The bargaining society requires effective negotiation skills in order to prevent calculating behaviour from frustrating constructive team projects. Management of teams and research project can be considered a very concrete form of constant negotiation or barter (➲A9). Even in courses and small group meetings you constantly engage in forms of formal and informal bargaining. All through your higher education you must also be able to negotiate effectively to 'survive' and optimise your learning (➲The Challenge; Part I). There is a considerable variety of negotiation and meeting *tactics*: salami – getting people to accept an unpopular solution gradually- , leaking information at the right time, sabotage, delaying, striking package deals and so forth. Fundamentally, these tactics always result in sub-optimal outcomes and precipitate calculating behaviour also by the people that did not start bargaining. Instead, this Skill Sheet focuses on the basics of negotiation *strategies*, and not on – short-term – bargaining tactics.

1 Four general principles for participants to negotiations

■ The most influential approach to effective negotiating has been developed by James Fisher and William Ury (1981) in their famous book 'Getting to yes', and by William Ury (1991) in 'Getting Past No' where he applies the basic rules to dealing with 'difficult' or 'uncooperative' people. Fisher and Ury identified four basic principles for successful negotiations, that also neatly follow the sequence of the Reflective Cycle (Figure G6):

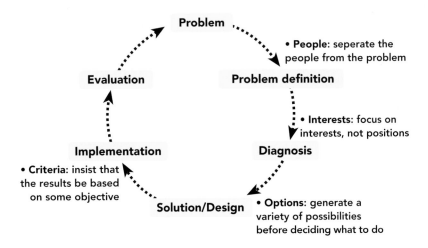

Figure G.6 Getting to Yes along the Reflective Cycle

These four basic principles can be elaborated further in a number of extra 'rules of thumb' to achieve effective negotiation behaviour:

- **People**
  - Put yourself in the position of the other person
  - Don't blame them for your problem
  - Be hard on the problem, soft on the people
  - Give them a stake in the outcome
- **Interests**
  - For a wise solution reconcile interests
  - Interests best define the problem
  - Behind opposed positions shared and compatible interests can exist. Identify them.
  - Realise that each side has multiple interests
- **Options**
  - Invent options for mutual gain
  - Consider brainstorming with 'the opposition' to come up with additional options
  - Try to broaden your options. This can limit the areas of contention
  - Change the scope for a proposed agreement
  - Invent agreements of varying strengths:

substantive	⇔	procedural
permanent	⇔	provisional
comprehensive	⇔	partial
final	⇔	in principle
unconditional	⇔	contingent
binding	⇔	non-binding

- **Criteria**
  - Insist on using objective criteria and/or fair standards such as:
    - professional standards
    - efficiency
    - equity or equal treatment
    - reciprocity
    - legal standards
    - existing precedents
    - moral standards, such as human rights
    - costs or market value
  - Frame each issue as a joint search for objective criteria

Following the abovementioned principles can limit the possibility of other actors using trick tactics, or basing their negotiation behaviour merely on their more powerful position. Common trick tactics include: using 'fake' facts or half truths ('how to lie with statistics' ➲A7, A12), ambiguity on who has authority on the topic, escalating demands during the negotiations, calculated delays, and 'take it or leave it' attitudes, which severely limit the openness of the negotiation process.

2 Before negotiations start...

Always try to establish your 'negotiation space' before you start the bargaining process: what is the optimum result of the bargaining and what is the minimum result beyond which you do not want to go. If the negotiation space of the participants does not overlap partially, there can be no solution to the bargaining problem, unless by force.

3 The actual process of negotiation

Effective negotiating and problem solving are often a matter of generating enough solutions. The process of problem solving in groups builds on the same principles of the Reflective Cycle applied throughout the whole Skill Sheets collection. Constructive negotiations are in principle organised as a 'dialogue' instead of a 'debate' (➲F3, G5). Debates can be very functional in sharpening argumentation, but as a negotiation tool they rarely function well. Table G6 shows the differences of debate and bargaining.

Table G.6 From debate towards dialogue

debate		dialogue
1 Competition with a single winner or only losers (either-or thinking; short-term oriented)	→ → →	Cooperation where everyone could be a winner (and-and thinking; longer term oriented)
2 Egocentric where the other is a threat or a means to personal gain	→ → →	Empathetic where the other party is seen as an opportunity and represents an intrinsic interest
3 Putting yourself in a better light	→ → →	Being yourself
4 Speaking while others must listen	→ → →	Listening to others before speaking yourself
5 Persuading	→ → →	Convincing
6 Confrontational, combative and destructive, seeking out weaknesses and set on proving the other wrong while negating commonalities	→ → →	Constructive, showing mutual understanding and respect so as to find commonalities from which to approach differences
7 A closed and defensive attitude because you have sole access to the truth	→ → →	A vulnerable attitude because many truths exist, and where all parties are open to criticism about their performance in order to learn from each other
8 Taking and keeping	→ → →	Giving and taking
9 Divide and rule	→ → →	Share and serve
10 Separate/isolated responsibilities	→ → →	Shared responsibilities

Source: Kaptein and Van Tulder, 2003; Van Tulder with Van der Zwart, 2006

The chair of the particular session should make sure that the session focuses on dialogue rather than debate. A dialogue entails a structured, interactive and proactive process aimed at creating sustainable strategies for the group. This requires that the following four dialogue phases be employed:

- **Inventory/problem definition**. It is very useful to have a phase of relatively unstructured *brainstorming* before arriving at solutions to the problem. Effective brainstorming is best served when:
  - criticising or making comments about each other or the group is not permitted (only positive ideas are generated);
  - an attempt is made to generate as many and varied ideas as possible, while participants are motivated to find new combinations of ideas;
  - all participants should have the possibility to contribute. One possible technique is to give everyone the chance to write ideas on a piece of paper, which is then handed in later in the storming session.

  The function of brainstorming should not be overestimated because free-rider behaviour in brainstorming can also appear in case the group contains members with largely differing interests (➔G2, G10).

- **Structure/diagnosis**. The group – or the chairperson – tries to summarise the most important ideas that were generated during the brainstorming phase. You can use the techniques listed in the Skill Sheet on argumentation skills (➔C6, E6) to compile a list of (1) pros and cons, (2) necessary and sufficient conditions, or (3) strengths and weaknesses on the list of options that came out of the brainstorming session.

- **Formulation/design**. The group – or someone especially designated for this task – assigns a priority ranking to the list of ideas that came out of the brainstorming phase. In group processes it is often better to search for acceptable solutions rather than for optimal ones to particular problems.

- **Editing/implementation**. The final ideas are written down and put into practice.

G7   Group Contract

More than in the case of individuals, it is important to make up a contract. Individuals can still operate on the basis of implicit rules and ambitions. By making an individual learning contract (➔B4) the learning process can be seriously improved. But, with groups, implicit rules and ambitions that are not explicitly specified can seriously hamper the project outcome. A group contract specifies the most important 'rules of engagement' that apply to each of the team members in relation to the ambitions of the whole group. The biggest challenge of a group contract is to make sure that there actually is value-added for the group activity, and that the end-result is more than the sum of the individual efforts of group members. The group contract takes the same form as an individual learning contract and consists of two parts: [a] the Group report, [b] the Group contract.

[A] The Group Report

1 Problem definition	Where are the individual members of the group now?	1 Strength and weaknesses of each individual (➔B4)
		2 Skill level of each individual (➔Skill levels)
		3 Research orientation (➔A3)
		4 Personal attitude (➔B2)
2 Diagnosis	What are the problems of the group?	1 Team roles (➔G2)
		2 Network topologies (➔G2)

The basic aim of the group report is to identify the starting position of the group and anticipate possible problems that might appear in further stages of the project due to initial weaknesses of the team. A detailed discussion of these aspects can be found in Skill Sheet G2.

[B] The Group Contract

3 Output/Design	Where do we want to go?	S.M.A.R.T. method
4 Implementation	How will we get there?	1 4W Model
		2 Timing
5 Evaluation	How can we test our progress?	1 Feedback (➔G9)
		2 Free-riders (➔G10)

The group contract defines the actual rules of engagement of the group. A smart contract takes the starting position of the group into account and on the basis of that decides upon goals, individual tasks and evaluation methods. Working in teams means that different people work on the same project at the same time, so it becomes vital to divide specific tasks adequately. This requires clear agreements on the subdivision of work. There are many methods to achieve this [⊕➔www.skillsheets.com]. For Goal setting, the S.M.A.R.T. method is particularly useful, for establishing individual goals, the 4W model can be applied.

1 Output/design: the SMART – method

S.M.A.R.T. is a technique to formulate functional and effective goals and agree-ments. It provides criteria to take into account when formulating goals. An impor-tant precondition for the SMART method to work is that all team members agree that these criteria are useful for the whole group. The SMART acronym stands for:

- *Specific*: goals and agreements are specific, formulated in terms of concrete results.
- *Measurable*: goals and agreements are measurable in terms of quantity, quality, and time.
- *Acceptable*: goals and agreements are acceptable for yourself and others.
- *Realistic*: goals and agreements are realistic in sense of its feasibility and practica-bility.
- *Time*: a certain time period is mentioned and are provided with a (end) date.

2 Implementation: Divided tasks: 4W model

The subdivision of smaller tasks can best be done when all team members are present. In the specification of tasks, people often tend to forget – for various rea-sons – a number of dimensions of the task, which later on in the process might become problematic. One of the reasons is that other team members are also not able to check progress with team members if the specification of the divided tasks is not done appropriately. In order to take all relevant practical dimensions into account, individual assignments have to answer four questions:

- **What** needs to be done exactly?
- **Who** is responsible for which task?
- **Why** does it need to be done?
- **When** does it have to be finished?

It is an essential part of effective team management that everybody, in principle, can indicate at every moment what all other team members are doing and how this fits within their own work. Fill out the following form:

Table G.6 A combined SMART/4W method

	Specific	Measurable	Achievable	Realistic	Time-framed
What					
Who					
Why					
When					

[⊕➔www.skillsheets.com for a more detailed analysis table]

In particular time management provides an important 'bottleneck' for most projects. Agreements about timing should be made *beforehand*:
- ☐ the time for feedback;
- ☐ time for layout process;
- ☐ study time;
- ☐ social time;
- ☐ how many times do we meet?;
- ☐ how quickly do we reach one another, and how do we establish how many times to meet?;
- ☐ how many agreements do we make at a time?;
- ☐ do we call one another, or do we use email to contact one another?;
- ☐ do we meet at the university or somewhere else?

Work backwards (start with the end date), in order to dedicate enough time to each phase of the project. A feasibility study (➔A6) can help you also as a group.

3 Evaluation: coping with unhealthy group dynamics and free-riders

To finalise your group contract, you have to think how you organise feedback effectively (➔G9) and how you would like to deal with 'unhealthy' group dynamics and conflicts (➔G10). Use these Skill Sheets as an input to the deliberations of your group. The issue of free-riders, however, is not just something to discuss. It should be part and parcel of the group contract. See the box for the most logical way to deal with the free-rider issue. Make sure that your decision on your approach to free-riding is taken *unanimously* (➔G5).

Preventing Free-riding

Free-riders are people who use the efforts of a group without making sufficient contributions themselves. Free-riding describes the act of trying to get the maximum result with the minimum of effort. Occasionally, everyone is a free-rider in a group. The reasons for this can vary. In general, however, free-riding – certainly when it involves always the same persons – jeopardises the functioning of the whole group. Therefore, it should be taken very seriously. The reasons for free-riding behaviour change along the stages of the team development process (➔G10), which makes it hard to deal with free-riding only at the moment it occurs.

Free-riders can only be dealt with if you have made it part of the group contract and/or have discussed *beforehand* what everyone in the group is expected to do. Only then, can the free-rider problem (1) be identified in time (which is very difficult even for the person who is the free-rider), and (2) addressed. **Basic rule**: A person who has been unable to carry out his/her responsibilities should *indicate this immediately* to the group. This person should come up with a proposal for compensating the deficiencies in his/her group contribution. It is not the responsibility of the group to do this, it is the responsibility of the (dysfunctional) individual member to come up with compensation. If the person does not do this, he/she can be considered to be a real free-rider: someone who *intentionally* tries to profit from the efforts of others. Talk about this problem openly with the person involved. Do this as soon as the problem arises. Real free-riders should be excluded from a group, but only when you have given the person a fair chance to offer compensatory action.

4 Individual checks

When the group has finished the above exercise, every team member should be able to answer the following six questions:

o What can I expect from the group? What are our shared expectations and what is the end-product?

o What happens when participants have not prepared for a meeting?

o Who will, in principle, take up which position in the group: will there be a chair, who will take the minutes, should there be a group secretary?

o How will we deal with free-riders?

o How to arrange effective feedback (for instance when to ask an external tutor for advice)?

G8   Effective Meetings

The effectiveness of meetings is strongly influenced by four characteristics: (1) whether the agenda is simple and covers the most important topics, (2) whether the chair is able to manage the 'hidden' agendas of the group members alongside to the formal agenda, (3) the extent to which minutes-taking functions as a support of the decision-making process and (4) the formal and informal communication patterns that develop in the group. The effectiveness of meetings drops considerably if one of these functions is not performed appropriately, or its importance is insufficiently understood.

A checklist: meetings can be effective when...
- the aim of the meeting is made clear beforehand;
- everybody respects the aims of the meeting;
- participants prepare for the meeting;
- the meeting runs according to the agenda and the intended time limit;
- only appropriate and useful contributions are delivered;
- the participation is limited to persons who are directly involved with the topics under consideration;
- all relevant information is available;
- relevant decisions are made and clear action is initiated;
- clear responsibilities and time frames for implementation are designated;
- formal and informal communication patterns are understood and managed adequately.

1 The agenda
Three conditions should be taken care of for every meeting:
a a fixed *agenda* (the box below contains the agenda for an average meeting);
b a *time frame*;
c *clear objectives for the meeting* (preferably put this in writing, but otherwise make these points clear verbally at the beginning of the meeting).

Components of an ordinary agenda
- opening;
- discussion of the minutes (of last meeting);
- announcements and treatment of incoming and outgoing mail;
- subjects to be dealt with (use annexes with written information if possible);
- other subjects to be discussed, suggested during the meeting;
- other business: questions remaining (chair asks each individual participant);
- close the meeting.

2 Being an effective chair

The chair *function* contains several tasks that were already explained in Skill Sheet G4. The chair*person* has a number of additional tasks to take into account during the meeting. One of the most important additional tasks is to try to reveal the 'hidden agendas' of each group member in order to make the 'setting' of the meeting clear:

- Do the participants have *other obligations*? Which could make it impossible for a participant to carry out task(s). Such a group member will burden the next meeting with 'excuses' and thus stall further decision-making. If you think group members will not be able to do what they have promised, it is useful to mention this immediately during the debate and discuss solutions.
- Make sure that each participant *feels free* to make suggestions. It is common practice in group discussions that the person who makes the suggestion is also responsible for the further execution of decisions taken. The result of this practice is that people (who may have many other obligations, for example) adopt a low-key participation profile, which then can hamper the effectiveness of the meeting considerably. Also make it clear during the first meeting who knows who in the group, and who already co-operates with other group members. Sometimes, you must actively debug 'old boys' networks' to overcome the negative group dynamism developing from *groups within a group*.

Checklist: Tasks of the chairperson (during the) meetings

- **Before**
  - sets the agenda;
  - anticipates the way each theme should be discussed: sequence, time frame, anticipating possible opposition.

- **During**
  - opens the meeting formally;
  - checks who is present and who is not (and what reasons were given for not attending);
  - goes through each point of the agenda;
  - gives a short introduction to each point;
  - makes sure that the discussion goes according to plan and reaches conclusions through summaries from time to time, and by involving participants who are not making themselves clear, or are not actively participating; deals with participants who use presentation tricks;
  - participates as little as possible in the actual discussion;
  - ensures that the amount of time scheduled for each part is not exceeded;
  - makes sure that people are designated operational responsibilities, which are subsequently listed in the minutes;
  - should be aware of 'groupthink' (⊕G10), reductive listening and other forms of negative group dynamism;
  - closes the meeting formally by summarising what has been achieved during the meeting;
  - ensures that everyone is in agreement about the next meeting date;
  - temporarily hands the chairperson's hammer over to another member of the group when his/her own position is up for discussion.

■ After
- makes certain that the minutes are correct (secretary first gives minutes to the chair);
- sees to it that the participants receive a copy of the minutes;
- controls the execution of the agreed tasks.

3 Taking appropriate minutes

Minutes should reflect the *decision-making process*. They are usually used to remind people of the most important decisions that were made, and not to record 'who said what'. With the 'who said what' type of minutes it is possible that people speak simply to be included in the minutes in order to prove later that they were present and active at a meeting. The nature of the minutes can affect the actual direction of the session.

Additionally, in meetings the phenomenon of *'non-decisions'* is as important as decision-making. Some participants have an interest in keeping decisions vague. The person who takes the minutes is often the only one (besides the chairperson) who feels responsible for the clarity of the decision-making process. For these reasons making functional minutes can be considered more of a social skill than a mere writing skill. The remainder of this Skill Sheet lists the 4W principles that should be applied by the person taking the minutes.

Rule 1: Make sure that you summarise all of the (non)decisions made. (What)

Often decisions are not identified as such. Make sure that the chairperson (➔F1) summarises the most important decisions. The minute-taker can summarise a decision during the meeting and thereby help the chairperson, or ask the chairperson to make a clear summary to ensure that the minutes are as complete as possible. If the minutes already include clearly identifiable decisions, this should function as a checklist for the rest of the minutes. If no decisions were made regarding particular issues, the minute-taker should mention this at the appropriate time.

Rule 2: Name of the person who is responsible for the execution of each decision. (Who)

Group processes are often a battle of different interests. In this bargaining game it is often in the interest of participants in a meeting not to have identified who is to be responsible for the execution of a specific decision. In practice, the decision can still become a 'non-decision'. A good chairperson will always name the people who are responsible. If this (for whatever reason) is not done, the minute-taker should request that it be done during the meeting. If no one has been selected the minute-taker should make a note of this fact, and immediately include this prob-

lem as a point for discussion during the next meeting. In minutes that are primarily aimed at covering decisions it is usual to include the names of the people
responsible in the following way: ACTION: JOHN, SUZY.

> **Rule 3**: Always include the time frame for the execution of each decision.
> (When)

Many people prefer not to have a plan, because it makes their function clear and
it is more difficult to 'get away' with free-rider behaviour (➔G10). If no one else
requests specific time limits, it is the responsibility of the minute-taker to ask the
chairperson to allot a time frame to the decision. If this is not done, the point
should be included in the decision making list for the next meeting.

> **Rule 4**: Finish the minutes as soon as possible, and send them to the partici-
> pants immediately so that they are confronted with their responsibilities.
> (Where)

Often, people quickly forget what they promised to do. This danger looms particularly large with difficult assignments. If the minutes are only sent a few days in
advance of the next meeting, people who are inclined to 'forget' their responsibilities will not have enough time to carry out their tasks. In the next meeting the
decision-making process will inevitably be hampered by these people searching for
excuses. Also include where the next meeting will take place, and where the minutes will be sent to.

> **Rule 5**: Minutes can be kept short.

Unless the minutes need to cover the various statements made by individual participants, they can be limited to around two pages with a clear layout. Short minutes should include the following:
- **A heading**: the date of the meeting, the length of the meeting, who was present,
  and who was unable to attend (with notice). If deemed necessary, you can also
  include the persons who did not attend without giving notice.
- **The documents** discussed and numbered, so that they are easy to file.
- **The decisions** made, the time frame and the persons responsible. List these decisions in a separate box or use underlining, so that the participants can see
  clearly what decisions were made.
- If possible, also include the agenda for the next meeting and the **date and meeting place**. Do this also in a separate box.

4 Understanding group dynamism: a communication topology

Besides formal positions and functional roles in a group, the actual group dynamics also depends on the informal networks that exist. Unclear ways of communicating are one of the main causes of conflicts within teams. Analysing how the interaction in a group normally develops is not that difficult. Just draw the topology of the table you are sitting at, and identify the intensity of the oral interaction between the members. After a while you can see that specific clusters appear. This is the communication topology of the group. In general it will reveal quite accurately who is in charge in the group (either formally or informally). Figure G.8 shows a simplified version of four rather common topologies:

- **Web or circle**: everyone communicates with each other on an equal and regular basis. In this case the chair and minute-taking functions, are just functions and not positions (of power)
- **Star** topology: there is one person (leader) in the group who is always addressed by everyone else. Normally this is the chair. In case of a revolving chair, the leadership can also change.
- **Hierarchical** topology: there is an informal order of merit within the group of specific groups that primarily talk to each other, and via a leader with the rest of the group. The informal leader (as is illustrated by the figure) is the factual chair.
- **Confrontation/debate** topology: two leaders talk to each other and within their own 'camp'. Camp members of one camp do not talk to the other's camp members. This topology is common in a negotiation or debate setting (hence the table topology), but can also develop in non-functioning groups even when the table setting suggests differently.

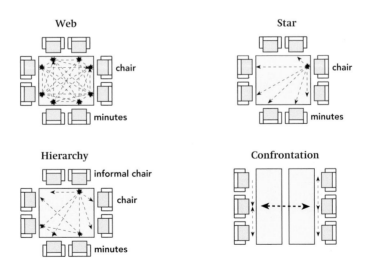

Figure G.8 Communication/Power topologies in groups

Ask yourself whether these communication patterns can lead to an acceptable and *sustainable* group structure. In particular, ask whether it is acceptable that some group members are 'followers' and others are 'leaders'. Who talks more often, and is that acceptable (➔G10)? If there is a more hierarchical topology in your group meetings – which implies that some people are doing most of the talking anyway – the chances are that free-riders will go unnoticed for a long period of time. If this continues, it becomes increasingly difficult to deal with the problem of free-riders effectively. A practice of (informal) condoning the free-rider could develop, which gives the free-rider the idea that the group accepts the behaviour. In case you do not like the structure and if it is permanent, first discuss the present situation in order to find a joint diagnosis, then actively search for organisational alternatives. For example, the group could agree to change positions regularly: different chairperson, different secretaries, and you can even decide to change the seating plan on a regular basis, in order to avoid informal hierarchies or vicious divisions of labour (➔G2).

Getting and giving feedback is one of the crucial activities that add value to working in groups. However, giving feedback is often one of the least developed skills. One of the principles of effective self-management is to generate and to receive sufficient feedback (➜B13). This requires a mental attitude as much as the awareness of its importance. In group processes, the organisation of feedback is much simpler, since teams are supposed to work together and comment on each other's work. Feedback therefore is a precondition for group work, but if badly executed it can also be extremely destructive. Effectively managing feedback is a *task for the giver and for the receiver*. Effective feedback depends on three conditions:

☐ measurable goals in close consultation with the group or the receiver of the feedback;

☐ positive feedback on the achievements of the person or group, and

☐ an appropriate reward to the performance.

In organisational theory and in management literature, these principles also lie at the heart of so called *performance management*. Feedback amongst group members or colleagues is also known as 'intercollegiate consultation' (De Haan, 2001), 'tutoring', 'peer-teaching' (Megginson, 1988) or 'coaching' (Cook, 2004). Effective teams consist of people that are willing and prepared to act as feedback giver on a regular basis. This has positive impact on the receiver of feedback, but often even more on the feedback giver. Consequently, there are many good reasons for becoming a coach, tutor or peer-teacher yourself. The box lists these reasons and lists a number of characteristics that are required to be(come) a good coach. Check what your present position is on these characteristics. The box also lists eight basic rules for effective feedback that will be further elaborated in this Skill Sheet. Effective feedback is positive feedback.

Why become a coach/tutor/peer-teacher?

■ it *deepens your understanding* of the literature previously studied or past experiences you have had, and which you now have to explain to others;

■ the experience helps you to manage a process of *mutual support in self-managed and active learning* (➜B series) and listening (➜D series);

■ requires you to read and use the literature more *actively* (➜C series). You read a book differently and more intensely when you ask yourself 'how can I explain this' than when you read it in order to be able to reproduce it for an exam;

■ research concerning the results of peer-teaching has shown that tutors themselves often learn more than the students that they support;

■ by engaging in tutoring and coaching you will carry a bigger *responsibility* in the management of the study or the organisation. This is bound to increase your *motivation*;

■ it gives you insight into the preconditions under which you can actually act effectively in a more collaborative style. Managers like to see themselves as 'coach' or 'mentor', whereas employees still tend to think of the manager as an 'instructor' and much less as a peer or a mentor (Megginson, 1988: 40).

Basic rules for effective feedback

1 Describe what you see first, and only then what you think
2 Do not make any remarks on the (perceived) feelings or thoughts of others
3 Use 'I' instead of 'we'
4 Say what you like, not only what you do not like
5 Assume a positive listening attitude
6 Do not ask 'why' questions, but search for solutions
7 Focus on the present and the future
8 Make clear appointments

Source: RSM Erasmus University, tutor programme

Personal coaching characteristics

	always	⇔	never
1 positive				
2 enthusiastic				
3 helpful				
4 trusting				
5 focused				
6 purposeful				
7 perceptive				
8 respectful				
9 patient				
10 clear				
11 assertive				

Source: Cook, 2004:26

1 Describe what you see first, and only then what you think

When providing feedback, others need to know on what observation(s) you base your thoughts. So, first describe the behaviour or facts that you have observed. By giving the other the opportunity to correct any mistakes in your observations, you will also create a common basis for further conversation. Only after all the relevant facts have been established is it appropriate to discuss your own conclusions, thoughts and/or feelings. Even in case your feedback only contains one line, first start with the observation and then your conclusion. For instance: 'I noticed that you did not attend the meetings Monday and Wednesday. I think it has a negative effect on the quality of our work'. The person whom the message is directed to, will immediately understand how the other person arrived at this standpoint. The first part is verifiable and is not open to debate. The only question that remains is whether the dissatisfaction concerning the absence of the receiver of the feedback can be removed, either by being present more often or by determining that being absent is not a substantial impediment to the quality of the work.

> **Positive feedback is descriptive, factual, specific and concrete.**
> **Tip:** ask the receiver of your feedback to summarize what you have said, to check whether the feedback has been concrete enough.

2 Do not make any remarks on the (perceived) feelings or thoughts of others

As feedback giver it is impossible to determine how someone else feels or thinks. Every statement in which you claim to know otherwise (or in which you state what the other should feel or think) will be followed by either an angry or a defensive response. The only way to find out what someone else thinks or feels, is by asking it, not making remarks about it. An equal waste of time for the coach or feedback giver is to tell someone 'what' he or she 'is'. The comment 'you are sloppy', for instance, is bound to elicit an angry or defensive response. Why? Because it is not very likely that the person is sloppy or careless in every respect. So the observation is probably flawed anyway. Secondly, 'sloppiness' relates to a very personal character trait, which is difficult to change quickly. As an alternative you could say that, by your standards, the work that someone has turned in is 'untidy', which directs the conversation to dimensions that can be directly adjusted relatively easily.

> **Positive feedback deals with actual behaviour (is objective and easier for the receiver to 'accept')**

3 Use 'I' instead of 'we', avoid should/must

Always acknowledge the other as a person with an own opinion and experiences. The feedback giver is only one member of the team; the coach is only an adviser. Respect for others is a basic condition for conducting a good feedback interview. Employing the 'I' form and avoiding 'must' or 'should' forms help in establishing a constructive conversation instead of a judgemental statement. It is less intimidating and therefore easier to accept. The use of the 'I' form dovetails perfectly with rule #2. In using 'must/should' statements, the feedback giver in fact tries to impose norms and values on the other, that might not be shared and therefore create further irritation. With the word 'we' the feedback giver in fact suggests that the opinion of the other is irrelevant. Moreover, speaking on behalf of others is risky, because they might not share this opinion. The effectiveness of the feedback immediately decreases.

Table G.9 Phrasing feedback

Type	Do's	Don'ts
Use the 'I' form	*'I would like you to listen first to what member B has to say.'*	*'You should first listen to what member B has to say.'*
Avoid 'must/should' form	*'I would like you to listen first to what member B has to say.'*	*'You must first listen to what member B has to say.'*
Avoid 'we' form	*'I would like you to listen first to what member B has to say.'*	*'We think you should listen to what member B has to say.'*

> **Positive feedback is clear about the interests of the critic**

4 Say what you like, not only what you do not like

The bargaining society favours negative over positive news (➔The Challenge, Part I) and therefore negative feedback is habitually favoured over positive feedback.

This does not only lead to calculating behaviour with the recipient of the feedback, but is also not very efficient as a feedback technique. The dominance of so-called 'corrective feedback' prevents companies, organisations and teams from reaping the best from their members (Morgen Roberts et al, 2005).

So, in a feedback session, in principle always start with the positive points of the other. It creates a more positive atmosphere in which the other is also more willing to listen to what you (further) have to say. You can also start by giving a compliment, but this has to be honest, otherwise you lose credibility with the feedback taker or with the other team members, who might notice that you are not honest. The feedback giver should be prepared to proceed by explaining 'why something is good'. This could provide a stepping stone for tackling consecutive less positive – or even plainly negative – aspects. This technique makes clear that on the basis of the same criteria the other has already done things right, so it is probably feasible to improve on the less successful areas as well.

> Do not worry if people fail to recognise your merits; worry that you may not recognise theirs—Confucius

5 Assume a positive listening attitude

An active listening posture is one of the most important preconditions for constructive listening during the presentations of others (➔D1). This requires first a positive mental attitude and the willingness to actively create an atmosphere of trust. Listen attentively and take notes. Then take some time to 'digest' the things you have heard. It is often important to take small breaks. It prevents impulsive reactions and makes it clear that you take the other person seriously. In a meeting, this 'break' can be relatively short – i.e. 30 seconds to a minute. A good way to simulate this is by asking people to fill out an observations form or checklist first before they start giving feedback. It provides the functional break needed for positive feedback. Then start by summarising the most important points and asking clarification questions. For the receiver of the feedback: do not feel under attack, do not defend yourself, explain your emotions (if they pop up), admit the other is right (if you feel so) (➔B13). A positive listening attitude should come from both sides.

> Positive feedback is 'open', it allows other members of the group to give their commentary on your observations

6. Do not ask 'why' questions, but search for solutions

Normally, the 'why' question constitutes the core of critical research (➔A1) and management (➔G1) practice. But there are three reasons for avoiding 'why' questions in direct coaching situations. The first is that 'why' questions often open old wounds, and lead to defensive or evasive answers. In response to a question such as 'why have you been absent three times?', one is apt to get a lengthy monologue about birthdays of sisters, football training, preparations for mid-term exams or intensive student parties. The result will be a lengthy rationalization that is basically not important for the feedback interview.

Secondly, a 'why' question will almost always come across as suggestive. 'Why didn't you put this in your document?' sounds like an accusation. 'Why did you use this font?' sounds like a direct rejection.

The third reason is that answers to 'why' questions are seldom useful. In the first example, it is not important why a team member has been absent three times. The aim of the feedback should be to find a solution by henceforth preventing the frequent absence. In the second example, you already know that there is something you would like to have in the document. You can simply mention that, if you wish. The other person then can let you know whether they agree. In the third example it is not important what kinds of considerations there were concerning the font used. The point is to agree on the fonts to be used from then on.

So, answers to 'why' questions are generally easy to avoid and induce irritation. The solution to these communicative problems lie in a reformulation of the question (not in evading the point): if the first question is reformulated as 'you have been absent three times and I would like to reach an understanding with you to prevent this in future', the reply will focus immediately on the understanding to be reached.

> **Positive feedback is respectful and takes the interests of the receiver of the feedback into account**

7 Focus on the present and the future

Feedback by tutors and coaches provides an assessment of a work process in which one looks for good solutions that could simplify and increase the effectiveness of the process in the future. Try to focus the interview on points of improvement and avoid unnecessary debate about the past. Of course, in the past, there were 'learning moments' for you and for the team. When referring to these moments, it is vital not to start a discussion on the correct interpretation of what 'exactly has happened'. It is better to silently learn from what you did, and in the feedback session focus on what you see and how to avoid mistakes in future. In talking about the future, the feedback giver should be explicit about limits. The following statements could be made that indicate future limits that are easy to accept by the team members: 'I will not work after midnight', 'I want to provide feedback on the documents of the other team members, but I don't want to correct any errors in language', 'if I write this chapter, I want to use this type of layout'.

Positive feedback deals with behaviour that can be changed; is aimed at good timing and given directly after the behaviour appears

8 Make clear appointments

The feedback moment should always end in clear appointments in which the reached consensus on what needs to be done, or the point of attention to focus on in the future, are summarised. Apply in particular rules #6 and #7. Constructive communication can only remain constructive if it leads to clear appointments, otherwise it quickly can turn into uncommitted, open-ended and therefore opportunistic behaviour. Good appointments as part of constructive feedback apply the 4W model (➲G7) and are based on the 'consensus' principle of decision-making (➲G5). Good appointments prevent conflicts (➲G11).

'Unhealthy' group dynamics occur in any group, but particularly in closed groups (➔G2) working on one project. Basically unhealthy group dynamics is caused by a lack of communication, or by non-constructive communication between the group members. In case you have applied the rules and tips contained in the preceding Skill Sheets, the chance that your group ends up in disarray, decreases considerably. In that case you should be able to deal with the following sources of potential conflict:

☐ Not listening to each other: can be due to a lack of constructive listening skills (➔D series), but is in group practice often strongly related to bad decision-making procedures (➔G5), including lack of brainstorming (➔G3) and lacking of feedback and coaching skills (➔G9).

☐ An unbalanced work distribution: is often caused by a lack of assertiveness of individual group members (➔B2), which in groups can cause an inappropriate assignment of roles and tasks (➔G4), in particular at the start of projects (participants not able to say 'no')

☐ Participants not keeping their promises: is very often due to bad individual time management skills (➔B8), but in group practice often is caused by an unsophisticated group contract (➔G7).

Two remaining dimensions of unhealthy group dynamics, however, remain that pop up during the 'performing' stage of group work, and that first need to be identified and understood as such before adequate action can be undertaken: (1) groupthink and (2) the changing causes of free-rider behaviour.

1 Groupthink: taking yourself too seriously

In small and closed groups there is a greater risk of unhealthy and particularly dysfunctional ways of group dynamism than when you work on your own. This happens firstly when group members constantly try to *outdo* each other. This is easy for individual group members to identify and belongs to the category of handling conflicts. A second category of unhealthy group dynamics is more difficult to recognise when group members strive too hard to *conform* to (perceived) group rules. Groups – and therefore individual group members as well – can become victims of the syndrome of 'groupthink', as Janies (1972) called it. Groupthink is a form of *collective autism*, which almost always leads to poor decision-making.

It is most important for individual group members to identify the causes of groupthink. It generally occurs when groups are too 'closed' to outside opinions, too self-confident, and aimed at avoiding controversy, resistant to working in a more rational manner, aiming too much at control and too little at learning. These group properties are similar to the negative individual properties in particular as regards self-management (➔B series) and feedback giving and receiving (➔G9). The solution to unhealthy groupthink therefore also builds on the insights gained in these other areas. In particular the positive properties (virtues) of powerful writing

(→E series) and creativity in research (→A4) could 'come to the rescue' of groups caught up in paralysing groupthink.

Except from abovementioned specific problems and solutions, a number of general resources are available for tackling problems:

□ *Self-criticism* – Next to creating an atmosphere in which individuals can come up with constructive criticism, use *structured controversy* in groups, by actively stimulating subgroups that can come up with alternatives. In general: create an atmosphere in which open brainstorming is acceptable (cf. Janis and Mann, 1977; →G3, G5).

□ *Empathy and 'reflexivity'* – Be aware of the mechanisms that work in a group; each group member should be interested in understanding and managing group processes – be it the chair or the minute taking functions (G4).

□ *Professionalism* (→B1) – Each group member should try to learn from past experience and design roles in which he/she performs best; but to stimulate the right group dynamism these roles should change from time to time (→G7).

2 The changing causes of free-rider behaviour

Free-riders are people who use the efforts of a group without making sufficient contributions themselves. Free-riding is a universal problem and cause of extremely unhealthy group dynamics. Free-riding can largely be prevented by discussing the problem beforehand and formulating a smart group contract (→G7). However, this formula only covers what individual group members should do once they have become free-riders themselves. The causes of free-riding behaviour, however, are not only individual but can also be related to the various stages of the Team Life Cycle (→G1). A team distinguishes itself from a group, because its members are dedicated to a goal – a purpose. Without a purpose (or when the purpose is achieved) individuals will pursue their own interests – i.e. develop free-riding behaviour – and handicap or even destroy the team. So there exists a trade-off in how the needs of the (1) task, (2) the team and (3) the individual are balanced. This trade-off can be pictured as a Ven diagram (Adair, in Whetten et al., 2004: 479ff). Figure G.10 shows how these various dimensions relate to each other in each stage of the Team Life Cycle. Each stage poses a functional challenge for the team members, which – if not dealt with properly – also creates different types of free-rider behaviour:

□ the forming group creates its own free-riders in case team members do not 'internalise' the task;

□ the developing team (storming) creates free-riders for instance in case one team member is too dominant, or the manager of the team adopts an authoritative leadership style; team members will not feel very committed to the task and attaining the goals from the start;

□ the consolidating team (norming) creates free-riders in later stages in case the norms decided by the team were not really accepted by some members, who will feel less happy in the assigned roles;

□ the mature team (performing) can suffer from free-riding in case the personalities match too much or in case the diverging (external) interests and obligations of the group are not managed very well; individuals can become less committed to the team in case tasks shifts without consultation;

□ the adjourning team creates free-riding in case team members take the sole responsibility to 'finish' the project. The hidden message can be that they don't trust other members for this task, which gives the latter sufficient reason to back off and let the others do the job.

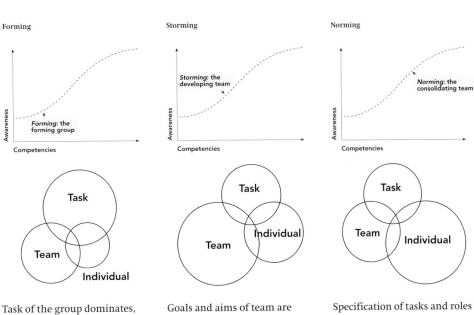

Task of the group dominates, decided who will join the team and under what conditions. Formation oriented.	Goals and aims of team are elaborated, brainstorming over approach and preconditions for collaboration. Input oriented.	Specification of tasks and roles per team member, formulation of group contract (either formal or informal). Process oriented.
Free-riding if:	**Free-riding if:**	**Free-riding if:**
□ task is externally imposed (no real motivation); □ team is already established and individual does not have to make an aware choice to enter the team.	□ task remains unclear; □ it remains unclear; who is part of the team; □ team leader adopts an authoritarian leadership style.	□ personal competition in team continuous; □ chosen roles do not match personal preferences; □ individuals did not accept goals.

Figure G.10 Stages of free-riding in teams

Performing

Adjourning

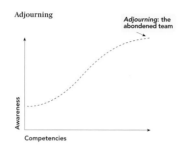

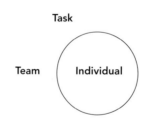

Execution of task; intensive feedback, more formal interaction between team members; output oriented.

Free-riding if:

☐ tasks shift without consultation;

☐ team process is inadequately managed;

☐ 'fit of personalities' is too good; no diversity or complementarity;

☐ team remains static.

Evaluation of team process; what can be improved next time; will we cooperate again? Learning oriented.

Free-riding if:

☐ one member takes the responsibility for finishing the project;

☐ participants do not want to enter a new cycle (but aim at unaware competencies).

G11 Dealing with Conflicts

Negotiations can normally be handled in a structured and orderly way provided you apply the rules of effective decision-making (⊕G5), negotiating (⊕G6) and organising meetings (⊕G8). But in some cases conflicts arise in groups. For example when parties have fundamentally clashing interests, when emotions are involved, which lead to misunderstandings between the members, if particular group members do not do what they promised, and when the degree of dependency on group members is either too high or unevenly distributed. Often conflicts start as a feeling of slight unease with some group members. If nothing is done about this problem, a small problem could grow into a real conflict. This Skill Sheet looks at the bargaining *tactics* that can be adopted by a negotiator. A general checklist for 'clever' negotiators has been included in the box below. But – depending on the particular bargaining dynamism developing in the conflict – two additional approaches can be used.

A clever negotiator:

- realises that it is more important to 'get it right than to be right' (is not interested in who is really right or wrong);
- is actively working for a positive atmosphere;
- knows that other people, who are not present at the meeting, could be important for the discussion;
- adjourns occasionally, to facilitate 'behind the scenes' bargaining: long breaks and short discussion periods are often more effective than long discussion periods and short breaks;
- knows that conflict between the bargaining partners is not necessarily bad. Conflicts (1) force parties to define the problem more clearly, (2) make the parties more aware of each other and each other's emotions (you can no longer ignore the other party), (3) conflicts can lead to new rules and norms which can be more transparent than the old rules which were clearly insufficient (⊕G6);
- is aware of the importance of the own posture and that of the participants (⊕G9);
- is a good listener and asks good/positive questions;
- actively searches for joint solutions to a problem and does not see that as giving in to one particular party;
- analyses the negotiation space of each participant and searches for the overlapping areas (⊕F9);
- takes time and creates time for the participants; is not impressed by the manipulation of time by some of the participants involved;
- only focuses on the relevant arguments, all other arguments could detract (and therefore be used as an excuse for not tackling it) from the main problem;
- always shows respect for each participant in the negotiations.

1 Approach I: adopt different and changing bargaining styles during conflicts

When entering into negotiations, try to analyse the position of the other participants and your own position on the following issues (based on: Mastenbroek, 1990):

	I	II	III
1 starting position on contents	indulgent, open to concessions	persistent, but flexible when confronted with good arguments	☞ clear, self-confident
2 dealing with power in the group	evasion, no discussion	☞ searching for a balance	aggressive, trying to force the other party into submission
3 mental attitude	personally involved, wanting to be liked, but therefore also unpredictable; making jokes; dependent attitude	☞ trustworthy, solid attitude, striving for informal relations, but in a more inter-dependent manner	often irritated, distant, sarcastic, striving for formal relations, based on the desire to remain as independent as pos-sible
4 procedural flexibility	☞ flexible and impro-vising, searching for alternatives	patient, open to alter-natives, but takes time	impatient, distant and awaiting

Effective negotiators *combine* a number of the characteristics mentioned above, indicated by the shaded areas: (1) they should be clear about their self-interest and can even be stubborn, as long as they (2) actively try to handle power problems in the group, show (3) collaborative mental characteristics and have considerable (4) procedural flexibility. Ineffective or naive negotiators only adopt the characteristics of column I, II *or* III. This may look consistent, but is not very effective.

2 Approach II: make a distinction between mediating and negotiating

If a conflict arises in a group, the person asked to tackle this problem can basically adopt two general positions: as mediator or as negotiator. The mediator is less involved in the group than the negotiator, but the effectiveness of each position can be equally high.

- **Mediating:**
  - let one party first tell the whole story; creating a receptive environment for this often 'solves' part of the problem;
  - show understanding;
  - ask for clarification on points that you do not understand;
  - make notes (also shows that you take the party more seriously);
  - do not enter into a discussion with the opposing party;
  - summarise the complaints, and ask if you have understood everything correctly;
  - find a proposition to solve problems once you have heard the arguments from everyone involved in the conflict;
  - do this in front of everybody; preferably in a meeting in which all parties have agreed to (1) accept the proposition, or (2) find solutions on the basis of the propositions within a specific time frame;

- come to clear and controllable appointments;
- check whether the appointments are implemented.

Tip from an experienced negotiator (CEO of a large company): **Learn how to read upside down!**

- **Negotiating:**
  - has almost the same properties as mediating, but now you are part of the bargaining process;
  - appoint a separate chairperson (other than yourself) and someone who takes notes;
  - try to specify and analyse the nature of the conflict;
  - try to asses the relative strength of each participant (including the relative dependencies of each group member on the others; ⊕G2). Conflicts often continue because the relative positions of the parties are not clear. Each group member who is capable of analysing the group dynamism should make this contribution, but individual group members may have opportunistic reasons for not doing so. In that case a mediator or a designated leader should create this insight;
  - exchange ideas on the nature of the conflict in a setting that is as 'open' as possible;
  - only once you have come to an understanding about this, can you try to work on the solutions;
  - list solutions in a setting that is as 'open' as possible;
  - only after listing many possible solutions, try to choose a specific solution;
  - come to clear agreements on the execution of the solution: time frame, responsibilities of individual group members.

Writing a paper or doing a research project with a group can create a number of additional and specific problems, particularly in the last phase, during which you finish your paper and/or prepare the presentation (➔A5). For example, all of the individually contributed input may not be of the same standard, information may be missing, or the group may not have agreed on the layout. Very often groups cease to function in this very phase, because one or two members take control. Time pressure is often the issue, but the (hidden) agenda could also be that one or two members simply want to take control of the end product. Whether this is justi-fied in terms of guaranteeing an excellent end product is not certain. But this move is bound to lead to frustration with all members of the group – including those who have taken control of the final paper. This Skill Sheet gives pointers for (1) effectively finishing a research project, and (2) what can be done afterwards to opti-mize the learning and decide whether or not you should engage in a new project with the same people.

1 Finishing the project

Finalising a research project is always a very hectic time. There is hardly any time left which require you to work under extreme pressure. Small irritations dur-ing the project stage can become major conflicts during the final stage. To prevent this from happening, take the following pointers into account:

- Make clear that everybody needs to be available or present during and immedi-ately after the final stages of a project. Do not allow people to plan a holiday. In case of a bigger project: do not allow that people take a holiday *immediately after* the deadline (how rewarding this might seem). It happens very often that you do not reach the deadline exactly, which requires that some people have to work on finishing the project even after the deadline. Make this decision not into a nega-tive one by making yourself unavailable. Another reason for not taking a holiday, is because you want to evaluate the project properly, which can best be done immediately after finishing the project.
- Make the specific tasks assigned to each group member as **concrete** as possible. In the last phase of a project your group should really develop a very functional division of labour, but without putting too much responsibility into the hands of individual group members.
- Designate a **final editor** or agree upon a procedure in which it is clear who is responsible for the final result.
- Give one group member the responsibility for the final **layout** of the report, but discuss the options before you make a choice as a group.
- Group projects often lead to sloppy and careless use of language. In particular differences in spelling are irritating to the reader. Make a **list of words** that require a specific spelling. Each member of the group contributes to this list on the basis of an own list, made during the writing process.
- Always take time to use a **spell checker**: use software programs and decide – in case you have not yet done this in advance which is to be preferred – whether

you want to use British or American spelling if you write in English (⊕➜www.skillsheets.com;➜E10). In addition to this, check the spelling yourself by proofreading carefully (➜E10-13). In principle, each group member should be responsible for this.

- Do a **final check**: did you explain concepts, have you given short introductions, have you written an executive summary (➜E3-5).
- Finally, never barter with **free-riders** (➜G7, G10) to **compensate** for their insufficient participation in the project during the final stages of the group process. Free-riders will not be able to bring the research to an end in an adequate manner, because they have not been actively involved. Do not allow the group to be dependent on weak group members.

2 Evaluating the project

One of the most undervalued aspects of group projects is the evaluation phase. Project groups tend to leave much of their irritation unspoken ('since I don't see the others again, why bother'), but thereby also leave much of the positive learning experience unmentioned as well. A few tips:

☐ Apply the feedback rules also to the whole project (➜G9). Plan a final group meeting *after* the presentation, and go through your learning experience.

☐ **Re-draft the group contract**: what would you do differently the next time. Check the principles of effective Team Management (➜G1): have they been well served in this project? Check in particular the following:
  - Tasks and roles effectively executed?
  - Sufficient complementarity and diversity in the roles (➜G2)?
  - Timing: appropriate time for each part of the research project?
  - Participation of each member: adequate (for the research project)?
  - Has the 'group' become a 'team' (➜G1)?
  - Has the end result become more than the sum of its parts?
  - What did you individually learn?
  - What did you (positively) learn from each other?
  - Where the rewards for the effort distributed evenly over the group members?

☐ Decide whether you would like to continue with this group:
  - New roles – to prevent you from 'getting stuck' in old division of labour and old skills.
  - New challenges – are there topics of mutual interest that we would like to address?
  - New rewards – should the rewards be distributed differently next time?
  - New members – what roles can add to the effectiveness of the group?

☐ **Ask for an exit meeting** with the teacher or tutor (1) in case you do not understand the grading of the project, (2) or in case of any major research project (like your PhD., M.A. or B.A. thesis for instance). Apply the rules of effectively receiving feedback (➜B13), but be prepared also to give the teacher/tutor feedback as well.

Of the following persons, the input for specific Skill Sheets is gratefully acknowledged.

A4	Cees Wiebes, Vitas Kersbergen
A7	L. Drijver
A8	Dolf Bruins, Fennie Lansbergen, Pieter van Gent
A13	Erik de Munck-Mortier
A15	Cynthia Piqué, Ans Kolk
B5	Ingwell Kuil
B6	Simone Schenk, Vitas Kersbergen, Cynthia Piqué
B8	J. Dirven, G. Nooy, M. Többen, Hand-out management skills, University of Groningen
B9	Marc Bleijenbergh, Kate Beeching and Paul Bonanno
B11	Simone Schenk
B12	Martijn van Loenen, Arjen Stroo
C5	Gerd Junne
C6	Anonymous author hand-out HES, Rotterdam
C7	J. Newton; Bureau Student Psychologists, Technical University Eindhoven
C8	Anonymous hand-out, HES Rotterdam
C9	Selma Rooseboom
C10	Bureau Student Psychologists, Technical University Eindhoven, Vitas Kersbergen
C11	Bjorge Verschure and Man Chau Hang
D1	Johan Guis
D3	Paul Aarts, Alex Fernández Jilberto, Cees Wiebes, Gerd Junne
D4	Simone Schenk, Cynthia Piqué, tutors of the Erasmus University and the University of Amsterdam
D7	Boudewijn Bertsch
E2	Jeroen van Wijk, Wouter Klinkhamer
E3	G. van Bruggen, A. Pruyn, H. Riezebos, A. Smidts
E4	Style sheets, Routledge
E6	Juup Essers, José Plug
E7	W. Michels, H.v.d. Westen
E10	Style Sheets of Berg Publishers, Routledge, Wiley and Pinter Publishers; and... many excellent dictionaries
E11	J. Newton, House Style Sheets Berg Publishers Inc
E12	Style Sheets of Berg Publishers, Pinter, Routledge, Wiley&Sons
E13	Paul Broholm, Ron Meyer
E14	Gerard van der Zaal
E16	Wil Sommeling
F3	Anonymous hand-out, HES Rotterdam
F4	FAKTOR Management advisors for Educators and Trainers
F5	Winfried Ruigrok, Tjeerd van der Meulen, Audio-visual Centre Erasmus University
F9-10	Geert van Deth, B-SM students
G-series	Suzanne Bax, Michel Lander & Stefan Leliveld
G6	H.Rijnsburger, W. Mastenbroek
G9	Simone Schenk, Cynthia Piqué, Linda van Klink, Mariska Keus, Geert van Deth

Abrahamson, E. and D. Freedman (2006) *A perfect Mess: The Hidden Benefits of Disorder*, Little, Brown & Company.

Aken, J.E. van (1994) 'De bedrijfskunde als ontwerpwetenschap. De regulatieve en reflectieve cyclus' (The regulative and reflective cycle), in: *Bedrijfskunde*, jrg. 66:16–24.

Alan, J. (1990) *How to write a winning C.V.: a simple step-by-step guide to creating a perfect C.V.*, London: Hutchinson Business Books.

Atkinson, Ph. (1988) *Achieving results from time management*, London: Pitman.

Barzun, J. (2002) *The House of Intellect*, Harper Collins, Perennial Classics.

Beck, U. (1992) *Risk Society, Towards a New Modernity*, London: Sage Publications.

Belbin, R. (1981) *Management Teams Why They Succeed or Fail*, Oxford: Butterworth.

Bell, T. (2001) Extensive Reading: Speed and Comprehension, In: *The Reading Matrix*, Vol 1, No 1, April 2001.

Berkeley Thomas, A. (2004*) Research Skills for Management Studies*, London: Routledge.

Berninger, V., A. Cartwright, C. Yates, M. Swanson and R. Abbott (1994) Developmental skills related to writing and reading acquisition in the intermediate grades: Shared and unique functional systems, *Reading and writing: an interdisciplinary journal*, Vol. 6 (2): 161–169.

Bigelow, J.D. (1991) *Managerial Skills: Explorations in Practical Knowledge*, London: Sage Publications.

Boekaerts, M. (1982) *Onderwijsleerprocessen organiseren, hoe doe je dat?* (How to organise educational learning processes?) Nijmegen: Dekker en Van der Vegt.

Bryson, B. (2004) *A Short History of Nearly Everything*, London: Black Swan.

Bunning, C. (1992) *Turning Experience into learning, Journal of European Industrial Training*, Vol.16 (6), 7–12.

Burka, J.B. and Yuen, L.M. (1983) *Procrastination: Why you do it, what to do about it*, Reading, Mass.: Addison-Wesley.

Burnard, P. (1992) *Interpersonal Skills Training: A sourcebook of Activities for Trainers*, London: Kogan Page Limited.

Burns, B.R. (2000) *Introduction to research methods*, 4th edition, London: Sage publications, 3–4.

Cameron, S. (2005) *The Business Students' Handbook: Learning skills for study and employment*, 3rd edition, Pearson Education LTD, Harlow.

Caproni, P. (2005) *Management Skills for Everyday Life. The Practical Coach*, New Jersey: Pearson/Prentice Hall, second edition.

Castells, M. (1996) *The Rise of the Network Society*, 3 vols., Oxford: Blackwell.

Cate, Th. Ten, Th. Tromp and M. Cornwall (1984) *De student als docent* (Students as teachers), Wolters Noordhof, Aula pocket 814.

Coady, J. (1979) A psycholinguistic model of the ESL reader. In: R. Mackay, B. Barkman and R.R. Jordon (Eds.), *Reading in a second language*, Rowley, MA: Newbury House.

Cook, M. (2004) *Effectief Coachen*, Den Haag: Academic Service.

De Bono, E. (1992) *Serious Creativity*, New York: HarperBusiness.

De Haan, E. (2001) *Leren met Collega's. Praktijkboek intercollegiale consultatie*. Assen: Koninklijke Van Gorcum.

Dewdney, A. (1993) *200% of Nothing*, New York: John Wiley & Sons.

Drucker, P. (2005) Managing Oneself, *Harvard Business Review,* Vol. 83 (1), January 2005.

Eco, U. (1977) *Hoe Schrijf Ik een Scriptie* (How to Write a Thesis), Amsterdam: Uitgeverij Bert Bakker (Dutch translation of Italian original 'come si fa una tesi di laurea'; English translation also available).

Van Eemeren, F. and R. Grootendorst (1992) *Argumentation, Communication, and Fallacies, A Pragma-Dialectical Perspective,* Hillsdale, New Jersey: Hillsdale.

Eisenhardt, K. (1989) Building Theories from Case Study Research, *Academy of Management Review,* Vol 14 (4), 532–550.

Eisler, R.M. and L.W. Frederiksen (1980) *Perfecting Social Skills: A Guide to Interpersonal Behavior Development,* New York: Plenum Press.

Elbow, P. (1981) *Writing with Power, Techniques for Mastering the Writing Process.* New York: Oxford University Press.

Ellis, A. and W.J. Knaus (1977) *Overcoming procrastination,* New York: New American Library.

Emory, C. and D. Cooper (1991) *Business Research Methods,* 4th edition, Homewood, Ill: R.D. Irwin.

Etzioni, A. (1998) *The New Golden Rule: Community and Morality in a Democratic Society,* New York: Basic Books.

Fendrich, J.C. (1979) *Präsentationen Vorbereiten – Ideen Durchsetzen* (Preparation of Presentations, Pressing Ideas), System-Management Hans O. Rasche + Partner GmbH. Heiligenhaus.

Fensterheim, H. and Baer, J. (1975) *Don't Say Yes when You Want to Say No: Making Life Right when It Feels All Wrong,* New York: McKay.

Fish, R. And Ury, W. (1981) *Getting to YES: Negotiating Agreement without Giving In,* Harmondsworth: Penguin.

Freeman, J.B. (1988) *Thinking Logically. Basic Concepts for Reasoning,* New York: McGraw-Hill.

Frey, B. (2003) Publishing as Prostitution. Choosing Between One's Own Ideas and Academic Failure, *Working Paper Series,* no.117, Zurich: Institute for Empirical Research in Economics.

Fry, E.B. (1963) *Teaching Faster Reading: a Manual.* Cambridge: Cambridge University Press.

Govier, T. (1988) *A Practical Study of argument,* 2nd edition, Belmont, CA: Wadsworth.

Griffiths, R.T. (2002) *History of the Internet, Internet for Historians (and Just about Everyone Else),* www.let.leidenuniv.nl/history/ivh/chap2.htm, visited 15 June 2006.

Guirdham, M. (1990) *Interpersonal skills at work,* London: Prentice Hall International.

Hallowell, E. (2005) Overloaded Circuits – Why Smart People Underperform, *Harvard Business Review,* Vol. 83 (1): 54–62.

Harris, R. (1997) 'The Art of Listening; Turn Listening into a Powerful Presence', *Training & Development,* 51 (7): 9.

Hayes, M.E. (1988) *Effective Meeting Skills,* Kogan Page, Better Management Skills.

Hedge, A. (2003) *Ergonomics Considerations of LCD versus CRT Displays,* Cornell University.

Hellriegel, D. and J.W. Slocum (1992) *Management, Reading,* 6th edition, Massachusetts: Addison Wesley Publishing Company.

Huff, D. (1954) *How to Lie with Statistics,* Penguin Books.

Janis, I.L. (1972) *Victims of Groupthink,* Boston: Houghton-Mifflin.

Janis, I.L. and L. Mann (1977) *Decision-Making,* New York: Free Press.

Junne, G (1986) *Kritisches Studium der Sozial Wissenschaften* (Critically Studying Social Sciences), Urban Taschenbücher, Kohlhammer, 2nd Revised Print.

Kaptein, M. (2005) *The 6 Principles of Managing with Integrity. A Practical Guide for Leaders,* London: Spiro Press.

Kaptein, M. and R. van Tulder (2003) Towards Effective Stakeholder Dialogue, *Business and Society Review,* 108 (2): 201–222.

Keefe, W. F. (1971) *Listen Management,* New York: McGraw-Hill.

Kersbergen, V. (2007) *On the Improvement of the Skills Development Programme at the RSM Erasmus University,* Rotterdam: paper.

Kolb, D. (1976) Management and the Learning Process, *California Management Review,* Spring, Vol. xviii (3): 21–31.

Kolb, D. (1984) *Experiential Learning: Experience as the Source of Learning and Development,* Englewood Cliffs, NJ: Prentice Hall.

Kolk, A. (1997) De Meerwaarde van Internet, *Tijdschrift voor Verantwoord Ondernemen,* no. 4: 64–65.

Lander, M. and S. Leliveld (2006) Linking Team Roles and Skills. Designing an Integrative Questionnaire, RSM Erasmus University, process report.

Leech, G.N. (1983) *Principles of Pragmatics,* London/New York: Longman.

Light, R.J. (1990) *The Harvard Assessment Seminars. Explorations with Students and Faculty about Teaching, Learning and Student Life. First Report,* Cambridge, Mass: Harvard University, Graduate School of Education and Kennedy School of Government.

Light, R.J. (1992) *The Harvard Assessment Seminars. Explorations with Students and Faculty about Teaching, Learning and Student Life. Second Report,* Cambridge, Mass: Harvard University, Graduate School of Education and Kennedy School of Government.

Louwerse, C. (1994) *Studeer Actief. Wegwijzer voor de Beginnende Student* (Studying Actively. Handbook for Starting Students), Nijkerk: uitgeverij Intro.

Mackenzie, D and P. McDonnell (1985) *How to Interview,* London: British Institute of Management.

Malhotra, N.K. and D.F. Birks (2003) *Marketing Research: an Applied Approach,* 2nd European Edition, Harlow: Prentice Hall/Financial Times.

Maloney, J.J. (ed.) (1983) *Online Searching Techniques and Management,* Chicago/LA.

Mastenbroek, W. (1990) *Onderhandelen,* Utrecht: Het Spectrum.

McNab, S.M. (1988) *On-the-Spot Revision of Science Papers Written in English as a Second Language,* European Science Editing, no.35, September.

Megginson, D. (1988) Instructor, Coach, Mentor: Three Ways of Helping for Managers, *Management Education and Development,* 19 (1), 33–46.

Morse, P. (1987) *Effectief Presenteren, Handleiding voor het Houden van Succesvolle Presentaties,* (Effectively Presenting, Manual for Successful Presentations) Utrecht: Het Spectrum.

Naisbitt, J. (1994) *Global Paradox,* New York: Avon Books.

Nederlands Huisartsen Genootschap (2005) *Slaapproblemen algemeen,* http://nhg.artsennet.nl/uri/?uri=AMGATE_6059_104_TICH_R187701209889722, visited 1 November 2006.

Newton, R. and K. Rudestam (1999) *Your Statistical Consultant,* London: Sage.

Olson, R.G. (1969) *Meaning and Argument: Elements of Logic,* New York: Harcourt, Brace and World.

Oomkes, F. (1992-1995) *Training als Beroep: Sociale en Interculturele Vaardigheid,* Meppel: Boom.

Parker, C. with B. Stone (2003) *Developing Management Skills for Leadership,* Harlow: FT Prentice Hall.

Patton, M.Q. (1980) *Qualitative Evaluation Methods*, London: Sage Publications.

Paulus, P.B. and H. Yang, (2000) 'Idea Generation in Groups: A Basis for Creativity in Organizations' *Organizational Behavior and Human Decision Processes*, 82 (1): 76–87.

Payne, E. and L. Whittaker (2006) *Developing Essential Study Skills*, 2nd edition, Harlow: FT Prentice Hall.

Peereboom, K.J., P.A.M Van Scheijndel, and P. Voskamp (2003) *Handboek Ergonomie 2003*, Alphen aan den Rijn: Kluwer, 93–104 and 375–402.

Pfeffer, J. (1992) *Managing with Power*, Harvard Business School Press, Boston: Massachusetts.

Phillips, E and D. Pugh (1987) *How to Get a PhD, Managing the Peaks and Troughs of Research*, Open University Press, Milton Keynes: Philadelphia.

Prein, H. (1988) *Trainingsboek Conflicthantering* (Training Book, Handling Conflicts), Alphen a/d Rijn: Samsom uitgeverij.

Raiffa, H. (1982) *The Art and Science of Negotiation*, Cambridge, Mass.: Harvard University Press.

Roberts, L., G. Spreitzer, J. Dutton, R. Quinn, E. Heaphy, and B. Barker (2005) How to Play to Your Strengths, *Harvard Business Review*, Vol. 83 (1): 74–80.

Schenk, S. (1986) *Leerstijlen in Termen van Informatieverwerkingsprocessen* (Learning Styles as Information Processing Activities) 1, Nijmegen: IOWO, 90.

Segers, J. (1999) *Methoden voor de Maatschappijwetenschappen*, Assen: Van Gorcum.

Sire, J.C. (1989) *Lecture Rapide: La Methode Flexivel* (Rapid Reading: the Flexivel Method), Paris: Editions D'Organisation.

Steehouder, M., Staak, J. van der, Jansen, C., Woudstra, E., Maat, K. (1991) *Leren Communiceren. Handboek voor Mondelinge en Schriftelijke Communicatie* (Manual for Verbal and Written Communication), 3de gewijzigde druk, Groningen: Wolters-Noordhoff.

Strien, P.J. van (1986) *Praktijk als Wetenschap. Methodologie van het Sociaal-Wetenschappelijk Handelen* (Praxis as Science. Methodology of Social Scientific Conduct). Assen/Maastricht: Van Gorcum.

Sudman, S. and N.M Bradburn (1982) Asking Questions; A Practical Guide to Questionnaire Design, *The Jossey-bass Series in Social and Behavioral Sciences*, California: Jossey-Bass Inc.

Tiggelaar, B. (2005) *Dromen, Durven, Doen. Het Managen van de Lastigste Persoon op Aarde: Jezelf*, Utrecht: Spectrum.

Troman, G. (2000) Teacher Stress in the Low-Trust Society, *British Journal of Sociology of Education*, Volume 21, Number 3, 1 September 2000, 331–353.

Van Tulder, R. (1996) *Skill Sheets*, The Hague: Elsevier.

Van Tulder, R. with A. Van der Zwart (2006) *International Business-Society Management: Linking Corporate Responsibility and Globalization*, London: Routledge.

Turley, J. (1989) *Speed Reading in Business*, Kogan/Page Better Management Skills.

Ury, W. (1991) *Getting Past No: Negotiating with Difficult People*, New York: Bantam Books.

Van den Brandhof, J.W. (1998) *Gebruik je Hersens*, Hoevelaken: Verba.

Vermunt, J.D.H.M. (1992) *Leerstijlen en Sturen van Leerprocessen in het Hoger Onderwijs: naar Procesgerichte Instructie in Zelfstandig Denken*, Amsterdam: Swets & Zeitlinger.

Verschuren, P. and H. Doorewaard (2000) *Het Ontwerpen van een Onderzoek*, 3rd Edition, Utrecht: Lemma.

Walton, D.N. (1989) *Informal Logic. A Handbook for Critical Argumentation*, Cambridge: Cambridge University Press.

Whetten, D., K. Cameron, and M. Woods (2004) *Developing Management Skills for Europe*, 2nd edition, Harlow: Pearson Education limited.

Yin, R.K., (2003) *Case Study Research: Applied Social Research Methods Series*, 3rd edition, Vol. 5: 1-11.

Zull, J.E. (2002) *The Art of Changing The Brain: Enriching Teaching by Exploring the Biology of Learning*. Sterling, VA: Stylus.

Index

abandoning
    meeting G7–8
    reading texts C7
abbreviations E13
    in interviews D6
    list E3
absorption capacity
    audiences D1, F7
    limit B7
academic writing E1
accreditation A8
acknowledgement E3
acronym E13
action research A2
active
    attitude B1
    listening D7
    reading A11, C10
advertisements A4
advice A2–3
agenda
    components B2, G11
aggressive B2, G11
aim
    group G7
    general research A1–2
    personal A3
alcohol B7, B10, B12
ambition A3, G2
analogy C6, C8
analysis/itical A5
anecdote F3
annex E5
annual report A8, E15
anonymous
    source E15
    referee procedure A8, C4
applied (research) A2, A7
archive/s A11
arguments/ation
    good/bad C7, E1, E6, F5, F7
    identifying C6
    misleading C8
assertive B2, B8
atmosphere
    interviews D4

attitude
    in groups B2, G2
    in meetings G4
    self-diagnosis B2
audience F2
    of books C2
audit
    first meeting A1, A5–6,
    A11–12, A16, B8, D8, G7
    progress meeting A9–10,
    C12, D2–6, F2, F5–7
    finishing the audit E3–5,
    E16, G10
authority B2, E6, F1, F9
authors E12, E15
    sequence in names C2, E3
autobiography C2, D2
automatic pilot B6
automatism B1
aware/ness B1
backup B1, F6
backwards planning A5, B1,
    F2
bachelor
    thesis B8, B13, *See also*
    ⊕ website
bargaining G1, G75–8
    society *The Challenges*
    strategies G6
    styles G11
barter A12, A16, B1, D2–4
basic research A7
Belbin
    (team) role/s G2
benchmarking C6
best-practice A9
bias D2
bibliography A6, E15
    systematic E15
bisociation *See* ⊕ website
blackboard F7
blue sky thinking A4, *See also*
    ⊕ website
body language D1, D5
    in presentations F7
    negotiations G11

observing D5
book
    review *See* ⊕ website
    selection C2
box
    pointers E14
brackets
    abuse E8
brain B5
    storming *The Format*, E1,
    G3, G5–7, G10
breaks
    function G11
budget
    time A5
    page A5, C5
    financial A5
business card D3
business plan
    See audit group assign-
    ments
calculating *The Challenges*,
    B1, G6, G9
capitals E3, E16
    heading/title E14
    in English E10
    on transparencies F5
    source E14
cartoons
    alternative source A4, F4
case
    lower ~ E3, E13
    ~ study A8
catalogue
    subject A6
causality C6, E6
    reversible C8
CD-ROM A13
ceteris paribus C6
Cf. E12
chair D5, G6
    checklist G4
    function G4, G8
chapter C7, E4
check/recheck A16, B11
checklist A6, C7, D2, D8, E1,

E9, F6, G4–5
class B8
    after the first meeting
    C5–8, C10, D7
    size level B1
    start of the course A16,
    B8, D7
cliché E6
closed
    ~ network G2
Coaching G9
co-producer
    status of listener D1, D7
coffee B7, B12
collective paper G10
colophon C2
comics F5
company audit
    See audit
competence The Format
computer supported learn-
    ing B1
concentration B7, D7
concepts definition A1
conceptualiser A3
conclusion
    book's C3
    contents A1, E3–5
conclusive words E6
conditions
    necessary/sufficient C6,
    E6
conference
    book C2
    reference to E15
conflict
    handling G11
confrontation G8
consensus G5
constructive
    communication The For-
    mat, D1, D8, F1, G9
    listening D1, D6–8
    feedback D8, G9
consultant/s A1, A3, A9
    disease The Format
contents (table of) B1, E3
contract

group G7, See also ⊕ web-
    site
    learning B4
contracted form (I'm) E13
contributors
    list E3
control G10
controversy
    structured G10
convergent thinking A4
co-production The Format,
    D1, F1–2
copyright C2, E3, E14
core competence
    research skills as The Chal-
    lenges
correction symbols C12
correspondence A16
course B11
creativity A4, See also
    ⊕ website
critical G4
    ~ research A1

criticise
    do not F3
criticism
    self ~ B1, E1, G7
CV (curriculum vitae) See
    ⊕ website
data
    base A13
    driven A7
dates E10
deadlines B11
debate G4
decision-making G5
    minutes G8
dedication E3
deduction/s A7, C6, C8, E6
    disjunctive C8
definitions A1, E3, E6
    on transparencies F5
delegating G5
dependency/ies G2, G7, G11
description A2
    interpretative A10
    journals C4

design B4
    of presentations F4
    See reflective circle
designer A3
desk
    ~ organisation B8
    ~ research A8
diagnosis B4, G7
'diagnost' A3
diagram C10, E6
dialectics E3
dialogue F5
diary B8
    See agenda
dictionary E10
dilemma C8, E6
disaster (presentation) F10
discipline B8, D6
discomfort zone B1
divergent/ce
    thinking A4
dots
    suggestive E6
doubt
    management of A1, A16
drafts do/don't A16, D2, B1
dress/ing See ⊕ website
    code B13
echoing D4
edited
    texts C2
editing E1
edition C3
editorial
    policy C4
editors
    final G10
    reference C2, E11, E15
effective/ness
    feedback G9
    meetings G5
    negotiation G6
    preparation (50/50 princi-
    ple) F2
    presentation F1
    speeches F4
electronic mail E15
empathy E1, G10

empirical A1, A4–A7, A10, C3, C6

endnotes C3, E12

endorsement C2

energy
management B12

English
spelling British-American
See ⊕ website

entrepreneur B1

epilogue E5

ergonomy/ic B12

essay *See* ⊕ website

ethos F1–2
See rhetoric's

evaluation *The Format*, B4, D1, D7, F7, G5

evasion G8, G11

exam B6–7, B10–11, B13
~ preparation B6

excuses B8

executive summary E3

experiment A8

experiential learning B5

expert A11

exploratory A4, A7

extra-curricular activities B1, B4, B11, G2

eyes D5

face
expression D5

fair A12

fallacies C8

falsification A8, A10, E6

fax *See* ⊕ website

feasibility
~ study A5–6

Feedback G9
avoidable ~ B13
listening for D8
generating ~ B5, B13
peer ~ B14
positive/negative D1, G9
receiving B13

feet
with presentations D5, F6

figure
list of E3

pointers E14, E16

reliability E16

files A11, A16, B1, B8

finishing
group projects G10, G12

flexibility G11

flipover F7

follower G7

footnotes C5, E3, E8, E10, E12, E14–15
abuse C3, E4, E8
interviews E8, E12
location in text E12

foreign language A16
interviewing in E8, E12
writing in B1, E8

foreword E3

formulation
See power writing

fragmentation B8

free-rider B1, G7–8, G10

full stop E12–14, E16
bibliographies E15
in abbreviations E13
in headings E14, E16
in job titles (prof.; dr.) E13
in numerals E10

fundamental research A7

general reference E12

generalisation C6

ghost writer C2

glossary E5

goal
of the Skill Sheets *The Challenges*
realistic B8, G7
See also aim

google/ing A14

government reports E15

group
contract G7
dynamics B1, B11, G1, G7, G10

group assignments
start A1–3, A5, B1–2, B11, C12, D8, E1, E8–16, G4–5, G7–8, G10
during A12, A16, B8, D5,

F2, F5–7
finish E3–5, G10

groupthink B1, B11, G4, G10

hand-out with presentations F4, F6–7

hands D5, F6

headers E16
on transparencies F5

headings C7, E4
figure/table E14
magazines/newspapers C4

health
balance B12

heuristic function C6

hidden agenda G4

hierarchy/ical G7

hyperkinetic society *The Challenges*, B1

hyphen E10

hypothesis
~ testing A7

I, when (not) to use E3
~ orientation B2

illustrations E14, F5

implementation B4, G5

'implementer' A3

improvisation G11

inaugural speech F3

indents E16

index E5
cards A11, C5, E15, F3, F5

induction/ive A7, C6, C8, E6

inertia
prevention B1

informants E5
create a pool/network of A16

input oriented skills
listening *The Challenges*, D-series
reading *The Challenges*, C-series

integration/ive A1, E11–2

integrity *The Challenges*, A1, E1, E12

interests G1, G6–7, G11

internalise

own arguments D8
Internet
    reference E12, E15
internship
    first meeting A5, A11–12,
    A16, B8, D8
    progress meeting E1, E3–
    6, E8–13
intersubjective/ity A7, A16
interview/er D-series
    managing ~ D2
    preparing ~ D2
intra-curricular activities B1,
    B4
introducing a speaker F3, G4
introduction A1, C7, E3
    presentation F4
intrusion
    territory D5
inventory *The Format*, B5, E1,
    E6, F2, G2, G6
italics E16
    in bibliographies E15
    in figures E14
    in quotations E11
journalists/m A1, D3
    investigative C3
journals B1, C4
judge(ment) A1, D4, D6
key word/s A6, A9, C5, F5
    concepts C10
    foreign E10
    in margin E16
knowledge
    ~ society *The Challenges*,
    The Format
Kolb *The Format*, B5
laboratory A8, B5
labour
    division A3, A5, G2
language
    ~ American/English *See*
    ⊕ website
    See foreign
lack of time B8–9
last lines E4, C3
laundry list syndrome D4
layout E16, G10

of bibliographies E15
leaders D5, G1, G5, G7
leading question D4
learning
    contract B4, G7
    cycle/circle *The Format*, B1,
    B5, F8, G1
    lifelong ~ B1
    report B1, B4, G2, G7
lectures
    attending D7
letter
    of application *See* ⊕ web-
    site
level of analysis A1
library
    librarian A6, A9, A13,
    B10–11, C4
    market C3
    memory as B6
linkage
    horizontal *The Format*
    vertical *The Format*
listening
    constructive ~ D1, G9
    checklist *See* ⊕ website
literature
    study A7, B5, E1
    supportive B1
logbook B1
logic E1, E6
logo E16
logos
    See rhetoric's
M.A. Thesis *See* ⊕ website
    first meeting C12, D8
    first planning meeting
    A1–3, A5–6, A11, A13, B8,
    C2–4
    start of the de-facto
    research process A9–10,
    A12, B8, C5–8, C10, D2–6
    writing requirements E1,
    E3–5, E8–15
magazines
    copying A11
    selection B1, C4
majority

absolute ordinary quali-
fied G5
management G1
    effectiveness A1, G5
manipulating
    gestures position D5, G7,
    G10, G11
margins E16
    notes in C10
marker
    use of C10
master
    thesis, *See* M.A. thesis *See
    also* ⊕ website
measurement
    notation E13
mediating G11
meetings
    characteristics G4
    effective G85
memo
    policy *See* ⊕ website
memory
    Short- Medium- Long-
    Term B6
memorising C7
mentor
    See peer-teaching
metaphor C6
meta-study A6
minimum skill require-
    ments *The Challenges*
minutes G4, G8
mission definition B1, B4
model/s A9
module/s B8, B10
motivation A5, B1, B10
multiple-choice questions
    B11, D4
negation A4, *See also* ⊕ web-
    site
negotiations
    principles G6
negotiator G11
nervous
    during presentations F2,
    F6–8
netiquette E1, *See also* ⊕ web-

site

network
author's C2
closed ~ G2
open ~ G2
~ position G2
social ~ G2
~ society *The Challenges*
neurotic *The Format*, B12
newspapers
selection C4
nicotine B7
non-decision/s G8
non-effective decision making G5
non-native spelling errors E10
non-quoting provision C4, D2
non-verbal B2, D5
See also body language
norm/ative A1, B11, C8, E6
note/s
making D7
taking D1–3, D7
while listening D6
numbers
See numerals
numerals (Arabic Roman) E3, E10
rounded figures F5
numerical signs C7
old boys networks
debugging G4
one minute paper D7, F7
open
network G2
opening C3, E3
opening line C3, E3
opinion
giving D4
opportunism
academic B1
original text C2
orphans E16
other-orientation B2
output oriented skills
presentation *The Chal-*

lenges, F-series
writing *The Challenges*, E-series
paperback/hardback books C3
paradigm C6
paragraph C7, E4
paraphrasing E11–12
parenthesis
with quotation E11
participants G6
participation
requirements G4
passive
writing E8
pathos
See rhetoric's
pause B6, D4
peak hours B7–8, B10
peer
~ feedback B14, G9
~ group C12
~ review *The Challenges*, A8
~ teaching B1
percentage / %
when to use E13
performance B7
management G9
Personal Efficiency Programme B8
phases
in groups G7
in research A5
phonetic spelling D6
phrasing
passive/active E8–9
plagiarism E11
plan/ning B1, B8, B10–11
plural
abbreviated ('nos') E13
pluralis majestatis E3, E9
policy memo *See* ⊕ website
portfolio
activities (literature teachers classes) B1, B4, B11
publisher's C3
positive/ist

~ feedback D1
postponing B8
posture D5, D7, F6, G11
See also body language
power G11
managing with ~ G7
~ topologies G8
PowerPoint F5, F7
preface A1, E3
prefix E11–12, E15
premise major/minor C6, C8
prescription A2, C6, C8
presentation F1
design F4
disasters F10
preparation F2
press
agency C4
~ release *See* ⊕ website
preventing problems B8
price of books C3
primary sources
See sources
principles
of active reading C1
of constructive listening D1
of effective presentation F1
of effective team management G1
of good research A1
of powerful writing E1
of successfully processing interviews D6
of virtuous/lifelong learning B1
priorities/ization B1, B8, D2
private activities B8, B10
See reflective circle
procrastination B9
process skills
management *The Challenges*, G-series
self-management/study *The Challenges*, B-series
professional/ism B1
profile *The Challenges*, B4

project/s
    management G-series
proof-reading A16, C12
publishers C3
punctuation
    numbers E10
pure (research) A7
qualitative A1, A7–10, A13,
    C12, E6, E14
quantitative A1, A7–9, A13,
    E2, E14
quasi exactness C8
questioning D4, G4
questionnaire A6, A8
question/s
    checklist in interviews D2
    choosing A9
    confrontational D4
    during presentations D7,
    F6
    formulating A10
    hierarchy A10
    open/closed D4
    open-ended A12
    qualitative A10
    rhetorical D4
    Socratic D4
quotation E11–12
    foreign words E11
    no-quote provision D3
    original spelling in E11
    secondary E11
quotation mark E8
    in notes D6
    double/single E11
rationalisation/s B8, E6
reader C2, E11
reading C-series
    readability E1, E4, E16
receive feedback B13, D8
recorder D2–3
rectification newspapers C4
reductive listening D2–4,
    D6, G4
referee
    procedures A8, C3–4
reference book A6
reference

Harvard Note E12
    shortened/ abbreviated
    E12
    See also source
reflective circle/cycle The For-
    mat, A2–3, B4, G5–6
    reversed The Format, A2
reflexivity E1
reification E8
reliable/ility C3
reporting E3–5
representation See ⊕ website
research A1, B4
    applied A2
    basic A2–3
resources
    See sources
responsibility G4
résumé
    See letter of application
review C5
peer The Challenges, A8
reward B8
rewriting A5, B11, E1
rhetoric's D8, F1
role/s G2, G4, G12
scan/ning See ⊕ website
    techniques C3
scenario G5
schedule
    week B10
Science Citation Index A6
search
    ~ engines A14–15
second
    opinion The Challenges
secondary sources
    See sources
secrecy interviews D3, E11
section C7, E4
selection C1, G5
    books C2–3
    newspapers/magazines
    C4
selective underlining C10
self
    ~ diagnosis B2
    ~ managed learning B1,

B4
    ~ management/er B1, B4
    ~ study group B1, B11
sentences lengthy/short E8
shopping-list D3
    See laundry list
simplistic argumentation C8
skill
    ~ profile B4
    ~ circle The Challenges, C1,
    D1, F1, G1
skimming B6
slide F7
small group meetings G6
    start of the meetings B1–
    2, C12, D8, G4–G5, G7–8,
    G10
    during the meetings B8,
    D5, F2, F5–7
S.M.A.R.T. B9, G7, See also ⊕
    website
snowball method A6
socialising B1
socially desirable answers
    D3
sociocratic G5
Socratic questions D4
solution
    aggregation G5
    See also brainstorming
sources
    anonymous E12, E15
    notation of newspaper
    source A11
    primary/secondary A6,
    A10, C3
    position of indication E14
    revelation of A1, A3, C3,
    E12, F5
    speculation E5
    spelling E14
speeches F3
speed reading C10
spelling
    American/British See
    ⊕ website
    check B1, G10
    errors E10

sponsorship A6, D2
stereotype C8, E6
SQ3R B6
stakeholder A1
statistic/s A7–8, A13, C6, F5, G6
stereotype C8, E6
stereotypical use of voice D5
stimuli
    positive B10
story
    line/plot A9
strategy in negotiations G6
strengths/weaknesses analysis B4, E3, E6
    of database A13
structure
    See power writing
study group B1, B11
study skills B1, G1
study planning B1–2, B4, B6–8, B10–11, B13
    semester B11
    week B10
style guide C4
subjective/ivist *The Format*, A1, A4, A7, A16
submissive B2
suggestive question D4
summary C2, C10, *See also* ⊕ website
    in mediating G11
survey A8
syllogism C6
    abusive ~ C8
synthesis C6, E6
system card
    See index
table
    as means of barter A12
    in support of presentation F7
    of contents C3, C5, E3, E5
    pointers E14, E16
    to schematise C10, E6
tactic/s G11
tape recorder D2–3
task G4, G12

tautology C6, E6
teachers *The Challenges*, B13
    correction C12
    thank-you line E3
team
    management *The Format*, G1, G5–7, G12
textbook E11
thank-you note D6
theory/izing
    grounded ~ A7
thesis
    B.A. B8, B13, *See also* ⊕ website
    M.A. A6, B8, B13, *See also* ⊕ website
think/ing
    ~ hat A4, *See also* ⊕ website
time
    indication E10
    management B8, B11
    preparation for presentation F4
    wasters B8
title
    catchy A10
    clear E13
    identify C3, C7
    page E3
(sub)titles
    See title
tolerance *The Format*, B2, G1
tools in presentations F5, F7
topology
    communication ~ G7
transcript D6
translation error A11, D6
translation programmes C9
transparency E14
    See also slide
triangulation A7
tribute speech F3
trust D2, G11
try-out F2
tutor B1, B13
typing B1
typography C7, E16

typos E10
unanimity G5
underlining C10
unhealthy
    group dynamics G10
unlearning F6–7
validation A7, A16
variables
    continuous ~ A7
    control ~ A7
    dependent ~ A7
    discrete ~ A7
    dummy ~ A7
    independent ~ A7, C10
verification A10, E6
vices (bad properties) E1
vicious *The Format*
video F7
virtues (good properties) E1
virtuous *The Format*, B1–2, B6, G1, G4
voice D5
voting procedures G5
white papers A11
whiteboard F7
wiki
    ~ pedia *The Challenges*, A15, E12
word
    ~association A4
    ~ processing E1, E16, B1
'W'
    4W G7–9
    5W G4
writing E-series, B1, B8
    powerful ~ C5, E1, E7, F2, G3, G10
    ~ style E1, E8–9
    ~ vices and virtues E1, G10

Skillsheets.com

'Do you know how to use references correctly?'

Skillsheets.com contains a large number of examples of skill problems, questions and challenges that every student encounters from time to time, and offers guidance on how to deal with these challenges.

Key elements of the website include:

- Self-assessment questionnaires
- Downloadable exercises
- Additional Skill Sheets
- Links to other skills websites

The website helps you with skills issues and challenges, such as:

- Giving a presentation
- Avoiding plagiarism
- Writing your Bachelor's / Master's thesis
- Speed reading
- Working in a team
- Performing quick scans
- Creating a powerful Curriculum Vitae / Resume
- And much more!

Check skillsheets.com for more information!

'Do you know how to prepare for an exam?'